Living between Worlds

LIVING BETWEEN WORLDS

ARCHAEOLOGY AND HISTORY AT THE SOUTHERN EDGE OF THE MAYA LOWLANDS

Edited by
MEGAN E. LEIGHT and BRENT K. S. WOODFILL

The University of Alabama Press
Tuscaloosa

The University of Alabama Press
Tuscaloosa, Alabama 35487-0380
uapress.ua.edu

Copyright © 2026 by the University of Alabama Press
All rights reserved.

Inquiries about reproducing material from this work should be addressed to the University of Alabama Press.

Typeface: Minion Pro

Cover image: Chixoy River, Chama Valley, Guatemala; photograph by Brent K. S. Woodfill
Cover design: Sandy Turner Jr.

Cataloging-in-Publication data is available from the Library of Congress.
ISBN: 978-0-8173-2256-4 (cloth)
ISBN: 978-0-8173-6238-6 (paper)
E-ISBN: 978-0-8173-9586-5

To Annika

Contents

Preface ix

Acknowledgments xi

Part I: Understanding the Northern Transversal Strip

Introduction: Shining a Light on the Borderlands between the Maya Lowlands and the Guatemalan Highlands
BRENT K. S. WOODFILL AND MEGAN E. LEIGHT 1

1. The Key to Understanding Both Maya Lowland and Highland Ancient Political Economies: The Trajectory and Impact of Research in the Transversal Interface Region
ARTHUR A. DEMAREST 11

Part II: Sites, Regions, and Regional History

2. The Transversal Economic Network: Forming a Breakaway Network through Economic Benefits and Ideological Seduction
ARTHUR A. DEMAREST AND PAOLA TORRES 41

3. The Archaeology of the Chixoy Basin
BRENT K. S. WOODFILL, CAITLIN EARLEY, AND ALEXANDER E. RIVAS 65

4. *Entre Dos Cuencas*: The Chaculá Region in Northwestern Huehuetenango
ULRICH WÖLFEL 87

Part III: Interrelations and Environment

5. Ceramic Interaction in the Northern Transversal Strip during the Late Classic Period
JORGE MARIO ORTÍZ DE LEÓN, SOCORRO JIMÉNEZ ÁLVAREZ, PAOLA TORRES,

Claudia Arriaza, Miryam Saravia, Juan Francisco Saravia, Carlos Fidel Tuyuc Nij, and Diana Méndez Lee   105

6. Changing Ritual Intent in a Stone Coffer from an Unlooted Cave in Central Guatemala
Erin L. Sears   120

7. Not All Distance Is Kilometric: Obsidian Procurement at Salinas de los Nueve Cerros and Cancuen
Chloé Andrieu and Edgar H. Carpio Rezzio   143

8. The Prehispanic and Colonial Exchange of Perishable Goods in and through the Northern Transversal Strip: Achiote, Cacao, Salt, and Exotic Feathers
Brent K. S. Woodfill, Mark W. Lentz, and Megan E. Leight   152

9. The Sacred, Urban Landscape of Cancuen and Salinas de los Nueve Cerros
Marc Wolf   177

10. Paleoecology of the Chixoy Alluvial Plains along the Northern Transversal Strip
Carlos Avendaño, Claudia L. M. Morales-Flores, Juan Carlos Berrio, Carla Paola del Cid López, Silvia Carolina Duarte Morales, Rosa Delfina Sunum Orellana, Mónica María Cajas Castillo, Nora Machuca Mejía, Sharon A. Cowling, Sarah Finkelstein, Ramiro Tox, Oscar A. Rojas-Castillo, and Carolina Rosales de Zea   206

11. Born in Xibalba: Kanek'-Kaweq Lineage History in the Franja Transversal del Norte
Ruud van Akkeren   247

Bibliography   277
Contributors   347
Index   351

Preface

When Wendi Schnaufer came to Brent Woodfill and asked him whether there were any book projects he'd be interested in bringing to the University of Alabama Press, a collaborative volume focusing on the Northern Transversal Strip in central Guatemala was the first idea that popped into his head. This area—a long, narrow band that straddles both sides of the Highland-Lowland Maya divide—is essential to understanding ancient Maya economics, politics, religion, and interaction. The strip contains one of the earliest Mesoamerican cities, Salinas de los Nueve Cerros, as well as multiple major pilgrimage centers that drew people from far-flung lands who were attracted to the area's unique and dramatic geology. It was cross-cut by multiple trade arteries that connected people and commodities through the entire western half of the Maya world. Moreover, its raw materials, natural communication routes, and great soil attracted multiple historical polities and empires, beginning with Tikal in the Early Classic and Calakmul in the Late Classic, and ending with the Hapsburgs.

Unfortunately, the Northern Transversal's resources and geography continue to attract the attention of empires. Recent and current policies, population trends, and economic interests have made research in the region much more difficult and much less appealing to foreign archaeologists, as they turn their attention instead to the national parks and jungle preserves to the north.

The Transversal region, in contrast, is less known for its archaeology than it is for the scorched earth military campaigns during the Guatemalan civil war of the 1980s, its fields of sour oil, the vast swaths of African palm and cattle now taking over Maya farming communities, and its clandestine air strips used for narcotics trafficking. Working there is a different experience than most Mayanists are accustomed to, with archaeological sites located in communities, on fincas, in cornfields, on private land, on military bases, and in the occasional park or preserve. As a result, projects are firmly rooted in community. We are expected to participate in inaugural season-opening ceremonies with Maya elders to bless their consecrated land, to the keep workers safe during the season, and to discuss and seek endorsement for the project goals. On the one hand, we are able to draw directly from the residents of our research zones their detailed knowledge of the local landscape and what it contains. On the other hand, there are some important sites and structures that remain tantalizingly out of reach, where our investigations push up against local, municipal, and transnational interests. Still, every pit we dig and every point we plot is a valuable addition to the field, and this volume is the vehicle for transmitting the results to our colleagues and the communities who are interested in what we have found.

To produce this book, the editors gathered a disparate group of scholars who have worked in the region, from established researchers who have directed long-term, big-budget investigations to Guatemalan undergraduate students who conducted thesis research on a shoestring budget. This motley crew passed around early copies of their work, sharing different chapters and even writing updated chapters together, using each other's results to rethink the nature of the region and their piece of it. We are deeply grateful to all of the volume's contributors for their enormous efforts in creating a critically important volume about the Transversal region.

Contributor Arthur Demarest wrote in an earlier version of Chapter 1, potentially the best endorsement for the book and its place in the field either of us could find. His words are a fitting end to this preface: "This volume is an important milestone in Maya archaeology. While that statement might seem hyperbolic, it is justified. By pulling together the disparate research from sites that are extremely different in material culture, scale, and regional geographical and ecological context, the editors and authors are defining a new 'region' for investigation."

Acknowledgments

THIS WORK IS the culmination of decades of research in the Northern Transversal Strip—living and working with local community leaders, encouraging young Guatemalan scholars to pursue higher education (and archaeology!), and pushing the boundaries of what community-based archaeological projects look like in Guatemala.

The Salinas de los Nueve Cerros (SNC) project would like to extend our sincere gratitude to the entire Tox family, who took care of us season after season. We fondly remember our dear friend Ramiro Tox. Ramiro served as one of the primary community partners for the SNC project as president of the local nonprofit organization, the Asociacion civil no lucrativa para el desarrollo Aj Waklesinel (ADAWA). Established in 2014 by members of the Q'eqchi' Maya heritage, ADAWA promotes education and collaboration to improve the lives of communities living in the Lachua region of the Alta Verapaz Department of Guatemala. They are dedicated to (1) providing better access to youth education, as only 20% of children are enrolled in school in the region; (2) building household infrastructure to limit illness and infection; they want all houses in the region to have access to wells, water filtration, efficient cooking stoves, and sanitary latrines; (3) bringing community health care and education to rural communities, with additional providers and support for the *comadronas* (midwives) serving these populations; and (4) teaching skill development and technical skill-building. Only 7% of Guatemalan households are able to access the internet. ADAWA focuses on construction projects (e.g., well-building, composting toilets); agricultural farming (e.g., organic farming, maximizing yield); innovative agriculture (e.g., hydroponics, aquaponics); medicinal plants knowledge (e.g., natural antibiotics); basic English language courses, eco-tourism, and so on. The term *Aj Waklesinel*, which is from the sacred Maya text the *Popol Vuh*, means "to lift up the people, to be united, that no one is separate, and to move forward together" (ADAWA website).

The editors would like to extend individual thanks for work completed on this volume over the last several years. At Winthrop University under Brent's direction, Kristin Scherpf, Anthony Dorman, Victoria Balberde, Kristin Smith, and Michelle Smith have gone out of their way to make this work possible. At West Virginia University, Samuel Hensley was a research assistant for Megan, and he reviewed several early chapters and the initial bibliography for months, paving the way for our first reviewed submission. Funding for their research was obtained through the Alphawood Foundation, the National Science Foundation, and InHerit Indigenous Heritage Passed to Present.

The SNC project spent the better part of a decade living in and working out of a concrete labyrinth of a laboratory house in Zona 7 of Guatemala City. We were always glad when it was finally time to go out for the night to celebrate a birthday, but it was a research space and a home-away-from-home for all of us. We are particularly grateful to the project members who coauthored chapters in this volume as well as Efrain Tox Tiul, Emanuel Tox Tiul, Judith Valle, Katerin Molina, Blanca Mijangos, Claudia Arriza, Gregory Odum, and so many others for their years of dedication to the Nueve Cerros project. This publication is the result of their perseverance and dedication to the site and its modern and ancient residents over the years.

Erin L. Sears thanks the late director Daniel Aquino de Lara, Victor Mendoza, and Josué García of the Guatemala Museo Nacional de Antropología e Etnología for allowing international access for research on the Hun Nal Ye coffer. Andrea Terrón graciously provided access to the Alta Verapaz collections at the Museo Popol Vuh. Thank you to Dorie Reents-Budet and Barbara MacLeod for feedback on this chapter. Sears also appreciates the efforts of Megan E. Leight for organizing and creating an academic avenue from which to highlight an alternative understanding of their discovery.

Ulrich Wölfel's fieldwork for the Proyecto Arqueológico de la Región de Chaculá (PARCHA) project was made possible through grants from the Deutsche Altamerika-Stiftung as well as permits and supervision by the Instituto de Antropología e Historia de Guatemala. Many thanks go to both institutions as well as the various incarnations of the PARCHA field team, in particular Victor Castillo, Paola Torres, Byron Hernández, and Julián Camposeco. He is grateful for being able to participate in the Cofradía Cartográfica Cuchumateca project, coordinated by Ana Pohlenz de Tavira and Carlos Salamanca Villamizar.

Chloé Andrieu and Edgar H. Carpio Rezzio thank the members of the Cancuen project (Instituto de Antropologia e Historia [IDAEH], Vanderbilt University, and Ministry of Foreign Affairs, France) and in particular Arthur A. Demarest and Paola Torres, as well as the Archeologie des Amériques laboratory of the National Centre for Scientific Research (CNRS, France) and the SNC project, in particular Brent K. S. Woodfill, Judith Valle, Blanca

Mijangos, and brothers Efrain and Salvador Tox. The X-ray fluorescence (XRF) analysis of Cancuen obsidian was carried out at the University of Missouri Research Reactor (MURR y) by David Glascock and financed by a project from the Fyssen Foundation. For the XRF analysis of obsidian from SNC, we also thank archaeologists Bárbara Arroyo and Javier Estrada from the Kaminaljuyu project.

Ruud van Akkeren sincerely thanks Brent K. S. Woodfill and Megan E. Leight for inviting him to participate in this first integral and multidisciplinary publication on the Franja Transversal del Norte. He is grateful as well to Mallary Tiul and Juan Moncada for their reprographics and maps. He is also indebted to the Maya whom he met during visits or in the courses he taught in the area, and he appreciates the history they shared with him.

All contributors to this volume are grateful for the organizers of the annual Guatemalan Simposio, particularly Bárbara Arroyo, who has selflessly continued this important tradition for decades. The opportunity to present and publish field research in Spanish remains an enduring legacy for archaeological projects in Mesoamerica. Contributors to this volume are regular attendees and participants in the *simposio* and appreciate how much it has fostered a community of scholars that crosscuts generations, nationalities, specialties, and career stages. This book is dedicated to Annika Wolf, a future archaeologist in training who has already accompanied her father, Marc Wolf, and her mother, Katie Miller-Wolf, to the field. They remind us of the importance of family and passing on knowledge to our future generations.

Living between Worlds

Part I

Understanding the Northern Transversal Strip

Introduction

Shining a Light on the Borderlands between the Maya Lowlands and the Guatemalan Highlands

Brent K. S. Woodfill and Megan E. Leight

In 1955, archaeologist A. Ledyard Smith called for future investigations to occur in the unknown area between the Chixoy drainage and Altar de Sacrificios, an area he viewed as key to understanding highland-lowland interactions. Over the subsequent decades, several others heeded the call, using data from the base of the Guatemalan highlands to understand larger theoretical issues related to the development and maintenance of Maya civilization, economics, and politics (e.g., Andrews V 1990; Dillon 1977; Hatch 1982), albeit their understanding was based on very preliminary research from a handful of small-scale projects.

Referred to today as the "Northern Transversal Strip" by the Guatemalan government, archaeologists use the term to refer to an area that crosscuts multiple modern departments, conquest-period ethnic groups, and Classic city-states that are all united by similar geography and interregional interactions. From the rise of civilization in Mesoamerica through the Spanish conquest, the Transversal was important both as a transportation route and as the source of the commodities cacao, *achiote*, and salt. The two principal rivers in the western Maya world pass through the Northern Transversal, leaving thick layers of highland soil that are much richer than the soil in the rest of the lowlands.

Unfortunately, our actual understanding of the region lags behind our understanding of other parts of the lowlands. There are several reasons for this. From an archaeologist's perspective, the dearth of monuments with hieroglyphic inscriptions, the paucity of stone architecture, and the poor preservation through much of the area of osteological and ceramic materials have all tended to discourage investigation. There were a few exceptions, beginning with forays by American graduate students. Members of the Seibal

Archaeological Project traveled to Cancuen and camped out there over Holy Week in 1967 to create a rough map of the site epicenter (Tourtellot et al. 1978). Brian D. Dillon and Patricia Carot conducted PhD research at Salinas de los Nueve Cerros and master's research in the Candelaria Caves, respectively, about a decade later (Carot 1989; Dillon 1977). Dillon was drawn to Nueve Cerros specifically because it was in the center of a giant knowledge vacuum (personal communication to Woodfill 2010), while Carot came when invited by a French spelunker who was attempting to develop an adventure tourism industry.

While these projects were working in the region, the political reality of the Transversal turned increasingly dire. The Guatemalan military became increasingly active here after the infamous Panzós massacre of 1978 (Falla 1992; Manz 2005), and by the early 1980s this strip of land was one of the most violent fronts in a civil war that pitted soldiers against largely unarmed villagers and the police against urban activists, all in the name of fighting communism (Brett 2007; Falla 1992; Manz 2005; Sanford 2003). A total of 161 recorded massacres occurred in this region during this time (ODHAG 1998, Tomo II:224–244), representing a loss of almost 2,500 individuals (CEH 1999, Anexo 2). Archaeologists began to return only after the fighting slowed down in the 1990s, beginning with a brief follow-up investigation by Dillon (1990) at Nueve Cerros and followed by several Guatemalan-led salvage projects associated with the growing oil exploitation in the region (Arroyo 1993; GEOPETROL 2005; Leal 2006).

Today, the Northern Transversal Strip is a complex patchwork of dense Maya villages and frontier towns, commercial cattle ranches and African palm plantations, oil wells and hydroelectric dams, interspersed with clandestine airstrips used by foreign and national drug cartels. Corporations and cartels are typically antagonistic toward archaeological investigation in their territory, and many of the communities and ranchers feel equally unsure about the intentions of any academic interested in beginning a project here. In spite of these hurdles, the region has become the focus of several multiyear investigations. Arthur A. Demarest and his team were the first to move into the Northern Transversal two years after the signing of the 1996 Peace Accords. While their work began at (and continues to focus on) the site of Cancuen, by 2001 they were working on both sides of the highland-lowland divide (see Chapter 2). Brent K. S. Woodfill, who conducted graduate research in the Candelaria Caves and other cave systems under Demarest, splintered off to found his own project at Salinas de los Nueve Cerros in 2009 (see Chapter 3). Bonn graduate student Ulrich Wölfel followed a few years later, drawn by early twentieth-century explorations by Eduard Seler to the western edge of the strip (see Chapter 4).

With three active archaeological projects and specialists in ethnohistory (Ruud Van Akkeren and Mark W. Lentz) and paleoecology (Carlos Avendaño) who regularly collaborate with us, we are finally able to answer Smith's call. Directors and specialists from each of the projects—ceramicists, figurine specialists, and lithicists, each with multiple decades of experience working in the region—provide current interpretations of the region's history and role in larger political and economic systems throughout the history of Maya civilization and through the Spanish conquest.

ROADBLOCKS AND BENEFITS TO UNDERSTANDING THE TRANSVERSAL

As this discussion shows, the Guatemalan civil war and post-conflict social order have made research in the region difficult, but several other factors have contributed to the lack of attention the region has received from the discipline as a whole. Unlike literature on much of the lowlands and even some of the better-known highland sites, most of the few extant writings about the region are hard-to-find "grey" literature—dissertations and theses (Carot 1987; Danien 1998; Dillon 1979; Garrido López 2008), reports to corporations and the Guatemalan government (Arroyo 1993; Dillon 1979, 1990; Garrido López 2012; GEOPETROL 2005; Graham 1965; Leal 2006, several of which had to be tracked down by Woodfill's contacts in the Ministry of Culture since they had been misplaced over the years), and short announcements or travelogs written by early explorers and gentleman looters (Burkitt 1924; Dieseldorff 1894; Habel 1878; Maler 1908; Maudslay and Maudslay 1889; Morley 1915; Seler 1908). More formal academic writing is either limited to preliminary findings (Arroyo 1994; Butler 1962; Dillon 1977; Tourtellot et al. 1978), published in obscure or defunct venues (e.g., Dillon et al. 1985, 1988; Dreux 1968; Pope and Sibberenson 1981), or out of print after a limited initial run (Arnauld 1986; Carot 1989; Hatch 1982). The resulting corpus of texts includes a daunting variety of languages—English, Spanish, French, and German—made more difficult by the archaic German stylings (even by early twentieth-century standards) of Eduard Seler (Ulrich Wölfel, personal communication to Woodfill 2015) and the idiosyncratic orthography of Burkitt, who was inspired by the calls of Noah Webster to experiment with new ways of spelling English words (Danien 1998).

Thus, unlike better-investigated Maya regions, the Transversal lacks a solid foundation for archaeological interpretation. Ceramics—one of the most important artifact classes for reconstructing regional chronology and interaction—has been particularly difficult to piece together as a result. As befits their location along a border zone, local residents adopted elements of ceramic styles from both the southern lowlands and northern highlands in addition to developing robust local traditions, often in dialogue with imports and locally made vessels in foreign styles. Of all of these ceramic spheres, only material from the southern lowland could be identified and dated with a high degree of precision before significant research was done by the projects represented in this volume (see Chapter 5). The understanding of local and northern highland traditions, in contrast, was largely limited to two short analyses of unprovenienced collections (Butler 1962; R. E. Smith 1952) and dissertations or ceramic monographs based on small-scale, short-term projects (Arnauld 1986; Becquelin et al. 2001; Danien 1998; Dillon 1979; Hatch 1982; Ichon 1992).

The lithic and figurine assemblages, architectural styles, and broader settlement patterns are similarly diverse, with local and highland traditions just as poorly understood as the ceramics (see Chapters 6 through 9). In addition, the region is largely devoid of hieroglyphic texts to provide dates, actors, events, and other historical data points like their neighbors to the north have. Because of all of this, the Transversal and highlands to the south have been poorly understood, broadly dated, and fundamentally unable to be incorporated into the increasingly refined chronology and political histories of the southern lowlands.

What makes these chronological and affiliative ambiguities more frustrating is the region's obvious importance for understanding several core themes in Maya archaeology. In terms of understanding the rise of complex society, the Transversal has provided some of the earliest ceramic assemblages in the Maya world—Salinas de los Nueve Cerros was established before 1000 BC (Ortiz 2022:12; Woodfill 2019a), and similarly early material was recovered from cave contexts around Cancuen (Woodfill 2010:107–108). The region is just as important for collapse studies—Cancuen successfully adapted to the fall of the Petexbatun until it was dramatically invaded and abandoned in the early eighth century (see Chapter 2), while Nueve Cerros, Chama, and the Coban Plateau continued to be important and active locations well into the Colonial Period (see Chapters 3 and 8).

As Demarest points out in Chapter 1, most of the writing about highland-lowland interaction has focused on specific sites and regions far from the Transversal (e.g., Adams 1978; Arnauld 1990; Hammond 1972; Kidder et al. 1946) rather than on where the two regions actually came together. Residents of both sides of the border depended on the region for a variety of commodities, from sumptuary goods like cacao to basic resources like salt (see Chapter 8). Jade, obsidian, quetzal feathers, and igneous groundstone tools were brought into the lowlands through the Transversal, and fine figurines and ceramics, feline pelts, and other lowland objects were brought back into the highlands along the same route (see Chapters 1 and 5 through 7).

Finally, investigations in the Transversal show the porousness of specific regions. Different parts of the Transversal were colonized by highlanders and lowlanders from multiple polities throughout its precolumbian history, and different lineages continued on to places as far flung as the northern Yucatan and the western highlands, where they founded some of the most important kingdoms of the Postclassic period. As we continue to reconcile historic texts and epigraphy with the archaeological record, we have the potential to reconstruct complex networks of interaction (Chapter 1) and family histories (Chapter 11).

A BRIEF HISTORY OF THE NORTHERN TRANSVERSAL STRIP BEFORE THE SPANISH CONQUEST

As mentioned, the earliest recovered evidence of occupation in the region is related to ritual cave use and salt production between 1200 and 900 BC, presaging the region's economic and religious importance in later periods. Throughout the subsequent 1,500 years or so, the Transversal was sparsely populated with the exception of Salinas de los Nueve Cerros, which emerged as an early Maya population center that produced salt for export into the southern lowlands (Woodfill 2019a, 2020; see Chapter 3).

During the Early Classic period (ca. AD 460), the eastern part of the Transversal underwent a radical transformation due to machinations at the lowland center of Tikal (Woodfill and Andrieu 2012). Residents of that city began to import massive amounts of raw jade and obsidian from the Guatemalan highlands, taking over the primary trade routes that they traveled along through conquest, through alliances, and, in the case of the Great Western Trade Route that passes through the Transversal, by taking over the local sacred geography. The Candelaria Caves, the Cave of Hun Nal Ye, and the riverine shrine at Tres Islas all became major ritual centers used primarily by merchants and other travelers passing along the route (Woodfill 2010, 2011a, 2019a; Woodfill and Andrieu 2012; Woodfill et al. 2012). Visitors would purchase locally made ritual paraphernalia (ceramic vessels, obsidian blades, and, presumably, incense and other perishable goods) to offer in small-scale ceremonies in order to ask for permission from the living mountains, caves, and other such beings who owned the land they wished to pass through (Henderson and Woodfill 2024).

In general, the local population continued to be found largely in small, dispersed settlements, aside from the aforementioned exception of Salinas de los Nueve Cerros. By this time, the disparate settlements surrounding the salt dome had grown together into one large urban area that was involved not only in various facets of the salt trade but in multiple derivative industries as well. Residents boiled down hard salt cakes on the western slope of the salt dome, which were then sold largely to lowlanders farther downriver or distributed through other neighborhoods at Nueve Cerros, where they were used to make salted fish and meat in addition to other secondary commodities (Woodfill et al. 2015; Woodfill 2019a, 2020).

Lowland rivalries heated up during the fifth and sixth centuries as Tikal and the Kaanxl kingdom (with the final vowel here represented as an "x," since there is debate within the epigraphic community as to how to read the glyphic texts) fought over the trade routes through direct warfare, diplomacy, and the establishment of military garrisons like Dos Pilas (Demarest 2006; Martin and Grube 2008). It was during this time that the Transversal began to be more densely populated, largely due to an influx of new residents. Northern highlanders appeared to have moved into multiple neighborhoods at Nueve Cerros (Woodfill 2019a) and founded new cities and towns like Raxruha Viejo, La Lima, and Sebol (Woodfill and Andrieu 2012; see Chapter 2). Lowlanders moved into the region as well, establishing a royal dynasty at Cancuen that was, for a time, able to harness the city's location along the trade route and connections to regions as far flung as the central Guatemalan highlands and Gulf Coast to become the primary site for processing raw jade into "blanks"—earspools, plaques, and other objects. These were then exported farther into the lowlands to be finished by royal artisans there (Andrieu et al. 2012; Demarest et al. 2014). Nueve Cerros was ultimately responsible for producing upwards of 10,000 metric tons of salt a year, which was consumed in neighboring regions on each side of the highland-lowland divide (Woodfill et al. 2015; Woodfill 2020). It is hard to overstate the revolutionary scale at which goods were produced in both Nueve Cerros and Cancuen for export in the Transversal, one that would be unrivaled until the Industrial Revolution.

Unfortunately, Cancuen's apogee lasted for only about 20 years, when the history of the city came to an abrupt end after an invading force executed the entire royal family at the beginning of the ninth century AD (see Chapter 2). Unlike the rapid boom and bust of Cancuen, Nueve Cerros, Quen Santo, and other cities in the western part of the Transversal slowly grew in size and importance throughout the Late Classic period, only to disintegrate around AD 1000.

After the collapse, the populations that remained took advantage of the new political landscape to feed into the northern highland economy and their demand for exotic lowland commodities like cacao, achiote, salt, and the pelts and feathers of jungle animals (Dillon 1975; Feldman 1985; see Chapter 8). The region was also important for ritual pilgrimage, with evidence of cave ceremonies held by foreigners in Quen Santo and on the outskirts of Salinas de los Nueve Cerros. In both of these locations, cave formations were modified to resemble the faces of ancestors and other beings; the portable sculptural tradition at the former focuses on deceased individuals, as indicated by their closed eyes and crossed arms (Earley 2023:131). At Nueve Cerros, the rituals are likely associated with the continued salt production at the site, with ceremonial offerings serving fundamentally as tribute to the living salt dome before his brine was boiled down (Woodfill 2019a).

ABOUT THIS BOOK

This book is a multidisciplinary, multiproject collaboration that is over 25 years in the making. The 11 chapters within include 34 scholars from eight countries, who are all united in their drive to shed light on this little-known region that is essential for understanding precolumbian Maya economics, politics, and religion. Contributors include archaeologists, art historians, ethnohistorians, biologists, and paleoecologists working on five different projects in the Transversal region of Guatemala.

The chapters are organized into three different parts. Part I includes this general introduction to the region. Chapter 1, by Arthur A. Demarest, is more explicitly theoretical, providing a potential framework for understanding the Transversal as a whole and how it fits into larger interregional Maya sociopolitical systems.

Part II focuses on synthesizing current and previously published data to describe the sites and history of the region. Beginning with Chapter 2, Cancuen project directors Arthur A. Demarest and Paola Torres describe the history and sites of the eastern Transversal, with a focus on trading networks and communication. Chapter 3, by Proyecto Salinas de los Nueve Cerros members Brent K. S. Woodfill, Caitlin Earley, and Alexander E. Rivas, focuses on the history of the Chixoy River, which cuts the Transversal region in half, attempting to bridge the highland-lowland divide that typically carves this river valley into isolated segments. Proyecto Arqueológico de la Región de Chaculá (PARCHA) director Ulrich Wölfel describes the principal sites and history of the Transversal's western section in Chapter 4, with an eye to linking ancient settlements in the western Usumacinta and eastern Grijalva watersheds to their counterparts in the Mexican state of Chiapas. Together, all three chapters bring together disparate data sets and the result of dozens of distinct archaeological projects in order to synthesize and update over a century's worth of research in the region for the first time.

Part III explores specific materials and themes that allow for a broader perspective on the region's history that goes beyond single projects. Chapter 5, by members of both the Cancuen and Nueve Cerros projects Jorge Mario Ortíz de León, Socorro Jiménez Álvarez, Paola Torres, Claudia Arriaza, Miryam Saravia, Juan Francisco Saravia, Carlos Fidel Tuyuc Nij, and Diana Méndez Lee, proposes a new ceramic sphere that spans much of the

Transversal region and demonstrates the close economic ties that united myriad sites throughout the Late Classic period (AD 650–800). Erin L. Sears argues in Chapter 6 for similar interregional ties in the latter part of the Early Classic period (ca. AD 460–550) based on iconographic similarities with cities as far-flung as Tikal and Copan.

Lithicists Chloé Andrieu, who works at Cancuen and multiple sites surrounding it, and Edgar H. Carpio Rezzio, who has been working on the Nueve Cerros collection, join forces in Chapter 7 to reconstruct the history of obsidian exchange in and through the Transversal region. In Chapter 8, Brent K. S. Woodfill and Megan E. Leight collaborate with historian Mark W. Lentz to reconstruct similar histories for four perishable commodities that were equally important for the Transversal region's residents—*achiote*, cacao, salt, and quetzal feathers.

Marc Wolf, a GIS specialist, conducts a deep dive into the cosmological underpinnings of the urban layouts of both Salinas de los Nueve Cerros and Cancuen in Chapter 9. Although both urban landscapes are vastly different, he argues they are deeply reflective of archetypal places in Maya mythology and worldview. In Chapter 10, the paleoecological team from Proyecto Salinas de los Nueve Cerros—Carlos Avendaño, Claudia L. M. Morales-Flores, Juan Carlos Berrio, Carla Paola del Cid López, Silvia Carolina Duarte Morales, Rosa Delfina Sunum Orellana, Mónica María Cajas Castillo, Nora Machuca Mejía, Sharon A. Cowling, Sarah Finkelstein, Ramiro Tox, Oscar A. Rojas-Castillo, and Carolina Rosales de Zea—reflect on the ecological and geological history of the city and its environs. They examine both the natural resources available to the region's residents and precolumbian land management strategies made visible through the charcoal, pollen, and other paleoecological remains. The final chapter, by Ruud van Akkeren, is the culmination of years of research into the profound changes in the region at the end of the Classic period and the new sociopolitical organization that emerged in the wake of the Classic collapse.

Together, these chapters create a nuanced understanding of this narrow strip of land between the Maya Lowlands and Guatemalan highlands, one that tied together these two regions, their residents, and their resources and commodities. It is the first book that attempts to bridge the gap, literally and metaphorically, between scholars working in these two halves of the Maya world.

Although contributors focus on the same region and confront many of the same issues—interregional and intraregional connections, culture-history reconstructions, exploitation of local resources, and so on—readers may note contradictions among the varied interpretations they present here. As editors, we accept that consensus is not always possible, especially when such diverse disciplines and data sets are presented. Ethnohistorians, paleoecologists, art historians, and archaeologists all examine the world largely through their own epistemological lenses, allowing them to see patterns and trends that are absent in other approaches. The most glaring example of interdisciplinary discrepancies in this book is the degree to which saltworkers at Salinas de los Nueve Cerros are interpreted to have interacted with their peers in the northern lowlands. Archaeologically (see Chapter 2), there is no evidence to date—no imports have been identified nor have pertinent hieroglyphic texts been recovered. Ethnohistorically (see Chapter 11), however, one of the founding families at Chichen Itza claimed to have come from Nueve Cerros! It is possible that archaeological evidence will eventually echo the ethnohistory—isotopic and genetic analyses of human remains are still in their infancies, and they have not been applied to the few recovered skeletons from the site yet. Exotic vessels, texts, and other evidence tying the two regions together might have been misidentified by laboratory specialists or still be in the ground. Yet the authors of colonial documents discussing the relationship between the sites may have been playing fast and loose with the facts or be mistaken. It is also possible that the relationship was sufficiently ephemeral and short-lived, making it irrelevant beyond establishing the legitimacy of a storied lineage from an exotic locale. Until some sort of concordance is reached, we are comfortable presenting both perspectives.

Fundamentally, as the diverse volume contributors make clear, the Northern Transversal Strip is an important, complex, and insufficiently understood region, albeit one that is necessary to understand if we are to create better models for Highland-Lowland Maya relationships over the millennia before the Spanish conquest. Its residents were a central part of multiple elaborate trade networks that extended deep into both the highlands and the lowlands, and they were responsible for producing, transporting, and consuming a variety of local and exotic goods. We hope that this volume serves as an important step toward integrating this often overlooked region more fully into archaeological interpretation.

1

The Key to Understanding Both Maya Lowland and Highland Ancient Political Economies

The Trajectory and Impact of Research in the Transversal Interface Region

ARTHUR A. DEMAREST

The Transversal interface region is not defined by an area of similar material culture, ecology, or political affiliations, or even by a shared language or "ethnicity." Rather, it is defined by sharing a critical part of the same research problem. It is an extensive region with a variety of sites, agencies, and linkages, many of which are central to our understanding of exchange between different zones of ancient and colonial Maya civilization. The fact that this region is not "unified," is diverse in every aspect, and has been minimally investigated with little integration of results is precisely why it has become so important. It therefore presents challenges requiring new methodologies, new concepts, and fundamentally different types of research designs and tools for interpretation.

Most notably, it exposes the current academic divide between "southern lowland Maya archaeology" and "Highland Maya archaeology"—a divide that is far more profound and damaging than most realize. The urgency of research in these regions lies both academically and geographically in their position as an interface between the "highland" and "lowland" zones, as well as in their central role in interregional exchange. Their economies can be interpreted only by understanding the linkages in the Transversal. By failing to investigate and sufficiently consider the Transversal sites and routes, a crisis has developed in understanding the agents and political economies of the systems on either side of the imagined divide. Especially in the lowlands, ignoring this region has added to the grandiose "splendid isolationism" and theoretical parochialism seen in many Lowland Mayanist publications.

Here, I critique the sources and impact of these problems and fallacies. Then, however, I briefly discuss the sometimes painful but eventually positive history of studies leading to new investigations in the Transversal. Those investigations led to an awareness of this zone in terms of its critical nature and role in "lowland," "piedmont," and "highland" culture-history. Along the way, the history and the challenges of Transversal research gave us new perspectives and tools that have the potential to transform Mayanist archaeology in general. In that sense, what we see in this volume could be the beginning of yet another revolution in Mayanist studies.

THE MACRO-SAMPLING PROBLEM

For decades, the greatest problem in Maya archaeology has been that of *interregional* "macro-sampling" (Demarest 2011). While some Mayanist archaeologists, ever fewer recently, do remain concerned with obtaining a more even and complete intrasite or "polity" sample, they fail to realize that in Maya archaeology the sampling problem has always been at the more global interregional scale. Vast regions of the ancient Maya world still have not been investigated by any type of archaeological project beyond some minimal test pitting or surface sampling or the recording of some monuments, if those were known.

We know that there have been major "game-changing" discoveries at the many sites in previously uninvestigated or little-investigated zones like the Mirador Basin, Calakmul zone, Petexbatun region, and Cancuen and Upper Pasión regions. Furthermore, there are the zones where findings are almost ignored, such as the southwestern Peten and piedmont Transversal zones. Findings that could change the "big picture" have been, and are being, found in the Transversal and the Verapaz and El Quiche regions. We can only imagine what is to be found in areas that have been even less sampled.

Instead, regions like the northeast and north central Peten, Belize, northern Yucatan, and the Copan Valley have continued to be the target of repeated and intensive study for over 150 years. There have been continuous and multiple annual projects for a century at specific sites like Tikal, Uaxactun, Kaminaljuyu, and Palenque, countless projects at Copan, and other long-explored sites with good previous data to build on and easier logistics. The ever-more-detailed evidence at those sites has been significant to Maya archaeology.

Nonetheless, it is impossible to understand even those regions and those sites, especially their economies, without a better sampling of the entire linked system and particularly the network of routes and agents of exchange that brought them their most critical resources, including obsidian, jade, salt, cacao, and even food. The movement of much—indeed most—of those resources was through the routes passing through the Transversal region. Until fairly recently this has been one of the most important "blank spots" on the map of Maya archaeology, and even now, with publications of large-scale investigations, the region continues to be largely ignored by Lowland Mayanists' interpretations.

THE COST OF THE MACRO-SAMPLING PROBLEM AND "CONNECTING THE DOTS" TO MAYANIST METHODOLOGY, INTERPRETATION, AND THEORY

A second great problem in Maya archaeology is linked to macro-sampling errors. For decades this corollary has greatly damaged method, interpretation, and theory: in order to compensate for our ignorance of large regions, scholars unwittingly use the fallacious interpretative device that I have for 20 years colloquially labeled as "Connecting the Dots" (e.g., Demarest 2009:258–259, 2011). We have continued to discuss exchange or other relationships as if they were between mythical *organic* entities, such as between "the highlands" and "the lowlands," between "Tikal" and "Caracol," between "Kaminaljuyu" and "the Pacific Coast," or with "the Olmec." That might be necessary as a starting point for more serious discussion, but instead such an approach has been dominant for a century and continues in Maya archaeology.

This is an archaic perspective in modern social theory, economics, sociology, and anthropology. The "highlands" and the "lowlands" are not organic wholes nor agents of any kind. On a more specific level, economic interaction was not carried out by "Kaminaljuyu" with "Tikal," nor between the "highlands" and the "Pacific Coast," nor were "the Olmec heartland" and "Izapa" actually agents, and it is often unlikely that their interaction was direct. We often simply construct interpretations between major known sites or areas, even if they are distant, and then do not sufficiently account for the many uninvestigated (or even investigated) sites between them. Also, we seldom investigate the possible routes and mechanisms for, as well as the agents and greatly variable methods and forms of, facilitating exchange. Instead, mythical economic landscapes are constructed and debated almost as if our sample was nearly complete. While all may understand this, many discussions go no further, because archaeologists often believe that they cannot, since more specific knowledge and closer investigation would be required. Yet that required search for agents and routes is precisely what we should be doing, as the Cancuen case demonstrates.

For example, it is almost normal practice to overemphasize imported ceramics or imitations to relate them to better-known "dots" far away, despite their often being only a tiny portion of those local ceramic assemblages, which often developed indigenously or regionally over time. Despite the minimal presence of these imported artifacts, subsequent analysis and discussion become dominated by anything that can connect the site to the well-known, more complex, and impressive distant centers or "cultures." Such emphasis also draws more attention to the archaeologist's work by connecting their finds to major known controversies about interregional systems. That is not necessarily the intention of the investigator, but such elements stand out when the ceramicist is struggling with unfamiliar new assemblages that are difficult to classify and relate to other assemblages in minimally investigated zones.

One "close-to-home" example of this is the Pacific coastal Early Preclassic site of El Mesak, Retalhuleu. In spite of having had a long and very detailed, well-dated, and continuous local sequence of ceramic types, wares, styles, and features (Demarest 1989), it was typically interpreted as an "Olmec outpost" on the Pacific trade route (see Demarest 2011) based only on the presence a small number of white-ware sherds, one with an "Olmec" jaguar motif that, upon reconstruction, appeared to come from a single vessel. Simple diamond-shaped designs on one other pot were widely distributed in eastern Mesoamerica. The less sensational tens of thousands of sherds of the local sequence, the local artifacts, the earthen architecture, and so on, drew little attention, as more time was required to analyze and interpret them in terms of local and regional development. Researchers have committed such mistakes, while many have had their data misinterpreted by others. At the core of this mistake, of course, is the interregional macro-sampling problem.

A more significant example of skewing in interregional sampling, and the resulting connect-the-dots interpretation, was pointed out as an obstacle in the 1980s and early 1990s by a number of scholars (e.g., Sharer and Grove 1989). In the "Olmec period" of the Early to Middle Preclassic, there were even more unsampled zones, but there were also many known but unexcavated sites with architectural patterns like those at La Venta that some pointed out (Demarest 1989; Sharer and Grove 1989).

Now, 30 to 40 years later, a series of innovative projects directed by Inomata and his teams (Inomata et al. 2020) have combined LiDAR identification of site features with subsequent ground excavation in several dozens of sites with the same layout, showing an even greater investment in labor in enormous platforms. Dozens of these, and still counting, have been identified well beyond the "Olmec Gulf Coast Heartland" into the Maya Lowlands from Tabasco and Chiapas to southern lowland centers like Ceibal (Inomata et al. 2013). Some of those, like Aguada Fenix (Inomata et al. 2020), are volumetrically larger than any contemporary or later Gulf Coast or Classic Maya constructions or ceremonial centers. More will be investigated, but already decades of interpretations of Middle Preclassic development and interaction have been negated and volumes of writing have been invalidated.

We will need to change our models and our future site targets for excavation. Current notions of the precocity and Middle Preclassic centrality of sites like El Mirador, Nakbe, and others will need to be seen in the light of this evidence of contemporary or earlier greater constructions and political complexity. Such progress was inhibited for decades by little investment in poorly sampled regions.

THE ELEPHANT IN THE ROOM: THE TRANSVERSAL

Very little investment in research has been carried out in the Transversal region of the far southwestern Peten border and the adjacent northern Verapaces and northern El Quiche zones. We have long known that, given its position, rivers, and routes (Figure 1.1), the Transversal region had to be a major zone of exchange between the southern lowland Maya civilization and the critical highland resources that it needed (e.g., Adams 1971; Arnauld 1990; Hammond 1972; Sidrys 1976; Woodfill and Andrieu 2012).

It is surprising that Mayanists did not investigate more in the Transversal

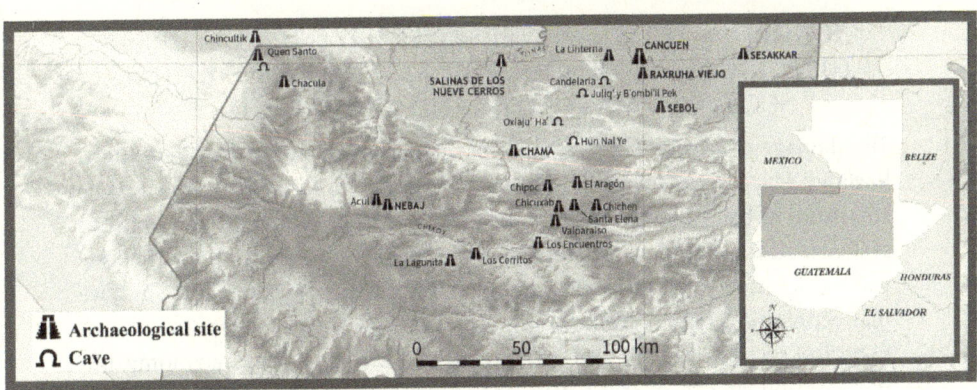

Figure 1.1. Transversal Strip and important sites within and around it. (Map made in Fresco. Courtesy of Luis Fernando Luin.)

and that they assumed it to be more or less passive in a totally unexplained process of highland to lowland trade, since the routes there had been pointed out and discussed 50 years ago. For examples, see articles in the New World Archaeological Foundation (NWAF) *Mesoamerican Communication Routes and Cultural Contacts* volume (Lee and Navarrete 1978), especially in the chapter by Adams (1978:27–36), who specified three different routes through the Transversal to the Pasión and Salinas Rivers, as well as land routes. Those interpretations were based on the obvious facts of geography but also on ethnohistorical evidence on the use of such routes, and a bit of archaeology (see also Hammond 1972:1092, 1973:601–607; Sidrys 1976).

Later Arnauld confirmed the necessary role of the Transversal routes through her excavations near Alta Verapaz close to Coban (Arnauld 1990). She also provided a map showing specific routes through the Transversal regions to both the Pasión and Salinas River routes (Arnauld 1990:349, Figure 1) and discussed the importance of the Transversal and its routes in other publications. Furthermore, excavations in the Transversal and Chixoy regions (e.g., Hatch 1982; Ichon 1979, 1982, 1992; Ichon et al. 1996) and especially by Sharer and Sedat (1987) in the Salama Valley identified ties, not only in ritual settings but also in artifacts, including some lowland Preclassic Chicanel ceramics. Chicanel and Mamom sherds have also been recovered in excavations at other sites in the Transversal (e.g., Ichon 1987; Sharer and Sedat 1987; Woodfill 2010; Woodfill et al. 2018).

There can be no doubt, as discussed below, that the Transversal routes and economic networks were critical to the culture histories of both the southern lowlands and all of the highlands. Yet most Mayanists, especially in the lowlands, still cannot see that elephant in the room.

IGNORING THE TRANSVERSAL ELEPHANT: CULTURE-HISTORICAL, METHODOLOGICAL, AND THEORETICAL COSTS TO MAYA LOWLAND ARCHAEOLOGY

The damage of myopia and regional parochialism in the study of southern lowland Maya archaeology has been enormous. Southern lowland reconstructions of basic culture-history, the nature of their economic and political systems, and the associated methodologies are flawed, as are their theoretical models due to insufficient interest and knowledge of their less spectacular economic partners to the south. The most obvious costs are to culture-historical reconstructions and interpretations of Classic Maya economy, but the "domino effects" of that have helped keep southern lowland archaeology decades behind in contemporary economic and social theory and its methodological and interpretative tools, as discussed below. The skewing of culture-historical interpretations is only the most obvious cost.

The centrality of Transversal research in understanding the history of the southern lowland Maya civilization should be quite clear. The findings to date show that we have no real comprehension of the critical economic relationships between the southern lowland Maya economies and those of the highlands. The Transversal and highlands are the sources for most of the central resources in Lowland Maya exchange and political economies, and they are a major factor in alliance and conflict throughout Maya history. This means, of course, that we have not begun to understand Lowland Maya political economies, networks, agents, or processes. The southern lowlands' interactions, alliances, marriages, and warfare were most often interconnected with control of those routes of trade. Without understanding the Upper Pasión and Transversal region and its routes and exchange relationships, we cannot understand the structure of lowland Classic Maya exchange and the agents, institutions, and mechanisms involved.

The very politics and history of Classic and Preclassic Maya societies in both lowland and highland regions are also obscured. That has been demonstrated by the findings of many small projects and the decade of the very large multi-institutional Petexbatun projects, the decade of large-scale Cancuen research, and then another decade of numerous Vanderbilt projects, and those of other institutions, at Transversal centers. They reveal quite different types of economies, political structures, and ideologies and the complex networks that connected them. The western routes through the highlands to the Transversal and then to the lowlands carried materials and products from the central highlands and Pacific Coast, as well as from the Transversal itself during the Middle Preclassic to Late Classic periods. Through or from the Transversal came much, and at times most, of the Peten obsidian, jade, plumage, and pyrite (from the Verapaz "biotopo del quetzal" area). The routes also carried the salt from the Salinas de los Nueve Cerros zone of the Transversal (see Chapter 8). Despite Dillon's work back in the mid-1970s (e.g., Dillon 1977; Dillon et al. 1988), the scale and importance of this source for the western Peten and elsewhere were greatly underestimated, perhaps in part because the scale of Dillon's work was small. Yet the importance of the source was clear from the deposits and the enormous brine storage cauldrons and other evidence of large-scale salt mining. Perhaps the architecture recovered was not impressive to Lowland Mayanists: the Nueve Cerros evidence was generally ignored or simply briefly mentioned in interpretations until more recent research (e.g., Woodfill 2011b, 2020; Woodfill et al. 2015).

The same problems can be said for the lack of identification and regional investigation of jade sources. In the eastern Quiche department, there is a large zone of clearly visible multiple-surface outcrops of jade, yet it was not generally known before the work of the Cancuen project and collaborating projects in the Transversal (e.g., Andrieu et al. 2011). Now that the Transversal/highland jade source has been identified and its distinctive jade has been analyzed, we will need to modify existing lowland route and exchange models and the related culture-histories. For example, a major aspect of the economy of Early Classic Tikal was based on its many workshops using both El Chayal obsidian and highland jade, which was then exported throughout the central southern lowlands (Woodfill and Andrieu 2012). The recent Transversal archaeological evidence includes many cave shrines with Central Peten Tzakol–style offerings and even a beautiful, albeit small, coffer carved with glyphs in central Peten style (Woodfill 2010; Woodfill et al. 2003; see Chapter 6).

This puts the Early Classic Tres Islas Pasión River shrine and those of the caves of the Transversal route in context. In the same way, recent seasons of excavations at Salinas de los Nueve Cerros and other sites in its region have increased our awareness of the truly massive scale of brine collection, processing, and export of salt cakes from the inland site to much of the western and probably central Peten (e.g., Woodfill 2020). The implications of the years of work on all these Transversal projects, discussed in chapters of this volume, are still largely pushed to the side by the belief that the Motagua was the main source of jade and that the Caribbean coast salt flats were the primary source of salt.

Obsidian was certainly the most critical material, and most of it had to move through the Transversal from the San Martin Jilotepeque source especially in the Preclassic, and from the El Chayal source in the Classic period, during which El Chayal constituted 80% of the obsidian in the southern lowlands (e.g., Andrieu 2009; personal communication 2021). Its movement through the Verapaces is geographically obvious and now confirmed. Of course, such routes would have carried much more than just obsidian, salt, and jade.

The lowland/highland academic divide is again the principal problem here and is at the root of much of the skewing of Maya macro-sampling and misguided interpretations. While this statement may come across as insulting, the citations and interpretations show that most Lowland Mayanists probably do not read articles and reports on the highlands in the Late Preclassic and Classic periods beyond Kaminaljuyu. Also, at meetings like the Society for American Archaeology or even the annual archaeological symposium in Guatemala City, sessions on the highlands always have few or no lowlanders in attendance to hear about the many sites and material culture exchanges. We can pretend otherwise out of collegiality, but this disciplinary schism is strangling economic interpretations in both regions.

Since I work and have always worked in both zones and the Transversal, I witness this lack of interest and parochialism from Lowland Mayanists as the core of the problem. When I give a talk on the southwest lowland/Transversal/highland interaction network, if the title sounds like it will be primarily a "lowland talk," I can expect up to a hundred or more will be in attendance, both lowlanders and highlanders, but if the title sounds more "highland," at most 20 to 30 will attend. This is one cause of the failure to understand that

Cancuen-centered talks are *not* about a "Classic Maya site" but about a lowland/highland hybrid site.

BROADER THEORETICAL AND CONCEPTUAL IMPACTS OF ENTERING THE TRANSVERSAL "MAZE"

In Classic southern lowland Maya archaeology, there have been great projects and breakthroughs in studies of paleoecology, offering new insights into infrastructure and settlement, as well as advances in epigraphy, use of LiDAR, and methodologies. However, when it comes to reaping the benefits of all of this for syntheses, theoretical implications, and new concepts, we are failing to truly reckon with the new data streams and, in turn, are maintaining the parochialism of studies of Maya political economics.

This situation became clear to our project researchers as the initially bewildering Upper Pasión, Cancuen, and Transversal data forced us to follow the same path of the Honduran research: the use of *network theories*. In turn, the many modes, variable forms, concepts, and methodologies in contemporary network approaches led to our direct collaboration with experts in large interdisciplinary fields that study economic practices and their "embeddedness" in and between societies or groups of all types, periods, and forms. Our theoretical work has greatly benefited from the logic, language, and critique in those fields, which is much clearer and "cleaner" perhaps because of the greater number of participants and more rigorous peer review. Additionally, the minimal use of rhetorical distortions and fallacies in critique may be attributed to the prevalence of case studies and quantifiable data. As a result of our 20-year learning curve in the Pasión Valley and the Transversal zones (Figure 1.2), we became more aware of our own errors in argument, outdated concepts, and flawed logic. This challenging process of trial and error changed our conceptual thinking and practice, all thanks to the labyrinthine and shifting networks of the Transversal.

IGNORING THE TRANSVERSAL IN HIGHLAND MAYA ARCHAEOLOGY: MISSING THE MOST IMPORTANT FACTOR IN HIGHLAND ROUTES AND ECONOMIES

The highlands present less of a "crisis" in conceptions and approaches. This is because highland sites and regions are more variable and also because there is less emphasis on "spectacular" sites, considering the lack of remarkable Transversal sites in the Preclassic and Classic periods. Kaminaljuyu, however, is too dominant in highland models, limiting their scope. Additionally, the macro-sampling problem in the highlands (due in part to the civil war) has led to limited knowledge and much speculation.

In general, the economic focus in the highlands has been on intra-highland

Figure 1.2. Area of some of Vanderbilt's 1999–2022 regional projects. (Map made in Fresco. Courtesy of Luís Fernando Luin.)

and highland-to-Pacific-Coast exchange. This ignores the enormous importance of the southern lowlands. During the later Preclassic and the Classic period, the principal consumers of highland goods and thus the central economic force in highland political economies would have been the millions of people at the many sites and sprawling cities of the southern lowlands—post-LiDAR estimates are between eight and 11 million (e.g., Canuto et al. 2018; Chase et al. 2012). Overlooking that crucial factor in highland study of routes, exchange, and economies has greatly limited interpretation and research priorities, leading to a skewed sample and unbalanced research designs. A principal interface for such exchange between the agents of the vast Lowland Maya cities and even within the highlands was the Transversal region.

One small example can be seen at the site of Semetabaj on the northern side of Lake Atitlan, where we are currently excavating. The site had an impressive florescence with adobe structures up to 12 m high, which is exceptionally large for the highland late Middle to early Late Preclassic. In an excellent new interpretation of the Atitlan region exchange, Davies and Ángeles Corado (2023) suggest that the period of success and construction at Semetabaj is attributed to its ideal location and probable role in the highland exchange of San Martin Jilotepeque (SMJ) obsidian.

Unfortunately, this Semetabaj-SMJ connection is viewed in terms of highland exchange, even though SMJ obsidian was the dominant source for millions in the southern lowlands during the same Middle to Late Preclassic periods. Beyond Kaminaljuyu, population levels in the highlands were comparatively small in the Middle to Late Preclassic and Classic periods, indicating that the large lowland populations would have been the major consumers of SMJ obsidian in that period. Given the location of the source, the routes of movement of SMJ obsidian would have passed through the Transversal, northern Quiche, and Verapaz regions, perhaps via the Chixoy, where the ceramics indicate a close relationship with the Semetabaj area. It is also not coincidental that the decline and near abandonment of Semetabaj corresponded to the later part of the Late Preclassic and the initial Classic period, when the popularity of SMJ obsidian declined in the southern lowlands and El Chayal obsidian rapidly grew to dominate. The change in preferences of obsidian types at the distant southern lowland cities could have been a cause of both Semetabaj's apogee and decline.

But again, the most important economic element is omitted: the consumption of most obsidian by the Lowland Maya cities. The purely academic highland/lowland divide continues to limit excellent research and insightful interpretations. Future research designs and global interpretations should focus on possible agents and centers along the highland/lowland exchange routes, as well as economic impacts on different highland groups, particularly in the Transversal in the Preclassic and Classic periods.

THE MYTHS OF THE CLASSIC MAYA CITIES OF THE SOUTHEAST REGION AS PRINCIPAL CORRIDOR OF EXCHANGE BETWEEN LOWLANDS, HIGHLANDS, AND CENTRAL AMERICA

Scholars have, since the beginning of formal investigations in the Maya region 150 years ago, largely overlooked the southwestern Peten and the Verapaz/Quiche Transversal. In contrast, far southeastern Maya centers, specifically Copan and Quirigua, have been central to the discussions of Classic Period exchange with Central America and the highlands since the latter nineteenth century (e.g., Arnauld 1990; Rathje 1971; Sharer 1983), largely because of the presence of spectacular manifestations of Classic Maya architecture, art, texts, and treasures. Dazzled by this spectacle, Mayanist archaeologists assumed that the southeastern Classic Maya states controlled the Ixtepeque obsidian and Motagua jade sources—the latter previously believed to be the only major source of Maya lowland jade. However, recent discoveries have shown that another important, likely equally common source was in the northern Verapaces and El Quiche, just south of the Transversal regions.

Indeed, compositional analyses and distributions of obsidian and jade, as well as the archeological evidence of the past 25 years, have rendered obsolete the interpretations that the Maya cities of the southeast region were the major agents controlling the corridors of exchange between the lowland Classic Maya and their neighbors to the south. To the contrary, in the Late Preclassic and especially Classic period, the evidence has shown that very little of economic significance from the south was coming through those centers and that they did not control or even culturally dominate those southeast "border" regions. Ixtepeque obsidian was far to the southwest and of secondary importance in the lowlands in the Classic period (e.g., Andrieu 2009). While Motagua jade was important and did come north from there, it was always simply assumed that Quirigua controlled that jade trade or was a major force in it. Yet there is no archaeological evidence to support that inference. This stands in stark contrast to the mountains of jade debris and preforms at Cancuen. Recent continuous research in the Motagua and adjacent regions by small Guatemalan teams has indicated that Motagua jade production usually took place at multiple smaller sites near local sources with no external and minimal internal elite control and no connection to Quirigua or Copan (e.g., Rochette 2014; Romero 1999).

THE WORK OF EDWARD SCHORTMAN AND PATRICIA URBAN: RETHINKING CLASSIC MAYA DOMINANCE OF AGENCY AND "PERIPHERIES"

Edward Schortman, Patricia Urban, and their teams have conducted more than four decades of directly relevant investigations, the findings of which have been published in books, articles, and annual meeting presentations (e.g., Schortman and Ashmore 2012). Despite the importance of their work to culture-history, it has often been overlooked or understated.

Their research negated the myths of an inflated economic role and southeastern lowland Maya dominance of the Honduran "periphery," but today the broader implications of their findings seem to have been forgotten. They revealed that Classic Maya centers of the southeastern region were not the primary region of imports from the east and south, and that their role in economic exchange was generally minimal at the Honduran sites.

No evidence has been found of Quirigua control or dominance of jade sources to the west. Instead, Schortman and Urban found that local independent elites at western Honduran sites formed their own networks with only some general stylistic elements from the Classic Maya.

Struggling to find alternative approaches to research design and interpretation, Schortman and Urban searched for other interpretative frameworks that could actually fit the evidence. Their progression of research was prophetic, anticipating the learning curve of the 1989–1997 Petexbatun project and especially of the 1999–present Cancuen regional and Transversal interregional network site projects. Our own investigations owe them much for blazing the path toward network alternatives.

AN EARLY USE OF NETWORK APPROACHES TO EASTERN MESOAMERICAN MAYA ARCHAEOLOGY

When Schortman and Urban's teams began to explore the many smaller sites in Honduras, they found that the then-popular "world system" and "core vs. periphery" models were simply incompatible with their evidence. Faced with those findings, how were they to proceed in research designs and interpretation of the data and patterns in the western Honduran sites? They came to realize that only network theory and network approaches would work to interpret the nature and relationships of the communities, their interaction, and even intra-site interactions in terms of the use of symbols, forms of production, and distribution of artifacts and styles (e.g., Schortman and Ashmore 2012; Schortman and Urban 1994). They found that many of those elements had symbolic significance and linked internal and external relations of the communities and the individuals in them—real "agents." The rest of their published work, mostly centered on the AD 800–900 portion of the Postclassic period, relied heavily on network approaches (e.g., Schortman and Urban 2011).

This approach aligns with the broader concept of social theory, which for decades has used network approaches in economics, political science, sociology, and psychology—as well as the physical sciences. Today, network methodologies and interpretations have become central to understanding linkages between individuals and other entities, as well as economic partnerships and systems. Shortman and Urban used a multilevel approach to networks in their Honduran research and interpretations.

Two decades later the Cancuen and Cancuen Regional Transversal projects, initially inadvertently recapitulated the earlier work of Schortman and Urban and slowly shifted research designs to general network theory and then to its more varied contemporary subfields. By 2005–2006 it became clear, just as it had earlier for them, that we had no further options for site and route investigation across such a "new" region with so few shared political and economic norms between centers.

One argument that has challenged and inhibited acceptance of network approaches is that in archaeology we cannot usually identify specific agents. This critique overlooks the very utility of network theory, or any clear theory, which provides a framework for scholars to investigate and gradually comprehend and identify the actions, practices, and resulting consequences of agents at various levels. In turn, this reflexively leads to broader insights into the interactions and processes. That is exactly the purpose of research designs—not just to make discoveries and interpret data but to investigate the unknowns and address those knowledge gaps in our research and conclusions.

THE MOVE SOUTH: VANDERBILT PROJECTS IN THE MIDDLE PASIÓN, 1986–1997

Over three decades, Vanderbilt and other institutions carried out investigations of the major western Pasión riverine highway in the lowlands, as well as its connecting land and river zones and routes (see Figure 1.2), beginning at Dos Pilas and the Petexbatun region. The Harvard projects at Ceibal conducted large-scale excavations there (Willey 1990). Aguateca and Dos Pilas had been explored with a few test pits, but Ian Graham later made preliminary maps of their epicenters, while epigraphic research was carried out by Peter Matthews, then Stephen Houston, and others (see Pasión Valley archaeological history in Demarest et al. 2012). Most of this large region was still unexplored, with no significant excavation except for Ceibal, located in the area that had been dominated by the Dos Pilas hegemony for only 20 to 25 years. In the decade of 1989–1997, the Vanderbilt Petexbatun regional projects carried out excavations and exhaustive large-scale investigations at all major centers in the region, as well as at many new major and minor sites, villages, caves, and rural landscapes (e.g., Demarest 2006a).

All of these projects seem to be primarily remembered for the study of the early collapse of Dos Pilas in AD 761 and the subsequent years of endemic warfare in this region, but there were other equally significant findings, especially concerning long-distance exchange. Ceramic analysis and instrumental neutron activation analysis (INAA) served as a central research guide for the project and all subsequent Vanderbilt projects. The first full "subterranean settlement pattern" project was carried out as an autonomous part of the hegemonic multi-institutional research (e.g., Brady 2009; Brady and Prufer 2005; Demarest 2006a), which demonstrated the central role of caves in all aspects of Maya civilization—not just ritual, but political and economic. The cave studies also pointed south to the Transversal, which was always thought to contain the major entrances to the Maya Underworld.

Those Petexbatun project priorities, as well as a multisite hegemonic structure of subprojects and collaborating projects from other institutions, became the modus operandi for the next two decades of Vanderbilt investigations. The Tikal and then Dos Pilas leaders aimed to control the Pasión trade route due to geography and its southern upriver connections. Those connections were underscored by Dos Pilas texts referring to "The Lady of Cancuen" as a major figure at Dos Pilas, where the extraordinary masonry of her own palace, throne, and panels with texts was far superior to that at the palace of the king. All evidence indicated the importance of an alliance with the then-modest but economically strategic site of Cancuen. Following the evidence, the Vanderbilt and collaborating multi-institutional projects moved south, upriver, to the Pasión interface with the highlands.

THE UPPER PASIÓN/CANCUEN LEARNING CURVE

The 1999–2022 Cancuen, Upper Pasión, and highland Transversal projects began with southern lowland Classic Maya hypotheses and templates for everything from ceramic analysis, house mound "types," and architecture types to obsidian and jade exchange and production. Also, as a team of primarily Lowland Maya archaeologists, we followed the general practice of imposing rather stereotyped economic interpretations based on Aztec or Postclassic ethnohistory and some inscriptions on monuments. Furthermore, some retrospective textual references to two Cancuen rulers being invested at Calakmul led many, including us, to initially believe in the "royal road" hypothesis of the Calakmul presence at Cancuen as controlling the Pasión Valley. Such assumptions misled us and still mislead most Lowland Maya scholars concerning the "Classic Maya" nature of Cancuen.

Later, after decades of excavations, research, recovery, and analysis of over half a million artifacts and historiographic critique, it became clear that Calakmul's role at Cancuen was only as a status-enhancing reference and symbolic connection and that Calakmul actually had no influence there. Indeed, Calakmul never controlled the Upper Pasión or even the Middle Pasión routes. There is no evidence whatsoever of Calakmul's presence or even influence at Cancuen—not a sherd, artifact, or architectural element at Cancuen, nor a Cancuen influence or artifact at Calakmul. Even in terms of epigraphic texts and culture-history, Calakmul's overall involvement even in the Middle Pasión fluctuated, occurring only between approximately 650 and 695 (Martin and Grube 2008). This contrasts greatly with the ample physical evidence at Cancuen of artifacts, architecture, ritual settings, stylistic elements, and ceramic types coming from each of its Transversal economic partners, and earlier from Dos Pilas and more distant partners in Veracruz, Chiapas, as well as other piedmont agents and communities along the El Quiche/Verapaz border zone.

Furthermore, in the period of the "kings" crowned at or by Calakmul, Cancuen was a tiny site. It began to slowly acquire size and significance only much later, during its period of a marriage alliance with Dos Pilas from approximately 730 to 760, long after the AD 695 defeat and decline of Calakmul's interregional influence or presence. Note that in contrast with Calakmul, the later Dos Pilas/Cancuen relationship was reflected in some elements of architecture, monuments, caches, and texts just before the beginning of Cancuen's 760 to 800 apogee. Even the Petexbatun's fluctuating connection to Cancuen was for about 25 years or less, just before Cancuen's own apogee as a major economic power, which occurred primarily after the 761 fall of Dos Pilas. Cancuen's apogee was correlated with its 760–800 economic network with the Transversal, but it was an economic alliance rather than a political one.

Our obsession with Classic Maya lowland kings added to the continuing failure to see Cancuen as being a Transversal/Maya site that was developing a totally different type of economic system from that of the southern lowlands. Despite the Dos Pilas and occasionally Cancuen references to their Calakmul connections, given the archaeological data and lack of chronological alignment, a more critical historiographic interpretation would see this as their desire to associate with a great prestigious center, a *tollan*, to enhance the status of the Dos Pilas and Cancuen rulers' alleged legacy, similar to the relationship between Tikal and Teotihuacan or Chichen Itza and Tula.

Regarding ceramics and chronology, we had begun with the idea of establishing a Tzakol- and Tepeu-related Late Classic ceramic sphere typology (e.g., Demarest and Barrientos 1999). Yet it gradually became clear that the

Cancuen ceramics were an assemblage not of Classic Maya but of interregional and "international" styles, types, modes, and pastes. By 2006 the ceramic and lithic studies reached a breaking point, when INAA studies of our Fine Gray and Altar Fine Orange ceramics demonstrated that those fine pastes were not ninth century at all. They were actually eighth-century Chablekal Fine Grays from Chiapas and Tabasco and seventh-to-eighth-century Campamento Fine Orange from Veracruz (Bishop et al. 2005). Cancuen had many more Transversal, highland, and Mexican types and pastes than Classic Maya types (Torres et al. 2014).

As excavation and mapping continued, we also found that the "Type I to Type IV" household groups typology borrowed from traditional Classic Maya projects did not correspond to mound or group variability at Cancuen. The structures and groups found had much greater variability in types, constructions, and patterns, which we later learned was evidence of the complex "hybrid" nature of its population.

THE SUDDEN RADICAL 2005 CHANGE LAUNCHING US INTO CONTEMPORARY THEORY

In 2005 the ceramic findings brought to a final end all of our lowland models of Cancuen as a "Classic Maya site": the jolting discovery from INAA ceramic compositional analysis (Bishop et al. 2005) that our Altar Fine Orange was in fact Campamento Fine Orange, a very similar fine paste ceramic, which was sourced to Veracruz. These vessels and sherds shared remarkably similar forms and pastes, but Campamento Fine Orange and Chablekal Fine Grey ceramics ended everywhere before AD 800. The INAA compositional analyses by Bishop and colleagues were confirmed by the leading Veracruz ceramicist in an examination at Cancuen (Chrisopher Pool, personal communication 2007) and 15 more years of laboratory studies (e.g., Torres et al. 2018b). Together with other evidence, this dating forced us to abandon preliminary ideas about the chronology, changing it by at least a century!

In terms of interpretation of the site and its regional culture-history, especially its economy and political economy, that chronological change also meant that the site apogee and period of large-scale production of obsidian and jade for export was extraordinarily short. Suddenly, everything changed. The shortened period meant there was a mass scale of production for jade and obsidian. It also meant Cancuen was economically engaged not only with the Transversal and highlands but also with distant Veracruz and Tabasco. This was evinced by the Veracruz Campamento ceramics as well as by the amount of obsidian from Zaragoza, Puebla—a source located near Veracruz—found at the site, which made up more of the Cancuen assemblage than at any other site in the Maya Lowlands (e.g., Andrieu 2009; Andrieu and Quiñónez 2011).

Yet Cancuen was still exporting some jade and obsidian to lowland centers from 780/786 to 800, a period of disintegration of the Classic Maya dynastic polities to the north. Note that the variable 780-versus-786 date is due to 780 being the ceramic and midden stratigraphy date (e.g., Torres et al. 2018b) and 786 being based on textual dedication dates for one of the sequential 760–800 reconstructions and expansions of the royal palace (e.g., Barrientos 2014). After that, correction of the previous lithic studies and new post-2003 lithics were begun by Andrieu, as well as detailed distributional studies of imported ceramic and lithics, which indicated that there was elite control of large-scale jade production in the 780/786–801 period.

These collective findings meant that we had to abandon the usual models of Classic southern lowland centers and apply new approaches to research design, analyses, and models for interpretation. It was necessary to expand our focus beyond the economic concepts typically used in Maya archaeology. This included collaborating and coauthoring publications with experts in various interdisciplinary fields and subfields such as comparative economics, economic sociology, strategic management theory, institution theory, crisis management theory, organization theory, partnership formation theory, and nonmoralistic forms of trust and contract theories (Das and Bing-Sheng 1998, 2001; Davis 2016; Sytch et al. 2012; Zucker 1986; and many others). Most of the myriad specialists in those fields use forms of network theory and field theory and apply it to economic, social, ideological, political, or personal networks of any kind. Most apply concepts of culturally embedded economies, institutions, practices, and "economic ethics" in their thousands of case studies on "modern," "ancient," "non-Western," and "Indigenous" economies.

NEW EVIDENCE, CORRECTED ANALYSIS, AND UPDATED THEORY ON CANCUEN ECONOMY

In 1999–2000 we began our study of Cancuen economy and production with the standard models and templates of Classic Lowland Maya archaeology. We incorporated these into our successful grant proposals and initial research designs, which included domestic household production, attached or independent artisans, and elite crafting of final precious artifacts. Subsequent excavations and lab work in the following decade, as well as the corrected chronology, revealed a huge quantity of imported ceramics, mass production in a short period, and grave goods. Also, the artifact architecture locations and forms, as well as their extensive excavations, revealed eight stages of reconfiguring the sprawling royal palace.

The short, new production period revealed by the excavations and distributional studies was 40 years for obsidian and only 10 to 20 years for jade—only 14 years from the palace sequence of dedication dates. This contradicted traditional Classic Maya models of independent household craft production of jade and fine crafting by elite artisans found elsewhere in the lowlands. Instead, it indicated that jade production at Cancuen involved literal "mass production" under the control of elites (Andrieu et al. 2011, 2014; Demarest et al. 2014; Demarest et al. 2020). The vast quantities of jade debris were not the result of over a century of small-scale production but were part of production on an enormous scale.

We then had to bring in top lithic experts to conduct years of complete reanalysis of previously excavated material and, in the following decade, to analyze all the artifacts and debris recovered at Cancuen, Raxruha Viejo, and other sites (Andrieu and Forné 2010; Andrieu et al. 2011, 2014).

Those analyses found that these materials and other products, as well as their production areas, were not distributed across the site but were concentrated in a northern zone near one of Cancuen's Pasión River ports. Nobles' range structures or small palaces were located right above the production zone and also just to the south of it. Jade was *not* exchanged at a site marketplace but was controlled by the elite in long-distance exchange. Surprisingly, there was very little jade even in the epicenter and tombs, including in that of the king, and almost none beyond it. As it turns out, this is a normal pattern in production and exchange systems, especially in the initial stages of economic network formation.

Meanwhile, the large obsidian core and debris deposits were concentrated in stela caches in the epicenter and on the edge of it (Andrieu and Quiñónez 2011; see Andrieu 2009). Unlike the jade debris, the elite obsidian caches are not an unusual pattern as at many sites, but again the *scale* was unprecedented. In this 40-year period, Cancuen had more worked or half-worked cores than in almost 250 years at Late Classic Tikal!

Cancuen was part of a much larger interregional market for its high-valued Transversal and highland materials and products. The findings contradicted models of "market economies" that are still used in Lowland Maya archaeology. While some market exchange was surely small, local exchange of subsistence and basic goods was present somewhere at Cancuen. Yet the city's core economic system was fundamentally different in nature from standard marketplace oriented interpretations. A real understanding of what a market economy actually is has nothing to do with "marketplaces." Instead, it involves networks of information exchange and knowledge of "equivalences" of the value of specific goods and commodities, which can be altered, restricted, or manipulated by factors such as sumptuary rules, status rank, kinship, or more often individual practices by economic agents. These factors exist in all societies, and there is no clear distinction between inalienable and alienable possessions, materials, or products until they are totally removed from human contract.

As it turned out, the problems we faced in our learning curve were due to both our attempts to force a Classic Maya southern lowland template onto Cancuen and the archaic nature of that template itself. For all our subsequent work, we put aside our Mayanist assumptions. Our investigations, analyses, and interpretations began to be guided by collaboration with scholars and gurus in other fields, using more universally applied concepts.

CORRECTION OF MODELS BASED ON 2000 GRANT PROPOSALS AND 2001 TO 2003 DATA: MISINTERPRETATIONS OF THE MOST IMPORTANT FEATURES AND THE VERY NATURE OF CANCUEN

Unfortunately, some of those early ideas based on our grant proposals in 2000 continue to be reported up to the present in publications and papers (e.g., Kovacevich 2011, 2013; Kovacevich and Callaghan 2019). The early 2000–2003 studies had imposed standard Classic Southern Maya lowland archaeological and ethnohistorical templates for domestic production, house mound typologies, fine ware identifications and datings, views on Maya economies and markets, and so on (e.g., Kovacevich 2006). In 2000 we were still in the steep learning curve described above and actually knew very little about Cancuen because few excavations had been conducted. Furthermore, even at that time there were numerous contradictions in the reports and publications that detailed the artifacts present in those contexts. A full inventory and review showed misreported numbers and types of critical artifacts for certain interpretations, and some artifacts reported did not even exist (e.g., Torres et al. 2016). The only "domestic jade workshop" specifically proposed at the time contains a total of only one small fragment of jade debris and one boulder of jade in a primary midden, like many others at the site.

Nonetheless, those grant proposal hypotheses have continued to be reported, even explicitly criticizing and dismissing the two decades of subsequent work by over 50 scholars (e.g., Kovacevich and Callaghan 2019). That is despite lab work, thousands of cubic meters of subsequent excavations at many network sites and Cancuen itself, and the analyses of over 600,000 artifacts from Cancuen and its connected Transversal partners and "hybrid sites." Contemporary analysis and reanalysis of obsidian and jade artifacts and debris (e.g., Andrieu and Forné 2010; Andrieu and Quiñónez 2011; Andrieu et al. 2011, 2014), and a chronology that by 2005 was a century shorter (e.g., Bishop et al. 2005; Torres et al. 2016, 2018b) narrowed the apogee to 40 years and the jade production period to 14 years or less, by some ceramic types at most 20 years.

It is important to begin more vigorously correcting the production myths about Cancuen regarding jade, obsidian, and Calakmul. Two decades of investigations, excavations, and lab work have resulted in precise documentation and understanding of the unique nature of Cancuen as a center with a specialized function in large-scale production and as an exporter of commodities in a greater *interregional* market. It also had another type of internal economic, political, and social structure resulting from its large scale of production and export economy, one deeply embedded in the non-Classic Maya Transversal network. The results of these findings could help change Mayanists' economic models and introduce to the Maya field new contemporary concepts and approaches to economy from a range of interdisciplinary fields.

INTERNAL ORGANIZATION AND ECONOMIC AGENTS

In other subprojects we began to see and understand that Cancuen's internal political structure and political economy were also different from most Classic Maya models and indicated the agency of various groups in the development of Cancuen and the initiation of the Upper Pasión/Transversal network. For example, deep and extensive excavations of the royal palace, one of the largest in the Classic Maya world, demonstrated that in the 750–800 period, its reconstructions changed the architectural structure and the nature of rooms, plazas, and its ceremonial axis. These elements reflected a change in political structure, with the power and even the physical space of the *k'uhul ajaw* (holy lord) becoming limited as elite merchant leaders took control of this economic center. During the major phases of palace reconstruction, it became a large administrative complex with many small offices, or *audiencias*, some with huge stucco portraits above them, and those were not of the *k'uhul ajaw*.

More recent excavations discovered a Postclassic-style colonnaded gathering hall in the same AD 760–808 period, about AD 780. That structure was amid courtyards and long terraces with many *audiencias* and central plazas. Fine range structures—nobles' palaces—were located above the sprawling jade workshop and at each of the Cancuen ports, the most critical assets of this site at the head of navigation of the Pasión River. The royal throne room and residence became quite restricted and surrounded by small nonresidential audiencia chambers. Overall, the palace had become an administrative complex, a ritualized economic headquarters for the most powerful but nonroyal agents in its economic networks.

THE NATURE OF THE AD 760–800 UPPER PASIÓN/TRANSVERSAL ECONOMIC AND RITUAL BREAKAWAY NETWORK

While working with collaborators from multiple disciplines, I learned about the various forms of contemporary economic theory and application using network approaches. Remember that such networks need not be between organic imagined "entities" like sites or civilizations. They are designated for any type of network in any aspect of a society, economic or political agent, individual, and so on. In analyses, my collaborators immediately identified clear network patterns. Most significantly they recognized the type of community network linking specific elements of the southern lowland Classic Maya entities, agents, and systems in the Late Classic period. As exemplified in Martin and Grube's famous "subway," or, as I call it, "intestinal graph," there were constant interactions between southern lowland centers in many different networks (Martin and Grube 2008:21). Note that they include royal marriages and family ties, diplomatic (i.e., political) contacts, war, explicit statements of hierarchy, and other relationships. They proposed different types of overlapping networks generally confirmed by the archaeological evidence. The number of different networks shows these would also have been *economic* networks for many forms of exchange.

Of course, today the number of players and networks would be even greater (now like a "twisted colon"?). However, I do not agree that Late Classic period interactions were Calakmul- and Tikal-centric to that degree, since many of the strongest network ties of those sites existed for only short periods in the late seventh century. The archaeological evidence now suggests changing some historiographic interpretations, because apart from "diplomatic ties," which were largely symbolic, Cancuen has proven to have no connections, especially political or economic, to Calakmul, as described above.

Despite those caveats, the Martin and Grube model does, perhaps inadvertently, move toward a network model, one showing multiple networks. It does not, however, address the obvious economic networks that would be necessary in such a system but that would leave few to no textual traces. What they are illustrating is part of an archetypical community network of partners identified by artifact imports and distributions, as well as necessary exchanges of critical imports like obsidian, jade, coastal shell and stingray spines, salt, cotton, and cacao, and by the late seventh century large-scale movement of foodstuffs (e.g., Chase and Chase 1998; Demarest et al. 2020; Demarest et al. 2021; Freidel and Reilly 2010; Freidel et al. 2016; Guderjan 2007). My collaborators in strategic management from the Mayanist readings, my own talks, and review of our evidence identified these patterns as well as the "breakaway" nature of Cancuen and the Transversal (Figure 1.3).

To clarify, a "community network" of economic partners and agents is a multipartner stable network. Network studies applied here model the opportunities in, and obstacles to, changing practices in the formation of new partnerships due to differing economic ethics or management "cultures." Some types of networks are innovative, first initiating dyadic relationships (Figure 1.4a) between just two new partners (e.g., Davis 2016; Sytch et al. 2012).

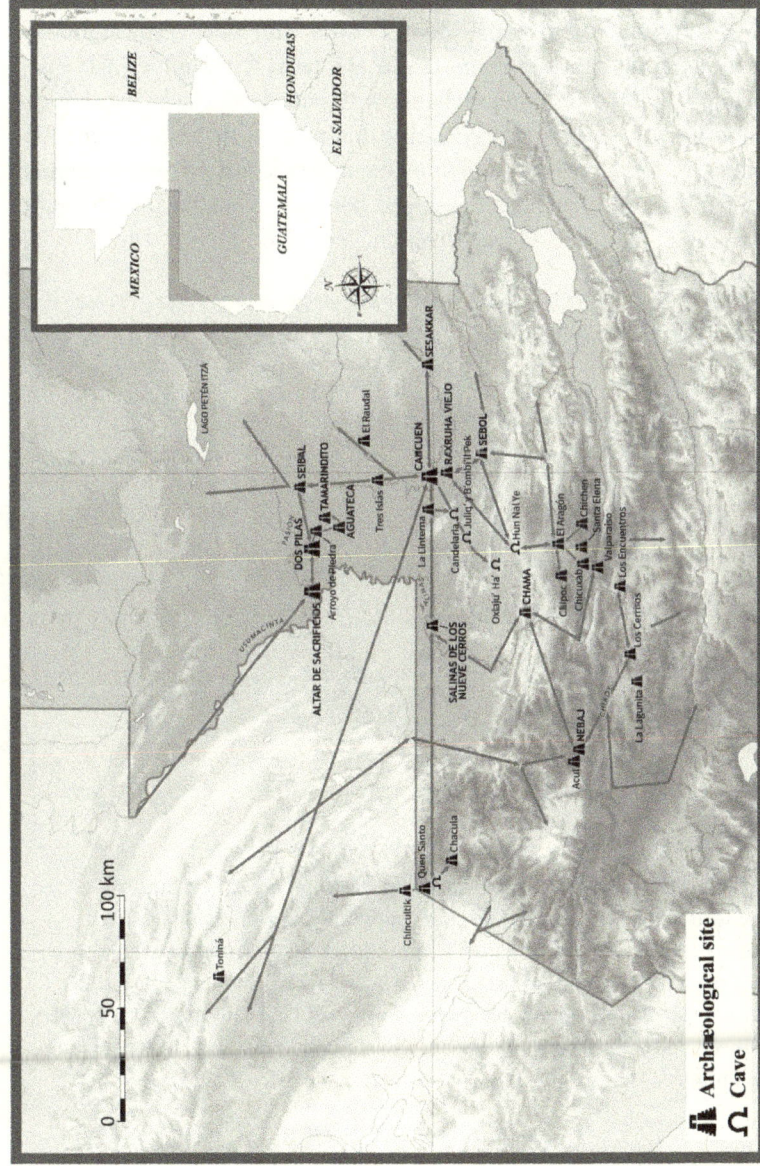

Figure 1.3. Some of the nodes and links of the Cancuen and Transversal network. (Map made in Photoshop. Courtesy of Luis Fernando Luin.)

Such dyadic, or subsequently triadic (Figure 1.4b), economic partnerships are characteristic of initial formation of a multipartner community network (Figure 1.4c). Considering the standard and ubiquitous use in Mayanist archeology of the "Fallacy of the Excluded Middle" or "False Dilemma," which dichotomizes arguments to make them absolute and thus easily refutable by any exception (a "strawman"), note that the term "community network" does not imply that they have no exchange with outside agents or economies. Rather, it is a relative descriptor indicating that most of the major economic collaborations or exchanges occur *within* that network and that an "economic culture" of norms and trust has developed between agents in that network (e.g., Davis 2016; Doz 1996; Oliver 1996; Zucker 1986).

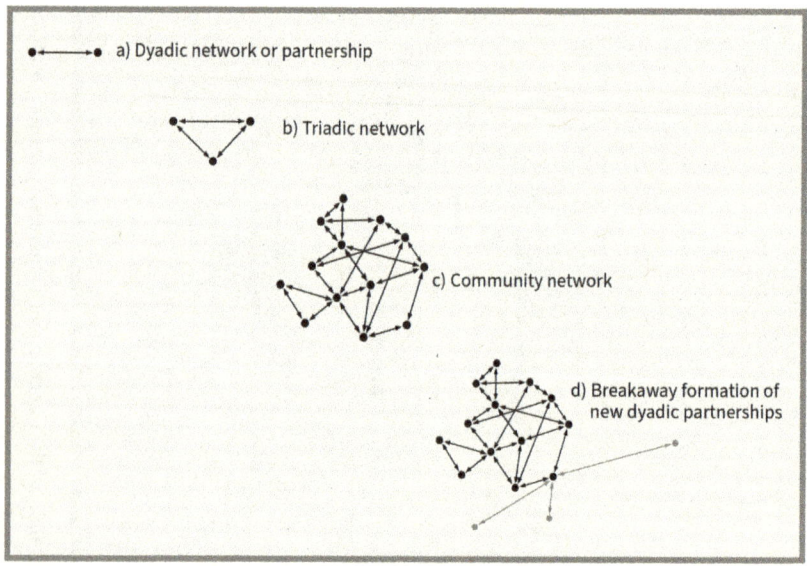

Figure 1.4. Schematic of partnership forms in the development of networks. All of these were seen in the Southern Lowlands: a community network (c) in the Peten, and the Cancuen/Transversal breakaway network (d). Cancuen's breakaway network created a series of dyadic links (a) but collapsed before it could develop into a stable network. These are not necessarily geographical routes but are conceptual schematics of the connections between economic agents. (Map made in Fresco. Courtesy of Luís Fernando Luin.)

Community networks tend to be far more stable, with lower risk since each participant *shares* multiple partners with the others over a long period, which creates shared norms, practices, and value equivalencies, and, above all, engenders trust, thus maintaining stability (Das and Bing-Sheng 1998;

Davis 2016; Doz 1996; Sytch et al. 2012). Conflicts and even large wars occur, but the multiple shared partners and concepts allow the integrity of the network to survive. Note that I am referring not to the "trust" that has been utilized in Mayanist interpretations but to the type that is based on the theological institution models of "moral communities." I am using the specifics of contemporary trust and contract formation network theory that are much further developed and objective (e.g., Das and Bing-Sheng 1998, 2001; Sytch et al. 2012; Zucker 1986).

While community network economies are more stable, over time they become less open to the addition of new external economic partners (Tatarynowicz et al. 2016). They have slower growth, less innovation, and long-term risks of economic decline (e.g., Granovetter 1985; Tatarynowicz et al. 2016; Uzzi 1996). Over time, increasing interdependence in the network can also lead to hyper-coherence. Those increasingly conservative aspects of community networks can lead to economic agents reaching out to form new "breakaway networks" (see Figure 1.4d). New dyadic one-on-one noncommunity partnerships are often a first step in a breakaway network formation (Breschi and Malerba 2007; Davis 2016; Doz 1996; Sytch et al. 2012). Dyadic partnerships can also result from later decisions by agents in a mature community network to look outside for new non-network partners for exchange or production activities (Tatarynowicz et al. 2016).

Such new dyadic connections in the formation of breakaway "innovation networks" exchange not only commodities or products but also ideas on economic practices and organization (e.g., Cowan and Jonard 2004; Whittington et al. 2009). These can bring rapid development, success, and wealth, as exemplified at Cancuen (e.g., Cowan and Jonard 2004; Davis 2016; Sytch et al. 2012). On the downside, new dyadic or open networks carry greater risks (Das and Bing-Sheng 2001; Freeman et al. 1983) because the ethics or economic cultures may differ between unfamiliar entities and can be problematic and potentially conflictive. Common exchange norms require shared partners and time to build trust (Das and Bing-Sheng 1998, 2001; Zucker 1986; see also Golden and Scherer 2013 for a parallel emphasis on "trust" in Maya political cohesion but one based on much earlier theological models).

Again, the above-cited applications of network theories, strategic management interpretations, and institutional analyses are often applied to non-Western, historical, ancient, and Indigenous economies since such features have been found to be particularly useful in addressing the functioning of institutions, agency, and strategies anywhere. Such specific features are found in all manner of economies in differing contexts and to different degrees (see discussion in Demarest et al. 2020).

"AGENCY OF LEADERS"

Our early years of struggles in understanding the striking economic and political differences of Cancuen from other Classic Maya cities were reflective of the often-cited "variability" between Maya sites, and they also indicated that Cancuen had an economic structure, as seen in its material culture, that contrasted with political economies of other southern lowland states and regions. Much of that difference was due to the simple fact that Cancuen was not actually a Classic Maya site but primarily a Transversal site. Many of its ceramics styles presumably exist because of the highland and Transversal population there having types, modes, and forms in the styles of the ceramics of nearby Verapaz sites, and its ritual settings reflect the interaction of the different cultures and economic ideologies that helped create new ritual networks.

Cancuen proved to be a late-eighth-century "hybrid" economic power with its economic agents, probably identified as "nobles," being in control, rather than the *k'uhul ajaw*. Through a complex strategy described in more details in the next chapter, Cancuen's economy agents stimulated the formation of a nonterritorial economic network based on commerce—like the Venetian maritime noncontinuous and largely nonterritorial mercantile "hegemony." However, the Upper Pasión, Cancuen, and Transversal network of interaction and exchange was even less militaristic than Venice was and had less political control over its partners. Agency was widely distributed at various levels of the system.

All aspects of that material culture also directed us to look at sites in the Transversal regions of the Verapaz and northern El Quiche. That required other new research strategies and use of different contemporary economic concepts to fill in the "blank spots" in sampling in eastern Mesoamerica and also a "blank spot" in the economic thinking of some Mayanists!

Thus, as we entered more deeply into that initially obscure zone of the Transversal and its new complex elements, we had to use not just network interpretations but the corpus of theory, concepts, and case studies on network formation, economic ideology, and the "network failure."

THE AD 750–800 TRANSVERSAL, UPPER PASIÓN, AND CANCUEN NETWORK: A SMALL WINDOW INTO TWO MILLENNIA OF TRANSVERSAL ECONOMIC EXCHANGE

One of the key facts about Cancuen's role in the late-eighth-century Transversal and Upper Pasión network is that Cancuen did not exist for two millennia of Transversal exchange and economics before and after its brief, but spectacular, apogee. The Cancuen-period network provides excellent detailed evidence that is only a brief view of the central role and great scale of Transversal exchange throughout the history of Maya lowland and highland civilization.

A host of scholars studied Cancuen for over two decades and invested even more time in exploration and excavations at the very different Transversal sites of the piedmont and the highland "frontier." Those networks were central to Lowland and Highland Maya exchange and economics in the late eighth century. Yet we must emphasize that other Transversal regions, routes, and centers, sans Cancuen, were always critical in the Preclassic, Early Classic, sixth and seventh centuries, Postclassic, Colonial, and even modern periods (see Chapters 2, 8, and 11).

The short-lived, though much more visible, network of Cancuen and its partners had more impressive architecture and monuments, and Cancuen displayed a huge concentration of materials involved in exchange, but in all other periods different types of Transversal networks and multiple routes (for example, Figure 1.5 shows some of the natural river and valley routes) channeled such massive quantities of needed materials to various regions before and after Cancuen, as glimpsed in the chapters in this volume.

For example, you can see in Chapter 5 that there was a Nueve Cerros-Chipoc-Cancuen ceramic network of exchange in materials covering the Transversal region in the 750 to 800 period, but such shared material culture "spheres" existed in the Transversal before and after the Cancuen era. Materials also moved using other multiple routes of transport. Critical Transversal resources and products were moving from and through these shifting networks to the consumers of every period. Note that we now also know that the products and networks of the Transversal included many materials, not just the lithic ones, for general needs of consumption of the lowland population, including cacao, cotton, salt, and foodstuffs, as suggested by the archaeological investigations and specifically described in the Colonial Period records on economy and tribute (Caso Barrera and Aliphat F. 2006a, 2012; see also this volume Chapters 8 and 11).

Although the investigation of the Transversal regions has just begun, it is already stimulating a broader revolution in research designs, methodologies, interpretations, and economic models and concepts. Even the initial efforts synthesized in this volume make it clear that without much more Transversal research we will never understand some of the most central aspects of both southern lowland and highland Maya civilization in all periods. This should provide motivation for the intensification of research there, for current and future generations of archaeologists.

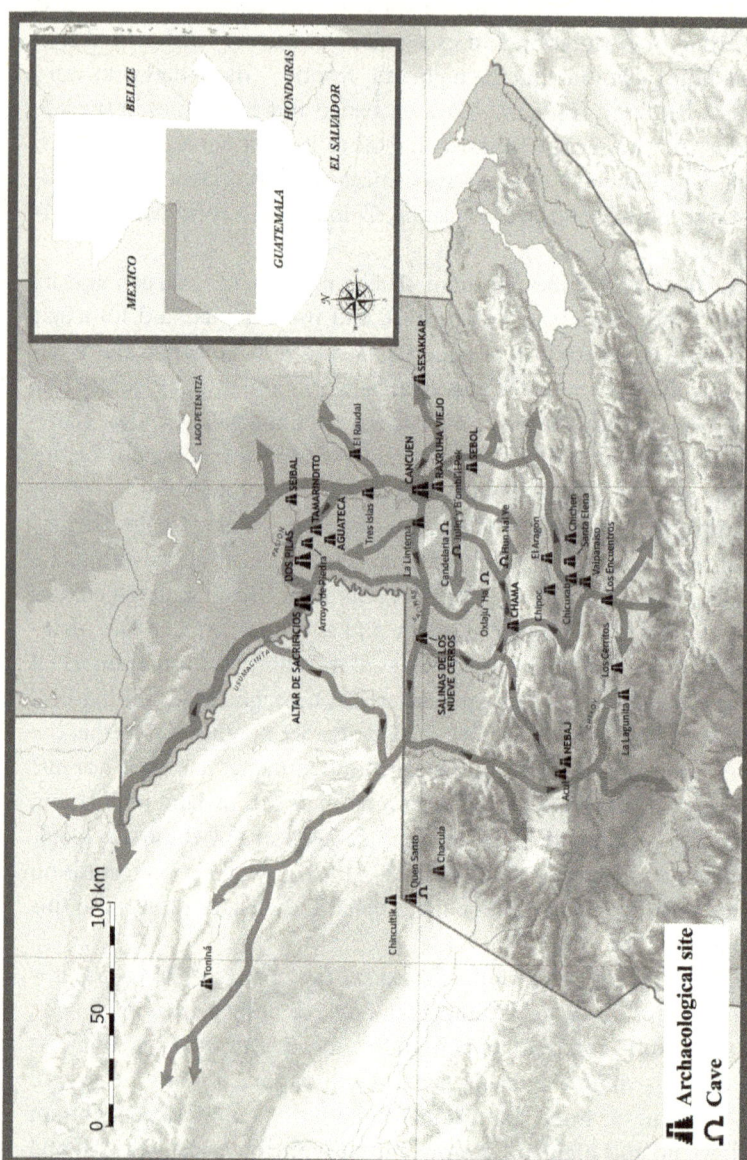

Figure 1.5. Principal river valley routes leading to and through the Transversal. There were many other land routes in all periods. (Map made in Fresco. Courtesy of Luís Fernando Luin.)

Part II

Sites, Regions, and Regional History

2

The Transversal Economic Network

Forming a Breakaway Network through Economic Benefits and Ideological Seduction

Arthur A. Demarest and Paola Torres

The AD 760–800 economic network of exchange of materials and access to routes in the Transversal is a textbook case of a "breakaway network." Some of the basic features of a community network and a breakaway network are discussed in Chapter 1, but here we see those concepts in successful application in the far southern lowlands and highland interface. These help to explain the baffling phenomena of the sudden leap to apogee and then disintegration—"network failure"—of the center, city-state, and kingdom of Cancuen. This failure correlated to a contemporaneous "apogee," at least in terms of epicenter or elite construction, at a number of sites in the northern piedmont and highlands of the Transversal. First, we review from Chapter 1 some of the primary characteristics of networks, the ones that are relevant to the Maya southern lowland and Transversal. Then we consider some of the centers and agents in this particular eighth-century network.

RELEVANT CHARACTERISTICS OF COMMUNITY AND BREAKAWAY NETWORKS

1. In a community network over time each agent develops shared multiple partners, economic agents, in the network. (In the Mayanist case they are usually labeled only as different "sites," but our resolution about agents and agency is slowly improving.)

2. In community networks those multiple links lead to a high level of sharing "economic cultures" and ideological values and a significantly higher percentage of interactions, including exchange, within that network rather than beyond.

3. Yet various factors, usually the perception of either new economic possibilities or a general decline of the community network and thus decreasing marginal returns, cause center agents to break away, in this case elite or "noble" economic agents like those at Cancuen, who reach out to exchange with new out-of-network partners (see Figure 1.4d).

4. It is literally "breaking away" from its previous close associations as a part of a community network that had stabilized over the years (in this case over many centuries). That does not mean that interaction and exchange with its previous community network ends, but that its economy or interactions become equally or more intense with new out-of-network partners.

5. Those partners often have very different economic, political, or ideological systems. They usually include different "economic cultures" and norms, like "economic ethics," regarding fair practice and distribution embedded into their culture.

6. Initial out-of-network economic partnerships are, by necessity, dyadic in nature (see Figure 1.4a) as relations are established in a one-on-one connection between agents. For that reason, they usually fail after some initial success because the agents involved do not yet share multiple economic partners; that is, a true multiple-link network has not yet formed. They also must bridge differences in the economic cultures of the two systems into which the economic practices are embedded, referred to as "the problem of embeddedness" (Granovetter 1985; also see for example Das and Bing-Sheng 2001; Freeman et al. 1983; Oliver 1996; Uzzi 1996).

7. The stabilization and building of "trust" in relations and contracts in a shaky new relationship with a different political economy and ideology is a difficult process that usually involves other forms of relationships, including ideological ones such as pilgrimages and, in Cancuen's case, the sharing of elements or even settings for ritual. They can also include social measures such as family ties, marriage alliances, or, almost naturally, the exchange of some personnel needed to span the logistics involved. It is these types of mechanisms that were used or developed between Cancuen and its Transversal partners (see Das and Bing-Sheng 1998; Doz 1996; Sytch et al. 2012; Zucker 1986).

8. Over time other partners can enter the new economic relationship, not just with the initiating breakaway center but with each other, at first triadic, and gradually with more participants with multiple links

between them. Usually initially more innovative, the relationships can form a more stable "community network."

9. However, discussed here and in Chapter 1, breakaway networks can rapidly bring great initial benefits, but they also usually fall apart quickly because of the risks of their formation discussed above.

THE AD 760-800 CANCUEN/TRANSVERSAL BREAKAWAY NETWORK IN CONTEMPORARY PERSPECTIVE

Cancuen and the Transversal network are textbook cases of the history of a new breakaway network. The incredible increase in wealth at Cancuen in such a short period, 760-800, and acceleration within that period led to sudden wealth and splendor, followed by a dramatic total collapse that affected the other sites in the Transversal that had dyadic relationships with Cancuen.

Our understanding of this breakaway network has been growing and changing with reversals and reinterpretations along the way. One reason for this is that even with clear evidence of network participation, there is little overall uniformity in the specifics of different partner centers—their agents, the nature of their relationship, and the specific exchanges involved. This challenging diversity is precisely because they were still dyadic. The agents, often elites, of each center or area had different forms of connection to Cancuen and thus varying physical manifestations of the links between them.

We have also slowly improved our understanding of these concepts through direct collaboration with experts in fields like crisis management, institution theory, field theory, and strategic management, all of which often apply network approaches. These sites and the zones and landscapes around them that we have surveyed or explored often had been unknown, unexplored, or minimally tested. The different forms of dyadic connections between these agents also make it challenging. Yet this dynamic in research and evidence has led to new hypotheses on the different connections involved and has driven our changing research designs, which is precisely what successful paradigms or theories must do. It is those more specific connections that we turn to below. Since each network partnership has different manifestations, in a short chapter we can give only a brief overview of a few of those. Here we provide a sketch of several sites in the Transversal network where the Cancuen economic agents collaborated with local economic agents to create this new network of transport, exchange, and, at Cancuen, production.

This description of networks and agency from the individual to "state" level may seem complex and perhaps arcane. That impression is only because we must explain concepts and interpretative frameworks that are not used in Maya archaeology but are the norm in much of the social sciences, including economics, the history of economies, and contemporary social "theory and applications, which often use network applications. Yet the most common network formations are of the type discussed above and below. This means that in our preliminary and developing interpretations, we should remember that changes were ongoing, and especially that specific routes are often monopolized by a single group of agents in a community or enterprise. One must keep in mind, however, that there are many possible routes that could be utilized, not simply the most efficient ones according to least-cost analysis. Routes and networks often operate, as in this case, on only *parts* of a political economy—for instance, exchange of only a specific commodity or interaction between specific agents utilizing their own individual networks of communication and bonding, and rules of exchange.

We must try to understand those industries and exchanges involving specific products by specific agents operating between two otherwise separate entities of agency. Although impossible at times, we should use research designs that can carry that objective as far as possible rather than be satisfied with the simplification of "site A trading with site B" or "region A trading with region B." We must always remember that sites or regions are not agents and are internally complex in ways that have been long studied.

This Transversal/Cancuen network was clearly not one with any type of unity or overall shared culture or political identity. It was about exchange and transport of specific resources, especially highland lithic resources (obsidian, jade, pyrite), but also many other things such as shell from the Pacific and Caribbean, obsidian and ceramics from Mexico, and so on. Ongoing ethnohistorical and paleobotanical studies (see Chapters 8, 10, and 11) have preliminary, yet convincing, evidence that Transversal cacao, cotton, and salt were also moving through these separate network relationships. Such perishable goods and foodstuffs would have been important to Cancuen and probably to the economic and ideological relationship between Cancuen agents and those, for example, in the Raxruha zone. All these elements were manifest in the discoveries at Cancuen, which was a central node but far from the only one, even in its 760–800 breakaway network apogee.

Such models and elements from contemporary economic subdisciplines can give us such hypotheses and clues about how to test them in the future. At Cancuen we believe that we have identified at least the types of principal agents and their elite offices and residences, although, of course, they are textually unnamed. At least two of them are presented on the beautiful Cancuen Panel 3, and others appear in large stucco portraits above the palace *audiencias* (see Figure 11.4). While such specific evidence is lacking at Transversal partner sites, we must remember in constructing our hypotheses that they would have existed as they do in all economies.

MILITARY OR POLITICAL COERCION VERSUS MUTUAL BENEFITS AND IDEOLOGICAL BONDING

One of the results of forgetting the specificity of relationships between agents is that we often invoke the most dramatic and disjunctive interpretation, coercion, conquest, political domination, or hegemony to explain inter-site connections. In fact, while most visible, especially in the historical record, such globally unifying political processes are the least frequent and generally least efficient forms of economic network formation.

In our Pasión River projects, we did in fact see coercion as the major tool of Dos Pilas creation of its Petexbatun hegemony, since that was clearly textually identified (e.g., Demarest 2006a; Demarest et al. 2012). While the intensive multidisciplinary investigations from 1989 to 1997 included projects on all aspects of the system at six major centers, small sites, and rural landscapes, there was ample evidence to identify other networks of different kinds beyond the textually identified rulers and queens. With the contemporary network understanding that we have now, such elements could be better explored (e.g., Eberl 2014). What we perceived was that one major goal of Dos Pilas's militarism and strategy was to gain a high degree of economic control of the Pasión Valley route and its highland resources.

As part of the 33-year-long learning curve discussed in Chapter 1, we did come to believe that the economic exchange aspect of the networks was the driving one. That gradually guided us upriver on the Pasión, including survey and extensive excavations at El Raudal and Tres Islas, and at the beginning of the river system, Cancuen. We later expanded through a network research design to study its region and then moved deeper south into the bordering piedmont and highland sites of the Transversal. We continued following a problem-oriented research design, which after 2002 became a network research design rather than the dominant "big site and its region" approach that studies no real ancient configurations. In doing that, it became ever more certain that what we were finding in Cancuen's most visible AD 760–800 period was the independent development and expansion (i.e., without Calakmul and after Dos Pilas involvement) of an economic network that was "international" but focused on exchange of specific goods. This network was linked to and largely "fueled" by resources and products by the non-Classic Maya agents in the Transversal region and piedmont to the south.

Nonetheless, initial interpretations of the monumental texts confused us with some claimed military encounters, not by the Cancuen ruler, Tajal Chan Ahk, but by a proxy lord (Fahsen 2000; Fahsen and Barrientos 2006; Fahsen and Demarest 2001; Fahsen et al. 2003). Better historiography and the findings at the proposed military "target sites" created ever-greater skepticism regarding the meaning of those texts. They recorded proxy victories by Tajal Chan Ahk, yet he was a Cancuen ruler whose power was increasingly limited, rapidly becoming only a figurehead for the agents creating or stimulating the new economic and ideological network. The actual textual references to militaristic action at Cancuen were two, and even those were hyperbolized or fictive.

Given the texts and material evidence at Cancuen and at its Transversal network exchange zones or sites, we doubt that war was a significant element in Cancuen's network strategy, albeit there might have been minor actions. As mentioned, the only other notable "wars" or "conquests" referred to in Cancuen texts were on one altar and Stelae 1, and the latter refers to a capture of "Torch Macaw" (Fahsen and Barrientos 2006; Fahsen et al. 2003), a name that often can mean something like "John Doe" or "Fulano de Tal" (David Stuart, personal communication 2003) and probably a reference to a nonroyal lower elite or perhaps a local leader. As an economic mercantile center, the elite class at Cancuen would have needed some royal references to enhance the image of their *k'uhul ajaw*. At Cancuen, the ruler's "macho" status was primarily enhanced by constant references to and images of him as a great ballplayer. Given the three impressive ballcourts at Cancuen, his own royal finemasonry ballcourt containing Cancuen's finest monuments and sculptures, this sentiment may even have been true.

The two "war" references that seemed credible were both on only one monument, Altar 2 (Figure 2.1), and we believe that those were probably not really "wars" in our colloquial sense and were not carried out by Tajal Chan Ahk but by a mysterious proxy, referred to as "The Captor of 'Sak Witz'" (Fahsen and Barrientos 2006). "Sak Witz" meant "White Mountain," which is the exact nature of the karst tower hills of the adjacent Chinaja ridge, where the sides of the hills are highly eroded to become almost vertical, with large patches of exposed white limestone. Raxruha, La Linterna, and other network sites have such hills around or near them, and we had considered the Raxruha zone, or La Linterna, to be the prime candidates for being "Sak Witz." This *yajaw*, or subordinate noble, is stated on Altar 2 to also have conquered or captured a lord of Machaquila; however, at best, this would have been some kind of suppression of a rebellion or attempted contract cancellation, or the like. Machaquila was located on the critical exchange route to the northeastern Peten and had long been dominated by or asymmetrically affiliated with Cancuen, whose *k'uhul ajaws* always used in texts the dual dynastic emblem glyph title "Holy Lord of Cancuen, Holy Lord of Machaquila."

Figure 2.1. Cancuen Altar 2 showing a ballgame between ruler Taj Chan Ahk (right) of Cancuen and a companion lord created through proxy wars (left). The horizontal inscription between the king and this mysterious lord credits that proxy agent with being the captor of "Sak Witz" ("White Mountain"). Later, a second horizontal inscription was added at the very bottom of the altar image that credits the subordinate lord with the capture of a lord of the great center of Machaquila. The exact significance of the text, particularly the "Sak Witz" reference, has been a source of much debate. (Courtesy of Luís Fernando Luin.)

The possibility of a Cancuen "conquest" of Raxruha or La Linterna seemed likely given the proximity of Raxruha and explicit evidence at La Linterna, including ceramics with a strong association to Cancuen. La Linterna's association to Cancuen can also be dated by the hieroglyphic staircase there, which puts it at 781–799. This corresponds to the Cancuen network expansion to Gulf Coast Veracruz, but it is too late to be relevant to Cancuen's initial network formation. In excavations and surveys, we have found no evidence of fortifications at Cancuen, Raxruha, or La Linterna. Only much later was there a rapid initiation of some piled stone palisade base walls, about AD 800, the time of the fall of Cancuen. Those were never completed and were left as surface deposits. Above all, there is minimal evidence of sufficient stratification at Raxruha and La Linterna prior to their late-eighth-century Cancuen-correlated epicenter constructions to have had "elite leaders" worthy of the typical meaning applied to most southern lowland Maya *k'uhul ajaw* or "war" references.

The fact is that, as discussed above, the most successful economic networks are primarily built on extending new benefits and relationships to the elite economic agents elsewhere who chose to join the network because of its benefits to them. Often, as with Cancuen, there is a bit of ideological bonding through ritual, symbols, and architectural elements. The Cancuen epicenter itself would have been very effective in courting and impressing regional visitors or leaders—potential economic partners. Cancuen was designed with its monuments, ballcourts, internal ritual canals, cisterns, and especially its royal palace to be an "ideological power generating device" (Demarest 2013:394; Demarest et al. 2020). The palace had the most grandiose, almost comically hyperbolic, elite entrance to the ritual procession way leading to the royal center of the administrative palace. Some buildings were nearly 9 m tall with almost fully round stucco sculptures above the doorways of each *audiencia* room and the central entrance corridor measuring 2–3 m in height (Barrientos 2014). Local benefits and such a variety of ideological devices could have helped initiate and then reinforce the different types of new economic connections. Such a pattern is normal in breakaway network formation, with partners voluntarily "joining" rather than being forced to incorporate through military coercion.

We now turn to some examples of the sites involved in such a network, each different in their relationships to the initial breakaway network formation process.

RAXRUHA VIEJO

At the Raxruha Viejo site, the only salient feature is its sudden and very short-lived "epicenter," which is actually a sacred ritual space. Large ceremonial constructions were added in the same late-eighth-century period of Cancuen's apogee. The new constructions there seem to formalize the ideology of hill (*witz*) and cave worship, sacred geography characteristics of the highlands and the Transversal interface. In the lowlands, the temples were architecturally created *witz*, sacred hills with tombs in them following the highland sacred geography pattern. In the late eighth century, in this unoccupied but sacred zone of Raxruha between the steepest towers with rockshelters, terraces of rough stones were built at the base of these natural karst hills and in open flat areas, natural "plazas" between them (Figure 2.2). Atop or near those were placed 19 plain stelae and four altars, and another stelae and altar were found in the periphery (Saravia 2014, 2016).

Figure 2.2. Reconstruction of the sacred center of Raxruha Viejo. The center is defined by its steep karst sacred hills, witz, and rock shelters, but in the 760-800 network period, the large platforms with stelae and altars were constructed at the base of the sacred hills. (Courtesy of Luís Fernando Luin.)

In addition to other stelae and altars, Raxruha Altar 1 was associated with Raxruha Structure 10 in the site epicenter. The exact primary context of this monument is unknown, but it was probably in front of Raxruha Stela 3, according to a photograph taken by Brian Dillon in 1975 (published in Sapper 1985). It is of the "truncated cone" forms characteristic only of the altars of Cancuen and previously not reported outside Cancuen (Tourtellot, Sabloff, and Sharick 1978:227), reflecting its stylistic influences on the sacred zone of Raxruha Viejo. It has a diameter of 0.83 m and a thickness of 0.32 m (Saravia 2014:74–75).

The relationship with Cancuen is reflected by many Raxruha ceramic types found at Cancuen and some Cancuen sherds and a vessel found at Raxruha. The strongest evidence, however, is that the many stelae, platforms, altars, and the flurry of construction at Raxruha were built during the same exact period as the apogee, and many constructions at the nearby magnificent Cancuen epicenter are just a 90-minute walk or a much shorter canoe ride away. Before and after this period, this zone of the Raxruha area was considered sacred geography, used for local rituals, and was probably shared with the central Peten traders/pilgrims active throughout this zone (see Woodfill 2010). Yet there were no constructions in the Raxruha epicenter after the Cancuen Transversal network existed. In addition to the terraces and structures discussed below, there were also two small structures with more lowland-style worked masonry. Yet the style of all the other constructions was highland or Transversal in nature.

Of significance is a highland-style elite structure that was placed during this same period in an open zone, one of the natural large "plazas" between the karst tower hill "temples" and stelae altar platforms (Sion et al. 2017). It is composed of two structures that form an L-shaped platform. Research conducted between 2016 and 2019 (e.g., Andrieu and Sion 2017, 2018, 2019, 2020) confirmed that the superstructures located on top of these platforms would have been made of perishable materials, *bajareque*, with signs of a wooden structure with a small base wall, some with possible parts of a stair and/or just staggered blocks. The nature of the structures, like most of the Raxruha material culture, especially ceramics, is much the same as nearby or more distant sites in Alta Verapaz. Close similarities between ceramics and simple earthen constructions are seen in the low structures at sites south and west of the sacred zone such as La Lima (Monterroso 2006; Monterroso and Woodfill 2005; Sion et al. 2018) and mounds along the San Simon river. Much of the material culture also corresponds to that of more distant sites like Las Tinajas (Smith 1955:58), Chijolom (Smith 1955:57), and many Alta and Baja Verapaz areas. Notably similar in structures and artifacts, recovered assemblages are also very comparable in material culture, especially ceramics, to that of small households in Cancuen's immediate peripheral zone.

The residence itself had several internal rooms, possibly storage rooms, defined by impressions and lines of small stones and small unworked cobbles, but without worked masonry and presumably with superstructures also constructed of wood. The artifacts recovered there and in the surrounding area included sherds of Transversal styles but also sherds in Peten styles and a number of Cancuen's distinctive La Isla Orange ceramics. There was one vessel that compares stylistically to the Kanalkan Gouged-Incised type, a ceramic ware that was found as a grave good in Burial 96 of Cancuen of the probable consort of K'an Ma'ax, adjacent to the last Cancuen ruler's burial (Torres et al. 2014).

That structure, while modest or even "rustic" in comparison with Cancuen and southern lowland Maya low-elite residences, is important since its location is in the most sacred space. We speculate that this might be the residence of a local leader, perhaps a very small highland-style "palace." In the highlands, elite residences or even palaces were long platforms with some base masonry, but with structures built of wood and canopies. Of course, it is also possible that it was a locus of ritual rather than the home of political leaders or elites, given its position in a natural space of sacred geography. It also existed only for a short time during the late eighth-century period, while mounds near it, in the areas just to the south and west, have more variable dates. Overall, the Raxruha Viejo epicenter, be it ritual, political, or both, was impressive in comparison with most other Transversal sites during the Cancuen/Transversal network period. It may have been either a locus of power or a shared sacred place for some large, unspecifiable zone.

RAXRUHA, CANCUEN, AND VARIABILITY IN DYADIC FORMS OF ECONOMIC NETWORK FORMATION

Given that the neighboring Transversal site of Raxruha is also the most excavated partner site to date, it merits a more detailed discussion as an example of the complexity of economic network relationships. Alternative hypotheses can be considered to guide future investigations and analyses. The relationships between Transversal network sites and Cancuen were individual and dyadic, and therefore challenging to interpret.

Cancuen's relationship with Raxruha has puzzled us, and still does, given their propinquity, which would be even closer or overlapping in terms of the area's local sustaining populations. The construction of the substructures was completed in highland materials, and forms and ceramics are typical of the piedmont/Transversal site. Yet such contrasting material culture of all kinds is normal in network development. That is also true of the fact that there is far more evidence of Raxruha and Transversal region materials at Cancuen, the network initiating center, than there is Cancuen material at sites associated with it. While the sacred zone constructions and other elements correlate with the Cancuen apogee, the low frequency of Cancuen ceramics with no concentrations suggests there were probably no Cancuen elites residing at Raxruha, again casting doubt on the probability of political or military dominance.

Also significant is that, at Cancuen, Transversal ceramics typical of Raxruha are primarily present in one extensive zone of the site. That more northern area lies between two principal ports with small subroyal palaces at both and the 780/786–800/801 jade workshop between them. This distribution suggests a local Transversal region population was present, yet the number of residences with Transversal/piedmont ceramics are few. It is possible that there was some type of day labor by the nearby non-Classic Maya populations. Also in this northern area, a purely highland-style ballcourt was present.

The nonterritorial network initiated by Cancuen was similar in these patterns to many such breakaway commercial networks. Their economic strategy was to bring resources into their own center or city-state to process and trade those commodities. That results in great "international" influences and materials in the omnivorous initiating center from the regions of its new trading partners. For a comparative example, there was enormous influence on Venetian products from all types of elements from its partner regions, but especially from its largest partner, Constantinople. Indeed, Venice is defined by Byzantine influences in art, architecture, and monuments, and some monuments and art actually came from Constantinople itself—much more after the Fourth Crusade's looting of that partner, but rival, commercial capital. There was less evidence of artifacts from Venice at most network centers, including Constantinople itself (see Formica 2017; Puga and Trefler 2012).

Such breakaway economic networks can have little or no population movement or minimal cultural impact since the initiator agents and centers are anxious to "court" new partners and are consumer centers in all respects. In the case of Cancuen, its agents would have been interested in specific elements of exchange. Such limited economic and cultural relationships can change and broaden as networks stabilize and the system develops into a stable multipartner community network. A close Cancuen-Raxruha economic relationship is clear from the correlation of epicenter activities and other evidence, but it may have been of a different, much closer relationship connection than seen at other partner sites.

It appears that the zone between the Raxruha population and Cancuen might have also been part of Cancuen's sustaining population in the 760–800 period. At and around Cancuen itself, there is very little agricultural land, since the area around the limited epicenter peninsular is largely water and swamps, and those types of swamps, *aguadas* and *bajos*, were unusable (Duncan Cook, personal communication 2003; Timothy Beach, personal communication 2009). This zone is at the base of the rainy highlands in the flooded headwaters of the Pasión River. The water level rises and falls an amazing 8–10 m a year on an unpredictable and erratic schedule, as we have observed every year for two decades (see Figure 9.2). This made agriculture impossible in the adjacent *aguadas*, swamps, and low-elevation land. The food for Cancuen would have needed to come from the fertile higher areas to the south, closer to Raxruha, and from the very productive Transversal soils of that region. A strong hypothesis is that Cancuen's subsistence base was provided by the farmers of that area in some type of individual or community exchange.

Furthermore, in that same short 90-year period, large-scale construction at Cancuen included six stages of erecting a spectacular palace, one of the largest in the ancient Maya world, with numerous internal ritual structures, two throne rooms, dozens of fine masonry *audiencias*, a large colonnaded assembly hall, paved plazas, many enormous stucco sculptures, one stone hieroglyphic staircase and another in painted stucco over porous stone, and other monuments in the palace alone. At the same time, they built large, impressive noble palaces and oratories near the central administrative palace complex, as well as smaller high-elite residences (or small palaces) near the ports and the jade workshop, three ballcourts—one with some of the finest sculptures of the Classic period. They also constructed a unique ritual water system with elaborate stone cisterns, artificial waterfalls, and stone-banked "streams" that wound through much of the epicenter. Those and other constructions in just the years of the apogee period would have required a continuous unbroken need for a significant labor force beyond the limited population of the epicenter and nearby scattered mound groups. Also, rowers and bearers would have been needed as laborers to move products and resources along the Pasión River and upstream on the Sebol River to the Transversal, as is done today by transfer to smaller canoes, and there would need to be bearers for movement by land to other network areas.

A different hypothesis from some of our earlier interpretations is that the relationship of the sites in the period of their contemporary epicenters would have involved subsistence goods and labor coming from the zones to the south between Cancuen around and near Raxruha. This intriguing possibility will need to be tested first by systematic survey and then by excavation in the areas between the two AD 760–800 epicenters. It is important to keep such common practices and economic complexities in mind to direct research designs and interpretations, rather than considering only the often mythical economics of archaeology involving simply "connecting the dots" between centers and labeling interactions "trade" or "hegemony."

We will also eventually understand more clearly the zone we call Raxruha itself, especially to the south and west of the sacred site. More survey and excavation there and along the San Simon river valley will give us a better understanding of the nature of the population configurations there, particularly in the periods before and after Cancuen. Indeed, further exploration of the peripheries of the other sites and their subregions is needed to understand this network and earlier and later exchange networks.

DYADIC CONNECTIONS TO SESAKKAR ON THE ROUTE EAST

As emphasized, any breakaway economic network initially involves highly variable, dyadic one-on-one relationships with new partners. This is illustrated by the nature of one such dyadic relationship, which is very different from that with Raxruha: the much-greater-distance connection between Cancuen and Sesakkar. Attention was first drawn to Sesakkar when reports noted the presence of stelae, including an eroded one (Sesakkar Stela 4) with the notched-top shape characteristic of Cancuen stelae (Saravia 2016).

The epicenter of Sesakkar combined sacred geography of hill worship with Peten-style monuments. This site had its unusual form dictated by the natural terrain of very steep karst hills separated by ravines or very narrow valleys (Figure 2.3). Hilltops were leveled into flat areas—low, wide terraces—to provide a surface for construction. Considerable labor would have been required for the massive movement of earth and rock and to construct its wide stone terraces (Torres et al. 2018a). The portions of Sesakkar investigated to date were atop two closely spaced natural karst towers. A small Classic Maya palace was on one hilltop facing across the ravine from the adjacent hilltop, which had an impressive plaza with 23 stelae (see Figure 2.3). Excavations uncovered rich lithic offerings in stelae caches under or in front of some stelae (Demarest et al. 2016; Saravia 2018; Torres et al. 2018a).

Figure 2.3. Sesakkar epicenter shows the central plaza with stelae and altars atop one steep hilltop and the palace facing it from the adjacent hilltop with a steep ravine between them. (Courtesy of Luís Fernando Luin.)

In essence, the Sesakkar layout is that of a small, typical Maya epicenter with a small masonry palace facing the main plaza with its stelae/altar complexes, despite the strange, separated positioning atop different adjacent, very steep karst hills. Moving between them would require climbing 40 m down the palace hill and then another 40 m up the adjacent hill to its ceremonial plaza. We have not yet investigated to see whether leveled paths with some steps were built to facilitate such movement between the two parts of the epicenter.

Sesakkar's location in the southeastern Peten but bordering the Transversal would help to explain both the mix of Transversal/piedmont and Peten ceramics there and the presence of Cancuen features in the epicenter and Cancuen-style ceramics. Sesakkar had some ceramic modes and types characteristic of the Cancuen assemblage, but more sherds were of types and pastes of the modified southeastern Peten Tepeu sphere and ceramics of the Transversal and piedmont zones just to the south. Its Transversal northern highland-style ceramics have a predominance of porous pastes elaborated with organic temper. This tradition extends from the northern zones of El Quiche and Alta Verapaz to the sites near the Lake Izabal Basin, as described by Hermes (1981) and Velásquez (1995). The most common of the Transversal ceramics are from the Cebada group. Within the modal variants that differentiate it from the sample of Raxruha Viejo and Cancuen, there is the presence of grooved decoration inside the rim of the pots. The broadly distributed piedmont ceramics correspond to the traditional notion of a "ceramic sphere" of shared styles and norms across a large region.

The Tepeu ceramic sphere of the Peten is parallel to this shared ceramic assemblage of the Transversal and piedmont sites. The Peten assemblage at Sesakkar is evident by the presence of the Tinaja group, represented with the types Chaquiste Impressed, Chinaja Impressed, and Tigrán Red, and the Cambio group, with the Chichicuil, Cambio, and Encanto Striated types. Of great interest is that those Peten types often have the porous pastes typical of Transversal ceramics, but in this case, they are in lowland, not highland types—truly hybrid!

Sherds of Cancuen types are specifically from the La Isla group with the La Isla Orange and Sebastián Fluted types, and the stamped Sebastián variety (Saravia 2018). The identification of a large representative sample of materials of Cancuen affiliation is another evidence of the relationship of the sites. Based on cross-dating of all these ceramics and the monument styles, the epicenter was contemporary with the late-eighth-century phases of Los Laureles (AD 760–780) and Chamán (AD 780–800) at Cancuen (Saravia 2018).

Given the location of Sesakkar, it is obvious that network links would be toward the resources east of Lake Izabal and the Caribbean (Figure 2.4). Therefore, the area east of Sesakkar should be a target for future investigations.

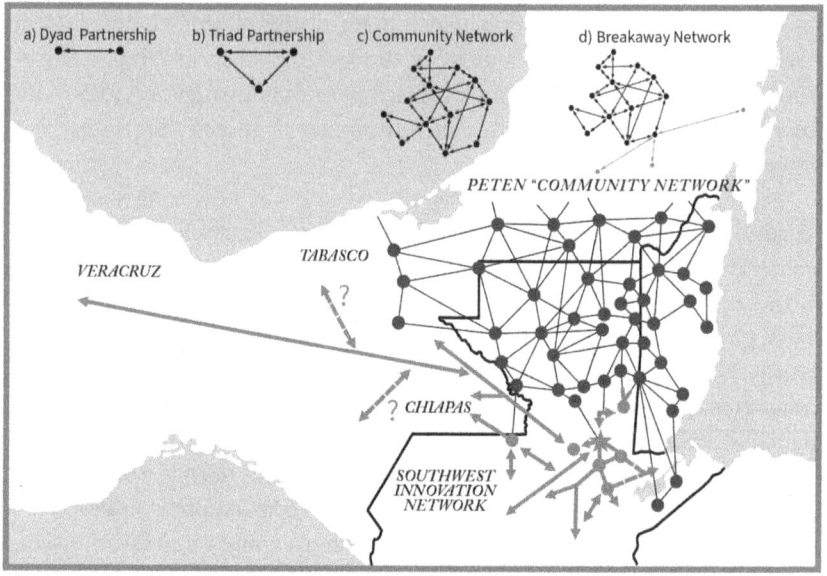

Figure 2.4. Schematic of the maximum AD 786 extent of the interregional economic networks of Cancuen. (Map made in Fresco. Courtesy of Luís Fernando Luin.)

THE CANCUEN CONNECTION TO CHIAPAS, TABASCO, AND VERACRUZ AND ITS ECONOMIC IMPACT: NEW PARTNERS, WEALTH, AND NEW IDEAS ON POLITICAL ECONOMY

One of the most important discoveries of the Cancuen site research and the entire investigation of the far southeastern Peten/Cancuen/Transversal economic network was the expansion west of its economic exchange network reaching to northern Chiapas, Tabasco, and even distant Veracruz and connecting those influences into the whole Transversal network. This would define the Cancuen/Transversal breakaway exchange network as one of the most interregional economic systems in eastern Mesoamerica in the Late Classic period (see Figure 2.4). That also helps explain the changes in Cancuen's economy, political economy, and production and exchange processes that led to it being unlike standing models of Classic Maya economic systems and partially explains its meteoric rise to wealth (Demarest et al. 2014; Demarest et al. 2020; Demarest and Victor 2022).

As described in Chapter 1, it was significant that the apogee period was associated with the highest proportion of Chablekal Fine Grey ceramics from northern Chiapas and Tabasco of any assemblage from the Classic Maya southern lowlands (Bishop et al. 2005). That proportion was greater than sites much closer to the source production areas of Chablekal. Those ceramics appeared shortly after AD 760, the beginning of Cancuen's transformation and intensification of obsidian blade production. Even more surprising was the discovery of Campamento Fine Orange ceramics from Veracruz.

The notable presence of Chablekal and later Campamento ceramics changed our economic interpretations. It was only after 760, corresponding to the importation of Chablekal, that Cancuen grew into a major site with massive production of obsidian flakes and partially worked and worked cores. It was only in the Chamán phase, probably Late Chamán 780/786 to 801 (Forné et al. 2011; Torres et al. 2016, 2018b), when the first imports of Campamento Fine Orange and Zaragoza obsidian from Veracruz were seen and the mass scale of jade preform production began.

Thus, the networks of exchange to northern Chiapas and the Gulf Coast were first correlated with the emergence of new major economic elements, including large-scale obsidian overproduction for export. Later, during the 780/786 period, Campamento and Zaragoza obsidian (i.e., Veracruz contact) drove more economic change. As a result, the palace and epicenter were further reconfigured into an administrative complex with more "noble" palaces, with additional palaces erected at its ports and jade workshop. At this point, Cancuen had completed the transition to a political economy managed by "merchant nobles" or, more accurately, "high elite bureaucrats" and principal "economic agents" of the polity. This is a familiar historical pattern, similar to the decline of the power of the Venetian Doges and the shift of real power to the two levels of councils of the merchant families (e.g., Formica 2017; Puga and Trefler 2012).

All the evidence indicates that each new economic link to another center and their agents, especially to those in Mexico, was correlated with radical internal changes and innovations in Cancuen's economic strategies, organizational structures, and types of production, leading to greater success of its political economy. This aligns with a historical and contemporary pattern, where stimulus diffusion of new models, in this case economic ones, leads to new network links and partners. In the fields of strategic management and economic history, this is seen in terms of new "network structure and the diffusion of knowledge" (Cowan and Jonard 2004) or the formation of new networks that can become "innovation ecosystems" (Davis 2016) through the exchange of new information about economic strategies, organization models, and forms of production. Study of such information network effects is its own subfield (see, for example, Breschi and Malerba 2007; Sytch et al. 2012; Whittington et al. 2009). Throughout history, forming links with new economic partners has been just as, if not more, important for acquiring new concepts and information as it has been for the economic exchanges themselves.

It may seem unusual or even exceptional for a southern lowland Classic Maya center or system to experience such rapid and significant changes in its political economy as a result of external relations, but perhaps such changes have not yet been perceived at other Maya sites. In contrast, Yucatan's Classic, Epi-Classic, and Postclassic culture-history has long been associated with the impact of new economic models and concepts of political economy from more commercialized political economies in the Mexican Gulf Coast and beyond. Study of those factors in Yucatan would benefit from the applications and interpretative structures of economic network approaches.

LA LINTERNA ON THE ROUTE WEST TO CHIAPAS, VERACRUZ, AND THE MEXICAN GULF COAST

La Linterna was located at the very base of the northern face of the Sierra de Chinaja, a steep range of eroded limestone hills running east to west, the final southern end of the lowlands. This zone lacks any subsistence advantages with its extremely thin soils and limited water on the north side of the Chinaja range. Surveys conducted thus far indicate a sparse population. Like Cancuen, Sesakkar, Raxruha, Salinas de los Nueve Cerros, and most northern Transversal sites, La Linterna is a challenging site for interpretation. However, it provides perhaps the best evidence of a direct and clear link with the Cancuen network, and there is a possibility that a small presence of Cancuen economic agents might have been present there or visited frequently for a brief period. Every aspect of evidence and monumental texts recovered thus far correlates with our hypothesis regarding the site, its function, and its alignment in nature and chronology with the Transversal/Cancuen network apogee.

La Linterna is located just to the north of the Transversal and piedmont, but directly on the route west toward Chiapas and Veracruz (see Figure 2.4). In 2018 and 2019, the Cancuen Regional Project's La Linterna Subproject conducted investigations and lab work, including careful review of previous research in the area (e.g., Lemus and Peralta 1996; Putzeys et al. 2008), subregional reconnaissance, surface collection, and excavations (Demarest et al. 2019). The earlier reports, notes, and interviews with older residents related great damage and looting during oil company construction and later by others. The community itself had greatly disturbed the site throughout, leveling mounds, building over others, and using structure masonry in their own house constructions and pathways. A notable problem was the placement of a large church atop the raised area that had been the core of the epicenter, just missing the hieroglyphic staircase and two reported panels by a few meters. Even the hieroglyphic stairway steps were moved, jumbled, and reset to form a line of blocks, not in textual order, with some blocks missing. The project was able to recover two of the stairway blocks that were buried in that area. Most significantly, seven carved stelae and two panels had been reported while still in situ, but they are not present today, probably looted. Nonetheless, the remaining evidence indicates a very close, and textually documented, relationship to Cancuen.

In our investigations (Demarest et al. 2020, eds.), we conducted subregional surveys, many small excavations, and large-scale excavations in three large and unusual groups in the "epicenter" area. We also tested a number of individual low mounds dispersed across the zone as well as isolated higher ritual structures at the site and nearby. In 2017–2018, after overcoming community opposition that had previously blocked research at La Linterna, including prohibiting photographs of the stairway, we excavated the area. During that excavation, we documented each step in situ with photographs and drawings, assisted by a trained sculptural text artist and the input of two epigraphers.

The largest-scale investigations (Torres and Tuyuc 2020) were into strange, high U-shaped compounds (Groups A, B, and C). Deep units and some wide, deep trenches, up to 10 x 3 m, were excavated to provide cross sections of those. Thirty units were excavated in the central area. Systematic survey and surface collections were carried out by three archaeologists over 45 quadrants, covering the surface of the areas near the epicenter in 25 x 25 cm units. Those operations found 11 low mounds less than 1 m high and 17 other even lower platforms (Demarest et al. 2020, eds.) but also some higher, steep mounds that had been small temples. There were some indications of equipment for obsidian work and salt grinding like those found at Salinas de los Nueve Cerros and Cancuen.

The ties to Cancuen appear to be very close during the late-eighth-century period of the creation and expansion by Cancuen economic agents of its breakaway network. The site contains a mix of piedmont/Transversal ceramics, far southern lowland Classic Maya Tepeu ceramics, and distinctively Cancuen-style ceramics. The same mix can be seen in some architectural elements, most convincingly in the hieroglyphic stairway, which we were able to redraw based on the pieces found.

In 2019, epigrapher Sven Gronemeyer worked with the project to study the new drawings and evidence, including the new monuments and texts from Cancuen. This was the first study with those advantages, as well as the benefit of his general access to related published and unpublished texts from across the southern lowlands (Gronemeyer 2020). The evidence shows a direct linkage to Cancuen during the period of Cancuen's exchange with Veracruz (781 to 799), apparently via La Linterna to the routes west. The earliest date on the stairway is 781 and the latest is 795, with some of the intervening dates marking the beginning and end of the network route to the west within the later period of the Cancuen florescence. Even more telling are specific parallel dates and the presence of the Cancuen emblem glyph and elements referring to the Cancuen ruler at this time, Tajal Chan Ahk.

There is a perfect correspondence between La Linterna's apogee, its texts, the presence of the Cancuen ceramics and artifacts there, and the entrance of Campamento Fine Orange ceramics and Zaragoza obsidian during the final part of the Cancuen apogee between 780/786 and 800/801. This also marked the beginning and the end of another step in economic change at Cancuen.

The portion of La Linterna adjacent to the Chinaja range karst towers has been suggested to be (and may be) the "conquered" center in the controversial references in Altar 2 of a lord's defeat of a lord from "Sak Witz." However, as expressed above concerning Raxruha Viejo, we are skeptical of what such texts may actually indicate. The Cancuen ruler and elites needed to include war and conquest references in their descriptions of military activities of a *k'uhul ajaw*, but at La Linterna these types of references have no convincing meaning. Prior to involvement with Cancuen, Raxruha had no impressive epicenter, and La Linterna was a very small site with unimpressive mounds and little evidence of a high degree of stratification or mobilization of labor. Therefore, it is unclear which "lord" Cancuen's proxy agent would have been defeating or capturing. In La Linterna's parallel apogee, there are well-worked facing stones on or nearby some structures, reported stelae, Cancuen ceramics, and the still-present hieroglyphic staircase with texts referring to Cancuen. Yet again, given its nature before that alleged "war" or "conquest," such a reference would be a great exaggeration or indeed meaningless. We suggest that La Linterna's local community leaders simply joined the new and profitable Cancuen/Transversal network.

RITUALIZED LONG-DISTANCE JADE EXCHANGE

Perhaps the most salient example of the different types of Transversal/Cancuen dyadic network connections may be the enigmatic form of jade import. The sources of Cancuen's jade are in the Transversal/highland from an area with visible jade outcrops along the border of the states of Quiche and the Verapaces. It is a distinctive jade of the highest quality in Classic Maya terms. The jade arrived at Cancuen in the impractical form of huge boulders weighing up to 18 kilograms, a jade-transport practice not seen at Late Classic Maya sites, probably due to its energetic inefficiency in transport (Andrieu et al. 2014). The probability that this impractical form of transport was due to ideological factors was supported by the discovery and thorough excavation of Cancuen's northern ballcourt, unique in the Maya Lowlands (Torres 2011). It had the exact form and function as the "feasting ballcourts" (e.g., Fox 1996) in the zone of the highlands that included the area of jade source for Cancuen's preform workshop (Andrieu et al. 2011).

This ballcourt was low, open, and sprawling, and thus more public (Figure 2.5). Its two defining platforms were of rough clay and stone, with highland-style construction, faced with large, unworked, inclined stone slabs defining a 24 m long playing alley (Torres 2011). It was, in all respects, a southern Verapaz, El Quiche, or Chixoy Valley–style "feasting" ballcourt (Torres 2011). At Cancuen the actual feasting is demonstrated by thick sheet middens of broken simple jars, *comales*, and serving vessels surrounding the ballcourt platforms. This same area has higher proportions of Verapaz ceramics than any other areas at Cancuen (Torres 2011; Torres et al. 2014).

Figure 2.5. Reconstruction drawing of Cancuen's Verapaz/Quiche style feasting ballcourt. The feasting is confirmed by large sheet middens of broken domestic serving vessels and garbage. (Courtesy of Luís Fernando Luin.)

All of this suggests the formation and maintenance of a dyadic relationship with agents from jade-extracting highland communities (Andrieu and Quiñonez 2011; Andrieu, Riverón, et al. 2011; Torres 2011). This new architectural setting at Cancuen could have served for ritual activities and as a typical form of building "trust" with new economic partners. One hypothesis is that this strong element of ideology legitimating and ritualizing jade exchange might have involved pilgrimage and games at Cancuen with its new highland and Transversal partners. Such settings and activities are always used to build economic trust, but this jade transport could also have been the actual mechanism of a network form of ritual economy (see Wells and Davis-Salazar 2007). Those speculative hypotheses further direct our network research design to carry out reconnaissance and excavations in the zone of the jade outcrops.

Although jade boulders probably arrived at Cancuen with some ritual significance, they were then treated at Cancuen like any commodity and only partly worked to enhance value (Andrieu et al. 2014; Demarest et al. 2014; Demarest and Victor 2022). The exact status of the preform products is difficult to discern, but the most pronounced changes in Classic Maya, historic, and modern jade value always occurred in the final carving stage, since it is one of the hardest and most cryptocrystalline stones. Thus, jade at Cancuen may have initially been considered an imported ritual good from the point of view of the resource region agents, but once integrated into Cancuen's internal system of production and export, it became a raw commodity. Then, it was enhanced in its economic value for export by working it into preforms of beads and earspools. Cancuen literally "moved up the production chain" in current economic terms. At receiving centers probably to the west and north, it could have been viewed as a material of high status, but only when it was finished into elegant carved artifacts did it become greatly significant or even sacred (Andrieu et al. 2014).

As described by Kopytoff (1988; see also Appadurai 1988), this "cultural biography" of jade—its multiple status and value changes—is seen in the Cancuen exchange networks. As is typical, that revaluation was manipulated by economic agents. Note that jade never became "inalienable property," since the vast corpus of ancient and modern evidence and current economic theory demonstrate that nothing is ever "inalienable" until it is completely removed from human circulation. It is the norm in ancient, historic, and modern economics that the most inalienable properties are routinely exchanged or sold, especially in times of economic pressure, such as in "selling the family jewels." Even popes and bishops often sold their cathedral and church artifacts, such as golden crucifixes and mass chalices, and this practice continues to this day.

That aligns with the Mesoamerican picture as seen in Freidel and Reilly's (2010) discussions of the exchangeability of jade celts and objects in times of drought or other existential crises facing leaders. However, these cultural biographies of resources and products not only result from gradual development in societies or responses to extreme stress, but also are driven by economic agents consciously revaluing the material. This occurs not just by production chains, but by manipulation of the object's social significance. Indeed, that is central to what economic agents of any kind have done in any period or culture. This pattern can become apparent to participants, and such consciousness of the possibility of exchanging such "sacred" items in times of stress quickly leads to more frequent use of such items or materials as a kind of "stored capital" (e.g., Demarest et al. 2020; Freidel and Reilly 2010; Freidel et al. 2016).

Sometimes we forget that humans, as participants in economic and social systems in any period and any place, can immediately see such obvious possibilities. These exchange complexities between distant partners with such a high- but protean-value resource would need much negotiation and legitimation—thus the Cancuen/Transversal use of differing symbols, architectural settings, and other elements, both at Cancuen and at partner sites.

SEBOL AND OTHER SITES FOR FUTURE INVESTIGATIONS

Our network research design covers many sites and areas—too many to list—where we have investigated, are beginning work, or will examine in the future. One important site is the region of Sebol, which may have been an important node in the Transversal networks before, during, and after the late-eighth-century Cancuen/Transversal network. "Sebol" is actually a "string" of occupations located precisely where the subterranean streams of crystalline water come cascading out of the caves at the base of the highlands to the south (Cambranes 2019). There the streams go north across only a 1 to 3 km fertile strip of land to create the east-west Sebol River. As more streams are added, the Sebol heads east as it grows in volume and then sharply turns north in an area just east of Raxruha and south of Cancuen to become the Pasión River, the much larger and more navigable "superhighway" of the western part of the southern Maya Lowlands. Each cluster of residences and some temples and large platforms (Transversal-style "acropoli"?) lie in between the streams coming out of the caves, and that pattern is almost continuous across the zone.

It was a strategic location because it lies at the intersection of the east-west Sebol River and the Transversal but also at the base of a land valley route south into the highlands (see Figure 2.4). It may be even more important in ideological terms since the sequence of caves with streams emerging from them is in the area often identified in ethnohistorical research as a major entrance to Xibalba, the Underworld. This might explain the variety of ceramics and artifacts collected by residents there from the caves and from our investigations of the sites.

Two seasons of field investigations at Sebol (Cambranes 2019; Joaquin et al. 2019) have surface sampled or excavated 20 low residences but also some elite or public architecture. A number of larger structures in one area were placed atop the wide platforms, and we explored two steep temple mounds, each 8 m high. Most material culture is of typical Transversal/highland ceramics and construction styles. However, a relationship to the general network is suggested by a significant percentage, just over 11%, of Peten ceramics and a small number of specifically identified Cancuen ceramics. The picture is further complicated by the presence of ceramics from the Late Preclassic and Early Classic.

Yet it is also difficult to generalize, since like the weird Sesakkar site, Sebol is a unique configuration, and the area explored is just one of the occupations separated by the streams. Some of the caves themselves have only been visited and must be further explored.

Clearly this is a very important site, given its strategic network exchange position and its more permanent status as a very sacred zone across many time periods. It presents great challenges to investigation, as do all the sites at the Transversal interface of the highlands and lowlands. Years of future investigation will be needed to better understand it. The same can be said about exploration at other unexcavated network sites and other not-yet-investigated zones on the key routes of network exchange.

THE CHALLENGE FOR FUTURE TRANSVERSAL NETWORK INVESTIGATIONS

As with all of the history of Upper Pasión and Transversal research described in Chapter 1 and here, investigators will face the same need to constantly retailor research designs, rethink hypotheses as they investigate, and repeatedly change either or both along the way. All of that can be explored in further research at the identified sites and as contemporary network research design guides us to new ones. Each site or area will require different approaches because, while in 760–800 this was a very effective network for a period, it was still in its formation—a breakaway network trying to establish *different* forms of economic exchange and ideological relationships with each set of partner agents in different regions for different objectives.

More challenging is the fact that the period of the more clearly marked network of the Cancuen apogee is only a very short piece of a long history for the Transversal networks. For a thousand years before and centuries after, the same vast quantities of materials moved from the highlands to the lowlands, and later, even through the Colonial Period, such goods moved through the Transversal to other regions. Those would have been different types of networks with different modes using many different mechanisms and routes. Transversal network research continues to be a frustrating, at times humiliating, but exciting long-term process.

3

The Archaeology of the Chixoy Basin

BRENT K. S. WOODFILL, CAITLIN EARLEY,
AND ALEXANDER E. RIVAS

THE CHIXOY RIVER Basin, which stretches from the volcanic western highlands of Guatemala well into the Maya Lowlands, is one of the largest understudied and largely unknown regions in the Maya world. The river is presently divided into four segments, each with its own name (Figure 3.1). It begins as the rather unimpressive Negro ("Black") River as it meanders from its origins near Chichicastenango to its confluence with the Salama and Carchela Rivers. The Chixoy segment passes through the northern highlands and tumbles into the lowlands. Once it passes the Maya saltworks of Salinas de los Nueve Cerros, the river changes its name again to the Salinas River, where it meanders through a deep, flat floodplain until it joins the Pasión River (see Chapter 2). It then forms the great Usumacinta River, which continues until it joins the Grijalva River a few kilometers before emptying out into the Gulf of Mexico.

In this chapter, we focus on the span between the K'iche heartland in the Upper Negro River and the saltworks at Salinas de los Nueve Cerros in the Northern Transversal Strip. While this approximately 350 km span drops nearly 1,800 m and passes through vastly different ecological niches, geological zones, and cultural regions, it was part of a major thoroughfare connecting much of the western Maya world, in addition to being the lifeblood of local agriculture. Travelers from near the headwaters of the Río Negro would have proceeded by land to avoid whitewater until Sacapulas, where boats could head upriver to the west. Land travel would resume once the river turned south near San Cristóbal Verapaz; travelers would walk northwest toward the Chama Valley (Morán and Akkeren 2016). From there, the river would have been largely navigable, at least during the dry season, apart from a few portages (Canter 2021).

Unfortunately, the entire Chixoy River system has received very little

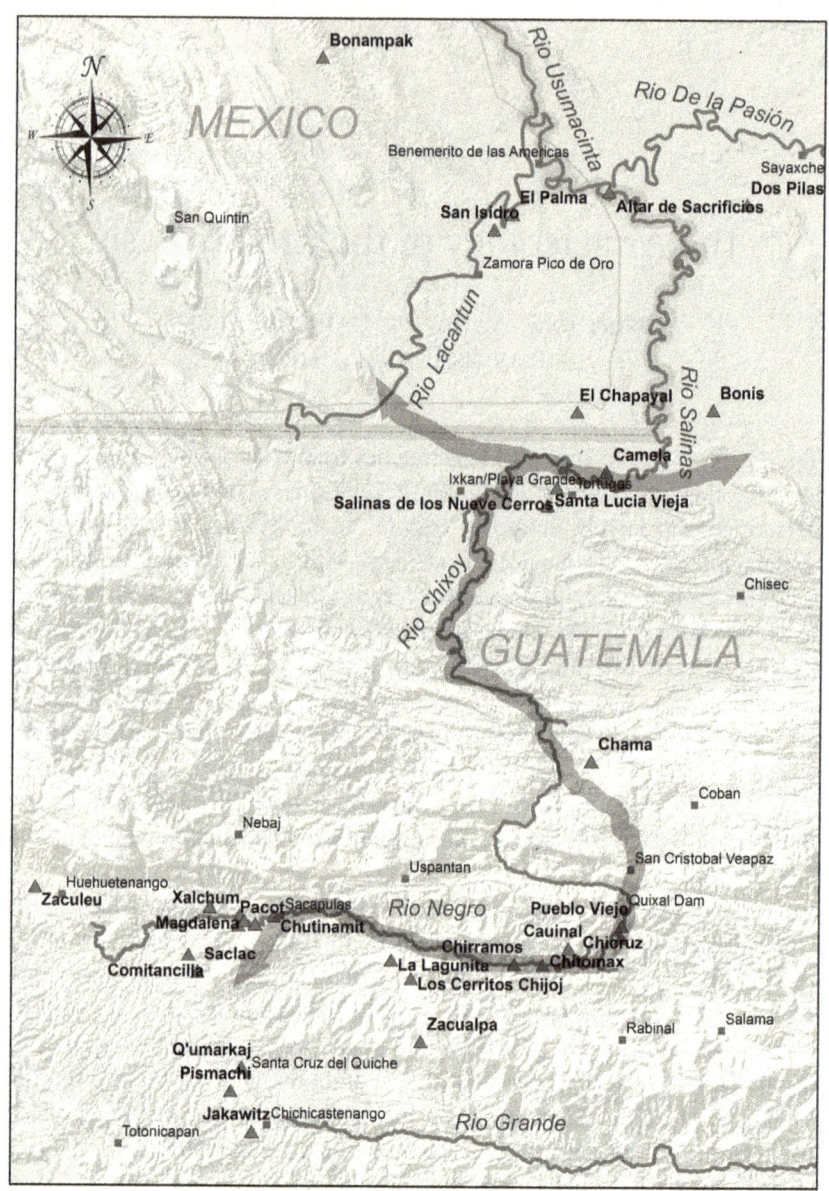

Figure 3.1. Map of the Negro/Chixoy/Salinas/Usumacinta River with principal sites discussed in this chapter and likely route between the river's headwaters and the southern lowlands according to Morán and Akkeren (2016). (Base map from ArcGis [ESRI]. Marc Wolf, modified by Brent K. S. Woodfill.)

archaeological attention relative to the better-known sites of the Usumacinta located downriver. This is due to several factors, from the intensity of the Guatemalan civil war that played out throughout the northern highlands during the latter half of the twentieth century and the distrust of outsiders there that continues into the present, to the construction of the Quixal Dam and other infrastructure that has flooded many important archaeological sites. As a result, much of the available data comes from mid-twentieth-century reconnaissance and salvage work associated with the dam's construction by Alain Ichon and his team.

Still, what we have glimpsed demonstrates the importance of this route and the communities on it over several millennia. There was a significant exchange of painted cylinder vessels between the Chama Valley and the lowland city of Altar de Sacrificios, located at the confluence of the Salinas and Pasión Rivers. Harvard excavations at Altar recovered two associated tombs with Verapaz-style ceramics (Adams 1971) as well as figurines proven to be part of a larger exchange network that included the Coban Plateau and most of the eastern and central Transversal sites (Cancuen, Raxruha Viejo, Salinas de los Nueve Cerros, and Chama; see Sears 2016). Conquest-era Indigenous histories document the migrations of multiple lineages along the Chixoy route into the highlands, which are also reflected in early census data (Akkeren 2012; see also Chapter 11). Combined, data indicate the river was a crucial means of interregional connections, facilitating trade and the movement of people and ideas from the Preclassic period to today. In the following sections, we trace available archaeological information from beginnings of the Upper Negro River to its eventual confluence with the Usumacinta.

HIGHLAND BEGINNINGS: THE UPPER NEGRO RIVER

The Río Negro begins near the modern town of Santa Cruz Quiche. Although this part of the Maya world has been settled since at least the Archaic period (Brown 1980), it is most well known for the Postclassic occupation of Q'umarkaj (Figure 3.2). Settled around AD 1400, Q'umarkaj was the center of the K'iche Maya empire, located on a plateau surrounded by deep *barrancas*, or ravines, approximately 2.5 km from Santa Cruz Quiche. Central Q'umarkaj extends less than 1 km^2 in area, but additional archaeological remains top the surrounding plateaus. Including its satellite sites, the total area of Greater Q'umarkaj is between 4 and 8 km^2 (Carmack and Weeks 1981; Fox 1978).

Information about Q'umarkaj comes from a variety of sources, including archaeological excavation and ethnohistorical documents. Archaeological excavation has been carried out by Robert Wauchope of Tulane's Middle

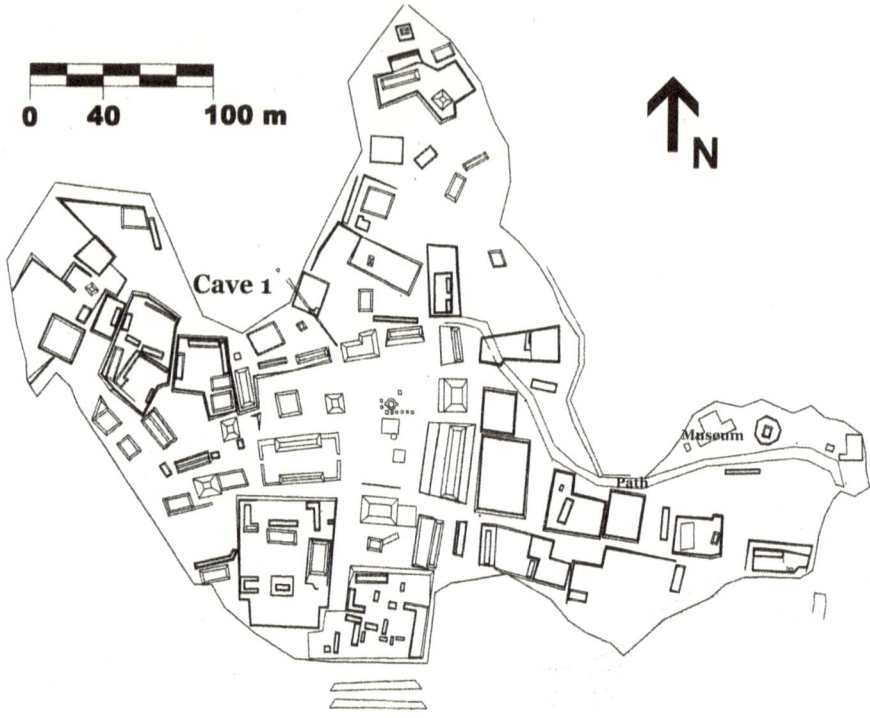

Figure 3.2. Plan of central Q'umarkaj, Department of Quiche, Guatemala. (Courtesy of Edy Barrios, Proyecto Q'umarkaj, CEMCA.)

American Research Institute, Robert Carmack (1977, 1981) of the State University of New York, and a variety of other archaeologists (Fox 1978; Wallace 1977; Weeks 1983). Recent archaeological excavation has been undertaken by Raquel Macario (2012; Macario et al. 2007). Study of Q'umarkaj also benefits from an extensive ethnohistorical record, including documents like the *Popol Vuh* and the *Annals of the Cakchiquels*. Sources indicate that Q'umarkaj was the last of several K'iche' capitals in the region; earlier capitals included Jakawitz, likely located on the outskirts of Chichicastango (Akkeren 2002), or Nahuala (Akkeren, personal communication to Woodfill 2023) and Pismachi, located on the southern outskirts of Q'umarkaj across a deep ravine (Babcock 2012:11). While the locations of these earlier sites are still debated, the K'iche' Federation that ruled from them represents the union of lineages from disparate places, most notably the Northern Transversal Strip (Kaweq'), the Pacific Coast (Ajaw K'iche' and Nijaib'), and central Guatemala (Tamub' and Ilokab'; see Akkeren 2000, 2012, 2016; see also Chapter 11).

Although efforts by the Guatemalan government to transform the site into a more tourist-friendly destination have begun to counteract the post-conquest history of the site, large parts of Q'umarkaj remain unreconstructed, and the buildings have suffered from the removal of cut stone for surrounding modern construction. The site center consists of a central plaza dominated by a large structure on its western side devoted to Tojil. A radial pyramid constructed using talud-tablero architecture, the Tojil Temple was first described for an American audience by Stephens (1841), who noted the remains of a jaguar painting on the west side of the structure. Two other temples around the plaza join Tojil to form a triangle reminiscent of a three-stone hearth—Awilix, on the eastern side of the plaza, and Q'aq'awitz (Fire Mountain), located on the plaza's southern side. Each of these temples refers to one of the city's three patron gods as discussed in the *Popol Vuh* (Akkeren 2002). In the center of the plaza is a circular structure perhaps associated with K'uk'umatz, or the feathered serpent (Carmack 1981).

Central Q'umarkaj also features a ballcourt and a number of palaces, which scholars have associated with specific lineages that occupied the site in the Late Postclassic period, including the Kanek', who are discussed in greater detail in Chapter 11. Archaeological research by Macario has also revealed evidence of hydraulic canals, indicating that residents constructed a sophisticated water management system at the Postclassic capital (Macario et al. 2007). Another important feature of Q'umarkaj is a series of at least four artificial caves carved into the plateau underneath the site (Brady and Veni 1992; Woodfill 2014). These caves are still used by local ritual practitioners and would have been useful tools in the Postclassic period for world-centering rituals designed to enhance political power (Earley 2008).

Q'umarkaj served as the K'iche' capital until 1524, when it fell to the Spaniard Pedro Alvarado. Excavations by Macario et al. (2007) revealed a burnt layer of occupation. Defensive walls near the incoming causeway may correspond with this event.

SACAPULAS AND THE MIDDLE NEGRO

From Santa Cruz Quiche, the river passes alongside Sacapulas, a major precolumbian saltworks still in use today. At the time of the Spanish conquest, the town was referred to as Tuja or Tujal and the river was known as Tujalha, which Akkeren (2008:63) posits all derive from the sauna (*tuj*)-like houses where locals boiled down brine into salt cakes, as they continue to do today. An early survey by A. L. Smith (1955:24) recovered artifacts dating from the Late Preclassic period at three sites in the region, registered as Xolchun, Xolcoxoy, and Chuchun. Populations increased around Sacapulas during the Epiclassic period (ca. AD 900) with most of the settlements dating to the Late Postclassic period (AD 1300–conquest; Chocano 2012).

John W. Fox (1978) identified six archaeological sites associated with the conquest-period Sacapulas K'iche. Of these civic centers, two large and two small sites were located along a nine-mile stretch of the Negro (Fox 1978:69). The two principal sites were Chutixtiox and Chuitinamit. The former is located at a bend in the Negro River, on a hill located approximately 100 m above the river. A. L. Smith (1955:17) noted that it was well positioned for defense and overlooks two minor agricultural settlements (Fox 1978:72). Of all the sites in the Sacapulas cluster, this one bears the greatest resemblance to architectural patterns at Q'umarkaj (Fox 1978:110).

Chuitinamit overlooks the salt springs from across the Chixoy (Smith 1955:20) and may have been the regional capital in the Postclassic period. The main plaza featured a radial pyramid as well as several long council-house-like structures. The site also featured a ballcourt, and archaeological investigation revealed stone-lined tombs and a sculpture of a jaguar at the base of Structure 3. Interestingly, the architecture of Chuitinamit also includes corbel vaulting, which Fox (1978) notes may be an import from the Maya Lowlands. While most of the documented occupation is Postclassic, Andrews (1983:91) does note "abundant . . . Late Classic and Late Postclassic materials" were recovered from eroding middens around the saltworks.

At the time of the Spanish conquest, the Sacapulas Valley was divided into three major territorial units, each run by its own *chinamit* (lineage group) centered on a Late Postclassic site (Hill and Monaghan 1987:65–73). Chuitinamit, as well as the contemporary town of Sacapulas, was located in territory controlled by the Ah Q'anil and the Ah Toltekat *chinamits* (see also Akkeren 2008). From their base of operations at Chuitinamit, the Ah Q'anil could have defended their claim to the saltworks below, while their eastern and western boundaries were guarded by the smaller sites of Xecaltoj and Papasca (called Chuchun by Smith [1955:25]), respectively.

The western edge of the valley was controlled by the Zacualpanec *chinamit*, who were based at Xolchun, located at the confluence of the Río Negro and Río Blanco. They controlled the western edge of the valley and nearly the entire stretch of the Río Blanco. Hill and Monaghan (1987) suggest the edges of their territory were secured by several defensible secondary settlements, which included Xoltinamit, Xolchun, Pacot, and Xolpacol.

The Coateca *chinamit* was sandwiched between these two *chinamits* and based at the site of Chutixtiox (or Chu'Taxtyoox; Chocano 2012), on a slope overlooking a broad curve of the Río Negro (Figure 3.3). Most of the territory they controlled was located in the mountainous lands to the south. However, it appears to have been far enough from the Río Negro and Sacapulas Valley that it did not need the presence of permanent defensible settlements.

Archaeology of the Chixoy Basin | 71

Figure 3.3. Reconstruction of Chutixtiox, Department of Quiche, looking north. (Tatiana Proskouriakoff, originally published in A. L. Smith 1955:Figure 12. Courtesy of Carnegie Institution for Science.)

Like Salinas de los Nueve Cerros (discussed below), Sacapulas was an economic powerhouse due to their control over their salt source. Communities throughout much of the northern highlands depended on Sacapultec salt, including the K'iche', the Ixil around Nebaj and Huehuetenango, and even communities on the Coban plateau (Andrews 1983:92–93). Sacapulas was also located at the crossroads of two important trade routes: the highland-lowland route discussed above and a shorter route between the central K'iche' region and the Ixil triangle that continued to be highly trafficked through the Colonial Period (Ximénez 1929–1931, Tome 1:191). Sacapulas was firmly a part of the K'iche' empire by the fourteenth century (Babcock 2012:303; Fox 1978:111), although this association could have even deeper historical ties. Akkeren (2008) notes that the Ah Q'anil trace their origins back to the Pacific slope, likely on the shores of the Río Nahualate downhill from Lake Atitlan (see also Bove 1989:49) and near the homelands of several important lineages at Q'umarkaj.

An additional saltworking site, Salinas de Magdalena, is located 6 km from Sacapulas (Andrews 1983:95). The salt source consists of a series of brine springs in a deep ravine, and a site that dates from the Late Classic through the Colonial Period is found atop the mesa behind it. Unfortunately, no formal research has been done at the site, and when Woodfill visited the contemporary village to inquire about the possibility of documenting it in 2019, he was kindly but strongly encouraged to move on due to the current distrust of miners and other extractive industries.

THE MIDDLE CHIXOY

The following section of river was densely occupied in the past and was home to multiple important sites that were investigated in the 1970s by a French team led by Ichon. Unfortunately, their work was a salvage project conducted before the construction of the Quixal Hydroelectric Dam. The dam was completed in 1983 atop the archaeological site of Pueblo Viejo Chixoy; the resulting flood raised the river level by up to 70 m and claimed around 2,000 hectares of land, forcing the eviction of nearly 500 households by the Guatemalan military, in addition to rendering follow-up investigations impossible (Ichon 1987, 1992, 1996; Ichon et al. 1996). This region is referred to in the literature, confusingly, as "the Middle Chixoy" in spite of the fact that it is actually the lowest section of the Negro River, with the official beginning of the Chixoy located just downriver from the dam. For the sake of continuity, we retain the term "Middle Chixoy" here.

PRECLASSIC AND EARLY CLASSIC OCCUPATION

Settlement in the Middle Chixoy Basin begins as early as the Middle Preclassic (700–300 BC; Ichon 1996) with some evidence for an Early Preclassic (ca. 800 BC) occupation at Los Encuentros (Ichon 1979:42) and Pueblo Viejo Chixoy (Ichon et al. 1996:55). Sites settled in the Late Preclassic period (300 BC–AD 150) were generally occupied until at least the eighth century AD, when archaeologists report dense populations with hierarchies of settlement including dominant centers, secondary centers, and residential sites. Ceramic analysis by Marion Hatch (1982) and Marie-Charlotte Arnauld (1985) places the local population in the broader Conchas (Pacific Coast) and Charcas (Kaminaljuyu) ceramic spheres during the Middle Preclassic and the eastern highland Providencia sphere during the Late Preclassic (Demarest and Sharer 1986).

The archaeology of the Middle Chixoy demonstrates ties to the southern Maya Lowlands by the end of the Preclassic period. One of the largest and most complete collections of Protoclassic (AD 150–400) material in the Maya world—approximately 300 complete lowland-style vessels—was recovered from a cave interred under a plaza at La Lagunita (Figures 3.4 and 3.5; Ichon and Arnauld 1985). Limited material of the same type was also found in elite tombs at three other sites—Chirramos, Chicruz, and Los Encuentros—and in surface collection at a fourth. La Lagunita, in fact, likely served as one of the primary interaction nodes for exchanging vessels and technologies during the latter part of the Protoclassic (AD 350–400), tying its residents with those in Kaminaljuyu, Momostenango, Atitlan, the central Peten, and Naj Tunich (Bonnafoux 2008; Brady et al. 1998; Ichon 1977; Ichon and Arnauld 1985; Ichon et al. 1996:59).

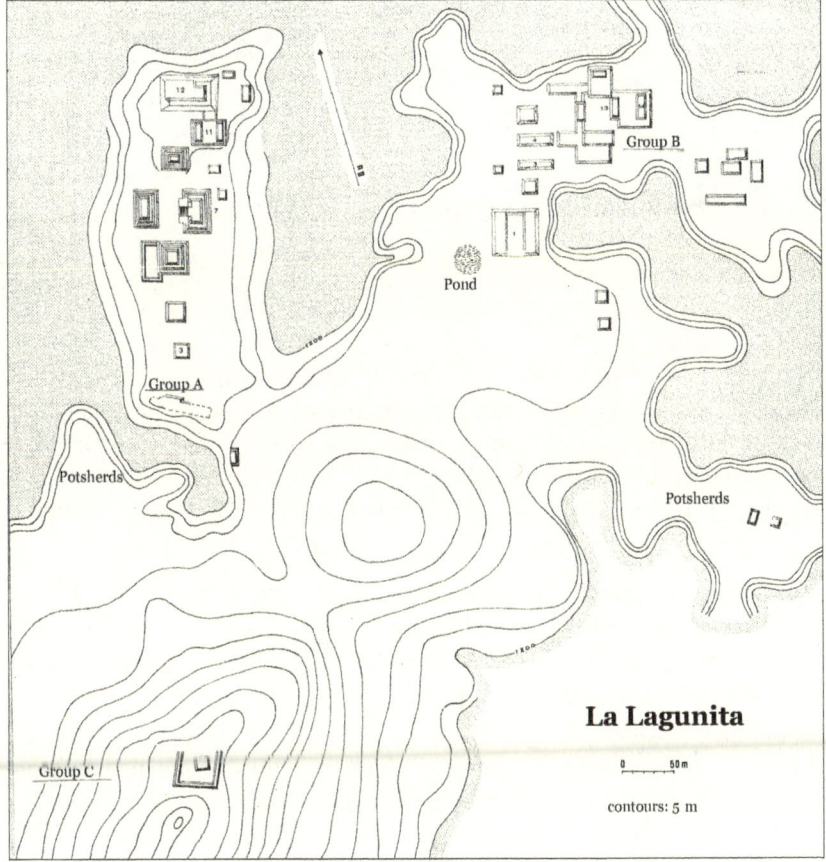

Figure 3.4. Site plan of La Lagunita, El Quiche, Guatemala. (Redrawn from Ichon 1977:Figure 57. Courtesy of Hannah Kitzmann.)

Figure 3.5. Ceramic vessels in La Lagunita cave (C-48), El Quiche, Guatemala: (a) southeast corner with limestone block; (b) southern pottery mound; (c) west wall and southwest corner; and (d) northeast cluster. (Photograph by Alain Ichon. Originally published in Ichon and Arnauld 1985:Figure 23. Courtesy of Archéologie des Amériques [ArchAm], UMR8096, CNRS et Université de Paris 1 Panthéon-Sorbonne.)

In spite of the presence of significant lowland material in special contexts, the majority of the Classic period in the Middle Chixoy was typified by the same ceramic stagnation as identified in the neighboring Verapaz (Arnauld 1986) and Izabal (Fialko 1982; Hermes 1981). The recovered Classic material dating to between about AD 400 and 900 is largely unchanging, making it difficult to refine the settlement chronology or identify potential hiatuses in occupation without additional dating techniques (Ichon et al. 1996:59).

Ichon and his team excavated two major Preclassic settlements and recovered surface materials indicating early occupation in at least six other sites. They found evidence of Early Classic habitation in six sites and Late Classic to Epiclassic habitation in 36. Some sites demonstrated considerable continuity: El Jocote, located near the center of the "Middle Chixoy" region, was a regional center from at least the Late Preclassic through the Postclassic periods. At this site, the French team uncovered evidence of monumental construction dating to around the beginning of the first millennium AD, including one platform that contained a cache of 23 complete vessels and a partial burial (Ichon et al. 1996:51). The site also contains the only securely dated Early Classic temple in the region, which was expanded on during its Late Classic fluorescence (Ichon et al. 1996:65).

Ichon considered Los Encuentros (Figure 3.6), located at the confluence of the Negro, Salama, and Carchela Rivers, to be the most important site in the region after the Late Postclassic site of Kawinal (discussed below), and Ruud van Akkeren (2012) identifies it as the probable location of Rax Ch'ich', an important Classic-period site. Los Encuentros grew to contain at least 10 architectural groups during the Late and Terminal Classic periods, although Ichon et al. (1996:45–46) noted a Preclassic occupation in at least two groups and the presence of several rich tombs dating to the Protoclassic. Hatch (1982) identified several imported wares, including part of a Tzakol 1 polychrome bowl from the Peten and a jar from Kaminaljuyu (Ichon et al. 1996:64).

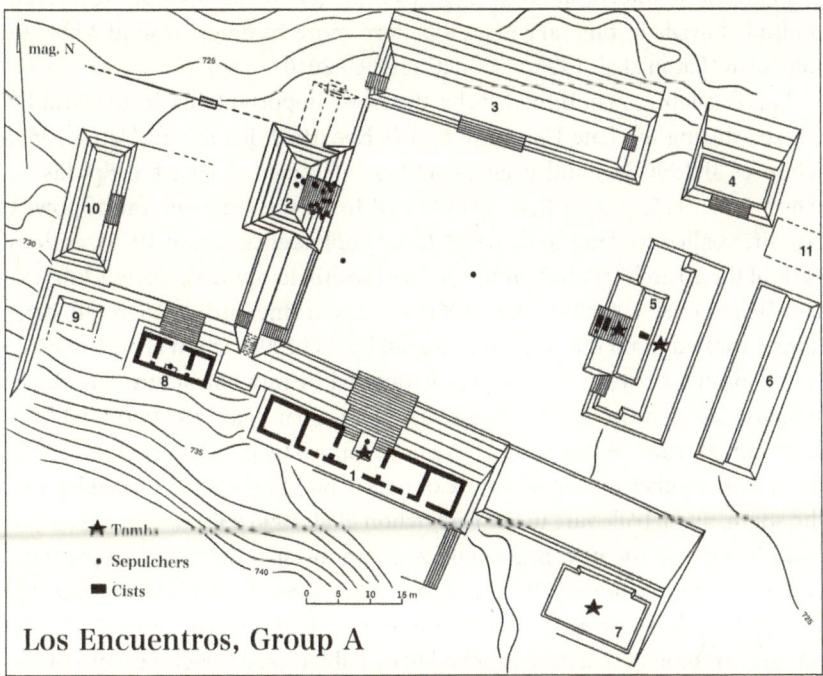

Figure 3.6. Plan of Los Encuentros, Group A. (Redrawn from Ichon and Hatch 1982:Figure 4. Courtesy of Hannah Kitzmann.)

LATE CLASSIC THROUGH POSTCLASSIC

The Middle Chixoy appears to have had its highest population density during the Late Classic (AD 600–900) period. Multiple settlements founded in valley floors during the Preclassic and Early Classic periods grew in size and importance, with the most important political and ceremonial architecture built atop earlier platforms, and new communities sprang up on natural slopes or hilltops surrounding them (Ichon et al. 1996:75).

The ceramics during the Late Classic are less international than during the Protoclassic and Early Classic periods and are closely related to styles from the Coban Plateau (Arnauld 1986; Ichon et al. 1996:98–99; Sears et al. 2021; Smith 1952). They include incised cream wares, bichrome and (occasionally) trichrome cylinder vases, miniature vessels, modeled figurines, and paneled ceramic "thrones." There is little influence from Chama and other sites farther downriver, however (Ichon et al. 1996:99), and as one moves upriver from Los Encuentros, the Verapaz influence decreases, replaced by a stronger presence of styles associated with the western highlands—Zacualpa, Zaculeu, and Totonicapan (Ichon et al. 1996:123). Other relations are seen in funerary practices: while most of the recovered human remains had been deposited in tombs or architectural fill during this time, Ichon and his team recovered multiple burials in funerary urns, a pattern more common around Nebaj to the north (Ichon et al. 1996:114; McCampbell 2010).

Los Encuentros continued to be the most important site in the Middle Chixoy during the Late Classic period (Ichon 1979; Ichon and Hatch 1982; Ichon et al 1996:84), and even as settlement waned during the Epiclassic, Ichon (1996:125) argues that it continued to be the regional seat of power. The site's ballcourt dates to its Late Classic fluorescence (Ichon 1979), as does each of the 10 architectural groups located within its approximately 1 km^2 extent (Ichon et al. 1996:84). The site's main temple, measuring 9.5 m tall, contains a vaulted tomb that was emptied out by AD 1000 (Ichon et al. 1996:84). It was located between two plazas surrounded by range structures; its single staircase led up from the larger eastern plaza. That plaza was bounded by a large range structure that would have been topped by perishable structures to the north, another masonry temple or palace building with five chambers to the south, and a ballcourt in the east (Ichon et al. 1996:83).

El Jocote was the next important center in the area. It had a 3 m pyramid and a ballcourt (Ichon 1979). It also had what Ichon et al. (1996:77, translation by Woodfill) describe as "a true ceremonial-residential complex . . . the unique ceremonial structure is boxed in by habitational structures very probably reserved for the elite."

Los Cerritos-Chijoj, one of the larger centers in the basin, also reached its florescence during the Late Classic period. It was first occupied in the Late Preclassic period between AD 100 and 300 (Ichon 1992:6). By the Late Classic, the site exhibits small ceremonial complexes and evidence of stone sculpture. While there is some overlap in ceramic types between Los Cerritos-Chijoj and other Middle Chixoy sites, the former appears to have been more closely related to archaeological sites to the southwest of Q'umarkaj around Totonicapan (Ichon 1992; Ichon et al. 1996:99).

Chitomax 1 is a Late Classic site complete with a ballcourt (Ichon 1979:49). Interestingly, the court's dedicatory cache consists of some possible Early Classic heirloom *camahuiles* (abstract anthropomorphic figures made of greenstone plaques), along with pieces of pyrite and jade beads inside a jaguar *incensario* (Ichon et al. 1996:65). Excavations in two structures revealed the presence of a Preclassic occupation (Ichon et al. 1996:44), again indicating continuous occupation in many sites in this region.

EPICLASSIC AND POSTCLASSIC OCCUPATION

The subsequent Epiclassic period (AD 800–1000) appears to have had a more restricted occupation, and local leaders appear to have reutilized and, at times, vandalized Late Classic tombs and ritual architecture in lieu of sponsoring new building projects (Ichon et al. 1996:126). Recovered materials continue to show strong associations with the Coban Plateau through multiple shared ceramic types and deep bowls with zoomorphic supports. Ichon's team recovered other imported wares including Tohil Plumbate; objects of jade, pyrite, and gold; and polychrome vessels depicting highland Mexican gods. All of these artifacts demonstrate the participation of the region's elite in larger highland exchange networks (Ichon et al. 1996:126).

Several sites in the region, most notably Pueblo Viejo Chixoy and El Jocote, survived the Classic collapse endemic to much of the Maya world. Chitomax 1 was abandoned by the beginning of the Postclassic, although the population likely moved to Chitomax 2, a large Postclassic settlement across the Negro River (Ichon 1979:55). By AD 1100, Los Encuentros was overshadowed by Pueblo Viejo Chixoy, located just 2 km downriver (Ichon 1979:49). The largest Postclassic site by far in the area, however, was Kawinal, which Ichon et al. (1996:84) consider to be the only "principal ceremonial center" in the Middle Chixoy. Akkeren (2003a) argues that it was the home of a branch of the Kaweq lineage, northern lowland merchants, which later became a central part of the K'iche' Federation.

Kawinal (also called Cauinal; Figure 3.7) had a relatively short history of occupation that was limited to the Postclassic (Ichon et al. 1980, 1996), although at least one of its ceremonial groups, Plaza C, was built atop a small Preclassic settlement (Ichon 1979:40) and a Late Classic tomb (Ichon

1979:47). Many characteristics of the site layout were typical of other contemporaneous highland sites (Akkeren 2003; Ichon et al. 1996)—radial pyramids, council houses, I-shaped ballcourts, hourglass shaped and handled censors. The majority of recovered elite burials were urns containing cremains, while commoner residential neighborhoods contained interred children and sometimes headless adults. The site does differ in one notable way. Kawinal is located in the rather unprotected valley floor, although it was surrounded by multiple smaller hilltop sites that would have allowed residents to protect and mobilize themselves from any incursions (Annereau-Fulbert 2012:264).

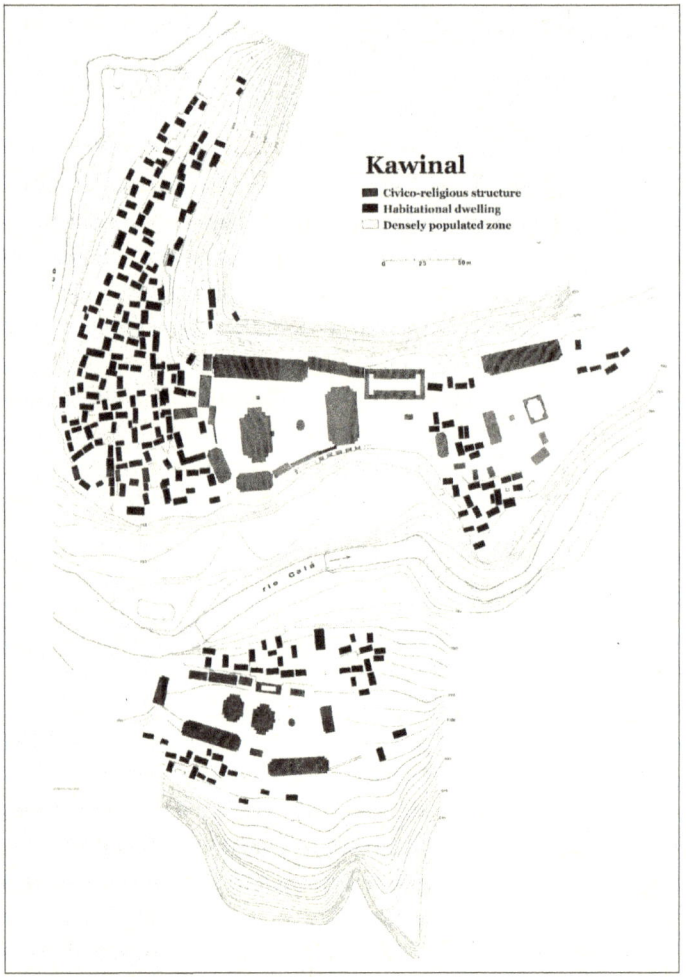

Figure 3.7. Site plan for Kawinal, Department of Quiche, Guatemala. (© and courtesy of Alain Ichon, et al [editors], 1980, Mission archéologique et ethnologique française au Mexique [CEMCA].)

During the years leading up to the Spanish conquest, the Chixoy appears to have served as the eastern border of the K'iche' kingdom, with Kawinal likely protecting the frontier from the neighboring Poqom (Hill 1982) or Poqomchi' (Ichon 1982). During the last phase of occupation, Kawinal's main pyramid was rebuilt as a double temple, which Fox (1981) suggested was a characteristic of frontier sites. The smaller site of Pueblo Viejo Chixoy, located to its northeast about 200 m above the old river level, might have been its farthest outpost (Hill 1982) during this phase, although Ichon did note an earlier habitation that spanned the Early and Late Classic periods (AD 100–1100).

THE CHAMA VALLEY AND THE COBAN PLATEAU

The Chama Valley, located almost a day downriver from the Quixal Dam, is the location of an important, eponymous settlement that has never been subject to formal scientific investigation. Explorer and scholar Robert Burkitt acquired a collection of archaeological material from this area in the early twentieth century that currently resides in the University Museum of Pennsylvania. Although not recovered as systematically as would be desired, the ceramics show a Classic-period occupation from approximately AD 250 to 800. Chama-style ceramics are well known for the chevron bands that frame a wide variety of scenes, including battle, palace, and procession activities (Coe 1973; Danien 1998; Doyle 2016). Ceramics indicate close links with the southeastern Peten during the Late and Terminal Classic period, especially with the downriver city of Altar de Sacrificios (Butler 1962; Danien 1998). Exchange between Chama and Altar de Sacrificios went both ways. In addition to the large quantity of Altar-style polychromes recovered from Chama, a well-stocked tomb at Altar de Sacrificios, excavated by the Harvard Altar project, included six Chama-style vessels associated with a middle-aged woman who died in the mid-eighth century (Tomb 128; see Adams 1971:59–68, 76–78, 131; Smith 1972:266–268; Willey 1973:50). As mentioned, recovered figurines and molds are part of a larger exchange network that includes both the Coban Plateau and the Northern Transversal (Sears 2016; see also this volume Chapters 6 and 7).

At the time of the Spanish conquest, the best-known settlement in the area was run by the local Xoy, about 10 km upriver from Chama in a place called "at the Xoy" (*Chi Xoy*). Spanish chroniclers mention that people traveled from as far away as the Middle Chixoy and the southern lowlands (Akkeren 2012:54). In addition, multiple Late Classic vessels from the Ixil Triangle show subordinates likely from the Chama region presenting achiote to lords as tribute (see K2206 and K2352; Akkeren 2012:56).

Woodfill visited Chama along with Marc Wolf and Carlos Efraín Tox Tiul in 2019, with the intention of beginning the process of starting a survey project there, which was to be undertaken in 2020. The global pandemic postponed these plans beyond the publication of this volume. What has been apparent from this and several previous visits, however, is the scale of the settlement, which consists of a Late Classic urban zone that covers much of the valley and includes multiple structures that are over 10 m in height.

To the east of the Chama Valley, the Coban Plateau was the primary source of quetzal feathers for myriad Mesoamerican groups in the centuries leading up to the Spanish conquest (see Chapter 8). In spite of this important distinction, the region has been largely overlooked by archaeologists. Most of our knowledge of the precolumbian history of the region came from a single short report written by Robert E. Smith (1952) in the mid-twentieth century that described Late Classic ceramic material recovered from a roadcut that nicked the corner of a mound within city limits at the site of Chipoc. The modes he identified were later recovered by other projects working in a wide region of the northern highlands, including the Purula Valley to the south (Arnauld 1986), Los Cerritos Chijoj (Ichon 1992), Nebaj (Becquelin et al. 2001), and the Cave of Hun Nal Ye (Woodfill et al. 2012). As described in Chapter 5, they are also common to sites at the base of the Guatemalan highlands to the north of the Coban Plateau such as Cancuen, Raxruha Viejo, Sebol, and Salinas de los Nueve Cerros, where they often appear alongside standard lowland types and the well-defined local ceramic tradition, referred to in the literature as "Transversal." Altar de Sacrificios Tomb 96, containing a human sacrifice associated with contemporaneous Tomb 128 as well as the famed "Altar Vase" (Figure 3.8), also contained a vessel probably imported from the Coban area (Adams 1971:77).

Figure 3.8. Altar Vase, Maya, Late Classic period, polychrome ceramic (18 cm x 11.5 cm) from Burial 96 at Altar de Sacrificios, Guatemala, now located in the Museum of Archaeology and Ethnography, Guatemala City. (Drawing courtesy of Hannah Kitzmann, based on the original by John Montgomery [JM03206].)

Two important archaeological sites atop the Coban Plateau have received disappointingly little attention. Preliminary excavations in 1964 and 1971 in Sakajut have revealed some of the earliest Maya ceramics dating to the end of the Early Preclassic (Butler 1962; Sedat and Sharer 1972), and the site continued to be occupied through the Classic period. Chich'en (Figure 3.9) is an adjacent site that was the primary city atop the plateau at the time of the Spanish conquest that was first excavated by George Léger in 1894 while serving as the Belgian consul to Coban (Montoya 2023). This settlement appears to have peaked during the Late Classic period, although it continued to be the most important Q'eqchi' city through the Spanish conquest, at which point its residents were resettled in the modern city of Coban (Escobar 1841; Montoya 2023). Each site contains a ballcourt and multiple pyramids and was located in strategic points along the Sakajut River.

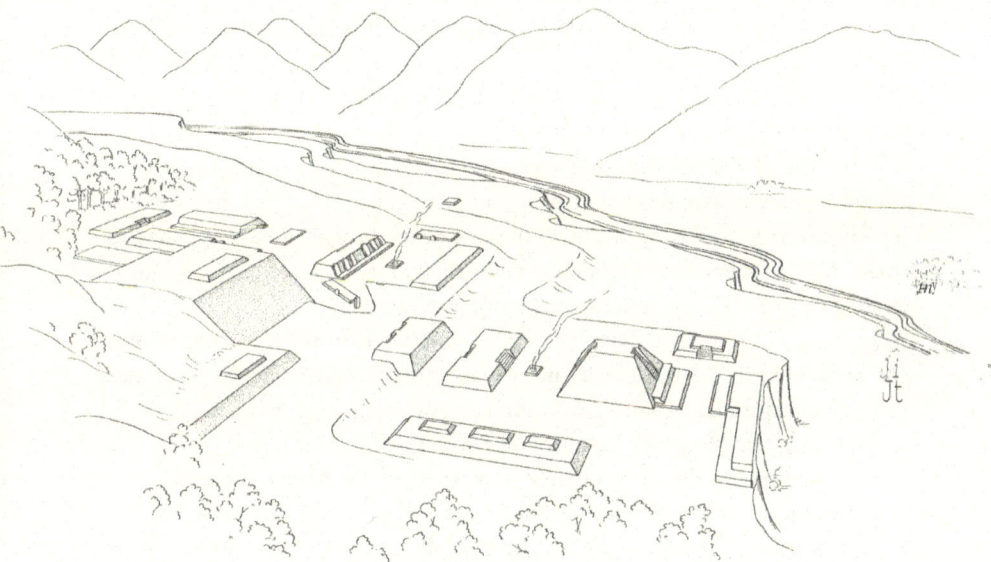

Figure 3.9. Reconstruction of Chich'en, Department of Alta Verapaz, looking south. (Kisa Noguchi Sasaki from sketch by Stephen F. Borhegyi, originally published in A. Ledyard Smith 1955:Figure 39. Courtesy of Carnegie Institution for Science.)

In 2018, Woodfill and his team were alerted to the surprise discovery of a ceramic production facility on private land on the outskirts of the modern city of Coban, and they were able to conduct a salvage project there later that year (Sears et al. 2021; Woodfill 2019b). The archaeological site, dubbed Aragón by its owners, was groundbreaking for several reasons. Not only does it more than triple the Coban-area ceramic collection with exceedingly well-preserved examples, but it also allows us to refine the settlement chronology of the area as well as document interregional ties through the inclusion of nonlocal materials. The new material spans the Late Classic through Early Postclassic periods (AD 700–1200). The material also includes at least one Fine Orange sherd, a ceramic type typical of the Gulf Coast that became increasingly important as a status good in the southern lowlands as trade to the central Peten was interrupted during the early years of the Classic collapse (e.g., Demarest et al. 2014).

The lion's share of the recovered assemblage is composed of large figurines, figurine molds, and other terracotta objects (see Chapter 6). All were created in the "Alta Verapaz" style—referred to as one of two "climax zones of the Maya figurine tradition" by Rands and Rands (1965) for their high quality of artistry. Artists made the figurines with the help of elaborate molds—often with two interlocking pieces to create a truly three-dimensional piece. They are typically hollow and often double as musical ocarinas. Similar figurines have been found from Chama to Cancuen, Raxruha Viejo, and Salinas de los Nueve Cerros (Sears 2016), the last of which has a small collection of molds associated with another figurine workshop.

What was strikingly different about the ceramic figurines recovered from the emergency rescue project at Aragón is that they include far more examples of initial production products than at other sites in northern Alta Verapaz. At Cancuen, for example, even with its large palace and surrounding sections of elite residences producing intricate jade products, nearly two decades of investigations have recovered only six ceramic figurine production molds (Sears 2016). The figurine workshop at Nueve Cerros does have a significant number of molds, and the ratio of molds to figurines is 14%. At Aragón, the ratio has more than doubled to 30%, suggesting that the site was a major figurine production center with a significant quantity of exports.

The ceramic and figurine material from Aragón indicates that its residents were closely tied to important trade nodes and economic centers in the southern lowlands. Sites throughout this region were located at crucial trade junctions: Chama was located at a strategic "choke point" along the Chixoy River where any canoe traffic would have to portage a dangerous set of rapids (Woodfill et al. 2014). Salinas de los Nueve Cerros was built atop the only noncoastal salt source in the Maya Lowlands and was a major production center for salt, salted fish, and a variety of agricultural goods (Woodfill 2019a; Woodfill et al. 2015). Cancuen lies near the headwaters of the Pasión River and was the largest producer of jade objects in the Maya world at the same time that its residents were exchanging figurines with Aragón (Demarest et al. 2014; Sears 2016). As a result, it appears that all of these polities were closely allied during the economic florescence of the region, and the gifting of these figurines, figurine molds, and prestige ceramics would have served as a mechanism to cement these alliances.

After the collapse of the southern lowlands during the ninth century AD, however, residents of Aragón appear to have continued to maintain their economic importance, albeit through alliances with other parts of the northern highlands. Presumably, the primary commodity they controlled through each time period was plumage. This is discussed further below.

THE LOWER CHIXOY: SALINAS DE LOS NUEVE CERROS AND ITS HINTERLANDS

Salinas de los Nueve Cerros is likely the largest archaeological site on the entirety of the Chixoy as well as one of the longest-occupied settlements in the Maya world. The city is named after its two most obvious geographic features: an 18 km long sierra called the Nueve Cerros Ridge, and the *salinas*, the only noncoastal salt source in the Maya Lowlands. The salt originates as a brine stream flowing out of the western slope of a massive salt dome called Cerro Tortugas. It then feeds a series of salt flats before the flow is diluted with fresh water from multiple springs along the ridge. About 2 km downstream, the water flows into the Chixoy River, at which point it becomes the Salinas River.

Research at Nueve Cerros began in the early twentieth century when Eduard Seler (1908) visited after hearing a report of its existence by eccentric explorer Simeon Habel (1878). Seler removed a monument but did little else, leaving the first significant investigation there to be undertaken by Berkeley graduate student Brian Dillon in the 1970s. His research focused on two parts of the site: the saltworks on the western edge of the Tortugas salt dome and two mound groups on the dome's northern edge. He concluded that the site was one of the most important Classic-period purveyors of salt (Dillon et al. 1988) as well as a potential breadbasket to meet the demand for agricultural goods in the southwestern lowlands (Dillon 1979).

Dillon returned in 1990 to conduct a salvage project at the saltworks after the site was invaded by a group of Q'eqchi' Maya seeking land (Dillon 1990; Woodfill et al. 2015). Three short surveys of the site followed at the behest of oil companies (Arroyo 1993; GEOPETROL 2006; Leal 2007). Proyecto Salinas de los Nueve Cerros conducted its first field season in 2010 with the goal of understanding the geographical and chronological extent of the site as well as its political and economic organization (Woodfill 2019a; Woodfill et al. 2011, 2015). In the intervening years between Dillon's work and our own, the region had transformed from unbroken jungle to a patchwork of villages, cattle ranches, and cornfields, allowing us to determine that the site was much larger than originally thought, with multiple major architectural groups that had been overgrown and overlooked.

Due to a complicated political situation—the area initially investigated by Dillon is owned by the municipality of Coban, a large highland city that has been encouraging oil production over archaeology—Proyecto Salinas de los Nueve Cerros has been working in other parts of the site, with most research focused on three specific areas. Pie de Cerro (also referred to as "the Epicenter" in several earlier publications; e.g., Woodfill et al. 2015) is an area of elite monumental architecture between the salt flats and the Nueve Cerros Ridge. Tierra Blanca is a sprawling zone located on the south bank of the Chixoy. Tortugas is located to the south of Pie de Cerro in the shadow of the ridge.

Pie de Cerro, Tierra Blanca, and the saltworks investigated by Dillon have more or less the same chronology. They were all founded around the beginning of the Middle Preclassic (ca. 1000 BC) and survived through the Classic period (ca. AD 900). Tortugas was founded during the Late Classic period (around AD 600) and survived into the Early Postclassic (after AD 1000), although one ritual cave located within this neighborhood was actively used in the fifteenth century, only about 120 years before the arrival of the Spaniards.

Residents of the city maintained close ties to the northern highlands and the southern lowlands as evinced by ceramics, figurines, and lithics (see respective chapters in this volume). The general trend from the Preclassic period through the Classic-period lowland collapse was to strengthen ties to the highlands at the expense of the lowlands. This may reflect increased interest in quetzal feathers, pyrite, obsidian, jade, and other highland goods that were in demand in the lowland market and could have been traded along with local salt, salted fish, cacao, and achiote (see Chapter 8).

The project has also investigated several sites in the hinterlands, notably Camela, Santa Lucía Vieja, and Chapayal. Camela, originally registered as a separate site by Dillon (1981), is now known to be part of the contiguous urban sprawl that includes Nueve Cerros and covers over 40 km^2. As a result, it is presently used to refer to the settlements on the northern bank of the Chixoy/Salinas. Unlike the southern banks, the contemporary Maya and *ladinos* (people of mixed European and Indigenous ancestry) who live atop Camela have proven to be more reluctant to allow archaeological investigation, so beyond a few simple maps and a surface collection by Dillon, there is little in the way of data at present.

Chapayal and Santa Lucía Vieja were secondary settlements that likely provided agricultural goods to Nueve Cerros. Chapayal was located 10 km north of the Salinas River on the outskirts of the Mexican village of Arroyo Delicias. Surface collection by Woodfill and a Mexican archaeological team in 2017 revealed the site was abandoned around the time of Nueve Cerros's florescence in the ninth century, suggesting that its residents were incorporated into the rest of the urban sprawl to the south (Woodfill et al. 2018).

Santa Lucía Vieja, however, continued through the Late Classic, although its residents were living in substandard conditions with limited access to useable chert and obsidian and only a few prestige goods—figurines, locally manufactured greenstone beads—to compensate for an otherwise marginalized life (Woodfill and Valle 2016).

LOOKING DOWNRIVER

Less attention has been paid to the section of the river between the Chixoy and the Usumacinta. This stretch, called the Salinas because of its association with and historical utility for reaching Salinas de los Nueve Cerros, is a void in archaeological knowledge. It is a sinuous, winding, and unstable passage that flows generally northwards, eventually merging with the Pasión (see Chapter 2), at which point it is renamed for the last time as the Usumacinta.

Dillon (1981) reported a cluster of monumental architecture near the Camela Lagoon, although a fuller survey by Woodfill and his team of the northern bank of the Chixoy and Salinas Rivers has revealed that it is part of the same contiguous urban sprawl as Salinas de los Nueve Cerros (Woodfill et al. 2017). Attempts to locate additional sites on the Guatemalan side of the border downriver from Camela were unsuccessful (Woodfill et al. 2018). Known sites on the Guatemalan side of the border include Altar de Sacrificios (Haviland 1971; Munson et al. 2019; Willey et al. 1960), located about 35 km downriver at the confluence of the Salinas and Pasión Rivers, and around Lake Petexbatun (Dos Pilas, Aguateca, and Punto de Chimino; Demarest 2006a).

As the river, now called the Usumacinta, winds through the lowlands, it traces the modern border between Mexico and Guatemala and merges with one last major river, the Lacantun, which allows for easy passage to the southwest into the modern Mexican state of Chiapas. The river continues to cut through the western Maya region, passing the famous Maya cities of Yaxchilan and Piedras Negras and eventually continuing into the Olmec heartland and flowing into the Gulf of Mexico.

CONCLUSIONS

Despite limited archaeological investigation, existing data make clear that the Chixoy River Basin was a flourishing part of the Maya world by the Preclassic period. From the salt springs at Sacapulas to the major centers of the Usumacinta, the river traversed a variety of environmental features and ancient settlements. Some sites in the area we have reviewed controlled large territories, affecting the nutritional and economic well-being of myriad other centers, and many were occupied continuously for centuries. Ceramic data, in particular, indicate that people in this region were in contact with other major centers, from the Protoclassic cache at La Lagunitas to the Chama vessels at Altar de Sacrificios. Additional archaeological investigation will help to establish occupational sequences and regional material traits in this important but understudied area. Understanding the connections between the Chixoy River Basin and Maya peoples from other regions, meanwhile, will help to clarify the trajectory of Maya history in the Northern Transversal.

4

Entre Dos Cuencas

The Chaculá Region in Northwestern Huehuetenango

ULRICH WÖLFEL

LOCATED IN NORTHWESTERN Huehuetenango, the Chaculá region lies below the western slope of the Cuchumatanes mountain chain (Figure 4.1). It is characterized by ascending terrain (west to east, from around 1,200 m to 1,600 m above sea level) that traverses various climate zones, from hot and dry country in the west to cooler and wetter climates in the east. The corresponding vegetation forms include short-tree savannas in the west, pine-oak-liquidambar forests toward the east, and cloud forests in the higher elevations southeast toward the Cuchumatanes.

This region owes much of its fame to the artifacts recovered by the German pioneer of Mesoamerican studies Eduard Seler during his research there in the summer of 1896. The artifacts were documented in a lavishly illustrated book (Seler 1901). A substantial number of objects resulting from these investigations was brought to the Königliches Museum für Völkerkunde (today's Ethnologisches Museum) in Berlin, where parts of the collection have been on exhibit over the last century (this collection has recently been restudied by Wölfel 2022). The region's particular sculptural style, with human figures in the round featuring crossed arms and adornments of reduced-size trophy heads, was studied by Carlos Navarrete (1979), who documented parts of an old collection at Chaculá. More recently, Caitlin Earley (2015, 2023) studied the related art style of the Comitán Valley in southeastern Chiapas. Of similar importance is the pioneering work by Seler on the archaeology of caves at Quen Santo, one of the principal sites in the region, which has recently been restudied and updated by James Brady and colleagues (Brady 2009).

Between 2013 and 2018, the Proyecto Arqueológico de la Región de Chaculá (PARCHA) conducted an archaeological survey of the region during

88 | Ulrich Wölfel

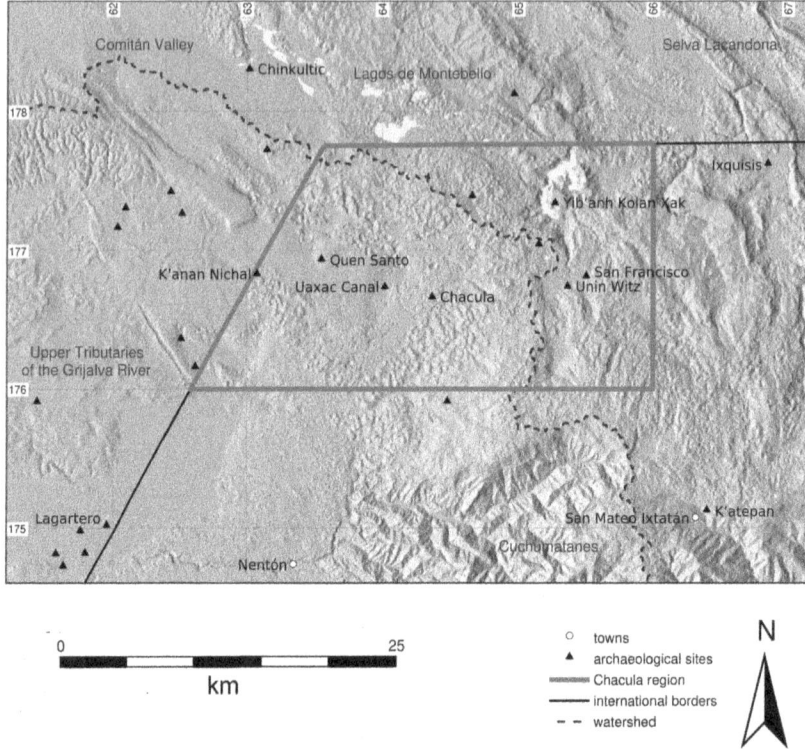

Figure 4.1. Chaculá Region of Huehuetenango department of Guatemala with principal sites investigated by Proyecto Arqueológico de la Región de Chaculá (PARCHA). (Base map from GRASS GIS, relief derived from ASTER GDEM V.2, water bodies derived from Landsat 8, borders based on humdata.org. Courtesy of Ulrich Wölfel.)

its five field seasons. The sites documented by Seler have been visited. Site maps, as well as test pit excavations, have been made at Chaculá (2014–2015) and Quen Santo (2015–2016), as well as Unin Witz, Yib'anh Kolan Xak, and Yalambojoch (2018).

It must be stressed that the concept of a "Chaculá region" is an artificial and arbitrary recent construct. In the sense that Eduard Seler (1901) talks about Chaculá as a region, it covers the lands formerly owned between the 1890s and 1920s by Seler's hosts, the Kanter family of German descent. Thus, no natural or cultural division was involved in the definition of this region. For the PARCHA project, the region has been delimited by a bounding box defined by Universal Transverse Mercator (UTM) coordinates (zone 15N, NW corner 1777700, 626000, SE corner 1760000, 660000) and within the borders of Guatemala.

As shown here, several traits observed in the archaeology of this region, among them the distinctive sculptural style, are not uniformly distributed across the whole territory. It thus makes sense to look for other ways in which to define subregions that help to better culturally understand this part of the Maya world. In particular, a notable distinction exists between the western and eastern parts of the region. The dividing line between the two parts seems to coincide with a major watershed. Whereas the sites discussed in the other contributions to this volume all belong to the Usumacinta basin, the division between this and the Grijalva basin runs right through the Chaculá region, roughly from the southeast to the northwest (see Figure 4.1). Covering 310 km², the Grijalva basin portion makes up around 60% of the region's surface, while the Usumacinta measures 204 km² and makes up the other approximate 40%.

This chapter explores the differences observed in the archaeological record of the two subregions. A summary of the current knowledge regarding the prehispanic Chaculá region is provided. It points out limitations and open questions, with the aim of stimulating further research in this part of the Maya world.

CHRONOLOGY

Navarrete's preliminary chronology for Quen Santo, in the western part of the region, places this site's florescence between AD 800 and 1000 (Navarrete 1979:49–53), although he based this on only a few diagnostic ceramic types (plumbate ware and modeled incense burners) plus the long count dates on the two "Sacchaná" stelae (10.2.5.0.0, July 16, 874 AD and 10.2.10.0.0, June 20, 879 AD), reportedly from Quen Santo (see below). His dates do, however, correspond very well with the results of a recent reexamination of the Seler collection in Berlin (Wölfel 2022), although they miss the apparently sporadic revisits to the caves at this site during the Late Postclassic.

The general chronology is confirmed by survey and excavation data from the PARCHA project. Despite a few sherds that date to the Early Classic (AD 250–500, Kau ceramic complex) and Middle Classic (AD 500–650, Lek ceramic complex), Quen Santo is essentially a Late Classic (AD 650–900, Mix ceramic complex) site that made a smooth transition to the Early Postclassic (AD 900–1250, Nichim ceramic complex) and was abandoned during the early part of this phase. Surface ceramics at other nearby sites were purely Late Classic and Early Postclassic. The site of Chaculá seems to have had an even shorter occupation, exclusively dating to the Late Classic.

A Late Classic florescence, followed by a steep decline in population at the beginning of the Early Postclassic, has also been noted for the neighboring region of the Upper Tributaries of the Grijalva (Pye et al. 2016:445–451), which Bryant et al. (2020:295) characterize as a "demographic vacuum" lasting some 200 years. In the western part of the Chaculá region, at places like Quen Santo or Uaxac Canal, people seem to have continued living at least during the initial part of the Early Postclassic, although these sites were also abandoned later during this phase. A continuing importance of the ritual caves at Quen Santo is evidenced by the Late Postclassic cremation urn burials there (French et al. 2009), but it is only in the eastern part of the region, at Unin Witz (located about 1 km east of Yalambojoch) that an actual settlement dating to this period has been found. This site preserves architecture that dates to the Late Postclassic (AD 1250–1530, Tan ceramic complex; Figure 4.2). Domestic pottery found here seems to have been produced locally, while polychrome types correspond with those documented at sites in the Upper Tributaries of the Grijalva region. On the other hand, the more elaborate architecture, with double stairways and a principal building that has stairs on all four sides, shows clear affinities to highland Guatemala, especially to the equally Late Postclassic site of K'atepan (Yolchonhab') at San Mateo Ixtatán.

Figure 4.2. Unin Witz, building A-2, exhibiting typical Late Postclassic architecture with double stairways. (Courtesy of Ulrich Wölfel.)

Ultimately, more extensive excavations, especially into major architecture, are necessary to grasp the full span as well as possible local variations of this region's occupation. Additionally, finer-grained chronologies are important to better understand how events in other parts of the Maya world align with processes observed for this and neighboring regions (e.g., the Late Classic "collapse" in the lowlands).

PALEOCLIMATE

The rejection of a simple and generalized drought-related explanation for the Maya collapse by Demarest et al. (2004:547–548) can be transferred on a very local scale to the Chaculá region: whereas the dry western part is highly susceptible to drought and was ultimately abandoned at the beginning of the Early Postclassic, the eastern part with its abundance of water sources and cloud forests continued being habitable during these times and is the only part with a Late Postclassic settlement. Recent investigations at the cenote K'ayil in the Usumacinta portion of the region show a very humid, albeit increasingly unstable, climate during the Late Classic–Early Postclassic transition, with a return to a more stable and humid climate by the Late Postclassic (Feller 2016:32–34; Stansell et al. 2020:6–7). A similar study near Chinkultic, at lakes San Lorenzo and Esmeralda, part of the Usumacinta basin, but not far from Quen Santo, shows droughts precisely in the Late Classic–Early Postclassic transition (AD 850–1200), again with a normalization of climate in the Late Postclassic (around AD 1350; Franco-Gaviria et al. 2018:87–88).

One may speculate that in search for access to water, populations moved upstream along river systems, especially in times of unstable climate. As viewed from the Chaculá region, the directions of flow that rivers in the two basins follow, while eventually converging near their mouth, are essentially opposing: west-southwest for the Grijalva, east-northeast for the Usumacinta. Assuming settlers moved along these rivers upstream, the Usumacinta basin received people from the northeast, whereas the Grijalva basin received people from the southwest. Thus, the watershed should not be seen as a barrier, but rather as a zone of convergence in which populations moved toward one another along vectors coming from the two river basins.

Pye et al. (2016:450) note that during the Late Classic period, settlement in the Upper Grijalva River basin "was densely clustered along rivers and tributaries." Although they also note that "most new sites were in areas away from primary bodies of water" (Pye et al. 2016:450), this selection of marginal locations for new settlements may be due to a significant increase either in population or rainfall, thus constituting either push or pull factors (Pye et al. 2016:457).

ARCHITECTURE AND SETTLEMENT PATTERNS

Standing architecture is largely absent in the region. This is due to most structures being mere stone foundations, whose walls and roofs were made of perishable materials. Fragments of burnt clay suggest the use of wattle and daub walls, possibly with thatched roofs. There are, however, a few buildings that originally had stone walls (e.g., Casa del Sol, Chaculá Structures B-1 and B-3, San Francisco pyramid), again probably with perishable roofs. Thus, the corbeled vault, characteristic of Lowland Maya architecture, was not employed in the region (also noted by Blake et al. 2005:415 for the Upper Tributaries of the Grijalva in Chiapas), although what can be called a very rudimentary form of this can be seen in some subterranean chambers, most of which probably served as tombs (for example, at K'anan Nichal). That wall and roof architecture was mainly based on supporting elements made of wood can be observed in the only building with preserved stone walls—a small chamber built into Quen Santo Cave III, where impressions of wooden posts and beams have been preserved (Seler 1901:164; Wölfel 2022:121–122, 304–305, Figures 4.56–4.58). Architectural monumentality is very modest, with no prehispanic structure reaching 10 m in height.

Eastern Part

In contrast with the western part of the region, where they are almost absent, pyramids are typical features of sites in the Usumacinta basin subregion, for example at Yalambojoch, Yib'anh Kolan Xak near the Laguna Yolnhajab', and the well-known pyramid of San Francisco (Figure 4.3). These are distinguished from buildings with residential or other functions due to their form, height, and volume, as well as the limited space in the building on top (e.g., Yib'anh Kolan Xak Structure A-1: 15.1 m^2) that provides too little space for living (and especially when also considering the great effort involved in their construction). Furthermore, the pyramids are usually facing large open spaces that correspond well with the plazas typically found in the centers of Lowland Maya sites. In front of the stairways of the pyramids, small, roughly square altars have been found at San Francisco and Yib'anh Kolan Xak, another feature typical of classic lowland centers.

Residential compounds, typically composed of two to four house foundations, sometimes arranged on a shared basal platform, look similar in both subregions: the eastern part lacks the "palace"-type elongated buildings with several superstructures, so typical of western centers. Also, there is only one known ballcourt, namely that at Yalambojoch, now partially destroyed by house construction. This may, however, be due to less survey work in this part of the region.

Figure 4.3. San Francisco pyramid. (Courtesy of Ulrich Wölfel.)

Western Part

Settlement density is relatively high in the area around Quen Santo. It continues toward the east until Uaxac Canal. In this part of the region, several smaller centers are located, each with its own principal building group (e.g., El Cimarrón, Rancho Viejo, Tres Lagunas, and the various parts of Uaxac Canal: La Ventana, El Llano, Piedra Parada).

Settlement in this part of the region varies between dispersed habitational compounds, often among extensive agricultural terraces and small centers with public architecture. This architecture often includes a main platform (range structure) and an adjacent ballcourt (Figure 4.4). In some of these centers, artistic expression takes the form of stone sculptures and modeled stucco fragments that formerly decorated the principal buildings (Seler 1901:35–38, 145, Figures 22 and 212; Wölfel 2022:259–266, Figure 4.44b).

Although open spaces are present, they do not conform to the typical Mesoamerican "plaza"—a large rectangular space bounded on its sides by major public architecture. At Quen Santo Group B, the ballcourt occupies most of the space in the "sunken plaza," leaving hardly any room for large gatherings of people (Figure 4.5). In Group E of the same site, another sunken plaza is surrounded by domestic and not monumental architecture. At Chaculá, the settlement pattern emphasizes household patios on platforms constructed to provide level surfaces. They are built against hillsides that surround natural

Figure 4.4. Ballcourt in Group B, Pueblo Viejo Quen Santo. (Courtesy of Ulrich Wölfel.)

depressions, thus forming clearly recognizable groups. Buildings are located on the side facing the hill and on the flanking sides, while the side toward the slope down remains open, although sometimes small altars can be found close to the edge. Status differences can be deduced from the size and elaboration of the buildings. Thus, the connection between domestic patios and public plazas (Inomata and Tsukamoto 2014:10–11) swings more toward the former in the western part of the region and more to the latter in the eastern part.

Agricultural terraces abound wherever the sloping landscape demands it. In contrast with terraces in the lowlands, these are generally very low and built with uncut stones so that much less effort was involved in their construction. Nevertheless, around sites like Quen Santo, they spread continuously for kilometers, so their horizontal extension gives them a certain monumentality. In some cases, these terrace systems are still being maintained today by the local farmers for their milpas, for example at Tres Lagunas (Wölfel 2022:93, Figure 4.25a).

The elongated main platform typically features several smaller platforms on top. Sometimes different heights or horizontal offsets indicate different construction episodes. In the case of Quen Santo Group B, the main platform grew to become a palace-type building, with a monumental staircase leading to its top. In several cases, such as this, one of the parallel structures flanking the ballcourt's playing alley is directly integrated into the principal platform. Such palaces are unknown in the Usumacinta part of the region.

Figure 4.5. Sunken plaza with ballcourt in Group B, Pueblo Viejo Quen Santo. (Courtesy of Ulrich Wölfel.)

Only a few pyramids can be found in this part of the region. For example, at K'anan Nichal two such structures face each other. Nevertheless, farther to the southwest, around Lagartero, pyramids are again more common.

Notable Late Classic architectural features include façades built with very regularly cut stones, sometimes with moldings as well as the occasional "megalithic" building (Navarrete 1981:76–77). Platforms and terraces are mostly constructed of irregularly cut or natural stones. Some buildings have stairways with *alfardas* (balustrades) and what seems to be an early form of the *talud-tablero* style so typical of the Postclassic.

Ballcourt density in the region is high, with a total of 12 ballcourts within an area of 514 km² (whole Chaculá region), resulting in 43 km² per ballcourt, not counting the "half" ballcourt with only one flanking building, found at Guayabal (Wölfel 2019:7–18, Figure 2.11). When only the Grijalva basin portion is considered, these numbers change to 11 ballcourts within 310 km² and thus 26 km² per ballcourt. A comparison of these figures with densities reported by Olivier de Montmollin (1997:Table 2) for the Grijalva basin region in Chiapas shows them to be well within the ranges observed in adjacent areas.

The name-giving site of Chaculá, in the center of the region, has a dense settlement arranged on the slopes surrounding several natural depressions. The many small patio-complexes are of a domestic character, although they vary widely in size. Some buildings appear to have had public functions, such as the I-shaped ballcourt, as well as a large pyramidal structure built against a hillslope.

The area closest to the watershed has very few archaeological remains. Although an archaeological site has been reported for the modern village El Aguacate (Kramer and Lowe 1940), no evidence of this site has been found so far. It may well have become obstructed by recent constructions. The only site known in this part is Yal Tzimin (Wölfel 2019:13), to the north of Laguna Mirabel (according to local informants, there are no other ruins locally known on lands that belong to El Aguacate). Likewise, Yuxquén, to the north of El Aguacate, has only a minor prehispanic settlement named Atz'am K'em (Wölfel 2015:23, Figures 2.41 and 2.42).

MATERIAL CULTURE AND TRADE

Slipped utilitarian ceramics, found at Quen Santo and other sites by Seler and the PARCHA project, belong mainly to the Tasajo Red (Late Classic) and Nichel Red (Terminal Classic–Postclassic, direct successor to Tasajo Red, according to Bryant et al. 2005:555) types, which are very common throughout the Upper Tributaries of the Grijalva and the adjacent Comitán Valley. Nevertheless, among the PARCHA materials, minor quantities of Chachalaca Red (Late Classic, typical of the Upper Tributaries, but not the Comitán Valley, see Blake et al. 2005:453–454) and Yerba Buena Fine (Late Classic, typical of the central highlands of Chiapas, but also found in the Upper Tributaries, see Blake et al. 2005:533–534) have been found.

The division between the two subregions did not impede the exchange of commodities. This is shown by the presence of ceramic types typical of neighboring regions in Chiapas (Upper Tributaries of the Grijalva, Comitán Valley) in the western part of the region as well as around Yalambojoch and the Laguna Yolnhajab'. There, for example, a mold-made ceramic fragment of a human face was recovered (at Yib'anh Kolan Xak) that fits one of the types identified in the materials recovered by Seler at Quen Santo (Wölfel 2022:219).

The Chaculá region was far from isolated in prehispanic times. People obtained goods from other places, near and far. Among the best archaeological material for understanding long-distance trade is obsidian, since it is nonlocal for most places, its narrowly circumscribed source areas are well studied, and objects can be confidently attributed to sources either by visual or trace element analyses.

The small collection of obsidian objects ($n = 15$) from the region (Quen Santo and Chaculá) in the Ethnologisches Museum Berlin (all collected by Seler) has been analyzed by X-ray fluorescence (XRF) at the Rathgen

Forschungslabor in Berlin (Röhrs et al. 2020). Of these, 10 prismatic blade fragments can be attributed to the El Chayal source, one is from San Martin Jilotepeque, and four objects come from Mexican sources, among them a large laurel leaf blade but also a prismatic blade fragment (Wölfel 2022:232–234, Fig. 6.44). Visual sourcing of obsidian objects from the PARCHA project indicates more balanced proportions between El Chayal and San Martin Jilotepeque for Quen Santo and Chaculá (Carpio Rezzio 2016:133–137).

In the eastern part, significant amounts of green obsidian have been recovered both on the surface and in excavations, at the sites of Unin Witz and Yalambojoch; these constitute around 13% of the total amount of obsidian in this area. Although the presence of green obsidian indicates access to different trade routes at the mentioned sites, it is quite possible this is also due to them having been occupied during a later period. On the surface at Yalambojoch, several sherds of plumbate pottery suggest a dating to the Early Postclassic, whereas the site of Unin Witz was inhabited even later, with most of its ceramic material dating to the Late Postclassic. Such finding would also explain why green obsidian is not reported from the Late Classic site of Ixquisis, located farther to the northeast (the most common sources are El Chayal and San Martín Jilotepeque, according to Garrido López 2012).

Imported ceramics have been found in small quantities. Among these are the three Fine Orange vessels recovered by Seler at Uaxac Canal (Seler 1901:Figures 23, 25, and 27) and fragments of plumbate pottery from Chaculá (D. García 2016a:Figure 8.66, 2016b:Figure 7.65), Quen Santo (Navarrete 1979:49; D. García 2016a:Figure 8.125, 2016b:150), and Yalambojoch (Hernández and Garnica 2019a:128). Polychrome types from the lowland regions of Alta Verapaz and Peten (Castillo 2013:65, Figure 4.12; García 2016b:Figures 7.75a, 7.76b, d, 7.79b, and 7.80) have also been found.

Other imported goods include reflector backs of either stone or ceramics. These were found by Seler at Quen Santo (Seler 1901:106–107, 118–119, 127–128, 152, Figures 130, 161, 186, and 224; Wölfel 2022:240–242). Pyrite tesserae were excavated at the site of Unin Witz (Hernández and Garnica 2019b:154, Figure 8.33), along with objects made of green stone, be it true jade or "social jade" (Seler 1901:Figures 20b, 133, 135, 138, 162, and 175; Wölfel 2022:237–240), and objects made of marine mollusks (Seler 1901:Figure 137; Wölfel 2022:273–274).Whereas the imports are thus identifiable, the exports from this region (if there were any) can only be speculated on at this point. The abundance of copal trees (*Bursera* spp.), especially near archaeological sites in the western part of the region such as Quen Santo, Copalar, or K'anan Nichal, might suggest incense was produced here in some quantity based on the resin of these trees.

The southern Peten region was connected to Tabasco via the Late Classic "Transversal" trade route (Demarest et al. 2014), so it seems reasonable to assume at least the Grijalva portion of the Chaculá region did have access to the route along the Chiapas central depression, termed the "Grijalva system" by Navarrete (1981:75), which continued toward Guatemala and in colonial times was known as the *camino real* (Navarrete 1978:99–102; see also Lee 2001; Tejada Bouscayrol and Lee 2019). The presence of additional trade routes that connected the Upper Grijalva region with places like Toniná and Palenque is highly likely. In fact, due to Chinkultic's position between the Cuchumatanes, the Comitán Valley, and important western lowland sites such as Toniná, it has been described as a "gateway site" (*sitio-puerta*) between these regions (Navarrete 1990). Whether the Usumacinta portion of the Chaculá region and places farther to the northeast, such as Ixquisis, had some connection to the Transversal route is unclear at this point and needs further investigation.

ART AND WRITING

The sculptural style, once held to be one of the defining features for the region (Figure 4.6 is an example of a human figure with crossed arms), has since been documented in several other regions (Navarrete 1979), including the Selva Lacandona (Rivero Torres 1992:Fotos 2–4, Figure 8; Schmidt 1979), and Toniná (Becquelin and Baudez 1982:Figures 113 and 114). It appears with particularly high frequency around Quen Santo (the current count for this site is 107 stone sculptures, including smaller fragments and plain stone discs). Furthermore, as noted by Earley (2020), the sculptural corpus of nearby Chinkultic in Chiapas, Mexico, shows clear stylistic and thematic connections with the Usumacinta region. No sculptures, not even fragments, have been found so far in the eastern part of the region.

Hieroglyphic inscriptions are mostly absent in this region. Apart from the two inscribed stelae that Seler bought at Sacchaná (Seler 1901:13–14, Figures 5–7) and that according to their previous owner had been originally found at Quen Santo (but see Blom and Duby 1957:56–57, who express doubts about this attribution), and the T510b glyphs (the logograph EK', "star") on a disc (Monument 20) found by Seler at Quen Santo (Seler 1901:122, Figure 174a; see Wölfel 2022:248–250 for an additional piece of this sculpture), only one inscription has come to light in recent years: three fragments of a Late Classic modeled-carved ceramic vessel have been found at Yalambojoch, near the current village center. The few legible hieroglyphs name the son of the divine lord of Naranjo-Sa'al in the eastern Peten. Although the precise archaeological context of this vessel is unknown, its presence in Yalambojoch indicates political connections into the heart of the Maya Lowlands did exist. This finding hints at a northeast direction of political relations for this part of the region.

Figure 4.6. Fragments of figure with crossed arms (Monument 52) in situ (Group C), Pueblo Viejo Quen Santo. (Courtesy of Ulrich Wölfel.)

Another feature that is abundant in the western part of the region, but so far has not been documented for the eastern part, is rock art. Ten sites with pictographs, mostly painted with red and blue pigments, have been documented so far and appear to be contemporaneous with site occupation (i.e., Late Classic to Early Postclassic; Batres et al. 2002; Ericastilla Godoy 2004; Seler 1901:83–84; Wölfel 2022:94–96, 97, 115–116, Figures 4.30, 4.51, and 4.62). Speleothems in caves have sometimes been carved with simple faces, such as those documented by Guerra Ruiz and Brady (2009:Figures 12–19) at Quen Santo Cave I.

POLITICAL ORGANIZATION AND ETHNOLINGUISTIC AFFILIATION

In the absence of hieroglyphic inscriptions that could shed more light on rulers, their realms, and their hierarchies, little is yet known about the political organization of the prehispanic Chaculá region. The only center in the western Chaculá region that stands out by its size and monumental architecture, and therefore is a potential candidate for a local capital, is Quen Santo, with its voluminous palace and ballcourt in Group B and the second, albeit minor, such complex in Group E. In fact, a case could be made for Quen Santo being a political microcosm (de Montmollin 1988, 1995:119–122)—that is, the two main plaza groups at this site replicate in their layout those of neighboring smaller, subordinate centers (such as Rancho Viejo and La Trinidad I). This would also explain the observed similarity between these sites, with ballcourts integrated into main platforms, as well as having the same general north-south orientation. The palace and ballcourt at Quen Santo Group B, in turn, could be seen as small-scale replications of the Chinkultic ballcourt and acropolis (Group C).

Generally, ballcourts have been located near major architecture and the nuclei of centers. Assuming that ballcourts played an important role in religious-political performances and served the elite's claim to power, besides being places for the exercise of sports, numerous smaller centers with ballcourts have been considered to be testimony to a fragmented local elite (de Montmollin 1997:29, 38). This appears to be related to the Late Classic phenomenon of smaller centers claiming independence and standing on their own that has been documented for parts of the Maya Lowlands (see, for example, Demarest et al. 2004:552) and that has also been proposed for the Upper Grijalva region in Chiapas (de Montmollin 1995; Pye et al. 2016:450).

Furthermore, political control of the region by the rulers of nearby Chinkultic is very much possible, although still far from proven. Iconographic themes observed in the sculptural corpus at Chinkultic do include warrior kings and subordination of lesser rulers (Earley 2020), likely from surrounding areas. The Late Classic kings at this site, identified by the Chan Ajaw emblem glyph (Grube 2002), also claimed highest titles, previously used only by the rulers of the largest centers in the Maya Lowlands, among them *kaloomte'* and *bakab'*, as well as unique titles, such as *k'uhul bakab'* (Wölfel and Wagner 2010).

A striking connection to a major center located further away has been found at Quen Santo. Excavations in the center of the ballcourt of Group B at this site revealed a cache below the central ballcourt marker (a plain stone disc) that contained a red slipped ceramic jar with nine obsidian blades, deteriorated bone fragments, and a disc-shaped bone bead (Hernández et al. 2017:77–78). The enclosure of this cache was constructed in a similar manner to one found under the central marker in the Toniná ballcourt playing alley (Becquelin and Baudez 1979:Figures 82, 89b, and 90a–b), with a round capstone sitting on an inner rim, protecting the contents. Even the contents are very similar, as they include nine obsidian blade fragments (Becquelin and Baudez 1979:166–167, Figure 145). Both caches have been dated to the Late Classic.

Regarding the ethno-linguistic affiliation of the ancient inhabitants of the Chaculá region, it has been suggested this region and its surroundings formed a multilingual frontier zone where speakers of Tzeltalan and

Q'anjob'alan languages were living together. This would provide the basis for the cultural and linguistic genesis of the group today known as the Tojolabales (for a summary and new evidence, see Wölfel 2022:311–315). For the Late Postclassic, Blake (2010:274) and Bryant et al. (2020:305–311, 317–320) consider the possibility of migrations from the Guatemalan highlands toward the Upper Tributaries of the Grijalva region.

Furthermore, as noted by Pye et al. (2016:450), the population surge in the Upper Grijalva region during the Late Classic was likely due to migrations from different parts of the Maya world. A particularly good candidate would be the lowlands, which at this time suffered severe depopulation. This contributed to a cultural mosaic with speakers of several Mayan languages.

Bioarchaeological investigations have the potential of resolving important questions regarding past biographies, including migrations. Additionally, they can also shed light on cultural affinities by looking at intentional head shaping. Tiesler and Lacadena (2018) have shown the distribution of certain shapes coincide with linguistic boundaries, and they suggest the observed differences served to reinforce group identity. A comparison with the regional distribution of artificial cranial modification forms (Tiesler 2012:Figure 25) shows that the skulls recovered by Seler from the Cueva de los Murciélagos, near Uaxac Canal (Grijalva basin) are consistent with the preferred form of broadened heads (tabular erect) found at other Late Classic/Early Postclassic sites in this basin (notably those from the Cueva de las Banquetas, Romano Pacheco et al. 2011). While the tabular erect type of modification is dominant at Toniná, as Tiesler and Lacadena (2018:42) note, is elongated head forms (tabular oblique) that predominate in the Usumacinta river area. It will be important to see in future investigations which head shapes are present in the Usumacinta basin part of the Chaculá region.

CONCLUSIONS

Differences in the archaeological record of the eastern and western portion of the Chaculá region, with the watershed between the Usumacinta and the Grijalva basin serving as the dividing line, have been explored here. What caused these differences is not yet fully understood. Different forms of political organization, perhaps combined with different ethno-linguistic affiliations and the corresponding cultural practices, may have been involved. In the absence of more complete and finer grained chronologies, it also cannot be ruled out that sites in the two parts originated in slightly different periods. Since surrounding areas are notoriously understudied, the spatial extent of the east-west division is unknown. It may well be that this is a strictly local affair. That the division by watersheds, especially large ones, does not necessarily translate well into political or ethnic divisions can be seen in the possible ties that

Quen Santo had with Chinkultic and Toniná (both part of the Usumacinta basin). On a more restricted, local scale, however, it seems to make much more sense, when also considering the geographic setting.

This chapter should be considered a formulation of hypotheses that need to be tested against new data to be collected in the field. The fact that the Chaculá region, itself having been submitted to an opportunistic (in contrast with a full coverage) survey by PARCHA, borders with two of the least known regions of the Maya area—the Selva Lacandona to the north and northeast and the Cuchumatanes to the east and southeast—results in problems when making comparisons, since we simply cannot establish links with these areas before archaeological sites are located and adequately described and investigated. Even the Chaculá region has several large, unsurveyed voids (e.g., in the northern part), and large-scale excavations have not yet been undertaken.

The observations about currently available data are nonetheless valid and in need of an explanation. Hopefully, they will stimulate and guide future research about the Chaculá region and surrounding areas, where still large gaps exist in our knowledge, even with respect to the most basic archaeological questions. Nevertheless, the differences between the eastern and western part of the Chaculá region described here are real, and the proposed ethnic and political affinities do make sense as working hypotheses. Answers can be provided only through more reconnaissance work covering areas so far untouched by archaeologists. Much work remains to be done.

Part III

Interrelations and Environment

5
Ceramic Interaction in the Northern Transversal Strip during the Late Classic Period

Jorge Mario Ortíz de León, Socorro Jiménez Álvarez, Paola Torres, Claudia Arriaza, Miryam Saravia, Juan Francisco Saravia, Carlos Fidel Tuyuc Nij, and Diana Méndez Lee

Although the history of interaction between the Guatemalan highlands and the central Maya Lowlands has been heavily debated (Adams 1978; Arnauld 1990; Hammond 1972; Seler 1993; Smith 1955), the nexus between these two regions has become the subject of sustained, active investigation only in the present millennium. Due to several recent investigations conducted within the Northern Transversal Strip (Figure 5.1), archaeologists have broadened their understanding of the dynamics of exchange between the two zones and its political and ideological context. These investigations have documented multiple cultural aspects and activities that are rooted in its position at a cultural frontier and its importance in the interregional exchange of salt (Woodfill et al. 2015), achiote, cacao, vanilla, jade, quetzal feathers, and so on (Akkeren 2012; Demarest et al. 2014, 2016).

These data have been contextualized by Demarest in the network theory model, in which elite groups controlled the flow of these goods into the central lowlands during the Late Classic period (AD 600–900; Demarest et al. 2017). This chapter synthesizes the ceramic data from the sites in the Northern Transversal that have been subject to intense archaeological investigation to date—Cancuen, Salinas de los Nueve Cerros, and Raxruha Viejo—to understand the dynamics of exchange from the perspective of material culture. We include some data from Sesakkar and Sebol, two important sites under the Cancuen sphere of influence that are still in the early phases of investigation, to reach a general understanding of some connections in the regional exchange network (Demarest et al. 2016).

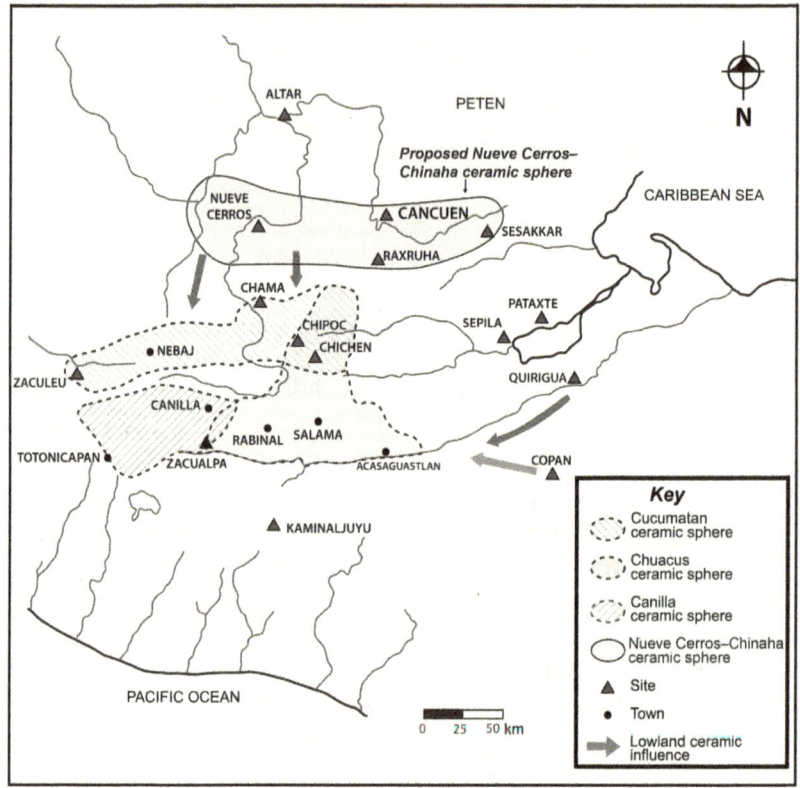

Figure 5.1. Ceramic spheres of the Maya Lowlands, Transversal, and northern Maya Highlands. (Map made with Illustrator. Juan Francisco Saravia)

Salinas de los Nueve Cerros (see also Chapter 3) is located in the municipalities of Coban, Alta Verapaz, and Ixcan, Quiche. Its proximity to the Chixoy River provided it with a strategic position along one of the three principal access routes into the southern lowlands from the Guatemalan highlands. In addition, the residents were able to take advantage of a natural salt source that provided the foundation of the regional economy; both factors allowed its urban zone to reach an area of over 40 km² surrounding the Cerro Tortugas salt dome (Woodfill and Valle 2016; Woodfill et al. 2017). The city was occupied by the Middle Preclassic and continued through the Terminal Classic and into the Postclassic.

Cancuen, in contrast, straddles the municipalities of Sayaxche, Peten and Raxruha, Alta Verapaz. The city's epicenter is located on a peninsula on the banks of the Pasión River, an important strategic location to allow for control of river traffic and an important point of contact to establish commercial routes and interaction networks at a local, regional, and interregional level

(Demarest et al. 2014). In this sense, the results from the ceramic analysis, based on over two decades of painstaking excavation at the site and the surrounding region, allowed for the identification of four complexes related to different ceramic traditions in distinct zones in the Maya area—Peten, Transversal, northern highlands, and Gulf Coast. The city's chronology is divided into three ceramic traditions, called Concordia (AD 650–760), Los Laureles (AD 760–780), and Chamán (AD 780–800).

Three other sites are included in this chapter's discussion (all discussed in greater detail in Chapter 3). Raxruha Viejo was subjected to archaeological investigation by the Cancuen Regional Archaeological Project in 2002, 2004, and 2013 (Demarest et al. 2014, 2016), with the goal of defining the dynamics of interaction with Cancuen and Salinas de los Nueve Cerros. It was an important regional center in its own right, one that was likely the capital of a large political entity with monumental architecture and a high concentration of blank monuments (Demarest et al. 2014).

Sesakkar, named after the hamlet founded on its ruins, means "the place of sardines" in Q'eqchi'. It is part of the larger village of Caxlam Pom in the municipality of Fray Bartolomé de las Casas, Alta Verapaz, in the Santa Isabel River Valley atop an outcropping of sedimentary rock jutting out of the surrounding alluvial plain (Martínez et al. 2016). Sebol is found in a *finca* (large landholding or plantation) of the same name in the same municipality. It is located at the base of the Sierra de Santa Cruz, close to the beginning of the Sebol River. It is located at an important position between multiple systems of commercial routes. It is the first major site when heading east from Cancuen and Raxruha on the way to Lake Izabal, southern Belize, and the Caribbean (Demarest and Martínez 2015; O'Mansky et al. 2009). Like Raxruha Viejo and Sesakkar, Sebol has multiple caves in nearby hills that were the object of ritual use for its inhabitants (O'Mansky et al. 2009).

METHODOLOGIES USED FOR THE STUDY

In addition to type:variety and modal analysis, two additional methodologies were used by members of both projects—instrumental neutron activation analysis (INAA) and ceramic petrography. The INAA is used to determine the chemical elements of clays and other included materials, which permits archaeologists to create chemical profiles of the raw materials that were used to create ceramic items in specific places or areas (Bishop 2003). The results of the elemental study, which uses radioactivity and analytical reasoning (in this case, statistical calculations that can be compared with archaeological data), can be used to make hypotheses about human activities related to the probable origin or "archaeological source" of ceramics recovered at a specific site (Arnold et al. 1991; Bishop 1980).

The analytic technique is nondestructive. In terms of application, ceramic sherds or whole vessels that are sufficiently dry are perforated through their walls with a tungsten drill to acquire a minimum of 150–200 grams of ceramic dust, leaving behind a small perforation. The acquired sample (the dust) is then irradiated in a nuclear reactor and stored for several weeks for a subsequent analysis based on the timeline of the decay of specific elements that become unstable when irradiated. Regarding the other method utilized here, ceramic petrography uses laboratory techniques adapted from geology, mineral chemistry, and pedology, among others. In this approach, specific minerals present in select ceramic vessels are identified based on their visual properties and texture as they appear in thin cross-sections, usually under a polarizing microscope.

This approach is used to acquire data related to the origin and manufacturing technology of ceramic wares, exploring the mineral composition and microstructure as well as the presence (albeit not further analyzed) of organic components (Freestone 1991). The majority of the investigators agree that there are various general topics that can be explored through ceramic petrography. It is useful as an analytic tool to assist with a preliminary understanding of how ceramics were made in a dynamic and complex way in past societies. The study of ceramic pastes provides important data regarding the physical characteristics of the resulting vessels before and after they are baked; the provisioning of resources and manufacturing techniques; even, with some limitations, potentially the nature of local or imported wares to deduce the origin of raw materials and their environment (Beaudry 1991; Rapp 2009; Riederer 2004; Stoltman 1999).

When applied, this technique is semidestructive, as the selected ceramic fragments are cut with a diamond blade and then, depending on their porosity, impregnated with an epoxy resin that does not alter the light diffraction of the minerals to be observed. Once the fragments are impregnated or cured, they are cut anew to create a thin section that is cemented onto a glass microscope slide and then ground down to 30 microns of width to be fully translucent. At this point, it can be analyzed to determine its mineral and textural composition (Castro 1989; Kerr 1965; Perkins and Henke 2002).

CHARACTERISTICS OF THE TRANSVERSAL CERAMIC SAMPLES DURING THE LATE CLASSIC

The ceramic tradition at Salinas de los Nueve Cerros (Figure 5.2) shares many characteristics with both its southern lowland and northern highland neighbors during the earliest periods during the Middle Preclassic (1000–250 BC). Throughout the subsequent time periods, the city's residents develop begin developing their own tradition, which dominates the assemblage by the Late

Classic (AD 600–900) and is typified by, among other things, a high volume of material related to the production, transportation, and storage of salt (Ortiz et al. 2017). The characteristics of the sample and the typological frequencies, together with their associations, have been discussed in other works (Ortiz et al. 2015, 2017).

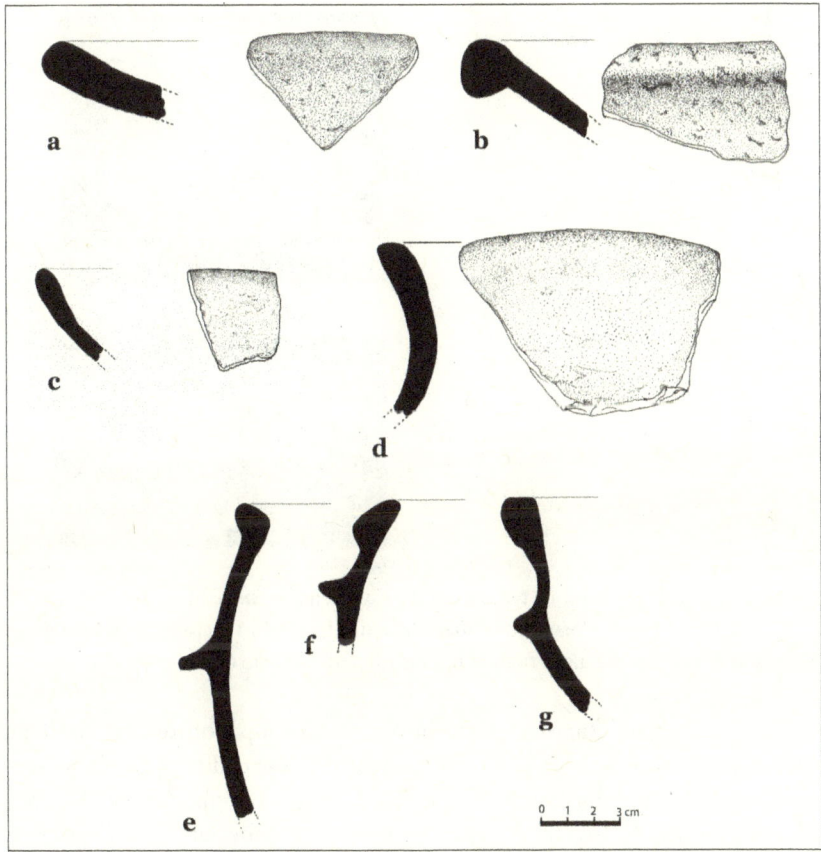

Figure 5.2. Common ceramic types from Salinas de los Nueve Cerros, Department of Alta Verapaz: (a, b) Camenac Red, (c) Infierno Black, (d) Cambio Unslipped, (e–g) Subin Red. (Courtesy of Carlos Efraín Tox Tiul.)

Cancuen is found on the northern limits of the Northern Transversal region. Its ceramics (Figure 5.3) correspond in their majority to the lowland Tepeu 2 ceramic sphere. However, some variants are atypical of the cities of the central Peten, due in great part to the residents' sustained interactions with Alta Verapaz to the south as well as farther regions like the Gulf Coast (Forné et al. 2011).

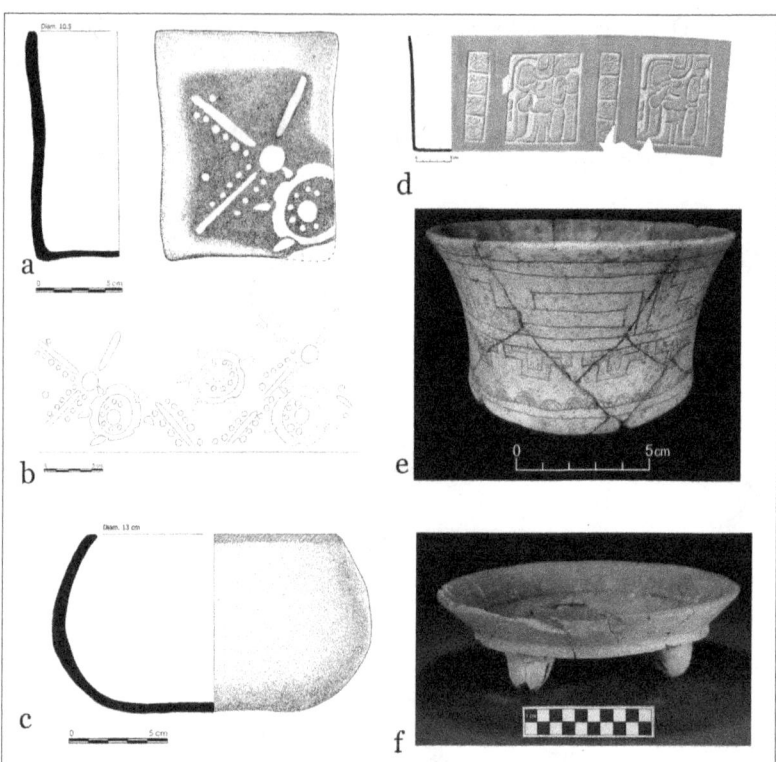

Figure 5.3. Common ceramic types from the Cancuen region: (a, b) Hinojo Negative, (c) Unnamed Red-on-Cream, (d) Kanalkan Gouged, (e) Nitro Incised, (f) Xelub Dichrome. (Courtesy of Luís Fernando Luin [a–d] and Proyecto Cancuen [e, f].)

The ceramics of Raxruha Viejo indicate an occupation during the Late Classic period (ca. AD 600–800) with a tradition steeped in the Coban 2 ceramic complex in Alta Verapaz in addition to the aforementioned Tepeu 2 (Forné et al. 2011). Together, these are referred to as the San Simón complex, although its phases are still in the process of being refined. There are at least two important occupation phases as reflected in the stratigraphy and architectural modifications.

Sebol's ceramic sample is scarce and suffers from a high degree of erosion and breakage, although it is possible to identify Chaquiste Impressed and Chinaja Impressed from the lowlands, as well as Chichicaste Brown and Cebada Porous from the Transversal/northern highlands. The settlement also dates to the Late Classic, with a possible earlier Preclassic phase (Forné et al. 2009). Sesakkar, for its part, has a ceramic tradition associated with the southeastern Peten during the Late Classic, characterized by the Tinaja, Cambio, and Encanto groups, with some examples that appear to have a distinct, local paste that is, at times, porous. There are also examples of ceramics local to Cancuen like La Isla Orange and Sebastián Fluted (Forné, Alvarado, et al. 2011). The Cebada Porous present at Sesakkar shows contacts with the Transversal-northern highlands complex.

PETROGRAPHIC EVIDENCE FROM SALINAS DE LOS NUEVE CERROS

Any ceramic analysis has the description and source of its component materials as well as the technology used to assemble them as an end goal. There are various analytic techniques to understand them. The most common are those that allow for a characterization of the chemical or mineral composition and its microstructural characteristics (Rands and Bargielski 1992:24; Rands and Bishop 2003:111; Rice 1987).

The ceramics from Salinas de los Nueve Cerros are classified into three cultural subregions: Transversal, northern highlands, and southern lowlands. To understand the mineral and textural characterization, we describe six thin sections (Table 5.1; Jiménez Álvarez and Obanda Acuña 2022): one corresponds to the Transversal sphere (SNC25TV/SNC5-17-1), one to the northern highlands (SNC8TA/SNC4A-2-1-10), and the other four to the southern lowlands (SNC3TB/SNC6A-1-5, SNC6TB/SNC21A-13-4, SNC8TB/SNC5-20-4, and SNC11TB/SNC24-13-2). The thin sections were studied by Socorro Jiménez Álvarez in the ceramics laboratory in the Faculty of Anthropological Sciences at the Autonomous University of the Yucatan (UADY) in Mérida. The semiquantitative petrographic descriptions were created by the geologist Luis Obando Acuña in the Petrography Laboratory in the Central American School of Geology at the University of Costa Rica.

In general, the pastes from Nueve Cerros have a maroon-color matrix with inclusions of volcanic glass and subordinate quartz minerals—undulose extinction, xenomorphic, chalcedony, plecroic, and oxidized biotite. There was also some alteration of the matrix and a minimal proportion of filomorphic iron oxide. The textures vary depending on the typology and the ceramic form associated with the fragments (Table 5.2).

The important features for each subregion include the following:

Transversal: The analyzed thin section belongs to a plate of the type Camenac Red (see Figure 5.2a–b; Ortíz 2022:20–22). Its mineral composition shows an abundance of shards of volcanic glass (30%), which is slightly recrystallized in round or globular shapes or in the form of needles or anvils. There are also inclusions of biotite, quartz, chalcedony, and plagioclase. This composition was of special interest because of the addition of colorless muscovite (7%), which is absent from the other samples. The matrix's texture is a clay paste

Table 5.1. Percentage of Minerals Identified in Petrographic Analysis of Ceramic Samples from Salinas de los Nueve Cerros (SNC).

Petrographic Analysis No.[a]	Matrix	Biotite	Muscovite	Iron Oxides	Glass	Pumice	Quartz	Chalcedony	Plagioclase	Augite	Epidote	Rock Fragments	Zircon
SNC25TV	52%	3%	7%	4%	30%		3%	1%	4%				
SNC8TA	55%	<1%		3%	30%	5%	2%	4%	1%	<1%			
SNC3TB	59%	3%		4%	25%	6%	3%	1%	2%	<1%	1%		
SNC6TB	59%	6%		<1%	12%	8%	5%	3%	5%	<1%		<1%	<1%
SNC8TB	49%	3%		3%	12%		3%	3%	2%				
SNC11TB	87%	3%		2%	8%		<1%		<1%				

Source: Socorro Jiménez Álvarez.

[a]TV = Transversal; TA = Tierras Altas (Maya Highlands); TB = Tierras Bajas (Maya Lowlands).

Table 5.2. Petrographic Analysis of Ceramic Samples from Salinas de los Nueve Cerros (SNC).

Petrographic Analysis No.[a]	Source	Region	Group	Type	Chronology	Form
SNC25TV	SNC5-17-1	Transversal	Camenac	Camenac Red	Late Classic	Plate
SNC8TA	SNC4A-2-1-10	Highlands	Olola	Olola Orange	Late Classic	Jar
SNC3TB	SNC6A-1-5	Lowlands	Cambio	Cambio Unslipped	Late Classic	Jar
SNC6TB	SNC21A-13-4	Lowlands	Subin	Subin Red	Late Classic	Bowl
SNC8TB	SNC5-20-4	Lowlands	Infierno	Tres Micos Impressed	Late Classic	Plate
SNC11TB	SNC24-13-2	Lowlands	Infierno	Infierno Black	Late Classic	Plate

Source: Socorro Jiménez Álvarez.

[a]TV = Transversal; TA = Tierras Altas (Maya Highlands); TB = Tierras Bajas (Maya Lowlands).

with mica lines. Like the highland piece described below, the matrix composes 52% of the thin section, which indicates that the artisan used similar proportions of clay and anti-plastic and fire-resistant inclusions while creating the piece.

Highlands: The analyzed thin section comes from a bowl sherd of the type Olola Orange (Ortíz 2022:29–31). For its mineral composition, it has a light maroon matrix with an abundant presence of shards of recrystallized volcanic glass that are globular, round, or in the shape of an anvil or needle. There are inclusions of pumice, quartz, chalcedony, plagioclase, iron oxide, and augite, the last of which was identified as a trace mineral. The texture of the matrix is a clay paste with alterations from lines of mica. The matrix comprises 55% of the thin section, which indicates the artisan used similar proportions of clay and anti-plastic and fire-resistant inclusions while creating the piece.

Lowlands: Four thin sections have been analyzed to date (Jiménez Álvarez and Obanda Acuña 2022:59–61), which consist of an Infierno Black plate (SNC11TB, see Figure 5.2c), a Cambio Unslipped jar (SNC3TB, see Figure 5.2d), a Subin Red bowl (SNC6TB, see Figure 5.2e–g), and a Tres Micos Impressed bowl (SNC8TB). At a mineralogical level, the primary inclusions in the paste are volcanic glass (8–25%); like the other thin sections described above, it is partially recrystallized and is globular, round, or in the shape of an anvil or needle. Other minerals present include biotite, quartz, chalcedony, plagioclase, and iron oxide. Pumice is present in some of the samples. The matrix is clay with a color range from light maroon to yellow-maroon with lines of mica. Since the thin sections were mostly inclusions (59–87%), it appears that antiplastic and fire-resistant materials were used more heavily than clay. For example, the Subin Red fragment had coarse-ground mineral inclusions, while the Infierno Black and Tres Micos Impressed fragments had finer-grained inclusions, which still dominated the composition.

In spite of the limited range of interpretation possible because of the extremely limited sample analyzed to date, it is possible to say preliminarily that each of the three subregions included a significant presence of material with a volcanic origin, above all the glass sherds and iron oxide. It is significant that the Transversal ceramic also shows the presence of muscovite. At present, there appears to be no difference between the mineralogical composition of the highland and lowland ceramic samples; however, the relative quantity of the glass, rather than simply its presence or absence, needs to be examined more closely as the analysis continues. In the same vein, texture is a distinguishing factor for the different classes of ceramic manufacture in areas or cultural subregions that exchanged objects made with locally available materials. The percentages between fine- and coarse-grained matrices in relation to ceramic types and forms will produce important data about the manufacture of the vessels. At present, it appears that the glossy wares, especially the plates, used temper or sands that are specially selected for their fine grade.

EVIDENCE OF CERAMIC EXCHANGE BETWEEN CANCUEN AND RAXRUHA VIEJO FROM INAA

The INAA is a compositional analysis for ceramics that permits the identification of subtle differences in the chemical composition of a ceramic sample (Bishop et al. 1984), and its results allow for a reconstruction of the nature of exchange between and among archaeological sites, creating an understanding of the production and distribution of ceramic goods. Of the material recovered at Cancuen, Raxruha Viejo, and other sites in the greater Upper Pasión drainage, Ronald Bishop (Smithsonian Institution) has analyzed approximately 876 sherds, which has allowed for a greater understanding of this zone's place in the Late Classic Maya world.

Of the total sample of sherds subjected to INAA, 31 samples had a chemical composition that indicated an origin in or near Salinas de los Nueve Cerros. This pattern is also seen in the figurines analyzed by Erin Sears (see Chapter 6; also Sears 2016). Of the material from Nueve Cerros, two samples come from the Upper Pasión—one from Oxib'chipek near Raxruha Viejo and another from Tres Islas (approximately 20 km downriver from Cancuen).

Twenty-seven of the 31 vessels manufactured in Nueve Cerros were found in Cancuen. Nearly half were found in the palace and nearby residential groups ($n = 14$), while lesser quantities were found in the northern part of the epicenter ($n = 5$), in an administrative and public ceremonial group and the northern ballcourt. Two samples were recovered from the jade production zone and the other six were without context. This pattern reinforces the general perspective that access to these imports was principally limited to residents of elite groups, administrative areas, and other places with connections to royalty, like the zones related to commercial production activities (the jade workshop) and ceremonies and feasting (northern ballcourt).

The contexts of these samples correspond primarily to three groups: middens, burials, and middens associated with burials. Middens (trash pits) are the most common with nine recovered examples. The presence of the mouth of an incised bowl with a polished black slip belonging to the Nueve Cerros type Cubuc Fluted (Dillon 1979:186) in the southeast patio of the palace complex suggests a very early influence of Cancuen's Sendero Group ceramics. These are characterized by black-slipped bowls with a variety of incised, fluted, and stamped decoration (Forné et al. 2011) that can be distinguished from the monochrome black wares of the central Peten (Infierno Group).

The materials recovered from burials are drawn from two contexts. Burial 96 is the resting place of the wife of Kan Maa'x, Cancuen's last governor. Her funeral assemblage included a polychrome bowl rim sourced to Nueve Cerros and a Kanalkan Gouged vessel manufactured in Tikal (Quintanilla 2013). Burial 2/7, located southeast of the palace, housed an infant associated with three whole vessels left as offerings. The vessels corresponded to Hinojo Negative, common in the Transversal and northern highlands and a red-on-cream polychrome related to Nueve Cerros. Five anthropomorphic figures were also recovered from the burial with removable headdresses and helmets; they appear to have been manufactured near the Candelaria Cave system in Raxruha, Alta Verapaz (Sears 2016:231).

Six of the sampled pieces correspond to burials associated with middens, a funerary practice common at Cancuen that has been previously discussed by Quintanilla (2013:115). Burial 2 stands out and includes four vessels associated with Nueve Cerros (three Xelub Dichrome vessels and a Nitro Incised bowl). Two rims were recovered and sourced from two additional contexts, the Patos *aguada* and a cobble floor in the northern part of the site.

The INAA results from burials indicate an open transmission of objects, ideas, and, likely, people between Nueve Cerros and Cancuen; the same pattern is seen in the Cancuen lithic assemblage, where salt-refining tools in the Nueve Cerros style have also been recovered (Mijangos 2014). Since Cancuen was a large commercial center, its residents must have maintained regular contact with people from different settlements in its network of interaction.

The presence of Nueve Cerros ceramics in each of the Cancuen ceramic complexes evinces the long-lasting relationship between the two cities (Forné et al. 2011). During the earliest phase (Concordia, AD 652–760), this link is established in the earliest context recovered from the settlement, a midden underneath the southeastern patio of the palace (Barrientos et al. 2001; Bill and Callaghan 2002).

Seven of the analyzed samples linking Cancuen and Nueve Cerros belong to the Los Laureles complex (AD 760–780). This includes the red-on-cream bowl from Burial 2/7 and six samples from the Laureles-Chamán transition. The latter includes three sherds and a whole vessel with a fine, greyish paste that are likely imitations of the common Chablekal Group. The complete vessel has a double bottom and belongs to the type Volcancito Composite, which was first identified at Cancuen and is common throughout the Transversal region.

During the subsequent Chamán complex (AD 780–800), there are four sherds belonging to Nitro Incised. These include a polychrome variety, one

Jekcha Red body sherd, and two fine paste rims belonging to unidentified types related to Fine Orange. Three additional sherds were dated to Chamán 2 (AD 790–800) of the types Sendero Black, Nitro Incised, and an unnamed highland polychrome from the burial of Kan Maa'x's wife.

As we integrate these data into the broader archaeological survey, it appears that vessels from Salinas de los Nueve Cerros were imported into Cancuen throughout the history of the site. For most of Cancuen's history, however, these vessels were found only in the immediate vicinity of the palace. After AD 780, however, the distribution opened up to include additional neighborhoods, including the northern part of the site. The presence of multiple imitation Fine Greys right as access to the imported wares loosens deserves future investigation.

Ceramic sherds recovered from other sites in the greater Cancuen area can be used to date additional contexts with Nueve Cerros. Four sherds recovered from middens in the epicenter of Raxruha Viejo were sourced to the saltmaking site. The samples, which include Nitro Incised, Nimha Gouged-Incised, and an unidentified type, suggest that a connection was established by AD 760. Additionally, a Kaleb'aal Incised sherd (Chichicaste Group) was recovered in a midden at the site of Oxib'chipek, and a Xelub Dichrome plate was pulled from Burial 3 at Tres Islas, pushing Nueve Cerros' network of interaction north of Cancuen.

Fundamentally, the results of INAA at Cancuen, Raxruha Viejo, and other neighboring sites have identified 33 sherds manufactured at Nueve Cerros. These formed part of prestige vessels. The presence of 11 different fine paste sherds in that sample suggests the city was an additional center of production for Fine Gray and Fine Orange.

An examination of the overlap between the Cancuen and Nueve Cerros assemblages reveals the importance of Nitro Incised ($n = 6$), including polychrome varieties with smudged interiors, suggesting residents of the latter incorporated this style into their local production even as it is associated with the central region of Alta Verapaz. Ceramic types that were developed locally at Nueve Cerros were also commonly observed at Cancuen and were included in the INAA samples like Xelub Dichrome ($n = 4$) and Jekcha Red ($n = 1$). Other general Transversal and northern highland types were recovered to a lesser degree, including those belonging to the Chichicaste ($n = 3$), Sendero ($n = 2$), and local polychrome ($n = 3$) groups. Erin Sears (2016) confirms the presence of at least 12 figurines produced in Nueve Cerros that were recovered from ceremonial contexts at Cancuen. Additionally, a figurine mold sourced to Nueve Cerros was recovered at the secondary center of La Lima, located 6 km west of Raxruha Viejo near the end of the Candelaria Cave system.

IDENTIFYING A NUEVE CERROS-CHINAHA CERAMIC SPHERE

Previously, Woodfill (2010) proposed that the frontier zone between the Pasión River and northern Alta Verapaz was home to a ceramic sphere during the Late Classic period that derived from northern highland traditions including the Chuacús and Cuchumatanes spheres (Arnauld 1986, 1987). The Cancuen region and sites to the north, in contrast, were largely ensconced in the Tepeu II and III spheres of the central Peten (Forné et al. 2009).

Recent investigations by members of Proyecto Arqueológico Regional Cancuen and Proyecto Salinas de los Nueve Cerros have documented a series of typological and modal characteristics that justify the creation of a new ceramic interaction sphere in the central zone of the Northern Transversal Strip, which we denominate the Nueve Cerros–Chinaha sphere in reference to the two major sierras that it incorporates. The proposed extent of the sphere (Figure 5.4) includes a western section surrounding the Nueve Cerros Ridge and the Chixoy-Salinas River, a central section under the control of Raxruha Viejo that includes the San Simón River Valley and an eastern section mediated by Sebol that extends perhaps as far as Sesakkar. Cancuen serves as the northern limit of this sphere. Both Sesakkar and Cancuen exhibit lower percentages of Transversal ceramics than their more central counterparts; the former presents stronger ties to sites in the southwestern Peten like Machaquila and El Raudal, and the latter to sites in the southeastern Peten. Still, both sites exhibit typical modes of the Nueve Cerros-Chinaha sphere, including an emphasis on porous pastes.

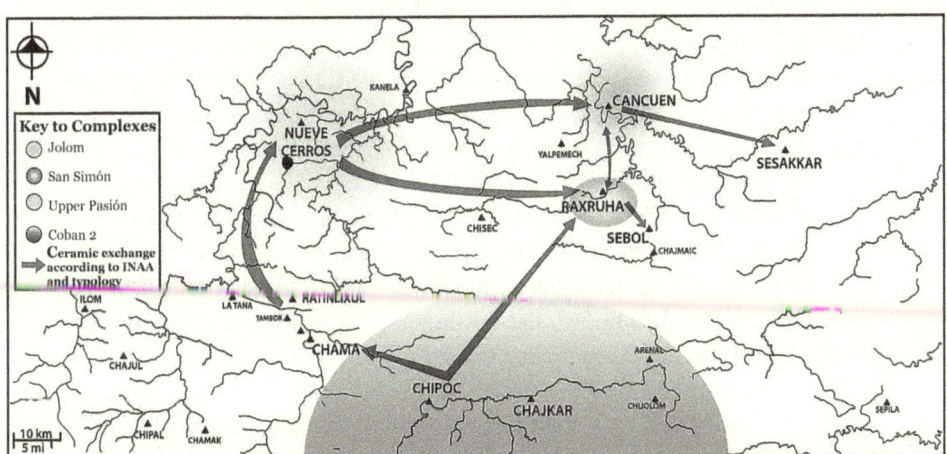

Figure 5.4. Geographic extent of the proposed Nueve Cerros–Chinaja ceramic sphere. (Map made in Illustrator. Juan Francisco Saravia)

CONCLUSIONS

Investigations undertaken in the Peten and adjacent parts of Chiapas have revealed that Tepeu II is a moment of great complexity in the Maya region. The necessity to acquire a wide range of imported resources in the central lowlands led to a struggle to control extant trade routes, and new political entities and alliances formed within this historic context. Each of the primary cities in the Nueve Cerros-Chinaha sphere took advantage of this moment and appear to have allied with each other to varying extents to expand their individual reach. The leaders of Salinas de los Nueve Cerros leaned on the city's advantageous location and long history of salt production. Cancuen, similarly, expanded its economic reach through controlling trade routes and different phases of production for important goods. Raxruha Viejo likely enjoyed similar interregional importance due to its architectural and sculptural richness that belies its status as a regional center. Sesakkar and Sebol, while secondary centers, were located at important choke points for interregional trade and would have been able to control much of the trade passing through their vicinities.

The settlements participating in this sphere were all located within a frontier zone that was important for commerce and pilgrimage to sacred caves. Their shared experience is evident in their ceramics, which includes shared modes and types throughout the zone—including Cancuen—and reflects a regional identity. All the settlements regularly used ceramic groups and types originating in neighboring zones, including the southwestern lowlands and the northern highlands. While fine paste vessels imported from the Gulf Coast were accessible only to residents of Cancuen, local imitations were manufactured in local workshops, at Nueve Cerros and elsewhere, and distributed throughout the region.

The relationship between Cancuen and Nueve Cerros is the lynchpin on which the Nueve Cerros-Chinaha sphere and the alliance it demonstrates hang. The act of bringing these two economic powerhouses together and maintaining a mutually beneficial relationship must have attracted residents from other cities to settle or establish commercial ties. The model proposed here focuses on the high probability that the principal sites at the highland-lowland transition came together to maximize their trading potential in the Late Classic period. It is hoped that the ongoing investigations at Nueve Cerros, Raxruha Viejo, and other sites along the Transversal will refine the region's chronology, and that the classification and analysis of larger ceramic assemblages will allow us to refine the chronological and geographic extent of this ceramic sphere and its importance in the history of the Transversal region.

To what extent was this relationship developed? What was the relationship and power distribution between Cancuen and Nueve Cerros? What role did Raxruha Viejo play? These questions arise from the analysis of the present data and provide avenues to orient future investigations for ceramicists and other specialists working in the region.

6
Changing Ritual Intent in a Stone Coffer from an Unlooted Cave in Central Guatemala

Erin L. Sears

THE CHAPTERS IN this volume illustrate the culmination of the first 20 years of exploration into a new millennia after many years of civil war and long-term modern economic reconstruction hardships within the Guatemalan southern Peten–Alta Verapaz regions. Arthur A. Demarest's excitement in Chapter 1 reflects these efforts and indicates the various scales of newly acquired, large ancient Maya datasets that incorporate this region under the auspices of "network," "interaction zones," or "community" rubrics. Other practices, such as museum exhibition and institutional collection-based research during this period, however, also created a space for renewed interest (Danien 1998, 2005, 2009). The acquisition of Maya material remains from this region (recovered under less-than-current palatable archaeological documentary standards) are part of the early twentieth-century history of Maya archaeological exploration and the global race for acquiring large-scale collections for building national public educational centers (Alexander 1996:5-15; Danien 1998; Martinez et al. 2022). Scholars and wealthy Guatemalan landowners of that era would send or sell their collections to large nation-supported and university-focused museums to display the range of "representation" of Central American ancient and ethnographic cultures. These collections (both international and United States based) are always awaiting a future "network" association that builds on or creates an alternative perspective as these objects sit patiently on shelves. There are always limitations when using museum collections (such as the lack of context, the absence of provenience, or an accidental incorporation of modern fakes). In this chapter I contextualize a few of these collective ancient remains from the Transversal region and elsewhere with millennial discoveries into a different narrative.

Unlike many northern lowland Maya polities that seek to facilitate communication with the gods by constructing large pyramid-shaped temple structures and residential compounds over small fissures in the limestone bedrock, the ancient Maya in the region of the Alta Verapaz exploited their mountainous environment, performing ceremonies within large cathedral-like cave systems (Brady 1989; see Wolf, Chapter 9, for other relationships of sacred spaces and human habitational zones within the Transversal). In 2005, Brent K. S. Woodfill and Mirza Monterroso were exploring the Hun Nal Ye cave system located north of the modern city of Coban in the Alta Verapaz region and discovered one stone and two ceramic coffers within the upper reaches of the first dark chamber (Woodfill et al. 2012:98; see Figure 1.1 for a regional map). The subsequent archaeological report described the layout of the two cave chambers, the descriptions of the deposited ceramic vessels within the chambers, and focused on one stone coffer that had incised hieroglyphs and imagery, which was placed in the back of the primary cave chamber (Figure 6.1; see also Woodfill et al. 2012:Figures 8–12; Woodfill 2019a:Figures 8.2 and 8.3). Other artifacts within the cave chamber the investigators exhumed were a human juvenile pelvis, one obsidian blade, and a calcified tapir bone interred within the incised box (Woodfill et al. 2012:98). A large portion of their report focused on the carved imagery and the decipherment of hieroglyphs found on the lid and sides of the stone box. They conclude, based on the construction and the hieroglyphic expressions and the presented imagery, that the lid and the coffer were created separately in different far-distant regions, and the coffer was attributable to the end of the Early Classic period. They additionally mention that the interior of the box likely housed a paper codex; however, a separate ending event may have replaced it with a tapir bone (Woodfill et al. 2012:107).

I add another level of perspective by reexamining the ritual intent and imagery carved into the Hun Nal Ye stone coffer in comparison with other material remains. I argue that while the imagery is cosmopolitan in the programmatic intent, both the incised lid and the coffer may have other directional connections within the Alta Verapaz, as well as toward the eastern Maya region. Other scholars have incorporated the Hun Nal Ye stone coffer within a greater context of imagery and cultural material that pertain to the ancient Maya worldview. The calculations by Houston et al. (2017) find that the regularity of the interior dimensions of eight examples of stone coffers from various Maya sites align with the dimensions of a few surviving codices. By these same metrics, the Hun Nal Ye coffer could potentially fit a paper codex within the parameters of its interior. From Houston's analysis, these boxes were valued highly for their purposes of housing ritual instructions written on bark paper to keep them safe from harsh tropical elements. The elaborate decorative imagery on the exterior of the stone coffer serves as a warning to an ancient, illiterate public to keep away from such intimate secrets that were

Figure 6.1. Incised sides of the stone coffer recovered at the Hun Nal Ye cave: (a) lid, (b) Side 1, (c) Side 2, (d) Side 3, and (e) Side 4. (Courtesy of Erin L. Sears.)

reserved for only the most privileged. The comparative method with the Hun Nal Ye coffer may reveal other connective designs that alter or assist in evaluating directionality of production for such a unique piece. By keeping with the general format of the original report's analysis of the incised imagery that is contained on both the lid and the sides of the coffer in a linear manner, the new connections to regional associations will become evident.

THE LID

Interpreting ancient visual media is, at best, an attempt to reconstruct past Maya intentions by stitching together meaning from other sources, either working back to the imagery by chronological means or creating an accumulation of regional patterning that demonstrates some form of regularity.

While the Hun Nal Ye lid (see Figure 6.1a) is carved in a different manner than the stone box on which it sits (see Figure 6.1b–e), it is how choosing aspects of the imagery may determine our ability to see how both are either connected or not connected. The original interpretation was to view the coffer's imagery as a separation of the night sky and the Underworld (Woodfill et al. 2012:98, 107); this current reading views an alternative mythological narrative—the Lunar Maize God as he passes through the Underworld.

The original 2012 report describes the lid as having 16 hieroglyph elements constituting a circle of text that surrounds a multicomponent scene showing an elongated left sided profile of the Moon Goddess. In the crook of her left arm, she holds the trusty *way/wayhel* companion, the rabbit. The curved right parenthesis form on the right side is the representation of the waxing crescent phase of the moon (Woodfill et al. 2012:98). In polychrome ceramic examples, these three elements on the stone lid are usually connected with other deity characters in the narratives of ancient Maya cosmic creation (K2733; see Miller and Martin 2004:96–97 for other material imagery depicting the Moon Goddess with her representative elements as well as the LACMA example of a stone lintel depicting an Elite Female in Moon Cartouche [AC1992.76.1]).

An alternative perspective of the stone lid views the imagery as an indication of the mythological telling of the Maize God becoming a lunar hero (Chinchilla Mazariegos 2011:204, Figure 89, 2017:202, Figure 107). The appearance of glyph C (Glyph 10A on the lid as the Maize God; Glyph 9A as the feminine representation) as part of the hieroglyph elements surrounding the image is part of the evidence indicating the humanoid at the center is not female; instead, it is the depiction of the Maize God holding the transformed Moon Goddess in her rabbit form (Houston 2012:Note 1). Identifying the exact character is difficult in this instance because these two characters tend to take on the same duties of transformation alternating every six lunar events (Milbrath 1999:150). Two polychrome ceramic vessels (Figure 6.2) best represent the visual mythological tale in relation to what is occurring on the Hun Nal Ye coffer: a Naranjo region vessel (K1398) and a red-beige vessel mentioned by Chinchilla Mazariegos (2011:206, Figure 110) located at the Los Angeles County Museum of Art (K5166, M.2010.115.628). Both vessels portray versions of the tale of how the Lunar Maize God played a role as the *way/wayhel* rabbit absconding with God L's clothing while in the Underworld (Milbrath 1999; Stone and Zender 2011:147). The Naranjo region vessel (K1398) has two scenes surrounded by glyph columns (just like what is presented on the Hun Nal Ye box); the first scene indicates the Lunar Maize God with a small rabbit positioned to the left of his waist in a similar arrangement as the rabbit portrayed in the Hun Nal Ye lid. Both characters are seated on a puffy throne on top of a *witz* monster that represents the sacred mountain with access to the Underworld through its cave maw (e.g., see the stalactite, three dots on the skull of the monster in K1398; see Stone and Zender 2011:139). The second vessel (K5166) depicts a palace scene with the Moon Goddess holding her wayward rabbit among her lunar courtiers as God L acts in obeisance. The architecture is of note in reference to the Hun Nal Ye coffer; both the wall and her extended throne are decorated with circular dots, a reference to floating water droplets, indicating this courtly activity is not occurring within the human plane.

Figure 6.2. Top: Rollout photograph K1398 depicting a mythological narrative of the Lunar Moon Maize God. Bottom: Rollout photograph K5166 of the Moon Goddess and her celestial court. (Collection of the Kerr Archive, Los Angeles County Museum of Art [M.2010.115.628]. Photo courtesy of Justin Kerr.)

In building his case for the idea of the Lunar Maize God's importance in this mythological line, Chinchilla Mazariegos (2011:224-225, Figure 104, 2017:207, Figure 112) compares two analogous examples excavated within a public/private cave-like interior space that originates from an elite compound in the center of Copan. The first example is an elaborately carved bench uncovered in Room 1, Structure 66C, as part of a subroyal elite residential unit (8N-11), or the Skyband Group, located to the northeast of the main palace of Copan (Webster et al. 1998:332-334, Figure 12). Along the front of the edge of the raised bench, a horizontally stretched version of the Lunar Maize God and Moon Goddess characters is quite similar to the Hun Nal Ye lid figures (Figure 6.3a-b). The nine carved panels along the front of the 5.6 m Skyband Bench contain imagery of the gods that rule the sun, moon, and stars, and the personifications of cardinal directions with four supports carved with humanoid forms (*Pauhatuns*) holding up the physical bench and, thus, the personified universe (Bricker and Bricker 1999:435-436). Yet another bench, originating from Structure 9M-146 in Copan, has a similar figure of the Lunar Maize God reclining with his moon symbol under his armpit. This recalls the painted image of the Moon Goddess, rabbit, and symbols portrayed in the LACMA vessel (recall Figure 6.2b, K5166; Chinchilla Mazariegos 2011:201, Figure 87, 2017:203, Figure 106).

CONNECTING WITH OTHER REGIONAL INFLUENCES

While Chinchilla Mazariegos was focused on arguing the mythological veracity of his analysis, it is interesting to consider that he did not connect the Hun Nal Ye lid (located in the Transversal zone) with the Copan Skyband Bench panel and the 9M-146 bench, which are in "close" regional proximity to one another. The imagery of the carved rabbits on the Hun Nal Ye lid and Copan Skyband Bench face to the right in the scenes, suggesting there is some form of regional stylistic interaction. Consideration of what is portrayed at other Maya sites may assist in understanding more about the production and meaning of the Hun Nal Ye coffer.

Within the Transversal zone, the representation of the Moon Goddess in ceramic figural form is not always associated with her *way/wayhel* rabbit creature but connected to what scholars interpret as either the Old Sun God or the Lunar Maize God pairing (Figure 6.4). Two versions of this paired representation occur at Cancuen (see Sears 2016). The first example (see Figure 6.4a, CANF2125) was recovered from an *aguada* (water reservoir) of an elite residence located to the northwest of the palace. Portrayed in figurine form is a highly eroded Moon Goddess sitting on the shoulders of an elderly form of the Sun God/Lunar Maize God with a tied ribbon connecting them

Figure 6.3. Photographs of (a) lid of the Hun Nal Ye coffer, in comparison to (b) an incised panel from the Skyband bench from the site of Copan, Structure 8N-11 to the northeast of the palace. (Courtesy of Erin L. Sears [a] and Justin Kerr [b].)

across his torso in the act of marriage. The second example (see Figure 6.4b, CANF0469) is a more common arrangement of two figures connected side by side that are found along Usumacinta riverine sites and as far north as Jaina Island. Another stylistic version of the side-by-side figurine type was also recovered at Salinas de los Nueve Cerros (see Figure 6.4c, S9C0143–0144 and S9C0154; see Sears 2016).

Figure 6.4. Moon Goddess in ceramic figurine forms from the Transversal region (sans rabbit): (a) with the Old Sun God/Lunar Moon Maize God in piggyback form at the site of Cancuen with her crenellated diadem and front flower tendrils (CANF2125); (b) traditional Usumacinta/Jaina arrangement of the Moon Goddess side-by-side with the Old Sun God/Lunar Moon Maize God excavated at Cancuen (CANF0469); (c) other side-by-side examples from recent excavations at the site of Salinas de los Nueve Cerros (S9C0154, S9C0143, S9C0144). (Courtesy of Erin L. Sears.)

The piggyback couple figurine from Cancuen (see Figure 6.4a, CANF2125) appears to have the same version of headdress arrangement as worn by the Lunar Maize God on the Hun Nal Ye lid. Both the female figurine and the Hun Nal Ye carving have the crenelated tiara with the protruding flower at the center. In the ceramic figurine version, the flower is represented as an eroded, long, raised line at the center of the forehead. Although the piggyback figurine was recovered at Cancuen, compositional analysis by means of neutron activation determined the figurine originated from the Dos Pilas region (Sears 2016:243). This highly eroded figure was recovered from an *aguada* at the Los Patos elite compound, northwest of the palace center. Contextually, the recovered ceramic figurine may be another example of ancient intent to represent this mythological program, as it could have been "sacrificed" in an attempt to access the Underworld through a watery environment during an ancient public ritual event (Sears 2016:242).

Other ceramic examples of the Moon Goddess connected to her *way/wayhel* creature are found in ceramic form at a site in Belize. At the site of Pacbitun, a subroyal burial (EC-burial-2) within the north residential area of the eastern court revealed multiple figurines arranged around an adult burial (Cheong 2012, 2013, 2020). One ceramic figurine example depicts a mold-made figure that is either a humanoid wearing a mask of a rabbit or perhaps the Moon Goddess in her animal guise since both bunny ears and buck teeth are intimated. The costuming also depicts the large, wrapped yoke with the long side skirts of the loincloth designating the role of this figure as a ballplayer—participating in a celestial game to begin "creation." Neither Woodfill et al. (2012) nor Chinchilla Mazariegos (2011, 2017) mention that the Hun Nal Ye rabbit may also be taking the guise of a boxer. The present study highlights the importance of connecting this imagery to other regional ceramic examples that display the ancient Maya cosmic creation narratives. The left paw of the Hun Nal Ye rabbit is extended forward, encased in a boxing glove that is carved with the mitt upturned to form a C-shape. The right paw is retracted to the torso with the paw in a relaxed, downward grip. This is similar to another burial tableau using ceramic figurines such as the miniature humanoid boxers from structure O14–4, Burial 39 at El Perú-Waka' in order to open portals to other worlds (Rich and Freidel 2010; Rich and Matute 2014:70).

Another potential site that bridges ancient connections of the Maya lunar myth with the Hun Nal Ye stone lid is documented at the site of Aragon, east of the modern city of Coban (Sears et al. 2021). This newly discovered ceramic production center lies in a valley between two large hills (Woodfill 2019b; Woodfill et al. 2020). Research is continuing to reveal unique highland forms that display god visages, elite women, and fantastic creatures. While future laboratory seasons will continue to augment the initial discovery, the 2019 season uncovered a new mold-made ceramic form (plaques) that contains hieroglyphs and celestial imagery (Figure 6.5; Sears et al. 2021:Figure 9). One example (see Figure 6.5 top FA0253 and production mold FA0269, bottom) is a square, thin, flat, mold-made plaque that displays a central figure surrounded by a celestial band instead of incised hieroglyphs. The old god is in an active pose, a similar arrangement to the *Pauhatuns* at the foot of the structure 8N-11 bench located in Copan, with hands held upward, holding up the universe. The encircling of the celestial band on the plaques is similar to the hieroglyphs enclosing the central design on the Hun Nal Ye lid.

Figure 6.5. Photographs of Aragon mold-made plaque depicting similar regional celestial arrangements FA0253 (top) and production mold FA0269 (bottom). (Courtesy of Erin L. Sears.)

THE COFFER: SIDES 1 AND 3, A REVISED ICONOGRAPHIC PERSPECTIVE

Nestled on the long Side 1 of the incised Hun Nal Ye coffer, between double columns of glyphs, reside two side-profile, seated figures facing each other on decorated thrones (Figure 6.6a; see also Woodfill et al. 2012:103, Figure 9; see Houston et al. 2017:Figure 3 for color photo). The seated figure on the left was originally identified as the "Fire God" because of the scalloped beard and nose bone under a substantial, crooked nose. The figure is balancing what has been interpreted as a folded codex between his outstretched left hand and the throne (Woodfill et al. 2012:105). The seated figure on the right, with extended hands, perhaps receiving the gift, is ambiguously identified in comparison to its mirror image on Side 3 of the Hun Nal Ye box (Woodfill et al. 2012:105).

The opposing long side (identified as Side 3) of the Hun Nal Ye coffer is a repeat of the imagery of Side 1, with the exception that different characters are seated across from one another in side-profile on their decorated thrones, facing each other, nestled between columns of hieroglyphs (Figure 6.7a; see also Woodfill et al. 2012:105, Figure 11). In the original analysis (Woodfill et al. 2012:105), the left figure on Side 3 was compared with the left figure on Side 1 in relative commonality of pose and items that are in the outstretched hand, while the right figure was designated as the Jaguar God of the Underworld. Given other regional material remains, these interpretations need to be reassessed.

The symmetrically aligned characters seated on the left-sided thrones on the coffer's Sides 1 and Sides 3 are a continuation of the Lunar Maize God's mythology. In this analysis I identify the first set of characters on both left sides as the personification of the Paddler Gods (Reents-Budet and McLeod, personal communication 2022; see Milbrath 1999:126–130; Schele and Freidel 1990:390, Figures 10:7 and 10:8). Because of the arrangement of the characters, the left-seated character on Side 1 of the Hun Nal Ye coffer is the Stingray Paddler God, indicating the day changing into night (see Figure 6.6a). He is characterized with his bloodletter piercing his nose, long chin/beard, and an additional *k'in* glyph on his belt to refer to his station of the daytime sun (Stone and Zender 2011:51). These long imagery sequences are not happening on the earthly plane, as noted by the circular blood/water/cloud droplets encased within the thrones (see Ixlu Stela 2 for the best comparison; Miller 1999:129, Figure 4.3b; Stone and Zender 2011:51, Figures 11.2 and 11.3). The scene is moving left to right, as indicated by the *ik'* glyph (A1 glyph on the coffer) or the action of the wind positioned behind the throne. The Stingray Spine paddler's counterpart on Side 3 (first, left) is the Jaguar Paddler, who wears identifiable mittens, a water-lily headdress, and designation *ak'ab/akbal* glyph bifurcated on the side of his thigh and buttocks (see Figure 6.7a;

Figure 6.6. (a) Photograph of Side 1 of the Hun Nal Ye stone coffer; (b) examples of the bone thrones carried and seated upon by denizens of the Underworld depicted in the polychrome bowl from the Museo Popol Vuh collection (Kerr 3395, Museo Popol Vuh MVP0420, MS730). (Courtesy of Erin L. Sears [a], and Ronald L. Bishop, Maya Survey Archives [b].)

Milbrath 1999:127; Stone and Zender 2011:145). In this case, these characters are not portrayed passing through different layers of existence, seated in a long canoe, but are floating serenely on their well-appointed thrones. They are enacting/creating the transformation not by passing a codex, as has been originally interpreted (Woodfill et al. 2012), but as the collective Paddler Gods who are distributing a bone throne to their respective incised counterparts on the right side. This is a different intention of presentation and a signal to cross over to the Underworld. Human femur bones are stacked and banded together or appear like an extended lawn-chair throne to signal the power of the Underworld and to identify where the mythological actors exist within specific planes during the various creation myths (see Figure 6.6; Reents-Budet 1994:272–273, Figure 6.44, MS0739, K3395; Stone and Zender 2011:95).

In contrast with the identifications of the left-positioned characters, the personage on the right of Side 1 is part of the cast needed to initiate this transformation, while the character on Side 3 is the final beneficiary of this "cloud riding." The first bone throne passed from the Stingray Paddler God is accepted by the God Chahk. His countenance is difficult to discern, but the downturned snout with arched, inflamed top lip, the fuzzy outlined bouffant frontal ponytail, and the potential *muyal* logograph (the "s" form on its side located on his skirt), denotes his realm (Stone and Zender 2011:41, 143). At times, there is a third character accompanying the Paddler Gods in their journeys in the glyph sequences (Stuart 2012). Stuart notes that the corresponding glyph has a wind feature.

Unfortunately, due to the heavy erosion, only the face and the headdress of the right character on Side 3 remain (see Figure 6.7a). Because of this, two interpretations can be considered. First, if there is a perceived loop at the center of the forehead, this symbol would indicate the character represents the elder Lunar Moon Maize God. Carved imagery on Altar 2 at Bonampak references a similar character, but this stone carving arranges the Lunar Moon Maize God in frontal form dressed in a ballplayer costume with an elaborate, birdlike headdress while carrying the Moon Goddess in her rabbit form in his left arm; he is encased in a large moon glyph (see Milbrath 1999:137; Schele and Miller 1983:46, Figure 18c). In this scenario, the Hun Nal Ye box has the Paddler Gods and Chahk delivering the Old Lunar Moon Maize God to his final destination. This theme is also presented on a series of four incised bones from Burial 116 at Tikal (Schele and Freidel 1990:413; Stuart 2012; Trik 1963:Figure 4a). The incised bones illustrate the same positions of the Paddler Gods as they are presented in the Hun Nal Ye coffer on Sides 1 and 3.

The second scenario of identifying these characters considers that God L may be the final deity and is being transported within another Underworld level. But this is quite unlike what is presented on a Naranjo regional vase, where God L needed to retrieve his clothing with lamentations and requests for his large, feathered sombrero and clothing from the Lunar Moon God and the rabbit-transformed Moon Goddess (see Figure 6.2 top, K1398). In this alternative perspective, the Hun Nal Ye representation includes his Muanfeathered headdress. By accepting the bone throne from the Jaguar Paddler, God L is returning to his realm (see Chapter 11 of this volume for examples of God L imagery in Alta Verapaz ceramic polychrome vessels).

Changing Ritual Intent | 133

Figure 6.7. (a) Photograph of Side 3 of the Hun Nal Ye stone coffer; (b, c) Jaguar-Way ceramic figurines from Chama (University of Pennsylvania Museum of Archaeology and Anthropology, Penn NA11208) and Salinas de los Nueve Cerros from Brian Dillon's excavations (S9C026); (d, e) God L ceramic figurines from Cancuen (CANF0165) and Roknima (University of Pennsylvania Museum of Archaeology and Anthropology, Penn NA10979). (Courtesy of Erin L. Sears.)

TRANSVERSAL VARIANTS OF THE CHARACTERS IN SIDES 1 AND 3 OF THE HUN NAL YE COFFER

The Paddler Gods are part of the Late Classic Maya canon in stone stelae and ceramic figurines within the Transversal region. For example, in front of structure 10L-16 at Copan resides Stela P. This highly carved monument is largely a testament to Butz' Chan's reign in early seventh century AD (Fash

1991; Fash 2011:55). At his torso, he holds a double-serpent bar with the heads of the Stingray Spine and Jaguar Paddler Gods emerging at his shoulders (Milbrath 1999:128-129, Figure 4.3e). The Paddler Gods are also part of the hieroglyphic translation history in the region, as Peter Matthews (1977) was the first to recognize the pair in glyph form on Stela 8 in Dos Pilas by means of their *k'in* and *ak'ab* details. In other glyph instances, such as what is written on Quiriguá Stela C, Stuart (2012) believes that the appearance of the Paddler glyphs are notifications of period ending/renewal sequences that are enacted for legitimation ceremonies.

The Alta Verapaz cultural material also contains the stylistic language of jaguar *way/wayhel* creatures that have similar elements to the Jaguar Paddler God and the eroded right figure on Side 3 of the Hun Nal Ye coffer (see Figure 6.1b, d). The Hun Nal Ye Jaguar Paddler God seems to be wearing a water-lily headdress, signified by the bifurcated curled trefoil tendrils in the front and a square-knot cape/neckerchief and elaborate side panels of the loincloth at the thigh region. A polychrome bowl in the Museo Popol Vuh collection demonstrates a similar *way/wayhel*-jaguar character actively somersaulting while landing on his front paws on a throne of long bones, costumed with the water-lily trefoil headdress and square-knot neckerchief (see Figure 6.6b, K3395; Reents-Budet 1994:272-273, Figure 6.44). The figurine examples of this transformative creature are found in two different sites within the Alta Verapaz region (see Figure 6.7b–e). One figurine, discovered in Chama by Robert Burkitt in 1920, is currently within the collections of the University of Pennsylvania Museum of Archaeology and Anthropology (NA11208; see Figure 6.7b). The figurine was exhibited and described first as a jaguar-man by Alfred Kidder (1959:104, Figure 75). The frontal imagery is a humanoid wearing a jaguar mask, with the square knot handkerchief enveloping the back of the head to hide the line of the mask. A shell-tinkler belt attached to a very decorative loincloth with side panels at the thighs and the body is covered in a netting. The second form of this figurine was discovered by Brian Dillon during his central royal elite excavations at Salinas de los Nueve Cerros (see Figure 6.7c, S9C026). Unfortunately, only the bottom half of the figure was recovered. The imagery contains the same costuming of the legs as well as the figure holding a deer rack in the right hand and what might be a small fan, or a trident, just like the ruler depicted as a Jaguar God from Naranjo Stela 30 (see Stuart 1998:406, Figure 23). Chemical analysis revealed that the two figurines are not similar, suggesting a mold of the frontal imagery may have moved between the Chixoy riverine communities (Sears 2009).

The right figure of Side 3 of the Hun Nal Ye box, while unfortunately eroded from below the head, may have features consistent with the portrayal of God L, the god of the Underworld (see Figure 6.7a). On polychrome-painted ceramic vessels, God L is frequently depicted in profile with square-shaped eyes, skeletonized facial features, and a beak nose, with his creature, a Muan owl bird, residing on top of his headdress. God L is usually relaxing on jaguar pelted cushions and leisurely smoking a cigar (Taube 1992:82, Figure b; Reents-Budet 1994:236, Figure 6.1, K2796). At times, he is associated with jaguars and has multiple powers over water, fertility, and death; he also served as patron to merchants (Miller and Martin 2004:61; Stone and Zender 2011:213). The head profile of the right figure from Side 3 of the coffer has some of the elements that would identify the figure as God L—the bird-head diadem, beak nose, and goggle/square-shaped eye.

Ceramic figurines of the Alta Verapaz-Southern Peten region depict God L as represented in different versions (see Figure 6.7d, e). One example of God L found in the Burkitt collection of the University of Pennsylvania Museum of Archaeology and Anthropology is an intact figurine example of God L (see Figure 6.7d). This seated version has all the facial hallmarks of God L, including a foreshortened sombrero with two Muan feathers curling at the top of the headdress. The feathered cape is attached vertically to the backs of the arms, which are positioned to connect with the thighs, allowing hollow space between the arms and the body. The right hand is near the chest with raised index finger, and the clasped thumb to the clenched fingers creates the gesture of the "in the presence" pose noted by Stone and Zender (2011:58-59). An additional figurine example was from a household midden northeast of the palace at Cancuen; it is a ceramic figurine head depicting the side-appliqued feathers, flame flanges, feathered sombrero, and the facial features of God L (see Figure 6.7e; Sears 2016:297, CANF0165).

Another example of a ceramic whistle box from Chajcar may illuminate a different version of God L (Peabody Museum of Archaeology and Ethnology at Harvard University 58-34-20/55524). Instead of the Muan bird or screech owl headdress, this version contains a diadem of a jaguar head. Because the Hun Nal Ye coffer is eroded at the midsection, the ceramic whistle-box imagery may provide clues as to what activities God L is doing. This God L from the whistle box depicts the right hand stretched out, but the left hand grasps a cigar with smoke trails.

THE COFFER: SIDE 2 AND SIDE 4

The short sides of the Hun Nal Ye coffer have hieroglyph blocks on each of the left sides and seated human figures on the right. Woodfill et al. (2012:105-106) note that Side 2 figure is writing on an open codex (see Figure 6.1c), while the Side 4 human is in a seated position (Figure 6.8a). Both texts inscribed on Side 2 and Side 4 are not organized in the normal manner and appear to be read from right to left (Woodfill 2012:107).

Figure 6.8. (a) Photograph of Side 4 of the Hun Nal Ye stone coffer; (b) examples of the Salinas de Los Nueve Cerros man discovered at Cancuen (CANF1008, 1308, 2182, 2705); (c) examples found at Salinas de los Nueve Cerros from old and recent excavations (S9C011, 033, 034, 525); (d) other ceramic figurines indicating the "in the presence pose" from the collections of the Museo Popol Vuh, Guatemala (MSF203, 208). (Courtesy of Erin L. Sears.)

The short sides of the coffer appear to exist on the human plane, but in "reverse" contrast to the directionality of the programmatic imagery that is occurring on the long ends of the box. The "backward" manner of the glyph blocks may be denoting a different way the human world is rotating (our existence runs clockwise versus counterclockwise in the celestial plane). Unfortunately, there are no known regional examples of a human with a codex in recently excavated figurine forms; however, an example of a rotund male with a book resting at his right leg originates from the Palenque region (Reents-Budet 1994:48, Figure 2.14, MS1072). Reents-Budet and MacLeod (personal communication 2022) note the Side 2 scribal character is looking up in the direction of the sky and may corroborate an artistic intent to connect the lid to the coffer.

The seated-human imagery carried on Side 4 is the strongest connection to Alta Verapaz and Peten regional parallels in connecting material remains to the imagery on the Hun Nal Ye coffer (see Figure 6.8a). Four figurines from the northern elite residential centers at Cancuen depict a petite-sized standing male wearing a cap headdress, and they were excavated in elite residential centers to the north. From my use of neutron activation analysis, these ceramic figurines were attributed to the site of Salinas de los Nueve Cerros, and they linked to the similarly styled excavated pieces from Dillon's collection (Sears 2016:336, Figure 8.17). From current excavations at the site of Salinas de los Nueve Cerros, there is a more intact example from the hinterlands (see Figure 6.8c, S9C525). Additionally, there are multiple variants of this male humanoid figure within the collection of the Museo Popol Vuh and La Ruta Maya Foundation (see Figure 6.8d). The stylistic arrangement of these figurines is interesting from a production method practice. Two molds are needed to complete the figure, and holes are usually punctured through the shoulder or side of the head. There is no indication of modeling whistle vents or ocarina holes, so these figurines do not function as musical instruments. The imagery of the frontal form of this figure presents a male with a loincloth and a three-jade-bead necklace. The reverse portion defines the necklace knot, the back of the loincloth, and the edge of the cap at the back of the head. The arm positioning is repetitive. The right arm is bent and angled across the torso, and the right hand is positioned at the left breast with the fingers touching the thumb with the index finger or first finger elevated upward. The left hand is clenched, resting underneath the right arm at the waistline of the figurine. The face is plain, and the eyes are "laurel" shaped, with some examples having a large, triangular-beaked nose. Some of the Cancuen examples have holes drilled into their cap headdresses, a design feature that would assist in allowing long human hair to be placed and cemented with beeswax or glue within the holes (see Figure 6.8b). This would allow for the ceramic figure to be more personalized by having the human hair formed into a ponytail-style arrangement, just like what is presented on the Hun Nal Ye coffer on Side 4.

Andrea Stone and Marc Zender have remarked that within a set of glyphs that focus on depictions of the human body, one glyph block has the arms crossed with the right hand at the chest with the index finger pointing up, and the other fingers are bent touching the thumb. They note this is the *ichon* glyph connected normally to the *yi-* and *-nal* phonetics to create the meaning "in the presence of" or "in the front of" (Stone and Zender 2011:58-59). They consider this gesture is also prevalent in visual representations of Maya court scenes in which high-ranking elites, vassals, or visitors are in poses subordinate to the human that is making the *ichon* gesture.

The positioning of the arm with a specific linguistic intent, connected to male imagery on Side 4 of the Hun Nal Ye, could be considered a regional representation. The seated figure on Side 4 with the glyph blocks to the left may be indicating a variant of an elite member within the royal court (Jackson 2013) or may be an example of elites that control considerable local territories within the Alta Verapaz region.

DISCUSSION

From the original report, the interpretation that the lid is separate in intent from the coffer (Woodfill et al. 2012's analysis) would mean the evening celestial occurrence of the Moon Goddess looks over the events that need to happen for the cycle of life. The Underworld gods are transferring codices to one another for correct events to take place in the human plane (Sides 2 and 4). The scribes and the elites "are in the presence of" marking these events, which are vital emergent celestial cycles and Underworld administrations.

In contrast, if the current interpretation is "accurate," based on the imagery depicted on the Hun Nal Ye coffer in its comparison with other regional ceramic and limestone cultural material remains, then the intention of the design is a representation of the Maya celestial occurrences that control the cycles of life and the notation of certain period-ending aspects to legitimate political activities in the Transversal region. The arrangement of the images on the lid and the box with this new interpretation are a connected physical alliteration of the universe in which the ancient Maya existed and attempted to control through their ritual practices.

While other cosmopolitan and unprovenienced examples were used as some of the best comparative visual narratives to explain the change of intent on the Hun Nal Ye coffer, the material remains from the Alta Verapaz, southern Peten, and eastern Maya region indicate similarities in cultural patterns that may modify the notion of locality for this coffer.

This narrative sequence concerning the ritual organizational structure of passing through different planes of existence for the ancient Maya aligns with contemporary interpretations of mortuary analysis excavated within the Transversal zone. At the site of Cancuen, Burial 2/7 was found in a residential compound that had a large kitchen to support the festivities performed at royal *aguada* near the south steps of the royal palace (Morán Giracca 2003;

Sears 2017). A set of five ceramic figurines surrounded a child burial placed with two highland vessels. Two figurines were dressed in ballplayer costumes. Farther northeast at the site of Pulsilha, in EC-burial-2, 12 figurines were recovered surrounding the deceased (Cheong 2012, 2013, 2020; Cheong et al. 2014). One ceramic figurine from this burial is the Moon Goddess, as mentioned, transitioning into her rabbit spirit, who is costumed like a ballplayer. Accompanying figurines are attendants and a sheltered ruler. Another figurine from Burial 39 at El Perú-Waka', a more distant lowland site, contains aspects of celestial gaming or boxing (Rich and Matute 2014; Rich and Freidel 2010; Sears 2017). Two of the 23 figurines portray masked dwarfs with one boxing mitt on their right hands, which are cocked low at the right hip, with the left in full extension. In contrast, the Hun Nal Ye rabbit on the lid has the same active positioning of the right paw angled back and the left extended but gloved (see Figure 6.1).

These two examples of mortuary remains interred with ceramic figurines near the Alta Verapaz region and one from far away in northern Peten have been previously interpreted as arranged specifically around the interred to open axes or portals to the Underworld (Sears 2017). In the case of the Cancuen burial, a sequence of events was interpreted from the archaeological record; the ancient living participants performed a sacrifice of the deer-headdress figurine dressed in ballgame paraphernalia to open such portals (Sears 2016:238–239). The verticality and horizontality of the mortuary analysis concerning the cultural material that is placed within these burials are similar in intent to the imagery of the Hun Nal Ye coffer (see Sears 2016:366–368). As observing and recording by the earthly scribes and sub-royal elites incised on Sides 2 and Sides 4, these 'humans' are there to witness such an auspicious event. These multihorizontal levels of ritual activities depicted on the coffer are necessary to correct or continue the cycle of life. The Lunar Moon Maize God participates in a vertical manner by activating these events by sending the earthly *way/wayhel* rabbit representative to perform in sacrificial boxing events for opening these different levels within the universe. If the ritual levels are all performed in a correct, timely manner, the centrally located, raised bump within the interior recess of the coffer (a representation of a raised belly button or small hill, possibly?) (Figure 6.9) touches the resting codex or the interred sacred objects to imbue what is within the Hun Nal Ye coffer with continued universal powers. The physical ritual placements of both the coffer, the figurine burials, and the Sky Band bench (Group N11-8) in an elite building all within restricted dark spaces (caves, internments, elite royal reception rooms) create additional sacred environmental zones between performers of the rituals and the audiences participating in such events.

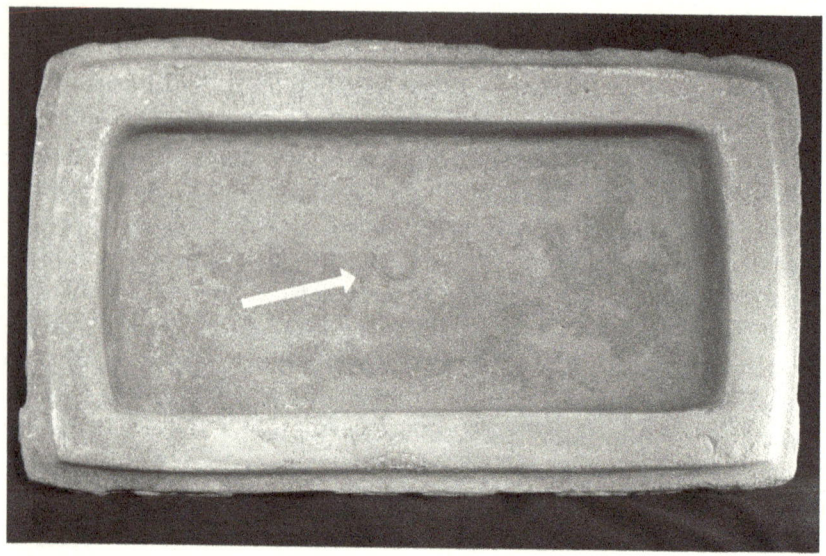

Figure 6.9. Interior of the Hun Nal Ye coffer containing a raised bump at center. This feature may act as a potential ritual connector (umbilical cord or idealized hill) to the ancient codex that was potentially housed in the coffer. (Courtesy of Erin L. Sears.)

In the case of the Hun Nal Ye coffer, Woodfill and colleagues (2012:112) surmise that because the ritual event occurred in a restricted part of the cave, there was no need to place elaborate polychrome vessels for large audiences to view. With the new interpretation concerning the imagery of the coffer, the placement within a physical cave feature is a necessary action for the ritual of the Lunar Moon Maize God and the celestial life cycle to be continually renovated. This event creates a specific political legitimation act and fomented relationships between regional royalty and the supernatural. In other case examples of figurine internments, the ritual practices were conducted into the ground and were most likely intended to continue the lineage of the elite residents that performed such ceremonies (Fitzsimmons 2010; McAnany 1995). This ancient mental template of opening portals to access the universe of Maya gods is found in regional caves, mortuary events, and elite residential structures in the Transversal area. This behavioral pattern intersects with other unique ritual practices (e.g., trade shrines) that have been discovered within the region (Sears 2017; Woodfill 2019a).

From the hieroglyphic sequence on the lid of the Hun Nal Ye coffer, Woodfill and colleagues (2012:101) translated parallels between the formation of glyphs 13 and 14 of the patron's name as a potential name-style to the fourteenth king of Copan, K'ahk' Joplaj Chan K'awiil (as cited by Martin and Grube 2008:208). The current analysis of the arrangement of the lid imagery, with the Lunar Maize God and corresponding identifying factors, is comparable to imagery of the Skyband Bench in structure 8N-11 located to the northeast of the palace at Copan (Webster et al.1998). In contrast with Woodfill et al.'s (2012) assertion that the pseudoglyphs on the Hun Nal Ye are unintelligible, perhaps the current analysis suggests that the design of the pseudoglyphs and the figure of Side 4 could represent a regional variant (or homage) to the naming of 11 Copan rulers. There is material representation of the first 11 rulers from Burial XXXVII-4 within a royal tomb of the Chorcha structure encased within structure 10L-26 at Copan (Fash et al. 1992:110-113, Figure 7). Large ceramic effigy figures placed atop lids arranged within the burial chamber have been interpreted as representing the previous 11 Copan rulers (Fash 1991). Conversely, the glyphs could represent the names of local elites or subroyals who participated in the actual interment ceremonies, or the representation of specific kingdoms within the Alta Verapaz region, whose emblem glyphs are not presently known. Or the tableau could be a combination of both interpretations.

The temporal interpretations of the Hun Nal Ye coffer's date of creation continue to be debated. Woodfill and colleagues (2019a; Woodfill et al. 2012:98) offer a late phase of the Early Classic period based on their estimate of the glyphs and other imagery. Others suggest the coffer is fully within the Late Classic sequence (see Houston 2018:82; Houston et al. 2017). Another alternative view is that the lid was constructed during the end of the Early Classic (AD 600) and the coffer well into the Late Classic period (AD 800; Houston 2018).

Comparative depictions such as the Lunar Moon Maize God from the Copan Skyband Bench and the ceramics originating from the interior rooms of the Cancuen residence fall within the Coner phase of chronology at the site, which starts at AD 600 (Webster et al. 1999:333-334). The ceramic figurines that have been used in comparison with the imagery are regionally focused within Late Classic contexts. This study therefore does not definitively end modern opinions concerning when the coffer was commissioned. Based on the regional comparative material, however, the analysis of Woodfill et al. (2012:107) that the construction of the lid was separate in creation based on hieroglyphic and programmatic iconographic differences from the coffer is implausible. While they suggest the lid and the coffer could be from lowland artisans, this study, based on the Lunar Moon Maize God designs and the Paddler Gods identification, suggests the lid trends more toward communities to the east or just south of the Hun Nal Ye site—potentially the large city-center of Copan or communities near the Coban Valley region. The tentative stylistic connections of the Hun Nal Ye area to the Copan zone are bolstered by a separate intraregional study using chemical compositional analysis, which indicated the two figurine pieces recovered from a test unit within the palace at Cancuen originated from the east of Copan, near the area surrounding the El Cajon dam (Sears 2016:158). The coffer box has not been scientifically sourced, and visual analysis of the pseudoglyphs did not assist in specifying a region other than a lowland tradition (Woodfill et al. 2012:107). The present study, based on the imagery in comparison with regional material remains such as the ceramic figurines and the ceramic whistle boxes (which also have pseudoglyphs), posits the coffer was created by artisans within or near the Alta Verapaz region.

CONCLUSION

This study attempted to expand how Late Classic Maya ceramic figurines can be invested into the interpretive schema of regional actions and ritual patterning, which are not usually considered with other Maya remains. This use of comparative analysis has historic precedents within the Transversal area. In 1969, Robert Rands turned from analyzing Palenque ceramics to initiate a stylistic analysis of monumental stone sculptures as connective points to seek generalized degrees of association between the long distant polities of Palenque and Copan. Rands used examples from Copan, Quiriguá, Salinas de los Nueve Cerros, Tenam, Toniná, Chuctiepá, Palenque, and Tortuguero. He was trying to demonstrate that there were patterns that he and Tatiana Proskouriakoff viewed as consistent elements of representation for the office of rulership through large stelae monuments within the region. He also compared a different class of material remains, large-scale censers, which had ruler elements projected in a similar manner as the stone stelae to connect hallmarks of shared elements produced among the western, central and eastern communities of the Transversal region (Rands and Rands 1959). While Rands thought there were strong stylistic similarities between the city-states of Quirigua and Copan because of their proximity to one another, he left the door open for further work, using only the paltry evidence of one monument originating from Salinas de los Nueve Cerros as the connective point of evidence (1969:521).

The Hun Nal Ye coffer continues this comparative tradition by illustrating the potential influences of the southeastern Maya communities into the Alta Verapaz region. The creation of this box demonstrates the importance of the political theater that was necessary for elite continuation for power, both local and at a distance. This current research on the coffer and other contributions within this edited volume suggest that connections between eastern and western highland communities should be reassessed as well, in Rands' (1969:521) sentiment, "to fill the spatial gaps" for understanding relationships at the edges of the Lowland Maya.

7

Not All Distance Is Kilometric

Obsidian Procurement at Salinas de los Nueve Cerros and Cancuen

Chloé Andrieu and Edgar H. Carpio Rezzio

Cancuen and Salinas de Nueve Cerros are two of the major sites situated along the Transversal route that enable travel from east to west along the Guatemalan and Chiapanec highlands. As described in greater detail in Chapter 5, ceramic studies have evidenced many interactions between these two sites that were both involved in the highland-lowland trade of goods such as *achiote*, cacao, salt, jade and obsidian (Demarest et al. 2017). The recently defined Nueve Cerros-Chinaha sphere demonstrates the existence of a community tradition along that route, which extends from the Chixoy-Salinas River and east through Cancuen and seems to flourish during the Late Classic period. However, this ceramic group is not represented in the same quantities in either site or all along the Transversal. The presence of Nueve Cerros material throughout each of Cancuen's occupational phases shows that the two cities did maintain a close relationship throughout the Late Classic (Forné, Alvarado, and Torres 2011), but these relations and influences, though evident in the ceramics, are still difficult to understand.

In particular, certain data—such as the lack of fine paste imported from the Gulf, which is very common at Cancuen (Demarest 2013; Demarest et al. 2014; Forné, Alvarado, and Torres 2011; Forné et al. 2013)—are absent from Nueve Cerros. In addition, the scarcity of Cancuen's ceramics at Nueve Cerros indicates that although these two cities were in close interaction, they probably also had different networks and areas of influence that we need to document and understand. In this chapter, we compare the obsidian procurement between both sites to shed further light on the complex interactions between these two major cities of the Transversal border and the rest of the Maya area and their respective role in these specific interregional exchanges during the Late Classic.

PATTERNS IN THE IMPORTATION OF OBSIDIAN INTO THE MAYA LOWLANDS

Obsidian, naturally occurring volcanic glass, is widely regarded to be a very good marker of long-distance trade and routes because it can be chemically attributed to a precise source. Since the beginning of sourcing analysis in the 1970s, obsidian has been one of the major elements used for studying trading routes and exchange. Indeed, most maps representing precolumbian trading routes are based on obsidian analysis (Arnauld 1990; Clark 2003; Hammond 1972, 1973; Nelson and Clark 1989, 1990, 1998). Most syntheses done since then have shown clear-cut changes through time that are still difficult to interpret. Throughout history, three major obsidian sources were imported toward the Maya Lowlands: San Martin Jilotepeque, El Chayal, and Ixtepeque (Clark 1981). These same obsidian sourcing analyses also showed that there were two major routes between the highlands and lowlands. The first is the natural route of the Chixoy River (see Chapter 3), seemingly correlated to the distribution of the San Martin Jilotepeque and the El Chayal sources of obsidian. The second route is largely coastal and distributed the Ixtepeque source (Andrieu 2009; Golitko et al. 2012; Golitko and Feinman 2014; Hammond 1972, 1973; Nelson 1985, 1994, 2004).

Chronologically, a clear tendency has also been observed since the very beginning of obsidian sourcing analysis that continues to be confirmed with the incorporation of new data. San Martin Jilotepeque (SMJ) represented the majority of the acquired samples until the Late Preclassic, at which point El Chayal became the most common lowland source by a wide margin (Ford et al. 1997; Moholy-Nagy et al. 1984:115–116; Rice et al. 1985:598). Ixtepeque, in turn, overshadowed El Chayal during the Terminal Classic (Braswell 2003; Golitko et al. 2012; Hammond et al. 1984; Nelson 1985, 2004). Therefore, an important pattern of the distribution of obsidian sources would be related to trading routes—notably, the shift from the El Chayal to the Ixtepeque source representing a shift from inland to coastal routes (Golitko et al. 2012; Hammond et al. 1984; Nelson 2004, see Daniels and Braswell 2014).

There are punctual variations, of course. In general, though, each minority source rarely represents more than 3 to 9% of the analyzed Classic Lowland collections (Andrieu 2009; Braswell 2003:135–136; Johnson 1996; Nelson 2004; Rovner and Lewenstein 1997). Despite these punctual variations, the general tendency is the overwhelming preponderance of El Chayal obsidian in the lowlands during most of the Classic period (Andrieu 2009:167–177; Braswell et al. 2011:17; Nelson 2004:931).

Such a pattern raises many questions, especially when knowing the political divisions within the lowlands: since the three major obsidian sources are situated at equal distance to the lowlands, we should have similar quantities of each source in each site, or at least a higher variation in the composition of the obsidian procurement from one site to another. On the contrary, we observe this strong homogeneity of obsidian procurement, with El Chayal generally representing between 70 and 90% of the lowland importations during the Classic Period, whatever the distance to the source (Andrieu 2009:167–177; Braswell et al. 2011:17; Nelson 2004:931). This relative homogeneity raises many questions and cannot be explained only by a competition between trading routes (the coastal versus the inland one), as has often been suggested (Hammond 1986; Nelson 1989). Even if this hypothesis could explain the Late Classic shift from the El Chayal to the Ixtepeque distribution network, it cannot explain why SMJ stops being imported to the lowlands at the end of the Preclassic period, since this source is only 40 km away from the El Chayal source and connected to the same inland routes (Nelson 1994:59).

One explanation could involve the sociopolitical alliances involved in distribution networks: the intermediary that distributed El Chayal obsidian probably developed significantly more relations with the lowlands than the ones that exploited SMJ. In fact, the quantitative data show that all lowland cities were not involved in the same way or to the same extent in obsidian distribution (Hutson et al. 2010; Sydris 1976; Woodfill and Andrieu 2012). Rather, some of them played more prominent roles than others as intermediary relays in these networks. These cities could have been more directly involved in the El Chayal network, serving as distribution centers for other parts of the lowlands. However, many aspects of these obsidian distribution networks are yet to be understood, in particular since the excavations made at SMJ by Geoffrey Braswell clearly showed that the Classic period was a period of major exploitation of these obsidian mines and corresponded to significant investment and development of the sites around the mines (Braswell 1996, 1998, 2002). The question is, therefore, where did that obsidian go after the Preclassic period, and which intermediary redistribution cities were tied to each source? The only way of understanding these patterns is by having a clearer idea of the provisioning chain between the highlands and lowlands as well as the distribution sphere associated with each obsidian source.

A critical examination of the obsidian recovered from Cancuen and Nueve Cerros, the two primary sites in the transition zone between the highlands and lowlands, is therefore crucial. Such an examination would enable an understanding of the way these different source materials were transported toward the lowlands and the mechanisms of such systems through time, as well as the economic interactions between and within each region. Both Cancuen and Nueve Cerros present numerous hints of being implicated in interregional trade. Cancuen is a major Late Classic river port with very strong evidence of large-scale production and exchange of both obsidian and jade artifacts, whereas Nueve Cerros is a site with a longer occupation, from the Preclassic to the Postclassic, similarly involved in the large-scale extraction and exchange of salt, figurines, and other goods. Both sites were contemporaneous during the Late Classic and in close interaction with each other, as shown by the ceramic and figurine analysis (Sears 2016; see also Chapter 6). Both sites had a possible redistribution role of the obsidian toward the rest of the Maya Lowlands. They are both situated at the same distance to both sources, though Nueve Cerros could be considered closer to SMJ since it is located on the banks of the Chixoy River.

CANCUEN: A MAJOR ACTOR IN THE EL CHAYAL DISTRIBUTION NETWORK

The obsidian collection from Cancuen represents 14,693 fragments collected between 1999 and 2016, mostly recovered from the site epicenter and dating to its very short occupation, between AD 600 and 800. For that reason, we can assume that the totality of the collection dates from the Late Classic. The majority of the collection corresponds to the prismatic blade production process. As a matter of fact, the Cancuen collection is composed of 9,954 prismatic blade fragments and 784 complete prismatic cores, as well as error correction of prismatic blade production. The remaining obsidian artifacts were composed of percussion flakes, a few flake tools (scrapers, drills), bifacial industries, macro blades, and small, unclassified fragments.

The overall lack of cortical fragments: ($n = 48$), the scarcity of primary series blades, and the absence of any flakes corresponding to the preforming of the cores indicate that the material was brought into the epicenter as already prepared cores. The high number of prismatic cores, in comparison with the quantity of prismatic blade fragments, likely implies that prismatic blades were exported outside of the epicenter (see Demarest et al. 2014).

The collection has been entirely visually sourced by us after years of training. The accuracy was verified by selecting 363 obsidian artifacts that were sent to the MURR for X-ray fluorescence (XRF) analysis under the direction of Michael Glascock in July 2014 (Glascock 2014). Of particular interest in the XRF sample was honing the differences between Ixtepeque and El Chayal, as well as possible Mexican obsidian, which is generally harder to recognize on a visual basis (Moholy-Nagy 2003).

The classification's success rate was 94%, enabling us to consider the visual classification of the rest of the collection correct (Braswell et al. 2000). Therefore, if we extend the XRF analysis of 363 artifacts to the rest of the collection that was visually classified, we would have a normal "Late Classic" lowland obsidian procurement pattern, with an almost exclusive majority (93.2%) of El Chayal obsidian at the site.

In spite of a few specificities in the composition of the assemblage, such as the relative abundance of Mexican sources ($n = 281$), the general tendency in its composition corresponds to what could be considered a very typical Classic lowland importation pattern. A full 98% of the prismatic cores could be attributed to El Chayal (Figure 7.1), and the very high quantity of cores in comparison with any other lowland site would clearly point to a pattern of exportation of El Chayal obsidian toward the lowlands in form of prismatic blades. Since the discrepancy between cores and blades in Cancuen is so high, and since the size of the cores shows that they were not all exhausted, it is also probable that much of the obsidian just transited through the site to be exchanged with settlements farther into the lowlands. Therefore, it is highly probable that Cancuen was one of the major actors in the distribution of the El Chayal source during the Late Classic period, responsible for exporting massive quantities of the glass into the lowlands.

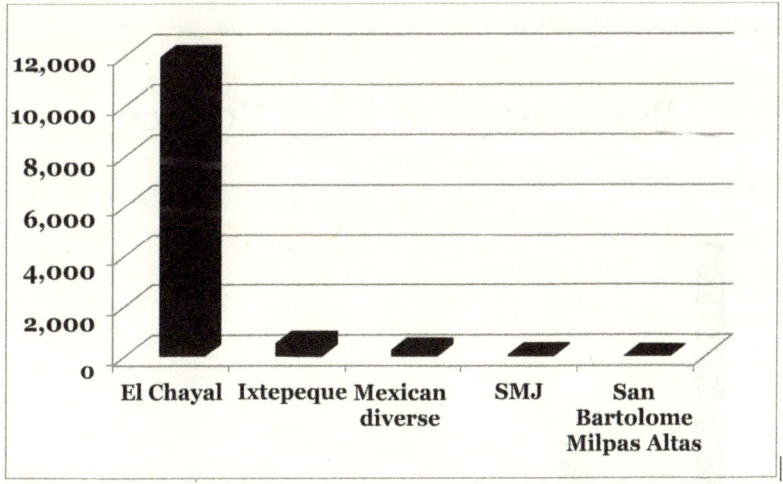

Figure 7.1. Frequency of different obsidian sources found from the Cancuen assemblage based on both visual sourcing and X-ray fluorescence (XRF) testing. SMJ = San Martin Jilotepeque. (Courtesy of Chloé Andrieu.)

SALINAS DE LOS NUEVE CERROS: A PREPONDERANCE OF SAN MARTÍN JILOTEPEQUE

The obsidian collection from Salinas de Nueve Cerros is composed of 30,257 obsidian artifacts coming from different neighborhoods within the urban zone—namely, Tortugas, Pie del Cerro, Tierra Blanca, and Santa Lucia Lachua, as well as from several caves. The composition of the collection is very different from the Cancuen one. From a chronological perspective, Nueve Cerros has a much longer occupation, from the Preclassic to the Postclassic period. However, 70% of the material from this collection could be securely attributed by ceramic association to the Late Classic period. Looking at the assemblage itself, project archaeologists recovered only 127 prismatic cores and 15,925 prismatic blade fragments from the site, indicating a very different pattern of use and making it unlikely that prismatic blades were exported from the site. Other artifact types like ridge blades and irregular blades are also present in the collection, as well as plunging blades that correspond to some error while reducing prismatic cores and indicate local blade production. Almost the half of the collection is composed of hard percussion flakes, a pattern that is much more common in highland collections and relatively scarce in the lowlands.

All the material has been visually classified (Figure 7.2), and 182 were additionally verified by a portable XRF machine owned by Bárbara Arroyo. Surprisingly, if we take into account only the Late Classic material, it appears that most of this material could be attributed to the SMJ source. These data are particularly surprising since it makes Salinas de Nueve Cerros a unique site compared with any other lowland Classic epicenters.

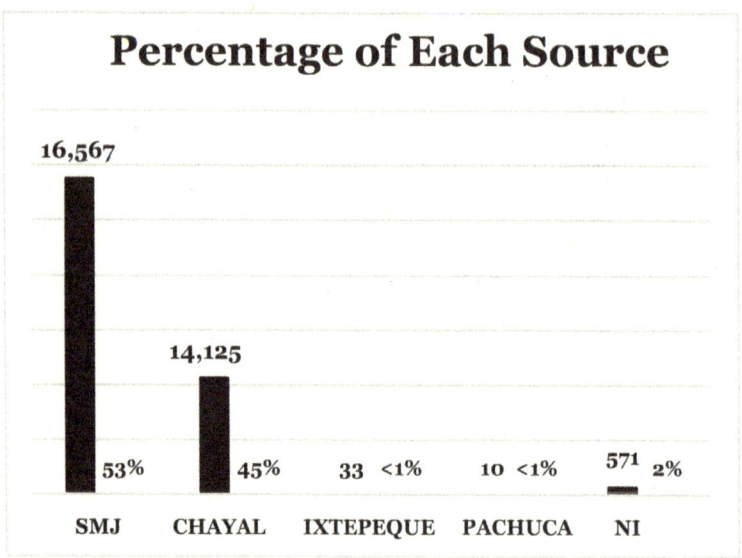

Figure 7.2. Frequency of different obsidian sources found in the Salinas de los Nueve Cerros assemblage based on both visual sourcing and X-ray fluorescence (XRF) testing. Note the dominance of the local Guatemalan sources (SMJ, Chayal) with little accumulated materials from the obsidian sources in Mexico. SMJ = San Martin Jilotepeque. NI = Mexican sources. (Edgar H. Carpio Rezzio)

However, the distribution of the obsidian sources within the site is very uneven. As a matter of fact, there appears to be a clear difference between the site epicenter (Pie del Cerro group) and the Tortugas group on one side, both of which present between 90 and 83% of El Chayal obsidian, respectively, and the Tierra Blanca group on the other, which has the highest percentage of SMJ, 82.2%, for the same period ($n = 22,872$). This highly variable pattern within the same site and same time period raises many questions that are yet to be answered on the social distribution of different obsidian sources. While not all obsidian is securely dated yet, if we take the sample from Tierra Blanca Sebol, one of the five compounds that constitute the Tierra Blanca group and the one that is primarily Late Classic, the SMJ obsidian represents 95% of the total ($n = 1,950$ total artifacts). It is therefore the first evidence of a Late Classic Maya Lowland site having a majority of SMJ obsidian. Such specificity could be related to the ease of transport from this source to Nueve Cerros along the Chixoy River but would not explain why multiple neighborhoods in the site have a majority of El Chayal obsidian.

If we look at the spatial distribution of the SMJ obsidian, 87.6% of the entire site assemblage is concentrated in the Tierra Blanca group, of which 86.2% corresponds to SMJ obsidian. Such data raise the question of the kind of activities that were held in that part of Salinas de Nueve Cerros and the possibility that this group had different networks of interactions compared with the rest of the site. There are therefore three important characteristics to consider about Nueve Cerros' obsidian procurement: the apparent increase in obsidian importation during the Late Classic occupation within the Tierra Blanca Group, the clear difference in the procurement between the epicenter and the Tierra Blanca Group (although this will have to take more refined chronological data when it becomes available), and, finally, the considerable amount of San Martin Jilotepeque obsidian in the Late Classic procurement of the site, standing in stark contrast to any known lowland Late Classic Maya city.

DISCUSSION

The obsidian evidence enables us to show that both sites had an important role in regional obsidian consumption and interregional obsidian distribution during the Late Classic period. However, the source analysis shows that they probably had different areas of influence and networks at that same period. The data from Cancuen clearly points toward the El Chayal network and shows that this site was very likely involved in the exchange of El Chayal obsidian toward the rest of the lowlands (Demarest et al. 2014). Nueve Cerros, in contrast, presents a pattern indicating that certain parts of the site were more connected to the San Martin Jilotepeque networks at that same moment.

The Nueve Cerros data are surprising for a lowland Classic Maya site. As a matter of fact, from the beginning of the Early Classic, SMJ obsidian has always been, without exception, a minority source in lowland Classic sites' obsidian collections. Therefore, the very first point to underline is the uniqueness of the Nueve Cerros results, which could indicate this site had developed and maintained other networks that were distinct from those of most of the lowland sites. Indeed, if SMJ was never very widely distributed in the Maya Lowlands during the Classic period, it did continue to be exchanged during the Classic period in other regions. In particular, it represents the majority of the Late Classic obsidian importation at most sites in Chiapas, Soconusco (Clark et al. 1989:Table 12-1; Nelson 2004), and in Late Classic San Andres Semetabaj (Carpio Rezzio 2016) in the Guatemalan highlands, as well as in the central Pacific Coast sites (Carpio Rezzio 2004). The Late Classic SMJ network was probably oriented toward the west and south then, with very little attention paid to the central and southern Maya Lowlands. In fact, Braswell underlined the importance of the nexus between the iconography found in the SMJ region and the Pacific Coast during the Classic period (Braswell 1998:154). This data would maybe indicate a kind of SMJ distribution sphere for the Late Classic that contrasted with the El Chayal sphere that covered the Maya Lowlands during the same period. If we follow that hypothesis, Nueve Cerros, or at least certain neighborhoods within Nueve Cerros, were probably looking more toward the Chiapan highlands to the west and the Guatemalan highlands to the south than they were toward the Maya Lowlands, at that moment at least, whereas the epicenter seems to be connected to the "traditional" lowland El Chayal networks. The political relations and networks between sites are more important than the geographical distance is in understanding the drawing of trading routes from one site to another.

However, there is a strong spatial discrepancy in the distribution of the SMJ source within Nueve Cerros that obliges us to fine-tune this hypothesis. Several neighborhoods at the site, including the Epicenter and the Tortugas group, do present a more typical lowland pattern, with a majority of El Chayal obsidian. These data point toward a difference in the procurement and function of the obsidian imported into the site as well as possible social or political factors. Such a hypothesis reminds us of Rice's interpretation of the obsidian pattern found in the rural area between Tikal and Yaxha (Rice 1984), which showed that in these particular zones far away from major cities, SMJ was still very present, even during the Late Classic period (Ford et al. 1997).

Since more material in rural areas is from the San Martin Jilotepeque source and "minor" sources, material from these sources may have been, for any number of reasons (functional or other), less preferred or valued than that from El Chayal and was shunted off to lower-status rural consumers (Rice 1984:191). This would imply that political or cultural parameters prevailed over geographic proximity in the distribution patterns of both obsidian sources. Indeed, SMJ, when present in Late Classic lowland assemblages, seems to be more associated with peripheral networks, unlike the central upper-class networks around the epicenters that El Chayal enjoyed.

In fact, few source analyses are available from peripheral zones, but when we do have access to such contexts, they show the same tendency. We do not have much data on areas far outside of the epicenters (places that are rarely excavated), and we can see that the SMJ obsidian seems to continue to be imported even during the Classic period. Haines and Glascock (2012) in Belize also showed that the SMJ obsidian tended to be distributed in modest or peripheral areas, whereas the El Chayal one was more exclusively concentrated in the civic ceremonial centers and especially in the lithic deposits. Therefore, that could indicate that SMJ and El Chayal distribution would have been socially conditioned within the Maya Lowlands: El Chayal perhaps would be more clearly associated with elite and civic ceremonial contexts in the Classic Maya Lowlands, whereas SMJ would be related to more peripheral groups. In that case, again, the most important factor to explain distribution patterns would be social, not geographic, proximity. Therefore, the famous "disappearance" of SMJ in the Maya Lowlands after the Late Preclassic would only be an effect of our tendency to focus on monumental architecture in and near site cores.

Therefore, the study of Nueve Cerros and Cancuen's obsidian enables us to fine-tune our perception of the obsidian distribution networks and trading routes. Future studies are needed to refine the El Chayal and SMJ distribution routes in the highlands and to try to eventually associate them with different cultural or political entities in that region, which is still so poorly understood.

8

The Prehispanic and Colonial Exchange of Perishable Goods in and through the Northern Transversal Strip

Achiote, Cacao, Salt, and Exotic Feathers

BRENT K. S. WOODFILL, MARK W. LENTZ, AND MEGAN E. LEIGHT

THE NORTHERN TRANSVERSAL, especially the Chixoy Valley around Salinas de los Nueve Cerros, had some of the most fertile soil in the Maya Lowlands because of the river's origins in the volcanic highlands. Thus, it would have likely been a breadbasket for multiple agricultural commodities, including achiote and cacao, among others. This hypothesis is still being investigated by the Nueve Cerros paleoecology team (Avendaño and del Cid 2017; also see Chapter 11).

This chapter focuses on four perishable commodities—achiote, cacao, salt, and exotic feathers—that are largely or completely invisible in the archaeological record due to the realities of preservation in a harsh tropical environment. They were, nonetheless, among the most important trade goods in the precolumbian and colonial economies. Each of these commodities likely traveled through the same economic networks, as detailed in Chapter 2. As discussed briefly below, the region was also home to an abundance of fish (Dillon 1981; Salazar 2000) that were dried and salted. There is indirect evidence of a local salted-meat industry at Nueve Cerros (Woodfill et al. 2015; Woodfill 2020).

TRANSVERSAL AGRICULTURAL GOODS: ACHIOTE AND CACAO

Cacao and achiote (Figure 8.1) were likely the most important agricultural commodities produced in the Northern Transversal Strip. Both are the fruit of trees that have a relatively restricted environmental niche. Cacao is cultivated in shady areas under 650 m above sea level with consistent precipitation and soil moisture and typically at least 127 cm of precipitation per year (Feldman 1985:84; McBryde 1971:33). Likewise, achiote pods grow on a tropical evergreen shrub most comfortable in regions with between 125 and 150 cm of annual rainfall (Donkin 1974:33). While both cacao and achiote were cultivated and exchanged in massive quantities both before and after the conquest, cacao has received the lion's share of scholarly attention, likely due to its central role as both commodity and currency along with its global importance today.

Figure 8.1. Primary and secondary cacao growing regions (light grey) and quetzal harvesting zones (dark grey) in eastern Mesoamerica. (Base map made in Fresco. Courtesy of Luís Fernando Luin, modified by Brent K. S. Woodfill with data from Feldman 1985, Guarino 2011, and McNeil 2006:2.)

In precolumbian Mesoamerica, multiple varieties of cacao and achiote, all of which fruited twice per year, were harvested and exchanged (Caso Barrera and Aliphat Fernández 2006a:290, 300; Feldman 1985:84; Lowe et al. 1982:47). Cultivated and wild varieties of *Theobroma cacao*, as well as a related species called *pataxte*, are treated as the same commodity in the chapter. Cacao trees produce large pods that contain 20–50 seeds, or "beans," suspended in a wet meat with a sour flavor reminiscent of a green apple. The meat was removed and the beans fermented before they were dried and roasted. Then they were ready for trade or consumption, typically as a cold, frothy drink. Cacao trees and pods figure prominently in the iconographic record, with examples ranging from the Maize God embodying a cacao tree to trees emerging from anthropomorphic figures (Figure 8.2; e.g., Green 2010; Martin 2006; McNeil 2006a; Stuart 2006a; Vail 2009). Cacao trees are often associated with the axis mundi trees of creation; the canopy offered by Maya forest gardens produced the shade needed to allow cacao to grow and thrive, leading to cacao's association with the Underworld and the birth of the Maize God. Martin (2006) has an excellent discussion of the fusion of the Maize God motif and cacao iconography as they occur repeatedly in the canon together.

Figure 8.2. Unprovenienced Late Classic polychrome vessel (K631) of a palace scene with a fruitful cacao tree emerging from a prone human figure. Woman at center on the ground uses a mano and metate to grind food into a powder or paste. (Photograph by Justin Kerr, Justin Kerr Maya archive, Dumbarton Oaks, Trustees for Harvard University, Washington, DC.)

Achiote (*Bixa orellana* L., also called annatto), in contrast, produces smaller spiny and nonbristled pod varieties that contain 10–50 tiny red seeds. The seeds contain a natural, edible red dye. Each tree can produce between 0.5 to 1 kg of seeds per year, with annual yields of between 300 and 600 kg per hectare (Math et al. 2016). The seeds were separated from the pods and converted to loaves and balls either by mashing the seeds in water and collecting the precipitation or by boiling them down into a thick paste that is strained and dried in the sun (Donkin 1974:40). Achiote was discussed in sixteenth- to-eighteenth-century ethnographic manuscripts (Donkin 1974; Ingram and Francis 1969; McBryde 1971; Miksicek et al. 1981; Miranda 1953–1954; Vázquez de Ágredos Pascual et al. 2010), but it had fallen out of favor in Europe and many of its colonies by the eighteenth century due to its unstable color and variation (Vazquez de Ágredos Pascual et al. 2010:97).

Achiote continued to be used as a red colorant for the chocolate drink and as a red dye for textiles well into the Colonial Period, as is particularly well documented among the Lakandon (Caso Barrera and Aliphat Fernández 2006a; Pugh 2006; Tozzer 1907). Ethnohistorical texts by Alonso de Zorita, Fray Diego de Landa, and Martín de la Cruz include specific descriptions of the use of achiote (see Vázquez de Ágredos Pascual et al. 2010:99). Several chroniclers likened the red-dyed drinks to blood; bloodletting rituals and bleeding cacao pods frequently occur during the precolumbian period (Figure 8.3; Alvarado 1924 [1525]; see McNeil 2006a:15 for a discussion).

Figure 8.3. Bloodletting ritual with cacao (or possibly achiote) and incense offerings from the *Codex Tro-Cortesianus* (*Madrid Codex*). Akademische Druck- und Verlagsanstalt, Graz, 1967. Museo de América, Madrid, Spain. (Courtesy of Hannah Kitzmann.)

The two most famous cacao-producing regions in the Maya world were Soconusco, on the Pacific Coast of Chiapas, and Chontalpa, on the Tabascan Gulf Coast (see Figure 8.1; Caso Barrera and Aliphat Fernández 2006a:291; Gasco 1996; Jones 1989:103; McNeil 2006a; Thompson 1956). Although the southern lowlands were a major consumer of cacao from the Preclassic through the conquest of the Itza in the late seventeenth century, only the Transversal, Izabal basin, and Belizean river valleys had the proper conditions for the trees to thrive (Caso Barrera and Aliphat Fernández 2006a:291, 297; Jones 1989:102–103). By the sixteenth century, these three smaller sources were the primary cacao producers for the southern lowlands. Soconusco, already separated from the lowlands by the Sierra Madre mountains, had been incorporated into the Aztec Empire, and the residents of Chontalpa were at war with the Itza (Jones 1989:103).

Recent studies suggest cenotes and other dry sinkholes in the Yucatan may have been used to cultivate a rare variety of the cacao plant associated with the Lacandon region (Gómez-Pompa et al. 1990; Vail 2009:7). While the peninsula boasts a climate typically too dry and too shallow to cultivate the crop, wild cacao discovered in three different shaded cenotes south of Valladolid confirm the ability to grow this precious resource in microclimates (Gómez-Pompa et al. 1990:247). This discovery aligns with sixteenth-century chroniclers' documenting cacao growth in "sacred groves" across the Yucatan, from Bishop Diego de Landa reporting from Valladolid in 1566 to Gaspar Antonio Chi at Mayapan in 1582 (Gómez-Pompa et al. 1990:250, quoted from Tozzer 1941:164, 230–232).

While scholars long continued to doubt the potential for cacao cultivation in the Yucatan, multiple eighteenth-century chronicles have mentioned cacao groves there (Roys 1939; Sánchez de Aguilar 1937). In addition, the ethnobotanical evidence of wild cacao cultivation in the Yucatan is supported by iconographic representations in the artistic canon. Several motifs long presumed to be cenotes supporting cacao plants seem to reflect these precious microclimates. An Early Postclassic capstone from the Temple of the Owls (Str. 5C7) at Chichen Itza shows the god K'awiil, who represents sustenance and abundance, emerging from the mouth of a serpent surrounded by a large U-shape symbol for "cenote" (Glyph T591; Figure 8.4; Gómez-Pompa et al. 1990:253). Cacao pods dangle above the god's head and below in the sinkhole, while K'awiil holds other precious foodstuffs in his arms (Gómez-Pompa et al. 1990:255; Vail 2009:8). This image corresponds to others noted in the *Madrid Codex* by Vail (2009:8).

Ethnohistoric records describe the nature of cacao production during the years leading up to and after the Spanish conquest. Individual landholders owned dense groves of cacao. Each hectare had about 625 trees that were

Figure 8.4. God K'awiil emerging from a sinkhole surrounded by cacao pods and quetzal feathers. Early Postclassic painted capstone from Chichen Itza's Temple of the Owls (5C7), Yucatan, Mexico. (Courtesy of Luís Fernando Luin.)

often interspersed with achiote and vanilla and could produce around 410 kg per year (Caso Barrera and Aliphat Fernández 2006a:290, 300; Córdoba-Avalos et al. 2001; Gasco 1996:391–392). Early colonial records from one village in Soconusco (Gasco 1996:391–393) show that every Indigenous head of the household had between 400 and 3,200 trees, averaging 1,580 per family. Interestingly, the village leader owned a grove that was under the mean size, with 1,200 trees, indicating grove size was not necessarily correlated with status.

Achiote and cacao were used as tribute items and medicine in addition to serving as prestige foodstuffs and ritual offerings. Scenes featuring these items are often laden with meaning and conflate one or more ideas regarding Mesoamerican myth. One complicated scene from an unprovenienced Late Classic polychrome vessel (K631, see Figure 8.2) depicts a large cacao tree, heavy with ripened pods, emerging from an anthropomorphic figure lying prone on the ground. Martin suggests the other figures are K'awiil and God L, who often accompany scenes with cacao (Kerr 1989:29; Martin 2006:169). God L, also known as the merchant god, is seen facing a large cacao tree laden with fruit pods on a mural painting at Cacaxtla. This seems to denote the use of cacao as a form of currency and exchange during trade (Dreiss and Greenhill 2010:90–91, Figure 10; Martin 2006:170). Other precolumbian scenes conflate the idea of fruitful abundance and human figures; the scenes lining the sides of King Pakal's sarcophagus from Palenque feature ancestors sprouting from nance, cacao, and even avocado trees (see Martin 2006:161–162; Schele and Freidel 1990:221), and another Late Classic polychrome (K5615) features the disembodied head of either the Maize God or Hunahpu in the Underworld sprouting from a cacao tree in the shape of a pod.

Achiote, chile, and vanilla were often added to chocolate to improve the flavor, and in the case of achiote and chile, the aesthetics transformed it into a red drink resembling the blood to which it was already metaphorically linked (Bergmann 1959:28; Feldman 1985:86; see discussion in McNeil 2006:15). The key to successful preparation of the drink involved the creation of a large amount of foam (Durand-Forest 1967:163–164; Green 2010:315; Landa 2013; Reents-Budet 2006:217) produced by pouring the cold liquid repeatedly from an elevated position to allow for greater aeration of the beverage. Iconographic representations of cacao drink production emphasize the foam and the spectacle of cacao preparation, with images of women deliberately pouring liquid from one vessel to another at great height differences, as seen on the Princeton Vase (K511; Reents-Budet 2006:116) and others depicting persons holding vessels over their heads and pouring (Durand-Forest 1967:166; Green 2010:325–327).

As discussed below, cacao was one of the most important commodities in the Mesoamerican economy, with millions of kilograms of beans circulating Mexico and the Maya world annually. Achiote composed a much smaller percentage of the market but was still significant in its own right. In the seventeenth century, over 16,000 kg were exported from Verapaz and Izabal alone (Villagutierre 1983:106), and Friar Morán reported that just one Manche' Ch'ol town had a yearly yield of about 1,000 kg (Caso Barrera and Aliphat Fernández 2006a:302).

SALT FROM THE NORTHERN TRANSVERSAL

Salt is a surprisingly controversial topic in Maya archaeology, having been the subject of a long-standing debate as to who provided salt into the southern lowlands and even, for a spell, whether salt was necessary (Andrews 1980, 1983, 1984, 1998; Dillon 1988; Dillon et al. 1988; MacKinnon and Kepecs 1991; Marcus 1984, 1991; Márquez Morfín 1982; Mock 1994; Pohl 1985; Valdez and Mock 1991; White et al. 1993). For many years, Anthony Andrews (1980, 1983, 1984, 1998) suggested the Gulf Coast of the Yucatan provided the majority of the salt consumed throughout the Maya Lowlands based on the known importance of multiple saltworks there. This model has largely fallen out of favor within the field (Andrews and Mock 2002; McKillop 2002, 2005, 2019; Woodfill et al. 2015, see Hutson 2017), as the southern lowlands appear to have been largely economically isolated from its northern neighbors (at least as far as the archaeological record indicates, see Chapter 11) and had access to at least two much closer sources: Salinas de los Nueve Cerros and coastal Belize. Nueve Cerros had the added benefit of being located along the Chixoy/Salinas/Usumacinta River, allowing it to be easily transported throughout much of the western lowlands as well as into the highlands, although there they would have competed with saltworkers at multiple other sources, like Sacapulas and San Mateo Ixtatan (Figure 8.5). The Caribbean salt sources were part of an extant trade network, evinced by the presence of Belize Red ceramics, which were present as far inland as Ceibal (Chase and Chase 2012; Laporte et al. 2008).

Woodfill (2017) compared the salt production at Nueve Cerros with the southern Belize industry, focusing on the salt production methodology, the evidence for derivative industries, and the possible markets for each source based on imported objects. Nueve Cerros and southern Belize both produced salt cakes out of brine during the Late Classic period. They were both found in very different contexts—small coastal settlements drawing from the Caribbean versus an inland city surrounding a salt dome from which a constant stream of brine flowed into a major river. In spite of this difference, speaking in broad strokes, both sites used the same methods for salt production:

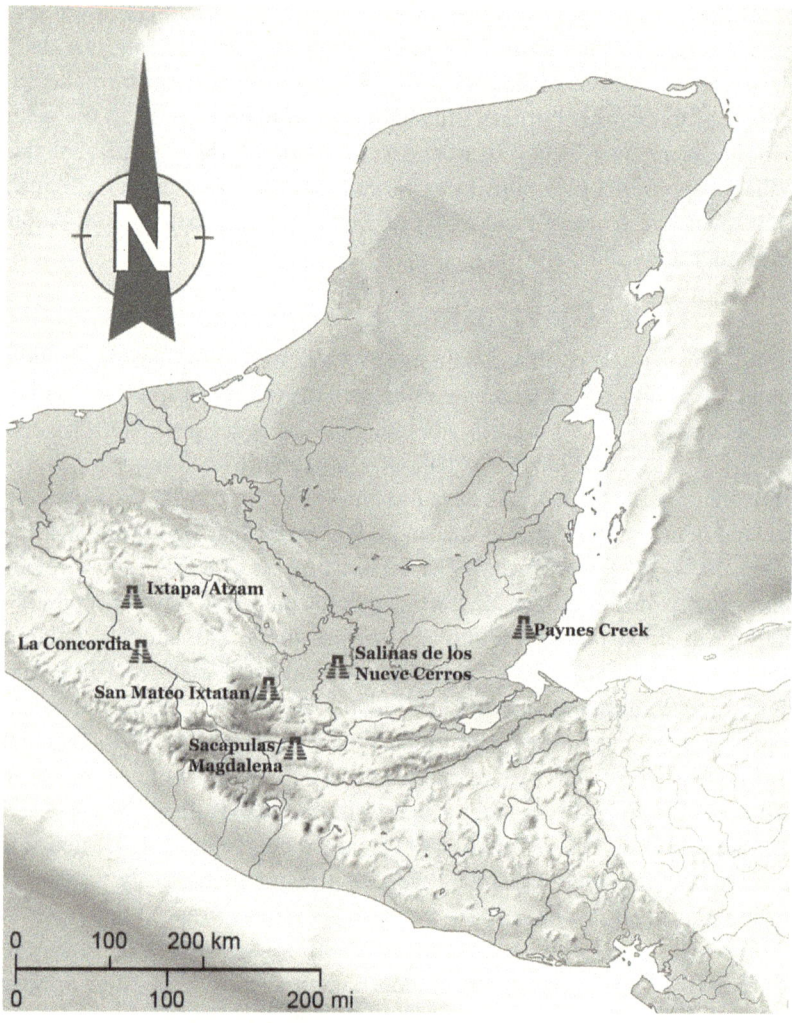

Figure 8.5. Salt sources in and around the southern Maya lowlands (Map made in Photoshop, modified by Brent K. S. Woodfill from Freiwald et al. 2021.)

boiling and leaching with some solar evaporation. Both sites focused primarily on briquetage (very coarse pottery) to make and shape the finished salt loaves—single-use molds were placed over an open fire to boil off the liquid. Residents of both sites took advantage of solar evaporation to thicken the brine beforehand, either through sections of the Caribbean with high salinity (e.g., the natural shallow lagoon at Paynes Creek, or the salt flats and large Atzam Red bowls [Figure 8.6c] scattered throughout the salt production zone at Nueve Cerros [McKillop 2002, 2005; Sills and McKillop 2013; Woodfill et al. 2015]).

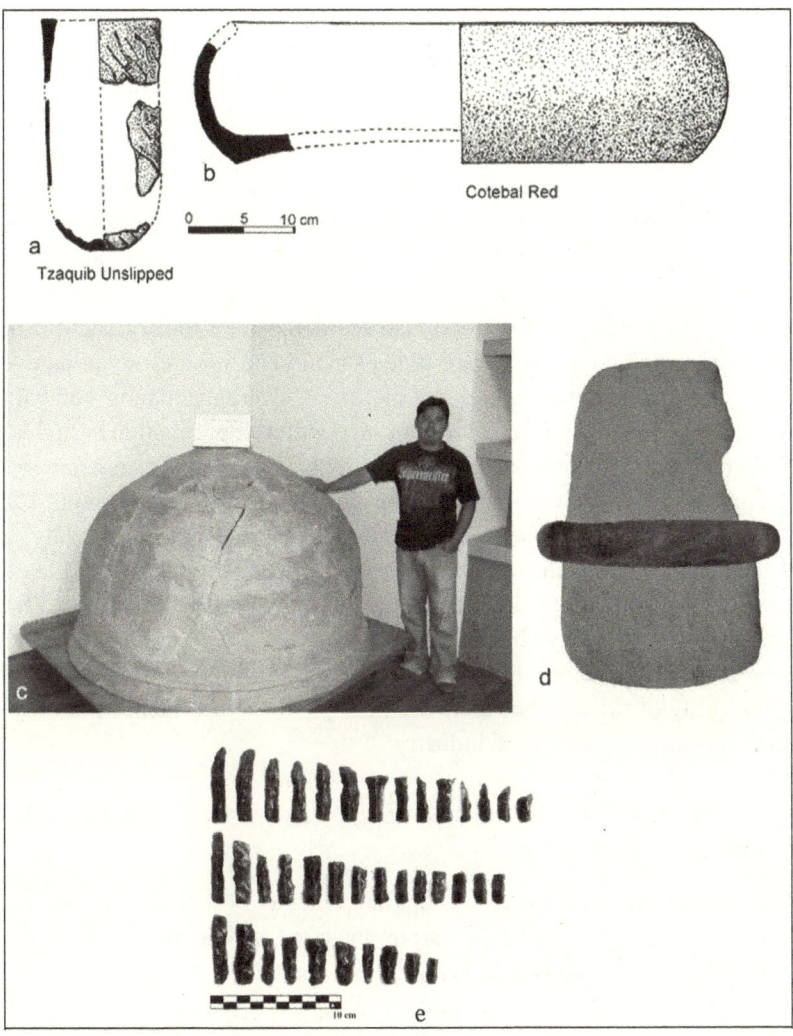

Figure 8.6. Specialized tools associated with the Nueve Cerros salt industry: (a) roughly made conical mold, (b) large flat mold, (c) brine storage vessel (upside down, with Carlos Efraín Tox Tiul for scale), (d) overhanging mano with associated metate, (e) probable obsidian fish descalers. (Courtesy of Carlos Efraín Tox Tiul [a, b], Brent K. S. Woodfill [c], and Blanca Mijangos [d, e].)

There were some differences in the details. Nueve Cerros focused on two different "types" of salt loaves—narrow, conical cylinders and wide salt cakes—which required two different mold types (see Figure 8.6a–b), unlike what appears to be a single form in southern Belize. Nueve Cerros also produced some of the largest ceramic objects in the Americas—the Atzam Red bowls—to begin to concentrate the brine, since it was harvested from an active stream instead of a shallow bay. It is likely they were also making shallow evaporating pools along the length of the stream, although neither Dillon nor the current project has found conclusive evidence of this so far.

The archaeological site of Nueve Cerros was located within a dense area of urban sprawl that covered about 50 km^2, although it is unclear whether it all represents the same polity. Because of its size, it is probable that not all the residents would have been directly involved in salt production, but there would have been multiple ways for people to take advantage of the salt and salt trade to work in derivative industries. The crux of the argument is that we have found an otherwise rare style of mano and metate—64 to date—in every neighborhood throughout the site. These "overhang manos" and paired metates (see Figure 8.6d) are still associated with salt production in highland Guatemalan saltworks and are, after testing by the Guatemalan Ministry of Energy and Mines, covered with salt residue (Mijangos 2014; Woodfill 2020; Woodfill et al. 2015). These tools would have been used to grind the salt cakes into small grains, which would have served a variety of functions. Along the river, for example, the residents who received the finished cakes could have produced dried, salted fish. Unfortunately, neither fish scales nor bones have been recovered through flotation of multiple soil samples, likely due to the high acidity of the soil, but there are multiple lines of evidence pointing to this being an important local industry:

1. Each of the excavated mound groups shows evidence of large-scale fishing.

2. At least two of the mound groups had evidence of specialized obsidian biface production that Edgar Carpio suggested were used as fish descalers (see Figure 8.6e, Woodfill et al. 2015; Leight 2018; Leight and Woodfill 2017).

3. This stretch of the Chixoy contains some of the best fishing grounds in the Guatemalan interior (Dillon 1981). During his reconnoitering on the northern banks of the river in 2015, project member Alex Rivas reported that the residents collected an average of 10 kg of fish per person in weirs and creeks every time the river floods; were they not to collect these fish, they said the entire valley would soon smell of dead fish (Woodfill et al. 2018).

4. Fish weights and other associated paraphernalia have been recovered from multiple mound groups close to the Chixoy River, indicating a large-scale fishing industry (Leight 2018, 2020; Leight and Woodfill 2017).

Neighborhoods in the rest of the site also appear to have been loci for secondary commodities involving salt due to the presence of the same grinding tools. At least one group in the southern part of the site away from the river had a dense concentration of obsidian scrapers along with the overhang manos and metates. This neighborhood was far from the river but near a vast swath of land that was archaeologically "empty" but was likely used for agriculture and arboriculture, which would have also been prime hunting or husbandry grounds. The presence of specialized saltworking equipment indicates they also depended on large quantities of finished salt made in elite workshops, which was likely used in preserving meat and/or hides.

The salt production at Nueve Cerros was dependent on two other industries that would have been present at the site or in the surrounding hinterlands: (1) the large-scale production of ceramic molds, and (2) the careful management (and likely regular importation of) firewood. Firewood was, in fact, the driving engine of the entire saltworks, as it was needed not only to feed the fires that boiled down the brine but also to make the salt molds, household and service ceramic wares, and hearths that kept the residents fed daily. According to estimates made by drawing together observations in ethnography, chemistry, and local archaeology, each metric ton of salt would have necessitated 6.67 metric tons of firewood for boiling the brine and an additional 182 kg for the molds (Woodfill 2020).

SALT PRODUCTION THROUGH THE CONQUEST

After the collapse of Nueve Cerros, the salt source continued to be exploited by various ethnic groups. Without the large population buffering the zone from the world at large, however, no one exerted the same degree of authority as the residents of Nueve Cerros, tipping off a series of political plays. Southern lowlanders, Highland Maya, Spanish priests and soldiers, *ladino* landowners, urban municipal councils, and foreign oil companies have all come to the salt dome and flats, although none have managed to hold onto it for long.

As discussed in Chapters 3 and 11, Nueve Cerros and its saltworks continued to be important after the city was abandoned. Dominant merchant and salt-producing lineages in both the Guatemalan highlands and the northern lowlands claimed to have come from the city as a way to ground their high prestige. The saltworks themselves were formally under the control of the Akalaha Ch'ol when the Spaniards arrived. Ruud van Akkeren (2010:16) suggests the conversion of the Vera Paz to Christianity under Bartolomé de las Casas in the 1550s might have ultimately been a power play to control the saltworks, since it would have made the Q'eqchi' lord of Carcha, Don Juan Matal B'atz, the most powerful ruler in the region.

Akalaha control over the saltworks weakened after they were reduced by the Spaniards into a community called San Marcos closer to the highlands. After the ambush and death of Domingo de Vico in 1555, they were moved again, this time to a neighborhood of Coban. Any Akalaha hold over the region was sufficiently weakened at this point, which explains the reports that the salt source was exploited by neighboring Maya groups like the Lakandon and the highland Q'eqchi' (Bassie-Sweet et al. 2015; Dillon 1979; Sapper 1985; Woodfill 2019a).

After another rash of uprisings in the Transversal region in the early seventeenth century, Friar Francisco Morán petitioned the colonial authorities to send troops into the lowlands in 1627. Capitan Juan de Santiago Velasco was brought in to pacify the area, and he ordered an advance group, which included Morán, to scout the best path forward that same year (Tovilla 2000a:114–115, 2000b:117–118). The squadron traveled by foot and raft as far as Nueve Cerros, where they noted its "large and good-quality saltworks" (Tovilla 2000b:117) and decided to set up camp while awaiting further orders. Unbeknownst to them, however, a group of 140 Lakandon men were camped at the site boiling brine. The Lakandon retreated to the other side of the Chixoy and, after a brief debate, called off an ambush and let the Spaniards live (Tovilla 2000a:114–115, 2000b:117–118; Woodfill 2019a). The squadron camped at the site for several days, even after Captain Velasco ordered a retreat. After another round of letters, the party begrudgingly returned home (Tovilla 2000b:118).

The presence of a highly productive salt source outside of Spanish control was likely one of the factors that allowed the Lowland Maya to maintain their independence. The lack of oversight at Nueve Cerros was not for lack of interest, however. Salt exploitation and taxation were a major focus of Spanish royal policy in Guatemala. A royal cedula of 1573 ordered crown officials to monitor, supervise, and tax salt production (Archivo General de Centroamérica, 1573, 00428).

The increasing presence of Spaniards in the seventeenth century did not immediately curtail Indigenous salt extraction. The Lakandon, the colonial Ch'ol and, likely, the modern Yukatek speakers continued to harvest salt in the area decades after Tovilla's expedition. A 1696 map produced under the auspices of a Mercedarian friar, Diego de Ribas, marked Nueve Cerros as "Saltworks (*Salinas*) where they make salt from the water of a small river" ("Plano del territorio reconocido por fray Diego de Ribas en los alrededores del lago Petén Itzá," Archivo General de Indias, Mapas y Planos-Guatemala, 13, 1696). The friar made the connection to the Lakandon clear by showing a route from Dolores, the largest and main Lakandon settlement in the region, to the Nueve Cerros saltworks.

Evidently, the intensified military incursions and relocations of the late seventeenth century did lead to a downturn in Indigenous salt exploitation in the eighteenth century. References to the harvesting of salt after the 1600s are less common, although one passage hints that Dolores, which was simply the rechristened capital Sak Balam, may have continued to control the source. In a series of letters between Spanish governmental and ecclesiastical authorities bemoaning the scarcity of resources and the limited number of clergymen able and willing to serve in the area, senior priest Domingo Faxardo described Dolores as the "only community of Indians with any funds" (Archivo General de Centroamérica, A1.11.7, Exp. 3813, Leg. 186, 1800, f. 40v.). Unfortunately, the clergyman did not identify how Dolores remained a more resource-rich town than neighboring communities, but their control of salt may well explain their better-off situation compared with nearby settlements.

NORTHERN HIGHLAND EXOTIC FEATHER PRODUCTION

The feathers of multiple birds were important for the ancient and colonial Maya. This economy included lowland species like the scarlet macaw and the alo, both of which were kept in aviaries and regularly harvested by their keepers (Feldman 1985:90; Somerville et al. 2010). The rarest and most prized plumage was the long tail feather of the male resplendent quetzal, emerald green and reaching 90 cm in length (Johnsgard 2000:47). Unlike the other prized birds, quetzals have not survived in captivity until recently. They are unable to process iron, but their native habitat allows for both a low-iron diet and tannin accumulations in the water they drink, which pools in plants and puddles and is able to neutralize the little iron they do ingest (Tremain 2016:401). As a result, the collection of quetzal feathers required specialists to find the wild birds and harvest their plumage. They also needed regulations to ensure the supply remained constant and the birds themselves were not endangered.

Spanish chroniclers identified two locations in Guatemala able to sustain quetzal populations (see Figure 8.1): a small area on the slopes of Volcán Atitlan in the western highlands (Bowes and Allen 1969:142; Paez Betancor and Arboleda 1964, both quoted in Feldman 1985:90) and the large cloud forests in highland Verapaz around Cahabon, Chamelco, and Tucuru (Dieseldorff 1904; Pineda 1925; Sahagún 1963:20, all quoted in Feldman 1985:90) to the south of the Northern Transversal Strip. This latter source was also important for multiple commodities in the precolumbian market, including liquidambar, copal, and precious stones. However, only feathers will be considered here.

Quetzal typically carve their nests into rotten trees, using their beaks to gouge out an area large enough to fit between two and four eggs. Males and females take turns incubating the eggs before they hatch—females at night and males during the day. As a result of the nest construction and labor distribution, the prized male tail feathers are easy to spot; the forest floor below the nest will be littered with rotten wood chips, and the feathers will be visibly emerging from the small hole throughout the day. The birds reuse the same nests over time, which means that once a nest is located, collectors can return annually to harvest more feathers (Tremain 2016:402). During the breeding and nesting season, the birds are most visible and have the longest tail feathers (Tremain 2016:403).

Quetzal feathers were among the most important sumptuary goods in all of Mesoamerica (Gage 1958:210; de Remesal 1932:390; Viana et al. 1982), and their harvest was tightly controlled by highland *ajaws* (lords), who bequeathed certain individuals the rights to harvest the feathers in specifically bounded zones in the years leading up to the Spanish conquest (Tovilla 1960:142). The quetzal was a protected species, and killing one was punishable by death (Feldman 1985:90; Las Casas 1909:617; Viana et al. 1982:208). Feather collectors would trap the birds with cages, nets, or blowguns set up near food sources or around watering holes during the dry season (Crandall 1939; Feldman 1985:90; Hagen 1946; McBryde 1971:72; Miller and Taube 1993:140; Tremain 2016:404). The collectors also invented special traps that would snag the feathers and allow the birds to escape and grow new plumage by the following year (Tovilla 1960:142; Viana et al. 1982:208).

The collectors, at least during the Colonial Period and the years leading up to it, were also protected by the *ajaws*. Dieseldorff (1904) recounted a conflict between the lords of Carcha and Chamelco. The former killed the feather collectors of the latter, prompting the ruler of Chamelco to ask for "400 bundles of green feathers, a silver 'crown,' a silver 'string,' and 'some precious stones'" in recompense (Feldman 1985:90). When he was rebuffed, an army from Chamelco invaded Carcha and took one of the quetzal harvesting territories for himself. The lords of Chamelco belonged to the B'atz lineage, who were themselves well known for working with green feathers (Akkeren 2012:145–148).

Finally, there are several Classic period examples of trafficking a complete quetzal instead of just the feathers. Quetzal skeletons have been found in Early Classic tombs at Tikal and Copan (Tremain 2016:403), although this was likely rare. Both were royal contexts that involved conspicuous consumption as a sign of extreme power—killing the goose that lays the golden eggs, as it were. Outside of a few rare exceptions, however, the quetzal was a distant producer of an exotic commodity to be harvested in the Guatemalan cloud forests and brought into the lowlands through the Northern Transversal.

THE CONSUMPTION AND EXCHANGE OF PERISHABLE GOODS IN THE SOUTHERN LOWLANDS AND NORTHERN HIGHLANDS

The commodities described here have largely or completely disappeared from the archaeological record, but it is still possible to reconstruct some aspects of interregional exchange and consumption patterns using archaeology, iconography, epigraphy, and ethnohistory.

Reconstructing the Late Classic Salt Market

Unlike the other goods described in this chapter, salt had a much larger market that included the entire citizenry of each city-state since it was not a sumptuary good. In addition to the fact that the market was much more open for salt than it was for other perishable goods, salt was consumed at a much larger scale. New excavations at Calakmul have produced incredible murals around the main acropolis, leading researchers to speculate the market may have been more centrally positioned than previously assumed. Several new glyphs have been translated to include the positions held within the market, including *aj azt'aam*, "he/she of salt" (Hull 2010:251; Martin 2012).

Clearly, Nueve Cerros and southern Belize were producing enormous surpluses of salt for regional and interregional exchange. The question, then, becomes where the markets were located. Unfortunately, salt is a soluble mineral that vanishes from the archaeological record, and while there are significant differences in strontium levels (Freiwald et al. 2019) and potentially other rare elements in different salt sources that could show up in the bones of the consumers, this is still speculative. As a result, this discussion of the potential market of Nueve Cerros salt relies on geography and established trade networks for nonperishable commodities.

Although salt is hard to track, other artifacts are not, and it is possible to examine larger trends in the market by looking at the importation and exportation of other goods. Residents of southern Belizean saltworks like Paynes Creek were part of the larger chains of obsidian trade and did have inland ceramics and figurines, which furthers the evidence that they were providing salt to much of the southeastern Maya. Nueve Cerros is tightly connected to other sites along the southwestern lowlands and northern highlands through ceramics and figurines. Erin Sears (2016) has shown that there was a tight exchange network for high-quality figurines that included multiple cities from Chama and Nueve Cerros to Cancuen and the Petexbatun, and Nueve Cerros was importing vessels and ceramic styles from people from lowland and northern highland cities from the Middle Preclassic through the Classic collapse.

From the perspective of regional topography and hydrology, both southern Belize and Nueve Cerros would have had easy access to myriad Classic cities. The former could have easily supplied markets throughout southern Belize and up to (and possibly beyond) Caracol, as well as cities in the southeastern Guatemalan lowlands and down to (and possibly beyond) Lake Izabal. The Nueve Cerros salt, in contrast, could be transported by boat into the Great Western Trade Route, where it could have supplied the Usumacinta drainage and much of the southwestern and central Peten. The most likely factors to limit the market expansion for both saltworks would have been geographic, such as the Maya and Cuchumatan mountains, and economic, such as the reach of other saltworks along the Belizean and Gulf coasts and in the western highlands at Sacapulas and San Mateo Ixtatan.

Within the southern lowlands and adjacent northern highlands/piedmont, the biggest competitors for the salt market would likely have been Nueve Cerros and southern Belize, and we will very preliminarily place the likely division between the two markets in the natural watershed divide, where the rivers flow into the Caribbean versus the Gulf. There are several caveats to this model, however. It is possible that inland and coastal salt were valued and conceived differently or that their production was affected by seasonality more than we are aware of, which would allow both of the salts to be consumed in the same areas. It is possible that there were internal or external factors that could have affected short-term or long-term production scales or disrupted trade routes. It is also possible that the entire capitalist "us vs. them" economic model is fundamentally irrelevant in this context. We do see diversity in the obsidian streams: Ixtepeque, Jilotepeque, and even Zaragoza, Pachuca, and other Mexican sources were present throughout the area dominated by the El Chayal source during the Classic period (see Chapter 7). Fundamentally, there is no reason to think that salt and other basic commodities would have been different.

The Tribute Economy for Perishable Goods

At the time of the Spanish conquest, cacao and quetzal feathers were among the most important tribute goods for Mesoamerican royalty, not only in the Maya world but up through highland Mexico (Dieseldorff 1904; Feldman 1985; Goetz and Morley 1950:228; Sahagún 1963:20). Iconographic and epigraphic evidence points to the deep history of this pattern: Late Classic polychrome vessels not only depict scenes of the "paradigmatic five" elite tributes (McAnany 2010:286)—cacao, cloth, jadeite, spondylus shells, and quetzal feathers—along with achiote (Akkeren 2012:56), but are often identified in the hieroglyphic text as vessels for drinking chocolate in the primary standard sequence (Stuart 2006a). Frequently, cacao pods and quetzal feathers appear on vases in tandem (see Figure 8.2). Often, those individuals with access to cacao are the same members of the elite with access to quetzal feathers. Tribute bearers and the tribute themselves often appear in painted scenes and murals (McAnany 2010:276–278). For instance, one Late Classic Maya scene (K453) depicts the gift of three-*pil* (bags) of cacao (12,000 beans) in front of the ruler, Ch'ok Wayis, and a quetzal feather bundle at his back—all gifts from the neighboring Lord of Calakmul (Figure 8.7).

Figure 8.7. Late Classic polychrome vessel from Topoxte (K5453) featuring K'ak' Hiix, an emissary from the Mexican city of Calakmul acting on behalf of ruler Yich'aak K'ak; he is presenting 12,000 cacao beans, a bundle of cloth textiles, and quetzal feathers to their enemy, Jasaw Chan K'awiil, the ruler of Tikal. (Museum of Fine Arts Boston 2004.2204. Photo by Justin Kerr. Justin Kerr Maya archive, Dumbarton Oaks, Trustees for Harvard University, Washington, DC.)

According to the Título de Totonicipan, the Poqom, Q'eqchi', Ch'olti', and even Itza paid a tribute of cacao as well as salt and gourds to the K'iche' Empire in the Late Postclassic period (Sacor Quiché 2007:104). Since most of these groups are found in too high an elevation to produce cacao, they depended on the Transversal to fill that need (see also Viana et al. 1982:210), which they acquired in multiple manners. Multiple colonial authorities describe merchant exchanges. Cobaneros would enter the lowlands with metal tools that they would sell for a heavily marked-up price (Gallego 2000:173–174). In 1677, for example, the Indian governor of Verapaz entered Manche'

Ch'ol territory with 30 axes, 20 machetes, and 19 knives. Sales of the first two tool types alone resulted in 325,000 cacao beans, about 60% of the annual tribute per town in Tabasco (Caso Barrera and Aliphat Fernández 2012:291).

While this is an obvious post-conquest example, there were certainly Classic and Postclassic equivalents with distinct but equally valuable commodities (e.g., obsidian, jade, pyrite, and quetzal feathers). There were other sporadic gatherings that are typically referred to as "fairs" in the literature—regular gatherings of merchants and retailers that would occur in easy-to-access locations at set times of the year, typically related to important pilgrimage events (Caso Barrera and Aliphat Fernández 2012:286; Gallego 2000; for an in-depth examination, see Feldman 1978:14). One of the most important fairs in the Transversal region was located about 10 km upriver from Chama and centered on the achiote trade and run by the Xoy. It was from them that the river that flowed past the fair got its name (Chixoy, "at the Xoy"; Akkeren 2012:48; Gallego 2000:177). At least during the Postclassic and Colonial Periods, these were especially important because they represented the only time that representatives from warring states would have safe passage and access to commodities that might otherwise be impossible to acquire.

Quetzal feathers had an even more restricted geographical source. While McAnany (2010:288) notes that there are conditions in Oaxaca—part of the Aztec empire—that would be conducive to quetzal habitation, Feldman (1985:90) documents that the internal economic system of highland Mexico, including Oaxaca, had no feathers of their own. Instead, the citizens who had a tributary burden to acquire the quetzal feathers had to "work six months or a year [in the Isthmus of Tehuantepec] cultivating lands" (Feldman 1985:90, quoting Barlow 1949:124) to build up enough currency to trade with the quetzal merchants who worked at the fringes of the Aztec Empire. Others apparently went right to the Vera Paz to trade directly (Feldman 1985:90). Once they acquired the quetzal feathers, they often had a double burden of tribute to carry, both to the Aztec Empire and to the local lord (Feldman 1985:87).

Since the Aztecs kept detailed tribute lists, it is possible to reconstruct the scale of tribute there. A total of 211,542 kg of cacao flowed into royal coffers in the Valley of Mexico every year (Molins 1956:34–35, quoted in Feldman 1985:84), about 22,540 kg of which came from cacao-growing regions (Durand-Forest 1967:177). The rest had to be purchased by the tributaries, leading to the same conundrum with the quetzal trade: people would have to purchase their mandated tributary cacao through selling goods or labor.

Unfortunately, it is difficult if not impossible to estimate how many quetzal feathers would have been collected annually during the Classic period, although it is likely that they would have needed to be replaced every few years because of their inherent fragility (Tremain 2016:404). Aztec records do allow for a window into their tribute economy, and it appears that during the height of the empire, 2,480 bunches were collected annually (Peterson and Peterson 1992). Tremain (2016:405–406) argues, based on iconographic representations, that each bunch was composed of four feathers, which would mean that 2,800 quetzals would have to sacrifice their tailfeathers to meet the demand there. Sixteenth-century records in Guatemala indicate that over 10,000 feathers were collected and sold annually (McBryde 1971:72)—more than enough to satisfy the demand in both highland Mexico and the Maya world.

Looking back to the Classic period, the settlements around the Verapaz cloud forests were surprisingly isolated from the Maya Lowlands beyond the Northern Transversal. As discussed in Chapter 6, there is a single ceramic sphere that incorporates Cancuen, Nueve Cerros, and the Coban Plateau during the Late Classic that draws some inspiration from lowland traditions, but most, if not all, of the lowland influence in the highlands seems to be filtered through the Transversal. Research conducted at the Terminal Classic site of Aragón atop the Coban Plateau shows how closely tied probable quetzal harvesters were to the cities of the Transversal. In addition to similarities in the ceramics, Aragón was a major ritual ceramic production facility, with hundreds of molds recovered in 2018 (Sears et al. 2021; Woodfill et al. 2019). Excavations also recovered the only long count dates in the Guatemalan highlands on multiple locally produced ceramic objects (Sears et al. 2021).

As a result of these close connections, we believe that the cities of the Transversal served as intermediaries in the exchange of quetzal feathers, much like what has been shown for jade at Cancuen (Demarest 2013; Demarest et al. 2014). Investigations at Cancuen, in fact, have uncovered several "empty" workshop areas where Demarest (2013) suggested the processing of raw materials such as plumage could have occurred, although since it is likely that the feathers were typically bundled and shipped, the processing would have been minimal to nonexistent.

It has long been assumed that the Spanish disinterest in tropical plumage and the end of tribute obligations to the K'iche' brought the harvest and trade of quetzal feathers to an end. Spanish conquest did indeed diminish the scale of the trade, but in 1574, the Dominicans of Verapaz reported that though younger Q'eqchi' no longer hunted exotic plumage, elderly men still did. They also reported that regional trade still included feathers in the commerce between "many towns" of the region (Feldman 2000:4, 7). In the seventeenth century (1635), Tovilla reported that Maya in the Vera Paz continued to use feathers in festivals, and as a result, ongoing hunting for quetzal feathers persisted (Feldman 2000:94, 96).

CACAO ECONOMICS

Chocolate was a celebratory drink in most feasts and festivals, a medicine, and a ritual offering (Durand-Forest 1967; McNeil 2006b; Thompson 1956), which explains its prominent place in tribute lists and the strict sumptuary laws associated with its consumption. While cacao was primarily cultivated for consumption, it served a secondary function as a form of currency that is well documented for the Aztecs (see, for example, Durand-Forest 1967:177–179; Feldman 1985:84; Millan 1955:220; Thompson 1956:96–97). Cacao was bundled into larger measurements: *zontli* = 400 seeds, *xiquipilli* = sack of 8,000 seeds (20 zontles), and a *carga* (or load) = 3 *xiquipilli*, totaling 24,000 seeds (the amount a person could carry).

One hundred seeds could purchase a canoeful of potable water, while a load could purchase an enslaved person. Cacao was not the only currency, but there were set exchange rates among the ones in circulation. One hundred seeds could be exchanged for one *quachtli*, or textile. In the *Codex Mendoza* (fol. 47), special straw bundles are marked with five flags, which McNeil (2006a:8) suggests indicates the base 20 count.

The economic specifics in the Maya world are not as well documented, but cacao did fulfill this same function. The mural in Bonampak Room 1 illustrates a similar standard Mesoamerican count for cacao beans. The five large bundles of beans placed in front of the main altar, which is surmounted by the royal family, includes a glyph that read "5 *pih kakaw*" on one of the white bundles. This correlates to 8,000 beans per sack (*pih*) and suggests 40,000 beans are presented in the scene (Miller 1997).

Cacao's use as a "coin of the realm" was taken up by colonial Spanish authorities due to its established importance and the rarity of copper coins in the Americas (Feldman 1985:86). Cacao seeds continued to be currency in Guatemala and the Yucatan through the nineteenth century. McBryde even observed its continued use in a market in Solola in the first decades of the twentieth century (Habel 1878:4; McBryde 1933; Pérez Romero and Cobos 1990:36).

Sahagún (1955:216) mentions "bad" cacao merchants who sell false cacao: toasting and covering with dirt, molding black dough or wax or ground "bones" of avocados. As a result of this and other fraud, Aztec markets were monitored by inspectors who policed the merchants and included the head of the *pochteca* (Aztec merchant class, Durand-Forest 1967:162; Steinbrenner 2006:263). Feldman (1978:11) notes that the conquest-period Maya had an equivalent group of inspectors monitoring their markets.

Likely in part due to the decline of the cacao production levels in Soconusco and Sonsonate in the late sixteenth century (MacLeod 2008:88–95), seventeenth-century chroniclers reported cacao plantations in regions outside

Spanish control. Fray Gabriel Salazar, writing in 1620, noted the presence of cacao plantations among the Manche' Ch'ol and the nearby Yukatek-speaking Xokmo'. Salazar also documented cacao plantations quite close to Nueve Cerros (Feldman 2000:36, 41, 44). Evasion of colonial rule and impositions likely led the Maya to produce cacao at sustainable levels both in terms of laborers and the environment. Though no cacao boom marked the region, locals were able to trade cacao and achiote for desired European goods, as described by Fray Gabriel Salazar (Feldman 2000:41). The Spanish-overseen boom and bust in Soconusco were not entirely atypical, though. Cacao producers were at risk of invasion and extortion by more powerful states throughout history. During the Colonial Period, the Manche' Ch'ol suffered the advances of the Itza, the Spaniards, and the Spanish-allied Q'eqchi' and Cahaboneros (Caso Barrera and Aliphat Fernández 2006b:300–301; Feldman 2000; Tovilla 1960:265). Villagutierre (1983:107, dramatizing the words of Francisco Gallego) described the situation around 1676, stating that the Q'eqchi' were interested in the region as a cheap source of achiote and cacao, and in order to maintain it, they

> defamed the priests and [faithful] by saying they were very avaricious in order to support themselves, and that the King's officials were tyrants who ordered people whipped and chained, and other things which horrified the Indians. And a machete, which cost four *reales* [about $0.50 in 2024] in Guatemala, was sold to those Indians for twelve [*zontles*] of cocoa [. . .].
>
> Any Indian fleeing from Cobán to the mountain forests would be asked by the people there what he was seeking, and he would reply, "I came here because in my village chains, jail, stocks, and the whip are waiting for me if I fail to pay the tribute." So the mountain Indians, out of pity, would give him a sack of cocoa or some pounds of [achiote], and he would pack his bundle and return to his village.
>
> At other times they entered the forest and seized the cocoa, negotiating for it more often by force; these Christian Indians were so bold they would frequently tie up and whip the Indians in their own villages, taking everything they had. Because of these stratagems, which they used to cheat them and profit from it, they impeded, or at least did not help in the conversion of those miserable infidels, since they thought it more to their disadvantage that they be converted and thereby deprive them of the things they were getting through their evil means. But this did come about. Whether or not it was worthwhile we shall see.

Gallego (2000:173) stated there was more than 36,000 pounds of achiote and cacao in the Vera Paz that same year, almost all of which was brought from the Transversal, principally by duplicitous and exploitative methods.

During the Colonial Period, the most important regional authority was called the *alcalde mayor*, or provincial magistrate. The position was typically filled by a Spanish citizen who purchased the post for a set period of time in order to facilitate business transactions in the region. Surprisingly for its relative isolation and lack of mineral resources like gold and silver, Vera Paz was one of the most expensive posts, due in large part to the amount of agricultural goods, including cacao and achiote, that the magistrate would be able to acquire through official and illicit means (Patch 2002:28–29). At least two *alcaldes mayores* of Verapaz got rich trading Spanish goods for Transversal cacao and achiote because of "the same greed that all of the governors drag with them" (Bricker 1981:37; Ximénez 1929–1931, Tomo II:382; see also King 1974:25, Sapper 1985:38).

Villagutierre (1983:356–357; Sapper 1985:37–38) outed one illicit network in his eighteenth-century *History of the Conquest of the Province of the Itza*. Shortly after the conquest of the Itza in 1697, the governor of the Yucatan ordered a shorter road to be built between his province and Guatemala. The route chosen by the Spanish authorities passed north through present-day Chisec, although the Maya guides took the survey team along a different path to the west of Laguna Lachua that was both more difficult and longer after being ordered to do so by the *alcalde mayor*. Eventually, the Spaniards took charge and traveled east to the designated location, where they saw multiple villages dedicated to producing cacao, achiote, vanilla, and cotton. Most of the villages were composed of refugee Ch'ol speakers who had escaped capture and relocation, although one, "Zocomo," was apparently inhabited by Q'eqchi' from the highlands who were farming achiote and cacao to pay the taxes imposed by the *alcalde mayor*. When the team returned to Coban, the *alcalde* had the Maya guides whipped for taking them through this route; he insisted the road be built along the longer western path, presumably so it did not interfere with his clandestine farming activities.

Other Maya and Spaniards benefited from the illicit trade in other ways beyond the regular contraband commercial networks. While the goods produced and exchanged in these regions outside of the control of the crown were not subject to taxation, people living there sought European-produced items. Hatchets and machetes, used elsewhere to lure unconquered Mayas into permanent settlements (Archivo General de Centroámerica, A1.11.7, Exp. 3813, Leg. 186, 1800, f. 28v.), were easily exchanged for commodities produced in the hinterlands. In other instances, *indios domésticos*, Maya under Spanish rule, traded desired European goods for Indigenous-cultivated, scarce products, such as coconuts and cacao, bartered by unconquered groups. Such trade continued into the eighteenth century, at least. Captain

Francisco Joseph García de Monzabal, charged with reporting on the situation of Maya groups outside of Spanish control into the mid-eighteenth century, observed that the Q'eqchi' of Cahabon defied colonial authorities and traded salt, hatchets, and machetes for cacao and pottery (*cántaros*) from the Xokmo's. Another native informant, Alejandro Monterroso, noted that the unconquered natives harvested coconuts before the Q'eqchi' were able to, which they also traded with those living in Spanish-administered towns (Archivo General de Centroamérica, A1(6), Exp. 3799, Leg. 185, 1754, f. 7v.). Notably, Spaniards had, by this point, brought the territory around Nueve Cerros under colonial control. Maya evading Spanish authorities now needed to trade for salt. Obviously, evading colonial taxes benefited both sides of the exchange.

CONCLUSIONS

Spanish reluctance to conquer and subjugate unconquered Maya, and especially the reluctance of the Maya under Spanish rule to collaborate with Spaniards in eliminating such settlements, likely stemmed from the same motivations that often led authorities to look the other way when faced with maroon communities (Lockley 2009). Like the maroon communities, begrudging mutual benefit occurred when either runaway Black slave settlements or Maya sites beyond the pale traded desirable Indigenous products with Europeans or complicit Mayas of other ethnicities for manufactured items, especially machetes and hatchets. Production of salt and cacao were more sustainable when the Maya mined and farmed the products without the severe exploitation imposed by Spaniards that led to short-term gains but environmental and demographic collapse in the long run. Indeed, cacao production in the Transversal endured for decades after the Spanish-overseen plantations of Soconusco and Sonsonate collapsed. Likewise, Colonial-era observers noted the large-scale salt production at Nueve Cerros under unconquered Indigenous groups. The consolidation of Spanish rule over the territory curtailed this large-scale economic activity. By the nineteenth century, the Salinas de Nueve Cerros saltworks were abandoned.

The sixteenth century did not halt the centuries-old regional trade in salt, achiote, feathers, and cacao. Instead, the process took centuries. By the eighteenth century, when salt production went into decline and cacao production beyond Spanish control was confined to smaller territories, Spanish justifications for increased incursions often included the need to bring fertile lands under cultivation. Their impact was the opposite. Instead, the once-vibrant Maya cultivation of cacao, processing of salt, and casting of pottery had nearly disappeared. One Q'eqchi', Cristóbal Battz of Coban, upon his return from exploring the abandoned lands of the Manche' Ch'ol, reported that he had not seen a single Maya. All he saw, he testified, were fragments of pottery of the "Chol Indians, who had been removed by the old priests" (AGCA, A1(6), Leg. 185, Exp. 3799, 1754, ff. 54–56).

9

The Sacred, Urban Landscape of Cancuen and Salinas de los Nueve Cerros

MARC WOLF

The archaeological sites of Cancuen and Salinas de los Nueve Cerros are physical embodiments of important aspects of the Maya worldview, reflecting significant paradigms of Maya ceremonialism and mythology (Ashmore 1991; Freidel et al. 1995). The spatial organization of these sites reflects the desire of Maya society to recreate landscape patterns of the sacred world in their settlement. Many aspects of Cancuen's sacred flowing water attributes are also present at Salinas de los Nueve Cerros. These cities shared important societal structures and controlled others and created their own regional contacts and permutations of the social diversity and community. Both sites highlight the inextricability of identity, land-use, and the sacred and economic landscape that was the Northern Transversal Strip. In this chapter, Nueve Cerros is discussed in terms of its sacred Maya directionality (north-south, center, and east-west land/settlement distribution), while discussion of Cancuen's sacred landscape revolves around its aqueous symbolism.

CANCUEN

Cancuen is located on the banks of the Rio Pasión, where the Peten and Verapaz meet in the midst of the slopes and shadows of the highland foothills of west-central Guatemala. It is the largest precolumbian site in this segment of the Transversal, straddling the borders of the contemporary departments of Alta Verapaz and the Peten (see Chapter 2 and Figure 1.2). The steep rises of the highlands are less than 12 km away and are an impressive landmark looming over the city's residents—recalling Barthes's writings on Paris's Eiffel Tower (1979) and Jeremy Bentham's panopticon theories of the eighteenth century (archaeologized by Michel Foucault in the 1970s). The mountains were an inescapable sight in most of the city and an integral part of the

Cancuen communal and political identity. The site's principal investigator at the time of writing, Arthur A. Demarest, often questioned the lack of typical Maya temple structures at the site in his early Cancuen works (Demarest and Barrientos 1999). Shortly thereafter, he realized these roles were filled by the mountains themselves, an obvious use of highland ideology (Demarest and Barrientos 2001, 2002). Cancuen is the first major destination, urbanized settlement, and link to other regions of the Maya world encountered after descending from the Maya Highlands in central Guatemala.

The department of Alta Verapaz is composed of intertwined yet vastly different ecological and cultural zones. This diverse area is unique in that it represents a major internal frontier within the Maya area as opposed to a peripheral border between Maya and non-Maya cultures. The northernmost part of Alta Verapaz is a region relatively easy to traverse, unlike the mountain ridges to one side and the ubiquitous swampy or riverine impediments to the east, adding to the volume of people and materials trafficked through the region. The Northern Transversal Strip, the main overland route of commerce and communication from the southern Guatemalan highland regions into the northern Peten, also connects Belize with Chiapas, Mexico, along an east-west route. The rivers also serve as major routes of connection throughout the area, skirting the mountains on one side and lowland inundated morasses on the other.

Water City

Cancuen is the epitome of a water city, embracing the curves of the Pasión River and flanked on all sides by smaller inlets, springs, and human-created water features. The most influential king of the Cancuen dynasty, Tajal Chan Ahk, was preoccupied with showing himself as a water king with symbolic water associations depicted in his headdress on numerous monuments (Demarest et al. 2014). To the north, the domineering presence of the Candelaria Caves merges into the highlands and symbolizes the Pasión River's origin. On the southern horizon, the Pasión's course seems destined for the domineering San Francisco Hills. Cancuen is bookended by culturally charged mountains on one side and caves on the other and is linked into a dynamic whole by the Pasión. The site core and most of the outer settlement are built within the folds of the sinuous river as it flows like a serpent toward the Maya heartland and the confluence with the Usumacinta, Lacantun, and Salinas (Chixoy) Rivers (Figure 9.1). Woodfill and other scholars have referred to this system as integral sections of the "Great Western Trade Route" of Peten commerce and interaction (Canuto and Barrientos 2013; Demarest et al. 2012; Woodfill and Andrieu 2012). The network would have connected Mexico's Gulf Coast and reached the Petexbatun region both on the Salinas and Pasión River sides before stretching into the Peten and continuing into the areas of the southern Yucatecan Coast, through Belize and into Honduras. The navigable Lacantun connects to important points in the west of the Maya world like Chiapas and eventually breaks into both the Mexican Plateau and the Guatemalan Highlands. Kilometers downstream from Cancuen, the Santa Amelia River branches off from the Pasión, overlooked by the site of El Raudal, providing a natural corridor for movement into the southern regions of the Peten and onward to the southern Yucatecan Coast, the Caribbean swamplands of coastal Belize, and the Gulf of Honduras. These riverine environments are emblematic of Cancuen's interconnectivity with the greater Maya region and indicate the importance of water in sacred Maya conceptions of the world.

Bluffs steeply ascending from the Pasión River and numerous seasonal swamps, drainages, and perennial springs frame the Cancuen landscape. The land recalls the Mesoamerican mythical crocodilian or tortoise, whose ridged hide or shell protrudes like islands from the primordial sea (Hammond 1977; Puleston 1977; Rice 2018). Buildings are bastions of civilization, breaking the uniformity of the jungle canopy. As early as 1893, modern urban planners subscribed to the ideals of the Garden City posited by Sir Ebenezer Howard, a settlement model particularly applicable to Mesoamerica (e.g., Chase and Chase 1998), and the discussion of possible garden plots, orchards, and other agricultural practices conducted within the urban environment (Barthel and Isendahl 2013; Isendahl 2012; Lentz et al. 2014; Stark and Ossa 2007). Cancuen is, similarly, a water city, where natural and modified hydrology is a constant backdrop to all activity in the area. *Cancuenites* identified their settlement and their own cultural identity with the Pasión River.

Water themes and features are ubiquitous at Cancuen, most impressively embodied by the Pasión River itself. Many of Cancuen's structures also evoke a water ethos and cascade into a hierophany of aquatic sacred symbolism. Buildings are decorated with water motifs, the sculptures that they house repeat this message, and they are usually associated with major water features. Mirroring elements of the sun's and moon's trajectory around the globe, the river marks a course around most of the Cancuen settlement. The steep riverbanks define the eastern edge of the Cancuen epicenter. East is a culturally significant direction for many peoples (Rybak et al. 2004), including those sharing the Mesoamerican worldview (e.g., Vogt 1969), as it is the "origin" of the rising sun as it travels westward. Maya cosmology also attaches a life-endowing sacred power to this east-west progression, particularly the life-fostering physical properties of the sun and water (the Pasión as the water role in the case of Cancuen). The western direction of the movement is likewise associated with life. At Cancuen, this western pole is more dynamic: a more privileged and epicentric view recognizing the palace and its associated

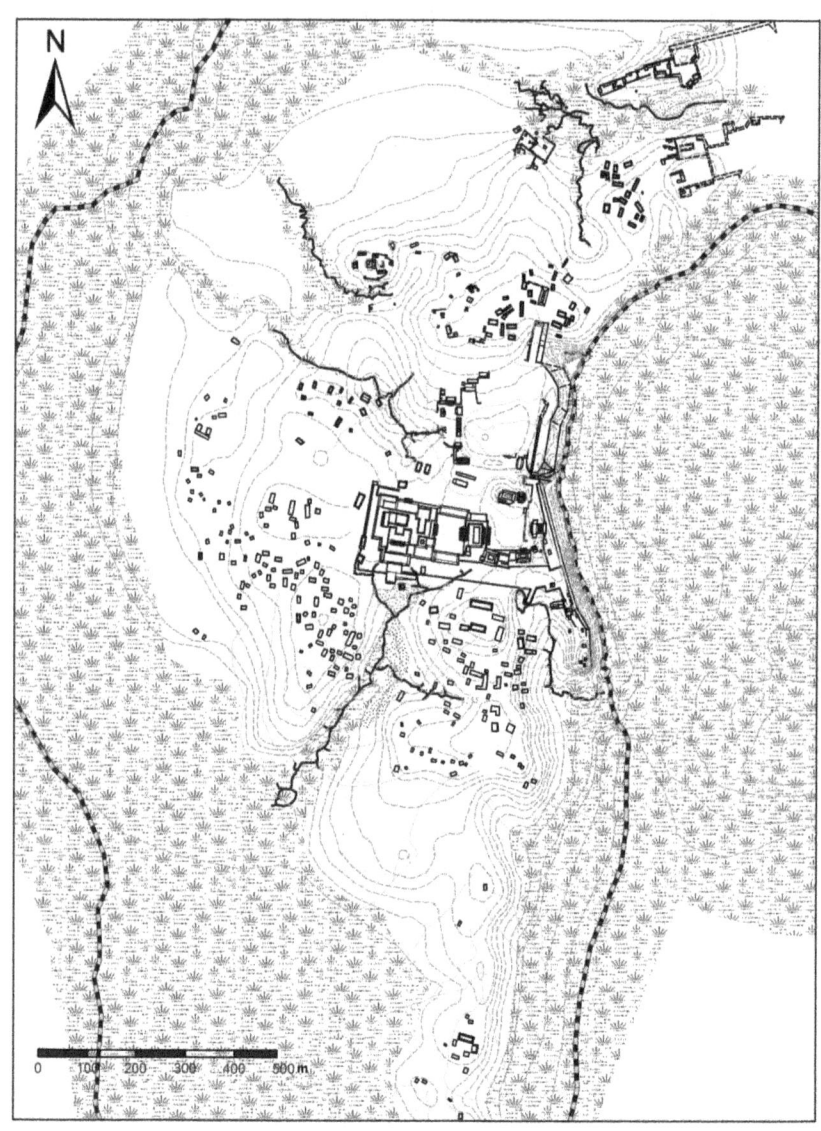

Figure 9.1. Archaeological site of Cancuen. (Base map from ArcGIS [ESRI]. Marc Wolf)

prestige and elite status as one side of the directionality or a commoner designation of architectural groups outside the site core, but both cases focus on the human element of the site.

Pasión River

Rivers were the highways of the ancient world, and the Pasión provided a major route within the Maya region. Almost all activity at Cancuen—work, leisure, ritual, communal, civic, and so on—was performed within sight of the river, its vegetation, or the acoustics of its rushing waters. Several ports and numerous potential portage locations linked important areas of the site directly to the river. Rivers are some of the most sacred landscape features honored in Maya society. Many cultures' origin myths revolve around a primordial sea, and, even though ephemeral and bounded by their shores, rivers can serve as a proxy for this sea of creation in Maya worldviews. Rivers, seemingly tireless and relentless, reach into the farthest and most exotic/foreign depths of the world; the flow of water is inescapable. They eventually penetrate the Underworld to be recycled as rain descending from the sky and Upperworld. This interaction is mirrored by an upstream association with the skies and ancestors of the Upperworld versus a downstream relation with the Underworld. Cancuen was a desirable cultural and social destination. This vibrant and active environment was made even more attractive as the system grew larger with more trade and people. Cancuen was not simply a commercial cornucopia but also a cultural nexus of migrants, religious pilgrims, political players, laborers, specialists, and other people curious about the bustling port, sacred features of a water city, and the most powerful settlement in the region (Demarest 2014).

CONCORDIA RIVER

The Concordia River drains the northern extremes of Cancuen's mapped area. It flows into the Pasión approximately a kilometer north of Cancuen's central precinct, passing many house compounds while also creating a mosaic of microenvironments. At multiple points, the river rushes downstream to the Pasión and has carved a distinct channel, while in other locations it becomes a wide and amorphous swamp system, only to reform into an active river again, and vice-versa. Several phases of this system are potential agricultural activity areas that might have supplied important products into the Maya sacred and utilitarian economy like cattail reeds (Schele et al. 2001) for woven mats, baskets, shades, and so on; cardamom (Thampi 2003; Wilson 1999) and achiote (see Chapter 8; see also Barrera-Bassols and Toledo 2005; Demarest et al. 2014; Marcus 1982) for food seasoning; and cacao (Hurst et al. 2002; McNeil 2006c, McNeil et al. 2010; see also Chapter 8). The reeds and cacao hold deep mythological significance as well as economic value as imports/exports within Maya society as discussed in the research of Cameron McNeil and others (Fash et al. 1992; Stuart 2006b; Vail and Hernández 2013). In a rolling landscape of small hilltops and declines, the Concordia serves as a water source and boundary for large expanses of shallow marshlands punctuated by slight elevations climbing out of the surrounding wetlands.

Water Sources

The perennial springs that add to the watery environments of Cancuen are distributed randomly over the site and are indicative of the fairly shallow water table of the surrounding landscape. Much of this water level is dictated by the volumes of rainfall and the corresponding rise and fall of the river, often changing within a single day. The sky can be clear and full of sun, but rain downpours in the adjacent highlands drain into rivers like the Pasión, which can swell significantly in a matter of hours. Notably, this environmental link between highlands and low is mirrored by the cultural links between these highlands and Cancuen. The pools and streams produced run fresh with unpolluted water, sustaining fish, amphibians, insects, and a variety of specialized flora and fauna associated with these wet microbiomes.

Incidentally, these shifts in water levels and saturation are as active today as they were in the past. The modern visitor's center of the Cancuen archaeological park is constructed on stilts to accommodate the sudden and rapid fluctuations (often several meters) of river waters (Figure 9.2). The swings in the riverine water level transform the environment as well, filling usually slow-moving or dry drainages with rushing waters, overflowing riverbanks and flooding vast areas of the low-lying land that mark the Cancuen topography. The daily backdrop of Cancuen already heavily imbued with water and river connotations is further drenched in seemingly endless waters that meander throughout the entire area, adding to the sacred symbolism that Cancuen's architectural assemblages are islands of human civilization in a worldly/celestial sea. Waters are commonly associated with cleanliness, freshness, clarity, and newness in ancient societies (Dunning et al. 2014; Mays and Angelakis 2019; Scarborough 1998). Ritual purification of body and spirit often relies on the effects of these cleansing waters, specifically in the ubiquitous use of Maya sweat baths (Hammond and Bauer 2001; Helmke 2006; C. Miller 2013). Water sources bolster the identification of Cancuen as a city of water—a source of purity given to Cancuen from the gods and the cosmos itself.

Northern Sacred Water System

In Cancuen, to the north of the palace ballcourt, leading from the west end of the playing alley is the head of a well-defined drainage system that delimits

Q'eqchi' Visitor Center, May 2013   Visitor Center, June 2013

Figure 9.2. Cancuen Visitor's Center, comparing flood water between May and June 2013. (Courtesy of Luís Fernando Luin.)

the northern extent of the central area (Figure 9.3). The drainage channel is wide and paved with closely fitted, large limestone blocks. It is commonly known from Maya mythology that the ballcourt is a figurative entrance to the subterranean world of the lords of the Underworld. Allegorically, the water of the system flows from this Underworld, notably associated with the mythic watery realm of creation in Maya cosmology. The drain continues for only meters before joining a much longer east-west running channel that helps define the northern extent of the site core, like a street defining a neighborhood, as Broadway does in modern New York City, Massachusetts Avenue in Boston, or the Champs-Élysées in Paris. Cancuen archaeologists posit that this drain was primarily a human-created feature, perhaps elaborating on an already present spring (excavations filled quickly with ground water). Silvia Alvarado and Elisa Mencos (2008) excavated this drainage, detailing the construction and recovering the remains of a canoe oar, cementing its water-portal symbolism. With a physical link to the known gateway of the Underworld—the ballcourt—the northern sacred water system also connects the living world of human civilization as represented by the expansive and stela-adorned monumental plaza.

Though often temporally associated with Preclassic or Early Classic period, a possible E-Group assemblage toward the east had been noted in the 2005 Cancuen seasonal report (Demarest et al. 2006). A longer north-south oriented multitiered platform may have been observed from a radial viewing platform constructed several meters due west and obscured by root and water disturbances due to the drainage. If substantiated, the water system would enter the Maya cosmos (indisputable laws of physics detail the cycle of precipitation falling to the earth to eventually return skyward in the form of

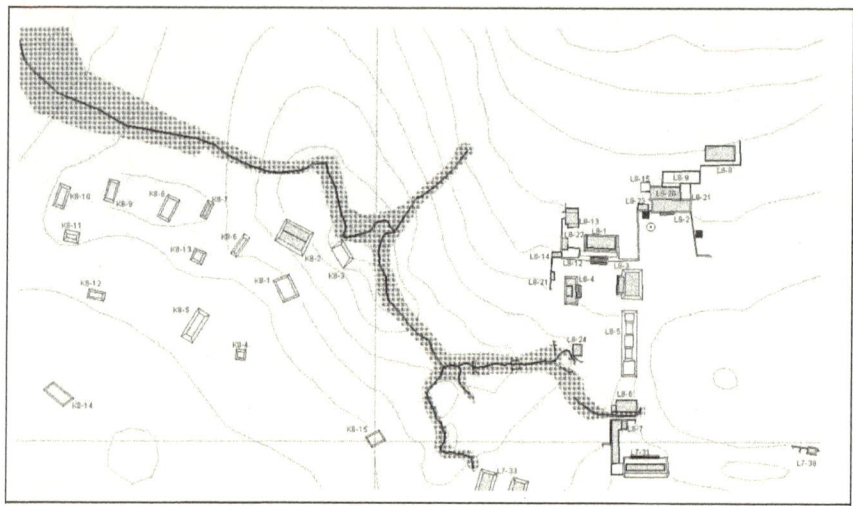

Figure 9.3. Northern sacred water system at Cancuen. (Base map made in ArcGIS [ESRI]. Marc Wolf)

evaporation), linking Cancuen to the stars and planets of the sky and Upperworld. This would be a perfect model of the Maya World Tree, with roots emanating from the Underworld at the palace ballcourt and the channel acting as the tree trunk, funneling water eastward toward the river. The tree's upper limbs reach into the Pasión, connecting with the heavenly realm of the celestial gods and ancestors.

Plaza Water System

Plaza B, colloquially the palace's backyard plaza, is also the setting of a complex and multilayered message of water symbolism (Figure 9.4). The plaza's eastern boundary, the Pasión River, is highly indicative of an aquatic undercurrent. The northern extent of the plaza is the aforementioned northern sacred water system, and its southern edge bleeds into the main plaza (Plaza A) and the northeastern sides of the palace. There is some variation, particularly where remnant fingers of the northern water system flow toward the palace and main plaza, but the ground predominantly slopes slightly upward to the palace and the ballcourt of Tajal Chan Ahk. Tomás Barrientos and associates excavated a series of trenches verifying the presence of probable water-disturbed limestone paving and concluded that likely the entire plaza acted as a rainwater catch basin, draining into the northern sacred water system (Alvarado 2013). Immediately before the downslope to the river, two long, plain stela mark the approximate northeastern corner of Plaza B. As mentioned by Maler in his early explorations, the monuments, like most of the Cancuen stela, are cut into a stepped square or an upside-down Maya "*Ik*" sign. Commonly, *Ik* is translated to English as "dark" or "wind," which are often harbingers of wet environments. In an analysis of Maya hieroglyphic writing and iconographic symbolism of taxes/payment details from numerous Maya polities, Kettunen and Helmke (2010:123) also associate *Ik* with tribute and regalia, elements probably levied, collected, shipped, and paid during different episodes within Cancuen's history. It may also be a reference to dark clouds and strong winds that often accompanied rain, clothing it in foreboding regalia. In either case, water is the stage where these monuments are set. The stela lies on a relatively narrow terrace that connects the secondary plaza to the main plaza and overlooks the river. This symbolic promenade is bisected by a relatively steep-sloped cross drainage that empties into the Pasión below.

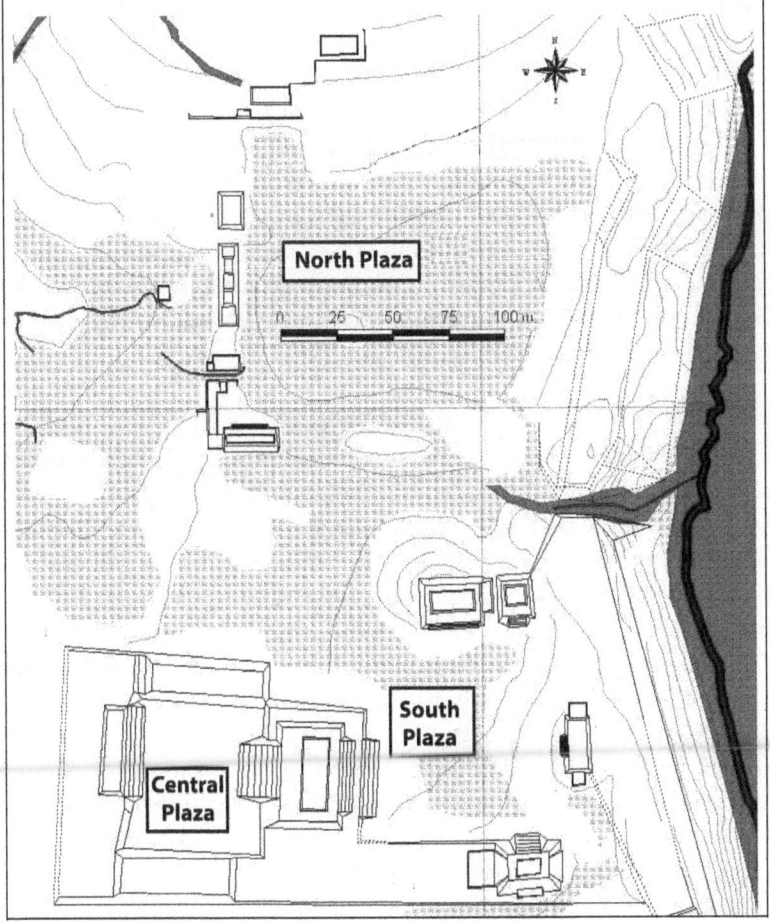

Figure 9.4. Cancuen plaza water system. (Base map from ArcGIS [ESRI]. Marc Wolf)

At the juncture of these plazas lies two structures that change the natural hydrology and drainage patterns of Cancuen's core. Structures L7–28 and M7–8 (Figure 9.5) are built such that they prevent the escape of water through the natural break in the landscape. They diverted rain and flood runoff waters toward the northern sacred water system or out to the Pasión. These structures likely functioned as a pressure relief when the water system was overburdened and could release or divert waters, symbolically controlling the flow. They were built only meters apart from each other, forming a tight and unified channel, or watercourse, between them, and both have complex and uncommon designs that seem both spiritual and utilitarian. A single small stela/altar combination lies a few meters south of the two buildings, anchoring them into the political, communal and spiritual order of Cancuen. Together, the buildings are reminiscent of water-associated double temples as reported from sites like Wari Camp and others in northwest Belize (Levi et al. 2019) and similar water temples, especially from the Aztec capital of Tenochtitlan underneath present-day Mexico City (Feinman 1988). The lack of upkeep, natural erosion, and mere clogging of that system undoubtedly resulted in large flood volumes forcibly pushing through obstacles, deepening the cross drainage over the time since the site was abandoned. In 2012, excavations were conducted into and around Structure M7–8 and yielded numerous stucco façade elements displaying aquatic themes such as water lilies and cormorants. In 2014, Structure L7–28 became the target of a large-scale horizontal excavation detailing an unusual architectural plan that exhibited traits of a hybridized political, secular, and utilitarian function.

Royal Pool

In 2006, the Cancuen survey team reexamined what was thought to be a natural sinkhole and modern cattle-trampled depression that flanked the main entrance to the palace (Figure 9.6; Thorton and Demarest 2019). Excavations led by Barrientos revealed a fine-cut stone block pool constructed over a natural spring that fills the chamber with crystalline fresh water. The pool's location in front of the palace, ethnographic evidence of cleansing (Buenaflor 2018; Groark 1997; Lucero and Kinkella 2015), and archaeological remains elsewhere in the Maya world (Child 2007; Katz 2012; Kinkella 2009; Lucero 2018; Lucero et al. 2017) suggest the chamber could have served as a ceremonial purification bath necessary to gain access to the palace. From another perspective, the pool and its waters are leveling mechanisms that strip away political, economic, and other social hierarchies, creating an environment of equality and community. In either view, the pool's water is emblematic of Cancuen and is a focal point of that aquatic theme, a landmark association or branding. The royal pool, as it is colloquially known, was also the

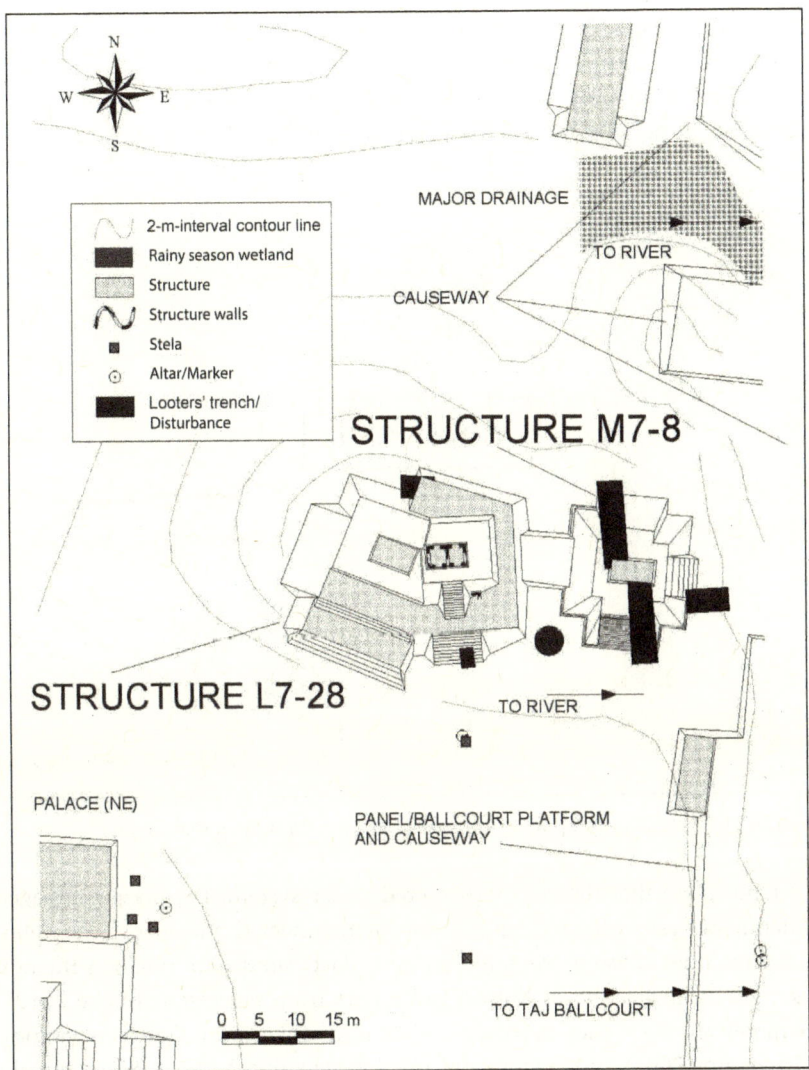

Figure 9.5. Cancuen Structures L7-28 and M7-8. (Base map from ArcGIS [ESRI]. Marc Wolf)

scene of the massacre of Cancuen elite (likely the ruling family at the time) around AD 779. Within the pool were the remains of multiple individuals—men, women, and children, likely the inhabitants of the palace, many marked as nobility by their association with jewelry, inlaid teeth, well-crafted lithics, and other luxury items. Analysis of the skeletal material was conducted in 2007 by a team of Guatemalan forensic scientists who also analyzed many of the burial remains from the Guatemalan Civil War (Suasnavar et al. 2007).

They hypothesized relatively merciful deaths of Cancuen nobility, whose bodies were then thrown into the water, ending the Cancuen ruling dynasty and again highlighting the role of the royal pool and water as symbolic of Cancuen, its political regime, and the people who made it their home.

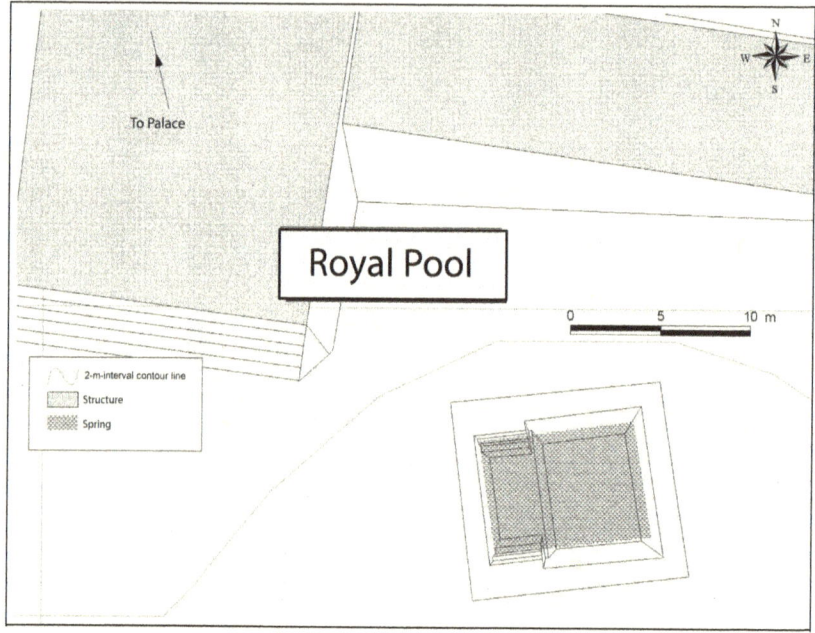

Figure 9.6. Cancuen royal pool. (Base map from ArcGIS [ESRI]. Marc Wolf)

I postulate that the northern sacred water system, the plaza drainage/catchment system, and the pools are interconnected and form a complex drainage/flow of waters centered on the palace, similar to Jonathan Ruane's example from the site of Xultun and others from the Peten (Ruane 2019). Symbolically the Cancuen palace is a water mountain from Maya cosmology (Barrientos 2008). This sacredly charged designation adds to the intangible importance and attraction of the Cancuen settlement in a Maya worldview and becomes a crucial cornerstone of the self-identity of the city's citizens.

Ports

The largest port at Cancuen, the main port of the city, is (as of 2019) a silt-infilled cove located at the northeastern corner of the Cancuen core (Figure 9.7). The area would have been able to accommodate numerous watercraft at once, with space for temporary moorings/slips for vessels not in immediate use, and possibly a dock system (now disintegrated by the wet extremes of the river and a tropical climate, and buried by centuries of silt accumulation) for the handling of materials and passengers. The port also likely provided storage for goods being transported by river when Cancuen was not the ultimate destination. Items could be guarded and stored in the area for quick loading, with supporting structures designed to manage the port's traffic. Soil analysis on the accumulated silt confirms its deposition after the port was active; during the apogee of Cancuen, the port was an expansive, sheltered inlet from the Pasión River (Cook et al. 2006). The port leads to a steep slope approximately 10 m via earthen ramp to the levee's top (depending on river water levels) and Plaza B. Rough or informal stairs, if present at one time, have long vanished with the accelerated erosion of steep topography and rushing rain or drainage waters. As this was the primary commercial access route to Cancuen's center, it was also fortified by a wall that served to restrict and control traffic from the busy port below (Alvarado 2003; Alvarado et al. 2006). The main port would have been a supernaturally imbued gateway for people and products to reach the impressive and epic Maya water city of Cancuen.

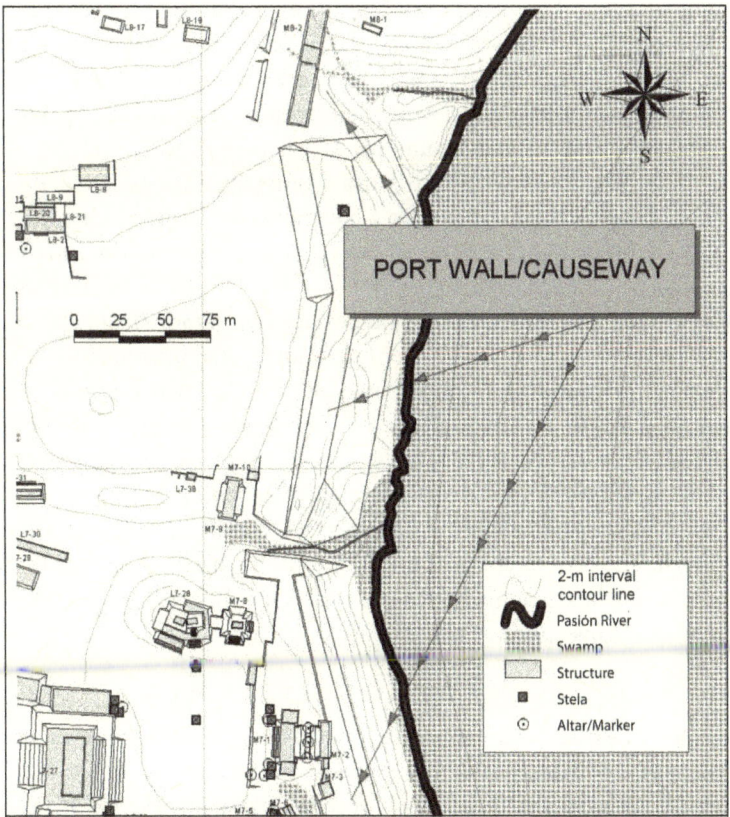

Figure 9.7. Cancuen main port. (Base map from ArcGIS [ESRI]. Marc Wolf)

A few ridges to the north of the main port and several hundred meters upriver, the Pasión bends inward to form another port, which was perhaps more private or specialized in function. Termed the northern port, it has considerably steeper sides, is much narrower, and is about half the size of the main port. This northern landing appears to have been seemingly controlled by a large architectural compound that overlooks it. This area probably had both residential and economic functions, providing housing and administration for the laborers who produced lithics in the nearby workshops (Andrieu 2014).

A smaller port or water landing was situated near the palace's main entrance, before the artificial pool. Aesthetically and functionally, the palace port was the most ceremonial and official route to gain entrance to the royal palace, via the royal pool. The port channel runs a short distance northward before bending east to join the Pasión, adding to the sacred symbolism of the landing itself by combining the cultural importance of the cardinal directions with the physical reality of an east-west passage. The waterway's north/south arm points to Cancuen's supernatural power manifested by the monumental architecture of the central precinct. The east-west segment highlights the human element of domestic architecture. It joins the palace—to the outside or etic archaeologist, the ultimate Maya conception of civilization—with the largest and densest residential settlement within Cancuen. This palace port was the connection, a symbolic umbilical cord, to the Pasión (linking it to the rivers of the world and tying it to Maya cosmology). The port was probably active only during the height of the Guatemalan wet season, when Cancuen was most saturated and at its most attractive as a visitation destination for political and/or other pilgrimage reasons.

Many other river landing areas and portages, both formal and opportunistic in accordance with shifting water levels and spatial practicalities of where goods were delivered or extracted, marked the Cancuen peninsula as well (Martinez et al. 2017). Although the Pasión carves a path northward into the lower regions of the Guatemalan Peten, it frequently and regularly twists into bows and bends as a sine curve. Each of these curves can represent considerable effort in transport, figuring not only the where of pick-up and delivery but also the seasonal strength of the current or fluctuations in river frontage. Regions of dry land seemingly far from the shore regularly flood, providing river access during specific times of year.

SALINAS DE LOS NUEVE CERROS

As alluded to earlier, many scholarly undertakings have focused on cosmological aspects of Mesoamerican settlement. In the following discussion "settlement" is an abbreviated definition of settlement patterns, terminology developed by Gordon Willey in the 1940s and 1950s to lend clarity to his survey study of the Virů Valley in Peru (and later in the Maya area at Barton Ramie in the Belize Valley), dictating that these patterns are the way humans inhabited or otherwise used and manipulated the natural environment (Willey 1953). With this foundation of what settlement *is*, researchers have long sought to understand the relationships between the human cultural environment and the natural landscapes where they are situated. There are countless strategies on which this dynamic is based. The justifications for a chosen locale have been attributed to a variety of reasons, from political to economic. Here, special attention is paid to conceptions of an idealized sacred landscape. It is not a novel idea; it is one that has enjoyed the deliberations of many insightful studies within Mesoamerica and for the Maya area in particular (Andrews 1975; Ashmore 1981; Ashmore and Knapp 1999; Fash 1991; Schele and Freidel 1990; Schele et al. 1998; Sharer 2006). This dialogue presents another narrative reflecting prior work within the Maya region, yet also moves the study forward by encompassing the natural landscape as a single unit mirrored and thus reenforced by architectural human-made assemblages. The cosmology or sacred aspect of the Salinas de los Nueve Cerros archaeological site provides a literal outline, shadow, highlight, or contrast to the ruins themselves. The natural world represents a cosmology echoed by the site's architecture, and vice versa. This duality reflects the unknown (and potentially dangerous, as commonly associated with the uncertain) power that both the natural context and the Maya structures within this setting inspire.

The ancient Maya displayed in architecture and iconography their worldview, detailing a cosmogram of their ideology in the layout and forms of buildings as well as the plans and adornments of the buildings themselves. Though this research posits ideas of past Maya traditions, their worldview is constantly evolving into newer forms to adapt to or confront the "outside" influences of world modernization or globalization. Modern Maya adhere to many of the basic principles embraced by their forefathers of architectural planning and layout such as the quadripartite alignments and divisions of agricultural fields (Vogt 1969) or house compounds (Andrews 1975). For the ancient Maya, researchers have postulated that cruciform shapes of urban settlement reflect the Maya ideals of a north-south world axis bisected by an east-west axis (Maca 2002; Tourtellot et al. 2000). In his seminal work at Tikal, Becker (1971) detailed and categorized the organization and plans of architectural groups within the Guatemalan site of Tikal. As mentioned, Schele and Freidel (1990) have discussed the mythic/ceremonial significance of individual structures, like that of the focal structure at Cerros in coastal northern Belize, and later the iconographic thrust behind architectural elaborations as the details and adornments of Pakal's tomb in Palenque, Chiapas, Mexico, and elsewhere in the Maya area (Mathews and Garber 2004; Schele et al. 1998). The sacred importance within

Maya settlement patterns transcends the buildings and adorning symbols themselves and also crucially echoes the significance of location and context. Where the Maya chose to erect their structures is a monumental statement. This discussion asserts that Nueve Cerros (though not unique in Mesoamerica) transcends the usual settlement patterns that result from obvious political hierarchies and agendas of a theater state and focuses primarily on ritual environments as the principal forces behind settlement.

General Description

The Nueve Cerros site, or "Saltworks of the Nine Hills," is located in the midwestern Transversal of Guatemala, in the transition zone between the Maya Highlands and Lowlands (Figure 9.8). The Classic Maya occupation (AD 250–800) was centered around a massive salt dome, the Cerro Tortugas or "Turtle Hill," whose salt was gathered by the city's residents from the saline stream flowing on the dome's western slope (Figure 9.9). The Chixoy River borders the northern edge of the city's core and served as a major trade route connecting the Maya world. Salinas de los Nueve Cerros is the moniker for several settlements situated within the omni-presence of the Nueve Cerros Mountains. The settlement pushes, perhaps establishes, the definition of cosmic space within Maya reality or daily activity. The Nueve Cerros area is a paradigmatic, if not the most compelling example from Maya cosmology based in the natural landscape, axis-mundi.

Figure 9.8. Site of Salinas de los Nueve Cerros. (Base map from ArcGIS [ESRI]. Marc Wolf)

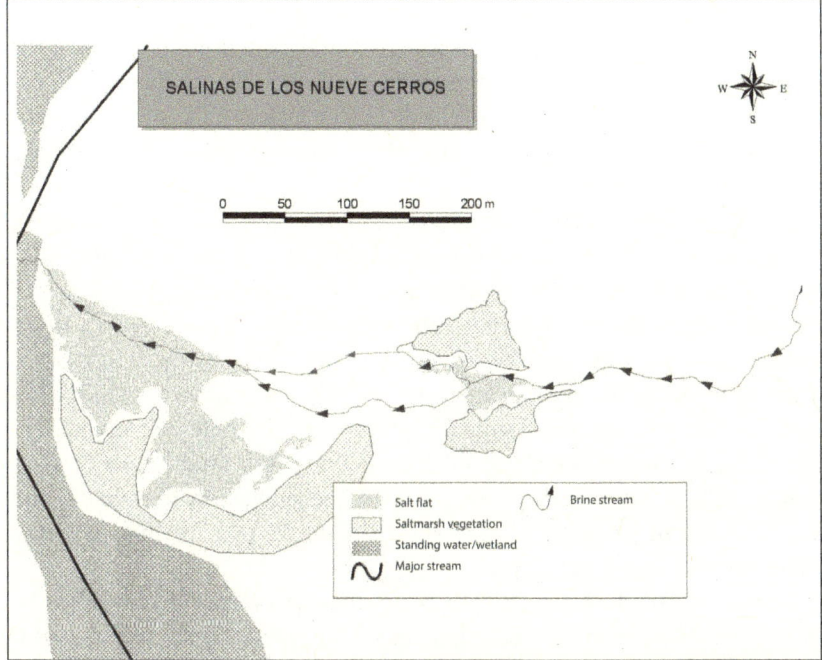

Figure 9.9. Nueve Cerros brine stream and salt flats. (Base map from ArcGIS [ESRI] .Marc Wolf)

The traditional model of the axis-mundi is a quadripartite division of the universe, distinguished by a cruciform shape of cardinal directions with an especially sacred convergence point in the middle of the two axes (Schele and Freidel 1990; Tourtellot et al. 2000). At Nueve Cerros, the salt dome lies at the east end of the cosmogram, the Nueve Cerros range at the western position, and salt flats, the ultimate transition, in the middle. Bisecting this east-west axis, a north-south axis is defined by several of the drainages in the area. The geographically enormous swamplands, generally trending northward, define the southern reference for the line, and the energetically flowing Salinas River is the northern point.

Site Overview

The north-south tangent of the Nueve Cerros axis-mundi encompasses both the vast swamp system and the swift Salinas River. Western culture fixates on north as the main cardinal direction; however, this was not necessarily the case in ancient Mesoamerica. Mathematically, two perpendicular lines defining two directions are nameless—simply tangents of 90°. They are assigned to east/west/north/south for the purposes of consistency and convention (the modern tradition dictates north is usually at the top of the page with other directions referenced tangentially). Many ancient populations anointed other directions as the seminal direction (Aveni et al. 2004; Krupp 1989; McCluskey 2007). The Maya maps of the Spanish contact and Colonial Periods, where east is the focal direction from which other directions are based, use an equally valid system.

At Nueve Cerros, water is the conjoining line or physical link between the four directions, with potable sweet water running from the mountains linking with the salt-stream flowing from the dome. This confluence defines the western limit of the salt flat and is the starting point for the Salinas River. The salt stream creates the shifting width of the flats, beginning as a single channel, breaking into multiple poorly defined smaller systems as it passes through the flats, and then recombining into one flow before emptying into the waters that together become the Salinas River. The swamplands lie adjacent to the flats, defining its southern extent. The salt flats are the tangible and liminal center of the Nueve Cerros world, linking Maya mythology to the architecture that surrounds them.

Maya iconography is replete with associations of a watery Underworld and stage of world creation (Scarborough 2003). The Nueve Cerros swampland is exemplary. Though future research will reveal more, these wetlands encompass a variety of different microenvironments. These range from a deeper central area to many horizontally larger shallows and differing degrees of morass and mud. Much of the entire urban zone is engulfed to varying degrees within this wet, often inundated environment. The ancient Maya architectural features of the site are islands within this wetland system. The Salinas wetlands embrace the settlement from all sides, reaching to the slopes of the Nueve Cerros Ridge and the topography of the salt dome. The salt flat—a dualistic and contradictory entity belonging to two different states of being at the same time—is both dry land and an integral part of the surrounding swamp. Water depth influences the vegetation of the different swamp zones, and these alternate from algae-covered waters and thorn and vine tangles of varying density to stands of inundated jungle trees and palms.

Important zones within the Salinas swamplands are the deeper water pockets that give the connotation of a larger clear waterbody. In Maya sacred world views, little distinction is made between lakes, oceans, and other larger bodies of water (Brady and Prufer 2005; Lucero 2003; Scarborough 2003). Maya creation myths commonly associate water as the stage for the development of humans and the physical world, detailing creation as sprouting from the carapace of an enormous mythological turtle floating in a primordial sea or from a world-tree with alligator attributes and other water connotations. Interestingly, the almost grid-like patterns of most species of turtle shells and the scales of mythological reptiles recall the forms of Maya agricultural fields or swampland raised field agriculture known from several Maya sites and elsewhere in Central America (e.g., the raised fields of the Aztec *chinampa* [floating garden] system of Tenochtitlan).

The more open areas of swamp are surrounded by tightly packed, pillar-like stands of wetland grasses, cattails, and other reeds. Like the columns of the Temple of the Warriors from Chichen Itza or Tula, the reeds cluster around these larger pools, acting as sentries guarding a crucial resource or restricting access. From afar, they resemble a military procession marching toward the site. These swampland reeds are important mythological symbols in a pan-Mesoamerican ideology associated with militarism, imperialism, and the Underworld (Sugiyama 2005). They represent an important day name in all Mesoamerican calendars and are tied to concepts of time and creation. Tollan, an important mythical or unidentified city or locale, especially important in later Mesoamerican and Mexican cultures, was known as "The Place of Reeds." As Cameron McNeil (personal communication 1999) has noted, these reeds are often indicative of the geological longevity of the wetlands they inhabit.

The Salinas wetlands represent further duality and paradox within Maya world views. The swamp's moisture and parasitic organisms readily deteriorate and rot most objects, but the swamp water is also a primordial "soup" of creation and development, mixing elements and rain runoff into a concentrated source. It throbs with an abundance of wildlife: birds, fish, reptiles, and myriad insects dwell in its rich organic life. Swamp soils are nutrient-rich, supporting both aquatic and terrestrial life-forms. They are microenvironments that encapsulate the life and death cycles of many animals. The swamplands provide the necessary drinking water for all life in the area, and the tender grasses are both a food supply and building resource for smaller game and birds. Deer use the reedy cover to avoid the attention of potential predators, raptors patrol the air for prey, smaller birds hide in the swamp vegetation while also feeding on the vast array of spiders, insects, and tiny fish, and larger carnivores can often find their game by the swamp as well. The environment would naturally be a perfect medium for aquaculture—from fish to turtles—and intensive farming of the wetland soils. It is a still quagmire of muddy water, yet it also flows slowly but surely from south to north, draining much of the entire area into the great Chixoy River. Enhancing the contradictory powers of swamplands, the aforementioned properties of decay are countered with incredible preservation powers in the anaerobic environs of deeper swampland waters. The famous Puleston Axe (an extraordinarily well-preserved ancient Maya weapon or agricultural tool with a stone head, sinew hafting, and wooden shaft—see Shafer and Hester 1991) was found in a swamp context in Belize and illustrates these preservation qualities.

The waters are a moving frame of mirrored, self-reflective repetitions of transformational processes, like the ideas of repetition detailed in other sacred contexts (Mannikka 1996; Schele and Freidel 1990). The greater symbolism of water itself is especially sacred to the ancient Maya and Mesoamerica in general (Fedick 1996; Lucero 2003, Lucero and Fash 2006; Scarborough 2003). From Aztec and Maya calendrics, Mixtec and Zapotec codices and Maya iconography, water has been associated with both the Underworld and the heavens above (Demarest and Conrad 1992; Lucero et al. 2006). Control over water resources has been touted as the factor behind the development of political power and state formation (Carneiro 1970). Water availability is one of the principal dictums of agricultural production and therefore of human populations and cultural systems. In its role as a mainstay of farming, water supplies are directly responsible for the development of craft specialization and, in turn, all the cultural elaborations that mark a hierarchical and developed society, including religion and worldviews. Terracing and drainage systems combat the erosive powers of rainwater run-off and other destructive flooding events pervasive in wetter climbs (Scarborough 2003). Water is a dualistic entity, capable of vicious currents and destructive inundation, but it is also the foundation of agricultural productivity and life in general. The ideological significance in Maya cosmology of the hydraulic cycle of groundwater evaporated into the atmosphere and then redeposited downward in the form of rain has been detailed in many academic discussions (Sosa 1985). This cycle links the realm of the Upperworld—the home of the gods and many ancestors—with the physical middle world (the daily world of the Maya people), and the mysterious Underworld into which this rainwater drains.

As noted, waterways are the arteries—the highways and communication lines—of the Maya world. Academic literature is filled with analyses of Maya trade and migration, and the rivers of Mesoamerica allowed for the dissemination of not only commercial goods but also ideas (ideology) and the movement of people (Demarest and Rice 2005). Central America in general and the Maya area in particular are often not conducive to traditional forms of terrestrial transportation. The geology and great variability of environments (impassable swamplands, highlands, rivers, canyons, impenetrable vegetative growth, etc.) render conventional wheeled vehicles useless and maintenance of overland routes difficult. Obviously, rivers were the preferred routes of commerce, aiding in the distribution of exotic and utilitarian items, and the route of sacred transformation of exotic goods into locally available items. The rivers facilitated the movement of peoples across the landscape. Recent books on Mesoamerican studies also stress how temporary incursions or permanent immigration often brings different customs and religious ideas into regions (Arnauld et al. 2021; Culbert and Rice 1990; Masson et al. 2020; Price and Feinman 2008). In many ways, the river systems of Mesoamerica formed the critical framework that unified Maya culture. Although local expressions of what was (and still is) defined as Maya might have been different in alternate regions, the rivers, through trade and other contact, promulgated a pan-Maya ethos. The Nueve Cerros area exemplifies this dispersion of people and ideas based around the salt resources.

In the large Salinas wetland, water moves south-to-north, changing dramatically from a stagnant swamp to a freely running river aided by the important addition of drainages from the Nueve Cerros range (the western extent of the cosmogram) and the salt dome (the eastern pole; see Figure 9.8). Strengthening the symbolism of transformation and creation is the complex relation of the heavy salinized salt stream and the fresh water from the mountains. Color is important in Maya myth as well (Tokovinine 2012; Tokovinine and McNeil 2012), and the salt-stream tumbles quickly as a cloudy grey or black, in marked contrast to the crystalline, lazy blue-green of the sweet water. It is the combination of these waters from the three very different sources that is the catalyst for transformation into one major waterway. All come together at the liminal meeting ground of the salt flats. The flats are the arena of metamorphosis and change—transformation of saline water into fresh water, mountains and firm land into a watery swamp, and the center point of the Salinas axis-mundi.

Currently, the salt flats of the Nueve Cerros region include the main flat and a significantly smaller one slightly to the east. These are probably part of one larger entity, itself dynamic and shifting in time from a larger mass to several linked smaller bodies and back again. Together they occupy approximately 500 m^2 in area. The flats are sandy, muddy landforms that appear incongruously in the surrounding jungle and wetlands. Their exact location moves on the landscape as well (Dillon 1981), reiterating their indefinable and ambiguous latent power. In the 1960s they were almost 100 m from where they are today (Brent Woodfill, personal communication 2009). Salt is an extremely contradictory substance. It kills vegetable crops, and its corrosive powers are rapid and total. At the same time, it is a crucial chemical in the dietary needs of most mammals, especially humans and the abundant animal life indigenous to the area. This dualism of life and death has been exploited throughout history; recall the Roman era's salting of the agricultural fields of defeated enemies or the tribute lists from Aztec codices or the modern commercial market exchange of salt today. Salt's destructive powers are intertwined with its power of preservation, especially apparent in its use to dry and preserve fish and game. It changes inedible raw items into safe consumables while also preserving it against decay.

Salt is transformational. Decomposition or putrefaction can be translated as inedible or unsafe. Salt alters the state of a freshly skinned hide or collected shell or other recently procured animal product into dried material for use as clothing or adornments. Prior to a salt treatment and desiccation, objects are laden with excess, such as pieces of flesh, blood, and other unstable biomaterials. After they are transformed by salting, they become suitable for use, consumption, or production. The Maya view different stages of life and death—life, death of the physical body, and death of the soul—not as a dichotomy of one versus the other, but as stages within a single process (Brown 2005).

The brine storage pots that were used at Salinas are enormous in size, with thick walls to withstand the wear and tear of the entire process. When the salt was properly reduced from the brine water of the salt stream or flats, it was placed in a ceramic mold was broken and the salt "cake" removed. The gargantuan vessels may serve as symbolic gateways, creating both a physical and hypothetical mirror in the reflections and dynamics of the surface and the depth of the transformational liquid they are designed to contain.

In addition to any symbolic properties, salt was also a heavily exchanged commodity (see Chapter 8; Guderjan 2007; Hewitt et al. 1987; Moga 2009). As control over water supplies helped beget the hierarchical society of the ancient Maya, access to salt resources was used as a controlling feature that strengthened hierarchical segregation. Demand for salt was a constant in the development of humankind, especially in light of its dietary importance in the humid tropics.

In addition to physical requirements, the existence of a redistributed resource (in this instance, salt) connotes a background of power. Salt economics reinforce the politics of a class-segregated Maya society. Salt trade, especially salt from Salinas de los Nueve Cerros, is also a means of combining religion and politics. The intermingling of politics with sacred ideology is a common theme in religious systems (Kertzer 1989). Salt was both an ideological symbol and a commercial (and thus political) item. At Salinas, salt was (and still is) a readily available commodity, but elsewhere in the Maya world its accessibility relied on market exchange. Although not an overtly exotic item, there is an element of luxury or privilege associated with Nueve Cerros salt, enhancing its value. The salt would not have been traded to distant regions of Mesoamerica freely for consumption by all; instead, it was limited to those with the means to purchase or otherwise obtain exchanged goods. The salt produced and traded from Nueve Cerros was a legitimization of Maya society, maintaining the divide between those Maya who had access to salt and those who did not. They were not only minimizing the danger in exposure to the unknown and powerful properties of the salt but asserting their own control over its ritual strength and sharing—proselytizing—its ritual importance with a broader Maya culture.

Cerro Tortugas Salt Dome

The most pronounced landscape features of the entire region are the Tortugas salt dome on one extreme and the Nueve Cerros mountain range on the other, about 6 km away on an approximately east-west axis. As Barthes (1997) mentions in his essay on the monumentality of France's Eiffel Tower—discussed previously for the hills and mountains within the Cancuen viewshed—the dome serves as a unifying point for all the disparate settlement clusters in the region. It is omnipresent in every aspect of daily life, from washing clothes and preparing food to hunting and working in the surrounding agricultural fields. Even today, one cannot travel any road or contemplate any activity without the salt dome looming in the background. The dome is bifurcated, a twin rise, reminiscent of the Olmec were-jaguar clefts and a clue to the probable antiquity of settlement and use of the site. The salt from the dome would have always been an attraction for animal and human life. The iconographic significance of incorporating pre-Maya, Olmec, or pan-Mesoamerican symbols raise issues of time in the conflation of traditions from a distant past with the Maya present. Adding to the sacred symbolism, from the salt dome flows the heavily salinized arroyo discussed earlier.

The dome is also home to natural gas sources, tapped by energy companies in recent decades, as well as some other fatal gasses (hydrogen sulfide vapor) that have notoriously killed several people—material proof of the dome's power. The dome is massive; up to seven cenotes (small lagoons or sinkholes) grace its peak of approximately 300 m in elevation. This highlights its contradictory qualities—its dualism or liminality—by inverting traditional concepts of space and relations between planes within the Maya cosmos. At Nueve Cerros, the Underworld as embodied by the dome is situated above a major settlement zone. One cenote on its summit routinely turns a deep and unnatural iridescent pink-purple during the rainy season, heightening the reflective qualities and potential power of the water and its association with an access point into the Underworld. Thresholds, or gateways, are integral to Maya cosmology with their seamless juxtaposition of water and inner earth; importantly, cenotes are usually confined to lower ground (Brady and Prufer 2005). Those of the dome exaggerate the dimension of earth and mountain as facets of the mythological Maya Underworld existing as a plane below the physical world. These cenotes are not simply envisioned portals of Maya ideology but actual submerged passages into the salt dome—symbols of the earth and the watery Underworld.

The Nueve Cerros Ridge, the west point of the cosmogram, rises sharply from the adjacent, often flooded flatlands and swamp grounds that mark the Nueve Cerros region. The peaks are not particularly tall; however, their precipitous rise creates the illusion of greater geographic distance from the ground below. The range is relatively well defined in a region of otherwise rolling hills and light topographic relief, forming a fence or boundary point (again a question of scale) for the area. They sprawl from east to west, rising suddenly and sharply. These mountains symbolically represent time in their almost instantaneous vertical shift and thus time travel to the pinnacle or sacred Upperworld—distant, inaccessible, or completely unreachable. The ability to combine and transform concepts of time from a single regression into multi-dimensions is paradigmatic of the axis-mundi. The summits of the Nueve Cerros mountain range are associated with the divine celestial world of revered ancestors and supreme gods (Watanabe 1990; McAnany 2000). The Maya occupation below, the world of daily living, is the plane of the present. The past is associated with the mortality of the Underworld as is the Salinas salt dome.

Temples have been found and caves reported from inside the Nueve Cerros Ridge (Schwab 2013; Schwab et al. 2012). No matter where one is within the region, one cannot avoid feeling the shadow of the dome or the Nueve Cerros range. They rise impressively from the surrounding landscape of rolling karstic hills and drainages of the important Chixoy River, only kilometers away. As noted, water and rivers have their own power and directionality in Maya cosmology (Lucero 2003; Lucero and Fash 2006; Scarborough 2003) and provide much of the reasoning behind the declaration of Nueve Cerros's position as the cosmogram of the central lowland Maya.

The freshwater drainage from the mountains counteracts the saltwater emitted from the salt dome. The concentrated mountain run-off is pure, coming from peaks too steep for feasible subsistence activities. There are neither domesticated nor animal concentrations nor recognized agricultural enterprises to pollute the drainage. Modern Maya who inhabit the area refer to this water as in the Q'eqchi' language as *chaab'il-ha'*, literally "excellent water," water given by the gods and ancestors of the Upperworld. Ideology often views mountains as the realm of the wild versus that of society and culture. The major local living settlements, the culture of the living Maya, lie below the Nueve Cerros heights. The relative inaccessibility of the peaks from whence the unadulterated water flows also charges this water with sacred power, adding to the city's mysticism.

Within this natural context, the Maya added their architecture into the equation. Mirroring the north-south axis of the cosmogram (the Chixoy-Salinas River and the main Salinas Swamp, respectively) is the Oxib' Kok group (Figure 9.10) and the Triadic group (Figure 9.11). The cosmogram's natural axis of the Nueve Cerros range to the west and the salt dome to the east is mirrored by the ballcourt group at the western position (Figure 9.12) and by the industrial zone at the eastern pole (Figure 9.13). Aside from the structures associated with the salt dome, all other architectural groups are built on slight rises out of the Salinas swampland. They form a mosaic of islands emerging from the primordial waters, like the rise of a crocodilian hide from the water is the stage of the Maya creation concept discussed earlier. The greater wetlands reach the slopes of the Nueve Cerros range, and much of the occupation zone has direct access to fresh water through a series of canals and reservoirs. The ballcourt area notably incorporates access to these waterways in its plan, both embracing the sacred water and socially avoiding it by orienting the main structure and the entire plaza to face away from the water sources. The drastic shift from swamp to mountain peak seems more extreme; spatial relationships and time are altered. The Upperworld is associated with the divine gods and future, while the Underworld below yields connotations of viscous water, evil or ambivalence, and past and future creation (Taube 1992, 1995).

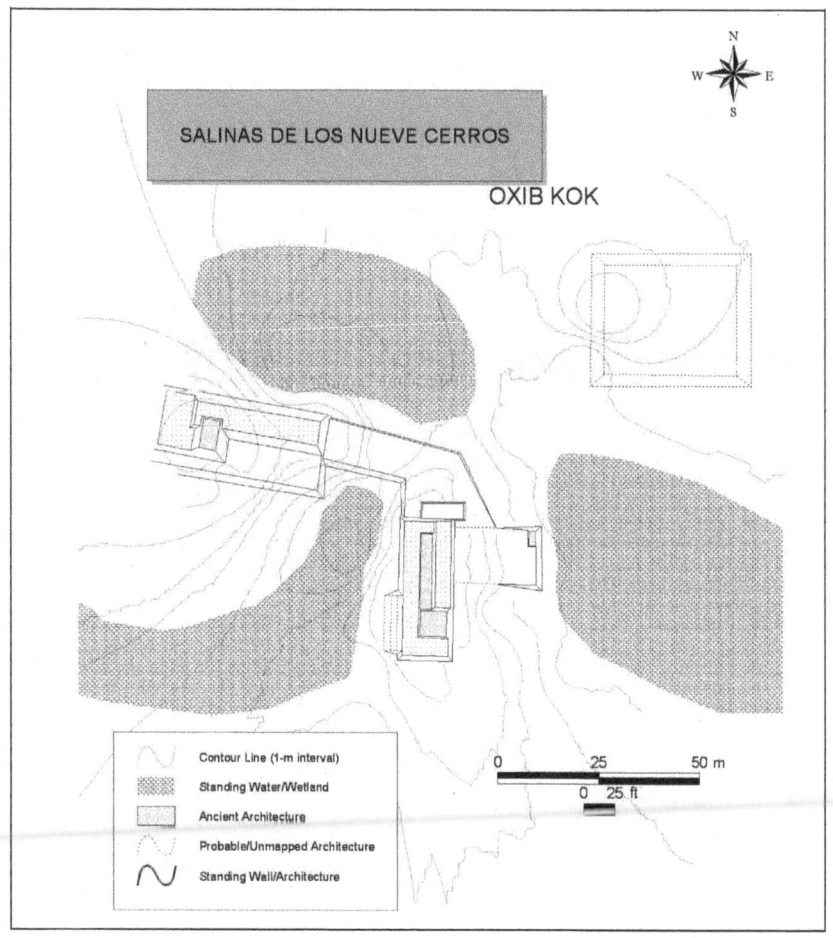

Figure 9.10. Oxib' Kok group, Salinas de los Nueve Cerros. (Base map from ArcGIS [ESRI]. Marc Wolf)

Figure 9.11. Triad group, Salinas de los Nueve Cerros. (Base map from ArcGIS [ESRI]. Marc Wolf)

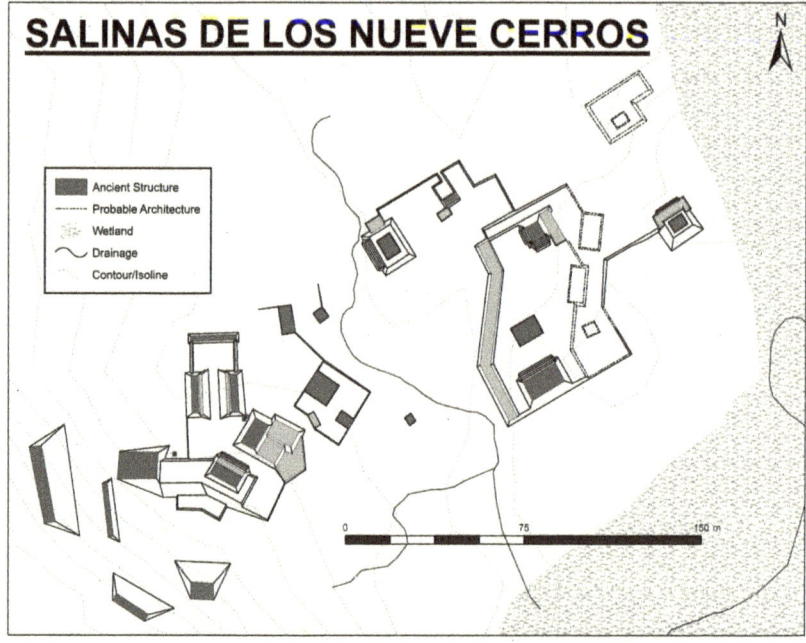

Figure 9.12. Central ballcourt, Salinas de los Nueve Cerros. (Base map from ArcGIS [ESRI]. Marc Wolf)

Sacred, Urban Landscape | 203

Figure 9.13. Salinas de los Nueve Cerros salt production zone. (Base map from ArcGIS [ESRI]. Marc Wolf and courtesy of Antolín Velásquez López.)

Architecture associated with the Nueve Cerros range—closer to the divine, celestial, or Upperworld—is more ceremonial in nature. The ballcourt (see Figure 9.12) lies at the heart of this assemblage, having cleft-earth and spiritual connotations (Scarborough and Wilcox 1991). The mythical story of the *Popol Vuh* is a clear example of the ties between ballcourts and creation (Tedlock 1996). In the story of creation from the Guatemalan Highland Maya Q'eqchi' peoples (ca. AD 1500), the *Popol Vuh* details the ballcourt as the context of the trapping, death, and rebirth of the Hero Twins. Their trials and eventual successes set the stage for the creation of the present world. The twins are tricked and are enticed into a heroic journey (and thus a significant transformation) into the Underworld in the setting of the ballcourt—a cleft or portal into the earth. Importantly, the ballcourt lies at the base of the Nueve Cerros Ridge. It is the downward pole in a three-dimensional reference to the Upperworld of the range and its heights. Several shrine complexes are known within these hills, looking down precipitous, almost vertical slopes to the playing court below. Symbolically, the ballcourt leads to the Underworld, exaggerating the vertical dimension of down in the earth versus up in the sky, on the heights of the mountains. The platforms and massive staircase of the associated plaza appear as if part of the topography of the hills themselves, creating a juxtaposition of both the natural and human developed world. Access to the mountains, the heavens, and the divine Upperworld begins from this ceremonial plaza and ballcourt.

Below the salt dome lies a much denser settlement of smaller workshop platforms, residences, enclosed plazas, and other activity areas called the industrial zone (see Figure 9.13). Most of these architectural compounds appear to be for storage, final preparations, or redistribution centers for salt and other resources within the region. The functionality of this assemblage recalls a more mundane, earthly, and common aesthetic than the ritualized ballcourt setting does at the opposite direction of the cosmogram. Central to this area are several expansive and walled plazas that have a closed, almost militaristic ambiance, defined on the northern edge by the salt brine stream. The area is a mix of activity locales and areas with restricted access, reminiscent of later Central Mexican defensive and imperial architecture. The symbolically powerful salt stream heralds the ideological strength behind these plazas. Similarities to compounds at Teotihuacan and elsewhere suggest an affinity to warrior-dedicated architecture and the death relation with the Mesoamerican Underworld (Braswell 2004; Storey 1992). Like the ballcourt occupying the base of the Nueve Cerros slope toward the heavens, this industrial and martial settlement lies at the foot of the salt dome—the Nueve Cerros gateway to the Underworld.

The north-south axis of the Nueve Cerros architectural cosmogram is created by several massive elite residential complexes in the Oxib' Kok Group (see Figure 9.10). The northern pole is a series of structures atop several greatly elevated basal platforms. The structures are generally taller (especially with the combined height of the shared platforms) and steeper and lack the expansive plaza of the Triadic Group that is the southern pole (see Figure 9.11). This larger southern plaza supports several large structures and is built on a single large rise from the surrounding wetlands as opposed to the several islands of construction in the north area. This opposition is symbolic of the change or a transition from a single unit into a dualistic or multidimensional one.

Many scholars have attributed this axis of the cosmogram as the ecliptic (Schele et al. 1998), the path of the sun and moon. At Nueve Cerros, the salt dome-Nueve Cerros Ridge axis is the principal line of the axis-mundi, east to west, representing the progression of nature from life to death. The north-south axis is represented by the then-living Maya people, mimicking the life transformations and developments of the residents of Salinas de los Nueve Cerros. As humans change into adults and history evolves, so the waters change from the deliberate and directionless swamp to the flowing Salinas River.

Sacred Geography

Salinas de los Nueve Cerros is the epitome of Maya sacred space. Its natural landscape embraces all Maya ideals of an axis-mundi. The individual components of the system are prime examples of Maya cosmology, and together they create an exponentially powerful complex. The salt dome, the salt flats, the swamp and drainages, and the Nueve Cerros mountains are deeply laden with their own sacred power, and the combination of these elements creates a dynamic system on which rests Maya expressions of creation, transformation, and afterlife. The Maya at Nueve Cerros inserted their own presence into this natural cosmogram by mirroring the system with their architecture. Buildings were constructed to reflect the ideals associated with the different segments of the axis-mundi. The east-west axis of the salt dome and the Nueve Cerros Ridge that illustrates the continuum of time and space from the Underworld to the Upperworld is mimicked by the martial and industrial area below the dome and the ceremonial aspects of the ballcourt group at the base of the mountains. At the center lies the Salinas salt flats with their own tremendous ritual power as both an economic and sacred resource and as a portal into time. The amalgamation of these natural formations and their complementary architecture irrefutably marks the Nueve Cerros region as a crucial microcosm of the Maya universe.

CONCLUSION

There are many ways of envisioning sacred landscape and water and how it interacts with human identity. Complex symbolism is described in this chapter at the archaeological sites of Cancuen and Salinas de los Nueve Cerros. The ideological placement of architecture in relation to the natural environment lies at the heart of both examples. This foundational tenant of landscape contextualization of architecture—that spirituality and human identification are inseparable from the physical and natural setting they occupy—should be extended to all conceptions of sacred landscape.

10
Paleoecology of the Chixoy Alluvial Plains along the Northern Transversal Strip

Carlos Avendaño, Claudia L. M. Morales-Flores, Juan Carlos Berrio, Carla Paola del Cid López, Silvia Carolina Duarte Morales, Rosa Delfina Sunum Orellana, Mónica María Cajas Castillo, Nora Machuca Mejía, Sharon A. Cowling, Sarah Finkelstein, Ramiro Tox, Oscar A. Rojas-Castillo, and Carolina Rosales de Zea

The Franja Transversal del Norte (Northern Transversal Strip) has been a biocultural convergent location since at least the Middle Holocene and into the present (Dillon 1977; Woodfill et al. 2015; Woodfill 2019). The Northern Transversal Strip is located approximately 170 m above sea level, spans the base of several mountain ranges (Sierra Chama, Sierra de los Cuchumatanes, Sierra Lacandon, and Sierra Chinaja), and is the result of complex geological processes, which explain its idiosyncratic hydroclimatology and highly biodiverse tropical rainforest environment (Andreani and Gloaguen 2016; Avendaño 2001; Avendaño et al. 2005; Avendaño-Mendoza et al. 2005; Castañeda 1997; Eisermann and Avendaño 2006, 2009; Granados-Dieselldorff et al. 2012; Pellecer et al. 2019). Furthermore, such geological processes explain its topographic diversity, exemplified by the Cerro Tortugas continental salt dome, the vast Chixoy River fertile floodplain, myriad caves at the foot of the 21 km Nueve Cerros Ridge (Nine Hills or Bolonppeluitz) and the approximately 200 m deep Lake Lachua. This geographic diversity elevates the region's sociocultural significance (e.g., spiritual, economic, and political) for current settlers in the Transversal, as it possibly did for the first settlers of the ancient Maya city of Salinas Nueve Cerros approximately 3,000 years ago.

In this chapter, we present the current state of paleoecological research developed at the heart of the Transversal, the so-called Lachua Region, during two main phases: 2006–2012 and 2012–2018. This chapter summarizes the findings of multiple projects developed collaboratively between San Carlos University in Guatemala (Escuela de Biología; Jardin Botánico; Centro de Estudios Conservacionistas; and Laboratorio de Análisis de Suelos, Agua y Plantas); the Departments of Geography and Earth Sciences at the University of Toronto; the School of Geography, Geology and Environment at Leicester University; the Proyecto Salinas de los Nueve Cerros; and the Center for Tropical Paleoecology and Archaeology from the Smithsonian Tropical Research Institute, with the primary goal of reconstructing the environmental history of the ancient city of Nueve Cerros. These collaborative projects utilize a critical and interdisciplinary viewpoint to propose explanations regarding the landscape paleoecology of this Maya city located in the transition between the lowlands and highlands of Guatemala. We also present the biophysical characteristics of the Transversal, the cultural history of Nueve Cerros, and the paleoecological reconstructions of the last approximately 6,000 years.

Our main goal is to document the achievements of individual research projects developed by the paleoecology team and collaborators (Avendaño and Del Cid 2017; Avendaño et al. 2018; Cajas et al. 2017; Del Cid 2018; Duarte et al. 2017; López et al. 2015; Machuca 2018; Morales 2014, 2016; Rosales et al. 2017) including the following: (1) the environmental history of the environs of Nueve Cerros (Middle-Late Holocene), and (2) related natural and cultural legacies in the Lachua Region landscapes. The proxies and resources integrated into this chapter include pollen grains, freshwater algal spores (i.e., zygospores), fungal spores, pteridophyte spores (i.e., ferns and the like), macroscopic and microscopic charcoal, sediment particle size, sedimentation rates, aerial photography, satellite imagery, vegetation inventories, community-based workshops, and ethnographic surveys.

GEOLOGICAL SETTING

The Transversal is located in the southern depocenter of the Peten Sedimentary Basin, which covers an area of approximately 60,000 km^2 across the modern Guatemalan departments of Huehuetenango, Alta Verapaz, Peten, and Izabal, as well as the Mexican states of Chiapas, Tabasco, and Campeche (see Figure 1.1; Fourcade et al. 1999). The Peten Basin complex geology is an outcome of vertical and lateral tectonic displacements occurring since the early Cretaceous (130 million years ago, Keppie et al. 2012). The main factors that explain this dynamic geology in the Proto-Central American region are the compressive tectonic forces between geologic terranes, primarily the Maya, Chortis, and Motagua (Solari et al. 2013). The basin stratigraphy shows the deposition of limestone bedrock and halites, which are indicators of past carbonate-evaporite platforms associated with marine transgressions and regressions (i.e., sea-level changes; Avendaño 2007). The geology of the southern depocenter, also known as the Chapayal Basin, indicates a dominant shallow marine environment during the early to middle-late Cretaceous (ca. 5,000 m deposition of shallow marine sediments; Fourcade et al. 1992). Subsequent regional tectonic vertical deformation resulted in the formation of deep oceanic conditions (ca. foredeep of 600 m, known as the Sepur formation) during the late Cretaceous–early Paleocene (ca. 72–61 million years ago).

The foredeep existed for approximately 40 million years until the Miocene, when sediments filled it and led to the development of the current terrestrial lowland environments (ca. < 1,000 m in elevation; Fourcade et al. 1999; Keppie 2004). Since the Miocene, the tectonic conditions in the basin have been relatively more stable, when the activation of transcurrent forces occurred because of the lateral displacement of the North American and Caribbean plates (James 2007). The sedimentary filling of the Chapayal Basin includes a combination of sources, from alluvial, brought from rivers cutting through the Cuchumatanes and Chama Mountains, to igneous from the regional vulcanism related to the Cocos Plate subduction under the Caribbean Plate (Vannucchi et al. 2004). The explanation of the geological configuration of the Transversal is critical to understanding the region's biophysical uniqueness and also why it became a scenario for cultural evolution since ancestral times.

BIOGEOGRAPHICAL SETTING

Paleobotanical reconstructions of the Miocene to Pliocene epochs in Guatemala (ca. seven to five million years ago), based on microscopic and macroscopic fossils (e.g., pollen grains and leaf remains), show the dominance of freshwater marsh and swamp habitats in the lowlands (due to higher sea levels of ca. 30 m), wet montane forests at middle elevations, and an association of mixed broad-leaved forests and cool coniferous forests in the highlands (Graham 1999). The existence of rainforests during these epochs may have been rare because of higher sea levels in response to warmer temperatures, which left a limited territory for its distribution (Graham 1999). In this period, the Laurasian flora that had previously migrated from the northern latitudes for millions of years was probably the ecologically dominant flora in Guatemala (Graham 2003, 2011). The great biotic migration around the timing of the Panama Isthmus closing (O'Dea et al. 2016; Montes et al. 2015) resulted in the eventual colonization of increasing available spaces in the lowlands and middle elevations, by Southern Amazonian and Andean Floras respectively, where both outcompeted the Laurasian one (Gentry 1982; Graham 1999; Jaramillo 2006).

Paleobotanical reconstructions indicate that the tropical rainforest extension may have experienced contraction-expansion cycles, in response to the Pleistocene glacial-interglacial cycles (i.e., alternating cool-warm temperatures; Correa-Metrio, Bush, Cabrera, et al. 2012; Hooghiemstra and Van der Hammen 2004). The paleovegetation biogeography of the last glacial (ca. 100,000 to 12,000 BP) is the basis for hypotheses about lowland and montane rainforests expansions from constricted areas known as refugia (Arruda et al. 2018). These refugia possibly had a sparse distribution across the Uxpanapa Arc, from the Oaxaca and Veracruz provinces in Mexico toward the Izabal Province in Guatemala (Wendt 1989). The Uxpanapa Arc may have functioned as the scenario for spared refugia at the foothills of a semicontinuous mountain range, where, on the one hand, higher precipitation allowed survival of biodiversity (Andreani and Gloaguen 2016). On the other hand, vicariant geographical isolation during glaciations (ca. 100,000 years), led to the formation of embedded biogeographical holding-pens in a complex topography where speciation occurred, and thus biodiversity levels increased (Cano et al. 2018; Correa-Metrio, Bush, Gutiérrez-García, and Vázquez-Domínguez 2013; Hodell et al. 2012; Pérez and Vázquez-Domínguez 2015; Schuster and Cano 2006). The current configuration of tropical rainforests in Mesoamerica (i.e., distribution, structure, and composition) most likely developed during the last approximately 12,000 years, when global temperatures increased during the Holocene. Parallel to the development of the current warm period, migrating human populations left a cultural landscape imprint across all types of vegetation (Correa-Metrio, Bush, Cabrera, et al. 2012; Ford and Nigh 2015).

Reconstructions of large-scale physical processes of the last approximately 130 million years allow a better understanding of the evolution of environmental settings of the modern drainage basin of the Chixoy River. These large-scale processes influence small-scale ones because biogeophysical factors exhibit autocorrelative and nonrandom properties (Dormann et al. 2012; Legendre 1993). Processes related to the development of soils and the establishment of plants (i.e., edaphogenesis and vegetation succession) are representative of the biophysical relationship across scales (Borrelli et al. 2012; Meunier et al. 1999), which ultimately affect where human societies settle and how they relate to their environments. Such is the case of the ancient Maya city of Nueve Cerros in the biophysical scenario of the Lachua Region.

THE TROPICAL RAINFORESTS OF THE NORTHERN TRANSVERSAL STRIP AND HUMAN OCCUPANCY

Currently, the 14,500 ha Lachua Lake National Park is the most extensive protected remnant of lowland tropical rainforest and wetlands in the Lachua Region (a total of 42,000 ha) along the Transversal (900,000 ha; Figure 10.1;

Monzón 1999). The territory around the Lachua Lake National Park where Maya villages have been established is known as the Buffer Zone (27,500 ha). Differential migration since the 1950s has resulted in a landscape mosaic composed of forest fragments among different land uses, all resultant of complex sociopolitical and economic processes (Monzón 1999), including petroleum exploitation, illegal logging, industrial agriculture, and animal farming. Since the 1970s, forced colonization and the development of a civil war front until the early 1990s left an imprint in the territorial arrangement along the Transversal (Hurtado 2008). As a response to this complex scenario, the Lachua Region lost 50% of forest cover loss, according to the 1954 reference baseline (Quezada et al. 2014). Formal biological research projects in the Lachua Region from the Escuela de Biologia at the University of San Carlos (USAC) started two years after the end of the civil war in 1996 (Poppema 2009). The implementation of these first projects aimed to support the management of the recently established Lachua Lake National Park by the Guatemalan government in 1996 (Monzón 1999). Until 2012, research projects at the Lachua Region covered contemporaneous forestry, landscape ecology, zoology, and botany, intending to support the management plan of the Lachua Lake National Park, Buffer Zone, and Mayan villages (Avendaño 1999, 2001; Avendaño et al. 2005; Avendaño-Mendoza et al. 2005; Ávila 2004; Baumgarten 2000; Cleaves 2001; García 2003, 2006; Granados-Dieseldorff et al. 2012; Quezada et al. 2014).

Before any paleoecological reconstruction at the Lachua Region, there was uncertainty about the age, origin, and history of the tropical rainforests at the Transversal (Avendaño and Del Cid 2017; Castañeda 1997; Monzón 1999). The provenance of these forests was explained mainly by biogeographic and geologic processes, without considering any partial historical contribution of humans in shaping their composition and structure (Graham 1999, 2003). The underestimation of human influence in forest composition and structure has been notorious when studying vegetation ecology in Mesoamerica (Campbell et al. 2006) and elsewhere in the tropics and the world (McMichael et al. 2017). However, more research over the last decade unearthed evidence about the millennial footprint of humans on the environment (Ford and Nigh 2009) and thus has opened discussions on the implications of cultural legacies (Piperno et al. 2007; Piperno et al. 2015). In 2012, the collaboration of our paleoecology team with Proyecto Salinas de los Nueve Cerros, led by Brent K. S. Woodfill and Judith Valle, expanded the research view at the Lachua Region by addressing a deeper historical perspective. This interdisciplinary collaboration fostered exploring and understanding connections between the origins and age of tropical rainforests at the Lachua Region and settlers of the ancient Maya city of Nueve Cerros (Avendaño 2012; Avendaño et al. 2017; del Cid and Avendaño 2015).

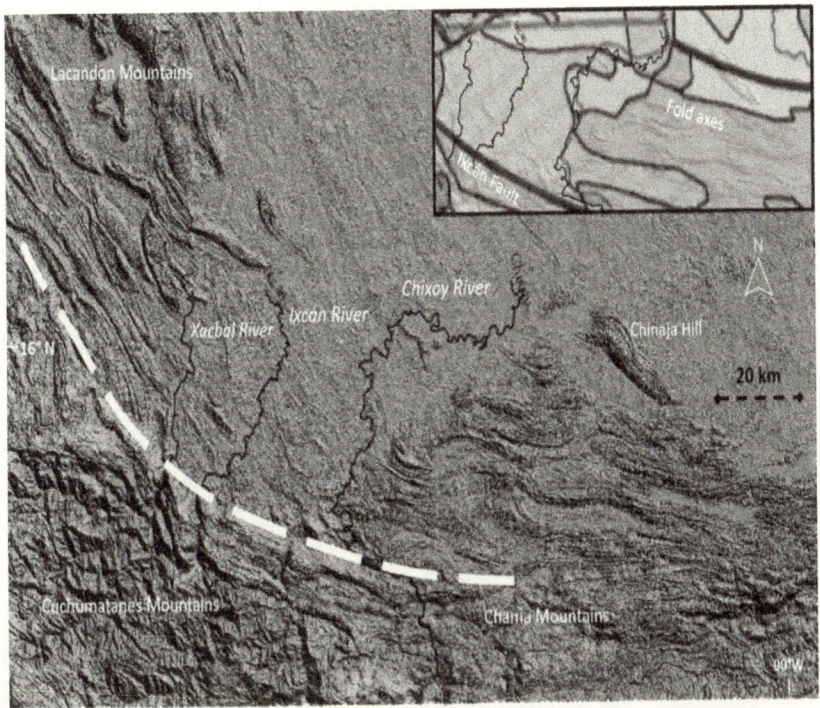

Figure 10.1. Topographic map showing the three main rivers along the Northern Transversal Strip (NTS): Xacbal, Ixcan, and Chixoy. The rivers' extensions are shown from their headwaters down to the lowlands. The geological map of the NTS is shown in the insert, where geological units are represented as polygons and separated by tectonic faults (thick black lines). The thick white dashed line represents the Ixcan Fault. (Base map from Global Mapper. Courtesy of Carlos Avendaño.)

The intermittent archaeological systematic research of Nueve Cerros led by Brian Dillon took place from the 1970s to the 1990s and established the epicenter location loosely confined to an urban pocket in between a 3 km² salt dome (Cerro Tortugas) and the 21-km-long Nueve Cerros Ridge (Dillon 1977). In 2010, Proyecto Salinas de los Nueve Cerros continued archaeological exploration and achieved an enhanced spatial representation of Nueve Cerros (Woodfill, Valle, et al. 2013). As the archaeological exploration has developed further, the occupation area of Nueve Cerros will likely be greater than the current 40 km² (Woodfill et al. 2015), as there are sparsely spaced satellite groups, or *barrios*, even north of the Chixoy River floodplain in El Quiche province and the Mexican state of Chiapas (see Chapter 3).

The archaeological evidence regarding the area and influence zone of ancient Nueve Cerros is a crucial element for contrasting paleoecological hypotheses about the origin and age of the tropical rainforests of the Lachua

Region. Research findings on ancient agroforestry in Mesoamerica (Ross 2011; Ross and Rangel 2011) support the hypothesis that Nueve Cerros settlers could have managed patched forest areas in epicentral and peripheral areas (as opposed to monocultures continuously in space). As the discussion about ancestral human influence on the contemporary composition of forests is increasingly recognized, the idea of solely "pristine" vegetation becomes less prominent. The recognition of humans in coshaping the structure, composition, and spatial patterns as part of a coevolutionary process acknowledges a more critical role in the historical domestication of biodiversity and modification of landscapes that still takes place (Gillson 2015a; Hightower et al. 2014; Nigh and Diemont 2013; Piperno 2006; Piperno et al. 2015). By enriching complementary views between the natural and social sciences, it is possible to achieve a more comprehensive explanation regarding the complex historical configuration of the lowland tropical rainforest along the Transversal (Gillson 2015b).

EXPLORATION OF MAYA FOREST GARDENS IN THE LACHUA REGION: CRITICAL HYPOTHESIS

The pollen quantification from sedimentary sources (i.e., sediment core L3) recovered from a nearby swamp to the Lachua Lake suggests a process of vegetation succession taking place close to over one millennium. The succession shows a shift from semiopen conditions (based on counts of Solanaceae pollen dominance) since the Late Preclassic (ca. AD 300) to a late succession stage (based on counts of Combretaceae-Melastomataceae pollen dominance) during the Early Postclassic (ca. AD 1100–1200; Avendaño et al. 2012). The reconstruction of this vegetation succession provides evidence of a transition from active forest management toward a progressive halt in operations matching the abandonment of Nueve Cerros. The paleoecological evidence might be pointing to the existence of Maya forest gardens in the environs of Nueve Cerros (Avendaño 2012).

Plant taxa from Maya forest gardens, based on the pollen record preservation at the Lachua Region and in Mesoamerica, point to the differential use of several species for multiple purposes, ranging from food, medicine, and timber to firewood (Ford and Nigh 2015). Firewood's historical abundance becomes critical in the history of Nueve Cerros, as this resource was very likely utilized in massive quantities to support the city's main economic activity of salt production. Tropical rainforest productivity estimates led to establishing that such activity did not deplete local forests, as such resource was sufficiently available in the Lachua Region (Woodfill et al. 2015). Paleoecological research supports these estimations, as arboreal to nonarboreal pollen-ratio calculations reference a forest cover of no less than 80% across the Classic-Postclassic indirectly (Avendaño 2012). The environmental reconstruction based on Core L3 suggests that the age of the current tropical rainforests in the Lachua Region is approximately 800 years, which matches the time since the abandonment of Nueve Cerros. It is likely that the structure and composition of such forests have an imprint of the ancient practice of Maya forest gardens that's been superimposed by Nueve Cerros inhabitants over an underlying biogeographic pattern. These findings have led to further exploration of such a hypothesis, which we are covering in the rest of this chapter.

SALINAS DE LOS NUEVE CERROS: SPECIAL GEOGRAPHICAL FEATURES

Recent investigations into the establishment of Nueve Cerros at least 3,000 years ago have revealed a larger city size, expanding across the Chixoy River floodplain. The vast floodplain may have provided appropriate extensive fertile soils for agriculture, flooded conditions for pisciculture, and excellent locations for ports to exchange goods up and down the river basin (Valle et al. 2017). The salt dome, where Nueve Cerros inhabitants placed their city epicenter, is a unique continental salt source in Mesoamerica, possibly connected to the paleomarine conditions that prevailed during the Cretaceous (Fourcade et al. 1999).

Research indicates that as younger terrestrial sediments cover ancient halite sediments (i.e., sea salt), the latter migrate vertically as a response to the downward pressure created by the former. Eventually, the halite mass outcrops in the surface, originating dome-like topographical features (Claringbould et al. 2013; Craggs et al. 2017). Along the Transversal, the fold axes of the Ixcan Fault provide superficial weakness (e.g., Andreani and Gloaguen 2016), which allows the halite sediments to outcrop. The continuous outcropping of the salt dome is possibly providing continuous positive feedback to the Ixcan Fault and associated secondary faults, which are known as halotectonics (Avendaño 2007).

METHODS: PALEOECOLOGICAL AND NEOECOLOGICAL PROJECTS

Paleoecological Reconstruction and Fluvial Geomorphology

The ideal location to collect sedimentary records is the bottom of Lachua Lake at approximately 200 m deep, which makes it one of the deepest lakes in Central America (Granados-Dieseldorff et al. 2012). Due to logistic difficulties to reach such depths, we instead extracted sediment cores with a piston Livingstone corer in its flooded shoreline environs (Figure 10.2). The collection of the Puente Mario 1 core (PM1; 114 cm in depth) was at the site known locally as "Puente Mario," close to 5 m from the lakeshore. Another location to collect sedimentary reservoirs in the Lachua Region is the Chixoy floodplain, which presents possibly the largest number of oxbow lakes along the Transversal. The mapping of young and ancient oxbow lakes in this floodplain (107.93°N direction lowering from 150 to 131 m in elevation over 18 km) aided in locating multiple sedimentary cores sites. Young and ancient oxbow lakes are generally U-shaped, but the former is still semiconnected to the main active river channel and filled with standing water. The latter is more frequently relatively far from the river channel (hundreds of meters or kilometers) and without standing water or at least holding swamp-like conditions. We collected core Tres Laguna 4 (TL4) from an ancient oxbow lake (1,040 m away from the Chixoy River) and analyzed it for paleoecological charcoal analysis (from the Tres Lagunas village, 108 cm in depth). The complete set of collected cores and pollen collection are adequately under storage in the laboratory facilities of the Proyecto Salinas de los Nueve Cerros in Guatemala City.

The nearby collection sites of the PM1 and Lachua 3 (L3) cores (2014 and 2006 fieldwork campaigns, respectively) in swamps of the Lachua Lake (1.74 km away) enabled cross-correlated paleoecological comparisons (Campbell 1999). We establish gradients and ordination of sedimentary data by applying principal component analysis and using Axis No. 1 and No. 2 eigenvalues (Legendre and Legendre 1998). We used nonparametric correlation analysis (Spearman) to quantify relationships between variables along the span of the sedimentary record (Legendre 1993). We applied a standardization technique to assess data deviation from a mean central tendency, by transforming measurements into z-scores: $z = x - \bar{x}/SE$ (where x = observed value; $\bar{x}$ = average; SE = standard error). This technique enables the assessment of extreme values according to the empirical rule (i.e., distanced more than two z-scores; Baker and King 2010; Cardoso et al. 2013; Legendre and Legendre 1998). We built stratigraphical charts (i.e., age-depth nonlinear models and paleoecological diagrams) by using the oldest- and younger-calibrated radiocarbon dates obtained through accelerator mass spectrometry from our sediment cores (Calib 7.10 using IntCal 13, Reimer et al. 2013; Stuiver et al. 2019).

Several samples interspersed from 2 to 5 cm along the PM1 core (a total of 21 levels) were collected to extract paleoecological proxies covering a size range from 5 to 150 micrometers (μm). We extracted palynomorphs and non-palynomorphs by using heavy liquid separation (Faegri et al. 2000) in the Paleoecology Laboratory of the Center for Tropical Paleoecology and Archaeology at the Smithsonian Tropical Research Institute (CTPA-STRI) in Panama City. By adding exotic *Lycopodium* spores (ca. 18,583 per tablet), we calculated

Figure 10.2. Satellite image of the Lachuá Region (Google Earth). Core locations in Lake Lachuá National Park (LLNP) and the Chixoy River floodplain are shown. PM1 = Puente Mario No. 1 core; L3 = Lachuá No. 3 core; TL4 = Tres Lagunas No. 4 core. SNC = Salinas de los Nueve Cerros; SD = salt dome Cerro Tortugas; LL = Lachua Lake; NC = Nueve Cerros Ridge. The black dashed line represents the LLNP limits. (Base map from Google Earth. Courtesy of Carlos Avendaño.)

the concentration of pollen grains, freshwater algal zygospores (Zygnemataceae), fungal spores (grouping ascospores, basidiospores, conidiospores, and teliospores; López et al. 2015), pteridophyte spores (Triletes and Monoletes), and microscopic charcoal (see below). We used tropical and regional pollen atlases for the identification of pollen grains found in the sedimentary record. To recognize pollen provenance, we contrasted pollen checklists with local and regional vegetation inventories (i.e., autochthonous—from the lowlands—or allochthonous—from the highlands transported by rivers or wind; Avendaño 2012; Barrientos 2006). Pollen taxonomic identification also took place at CTPA-STRI, in collaboration with world expert palynologist Enrique Moreno. Complementary microscopic photography took place at the Paleoecology Laboratory of the University of Toronto and CTPA-STRI. Existent modern pollen rain data from the Lachua Region were used to calibrate the significance of pollen abundance (Del Cid and Avendaño 2015). To complete the assessment of the representation of the sedimentary pollen composition, we compared it with checklists of contemporary forest stands located in the Lachua Lake National Park and its Buffer Zone (Ávila 2004; Cajas 2009; Del Cid 2018; M. García 2003). We also included forest inventories of plants associated directly with mahogany trees (*Swietenia macrophylla*, King, see below; Rosales et al. 2017).

Particle size analysis took place in the School of Geography, Geology and Environment at the University of Leicester (49 samples from PM1). To reconstruct fluvial and lacustrine environments, we matched the calculated D-values (D x 10, D x 50 and D x 90) to the sedimentary facies proposed by Torres et al. (2005). D-values larger than 200 μm indicate lower water tables or fluvial conditions; in the range between 63 and 4 μm transitional indicate fluvio-lacustrine; and smaller than four indicate μm lacustrine-flooded (i.e., higher water tables; Groot et al. 2013; McGlue et al. 2015). To test regional climatic synchronicities, we ran a Spearman nonparametric correlation analysis between PM1 D-values and stable oxygen 18 (δO^{18}) isotope databases from Lake El Gancho in Nicaragua (Stansell et al. 2013) and the Cariaco Basin off the coast of Venezuela (Lin et al. 1997, 2001). The study of marine planktonic foraminifera taxa, a source to measure δO^{18} in centennial to millennial paleorecords, has revealed correlations with annual-average past sea surface temperature (SST; Ravelo and Hillaire-Marcel 2007), mainly *Globigerinoides ruber* White (Gb; Lin et al. 1997). In lower latitudes, annual-average higher δO^{18} values have generally correlated to lower SSTs and precipitation and viceversa (Arellano-Torres and Machain-Castillo 2017). The addition of titanium concentrations from the Cariaco Basin database to the regional correlation analysis (e.g., lower values indicate lower fluvial discharge and precipitation regimes; Haug 2001a, b) complemented the discussion about the Lachua Region azonal (i.e., localized) to zonal (i.e., regionalized) climatic relationships.

Calibration of modern sediments included the analysis of samples from three soil pits in Santa Marta Salinas (SMS1, SMS2, and SMS3, in the Lachua Region, Coban, Alta Verapaz) and one in Vista Hermosa (VH1; in Ixcan, El Quiche) villages along the Chixoy floodplain. The paleoecological calibration included sediment texture analysis (percentage of clay, silt, and sand particles), organic matter content, and micro- and macro-elements analysis (e.g., phosphorus and iron measured in parts per million [ppm]). This calibration aided the understanding of sedimentation dynamics in response to climatic, hydrologic environments and cultural factors (Sarmiento et al. 2008).

A contemporary geographic analysis of the temporal evolution in four time frames—1962, 1987, 2006, and 2016 (available aerial photography) of the geomorphology of the Chixoy River floodplain in the Transversal context—revealed evidence about the temporal resolution of fluvial dynamics (Machuca 2018). The overlapping of topographic, geologic, and watershed database layers allowed a qualitative matching to identify geological hydrologic adaptation (Ziyad 2014) of the three major rivers in the Transversal, the Xacbal, Ixcan, and Chixoy (see Figure 10.2; Duarte et al. 2017).

Fire Management: Charcoal and Botanical Macroscopical Remains

When looking in the sedimentary records at the evidence that relates to fire events, it is critical to discern its cause, either natural or cultural (Snitker 2018). Natural fires occur in many ecosystems as a fundamental and functional process that allows ecological succession to take place. This process is especially relevant in dry-prone ecosystems, such as in savannas, and to a lesser degree in tropical rainforests and wetlands (Cochrane and Ryan 2009). The challenge remains to differentiate cultural fire against a climatic background because, for example, dry periods increase the likelihood of fires occurring and their frequency. In terms of the Nueve Cerros environmental history, the identification of fire events is critical for reconstructing cultural activities related to agriculture, forestry, and, its main economic activity, salt production.

Charred botanical remains, separated as macroscopic (visible to the naked eye) and microscopic, are used as past fire indicators, using the former to reconstruct local events (< 25 km in distance to the source) and the latter for regional ones (> 25 km in distance to the source; Cochrane 2009). The sampling of macroscopic charcoal was done by following a charred particle extraction protocol (López-Pérez 2015) from different levels of the PM1 (every ca. 2–5 cm) and TL4 (every 10 cm) sediment cores at the Inorganic Chemistry Laboratory at USAC. Each 1-cm^3 sample was immersed for 20 minutes in warm (not boiling) sodium pyrophosphate (10%) and then stored in cold conditions (4°C) for five days. Subsequently, samples were lightly heated, washed with distilled water and sieved through a 53-μm mesh, retrieving combined mesoscopic (53–150 μm) and macroscopic charcoal (> 150 μm; hereafter referred to as macrocharcoal). Finally, the centrifuged material kept in the mesh (2,500 rpm for 2 min), underwent washing and oven drying for 24 hrs. The material recovered from each sample was weighted on a high precision scale to estimate relative charred biomass (grams/cm^3). We used the same samples where we extracted pollen and nonpalynomorphs from the PM1 core (heavy liquid separation method), to determine the concentration of microscopic to mesoscopic charcoal alternatively by counting particles (range size 5–150 μm; hereafter referred as microcharcoal). Lastly, we calculated microcharcoal accumulation rates (CHAR, particles/cm^2/yr) according to Vachula et al. (2018) to extrapolate calibrated charcoal source areas to infer the spatial extent of fires. Exploration of botanical remains from archaeological sources is under exploration, and most likely future publications will reveal contextual information about the Nueve Cerros epicenter.

Neoecology and Cultural Legacies: Modern Rainforests and Household Gardens

We studied the population and community ecology of 12 mahogany (*Swietenia macrophylla* King) stands (six in the Lachua Lake National Park and six in the Buffer Zone; Rosales et al. 2017), because of the taxon's ecological importance in the tropical rainforests and cultural significance in the Maya culture (Steinberg 2005). As mahogany trees are well known for their longevity (Grogan et al. 2008), we assumed they represent a legacy of Maya forest gardens management of Nueve Cerros. By studying mahogany's neighboring tree composition, we hypothesized to find such management imprinted in the modern rainforests of the Lachua Region, as an anisotropic spatial distribution of beneficial tree clusters. The application of Rao's spacing test to quantify the neighboring tree community composition (Batschelet 1981) incorporated measurements from circular lots (radius 10 m, ca. 314 m^2) around each mahogany tree, where we counted and identified trees (> 10 cm diameter at breast height) and measured their distance and azimuth orientation.

An ethnoecological exploration of Santa Lucia Lachua, a Q'eqchi' Maya village neighboring the Lachua Lake National Park, provided a more nuanced understanding of the importance of household gardens among the contemporary Maya. In the study of 15 family household gardens, we explored plant diversity (plant habit and species relative abundance) and their ethnoecology in regard to beliefs, knowledge, and uses (including firewood use; Cajas et al. 2017; Morales 2014, 2016; Toledo 2002). Although still under debate, the modern analog of ancient Maya forest gardens could be the household gardens (Ford and Nigh 2015) because, as we observed, they reflect cultural assimilation of the local environment despite the recent colonization of the Q'eqchi' Maya in the Lachua Region (i.e., 40 years).

RESULTS AND DISCUSSION

Despite different regional climatic trends the Mesoamerican region may have experienced (Mueller et al. 2009; Wahl et al. 2007, 2014), the interpretation of the paleoecological reconstruction of the Lachua Region needs a contextual perspective (i.e., azonal geography). It then becomes critical to not homogenize and extrapolate findings to broader scales (i.e., zonal), especially in diverse and complex geographical, topographical, and cultural gradients such as those found in Mesoamerica (Douglas, Brenner, et al. 2016; Douglas, Demarest, et al. 2016). Even more, induction from the observations of both L3 and PM1 paleorecords brought awareness that caution is also needed when extrapolating findings from the local to the landscape scale (Hubbard et al. 2019; Legendre 1993; Robertson 1987). The advantage of using nearby sources for paleoecological reconstructions (proximity of 1.74 km) became apparent when we observed that their information was not entirely similar. We believe that their partial contrasting evidence enhanced the historical interpretation of ecological and cultural events.

We are presenting a historical progression starting in the Middle Holocene based on our paleoecological findings. This evidence is accompanied by and contrasted with neoecological results because of the natural and cultural links to paleoecological processes (Buma et al. 2019). Most of the Lachua Region studies cited in this section are a collection of collaborative projects among the peers of the paleoecology team during 2012–2018.

Middle-Late Holocene Environment (6000–4000 Cal BP): Climatologic Overview

The PM1 record shows the climatology of the last approximately 6000 BP in the Lachua Region has been highly dynamic and correlated with southern Central America and the southern Caribbean region (Figure 10.3). As expected, the comparison between the PM1, the Cariaco Basin, and Lake El Gancho records shows a climatic relationship due to an asynchronous rainy season as a result of the annual latitudinal oscillation of the Inter-Tropical Convergence Zone (Hastenrath 2002). According to decreasing titanium and depleted δO^{18} values in the Cariaco Basin, during the Holocene the Inter-Tropical Convergence Zone precipitation belt has exhibited a southern migration toward the Equatorial line (Haug 2001b), driven by a decrease in obliquity forcing (i.e., 41 kyr cycle; Bogotá et al. 2011). When obliquity reached last its maximum planetary inclination of 24.5 degrees during the early Holocene to Mid-Holocene Climatic Optimum, it led to an increased Northern Hemisphere summer insolation (i.e., 5%), which induced a higher thermal gradient from north to south, accompanied by a higher seasonality variability (Laskar et al. 2004). Since then, a progression toward a minimum obliquity of 22.5 degrees (for the next ca. 20,000 years) involves a southerly displacement of the Inter-Tropical Convergence Zone and, therefore, lower SSTs (i.e., an enriched δO^{18} trend in Lake El Gancho and the Cariaco Basin; Liu et al. 2015). In other words, at the centennial and millennial-scale, the southern Caribbean has become drier because of lower precipitation values reflected in lower fluvial discharge at the Cariaco Basin (i.e., lower titanium values).

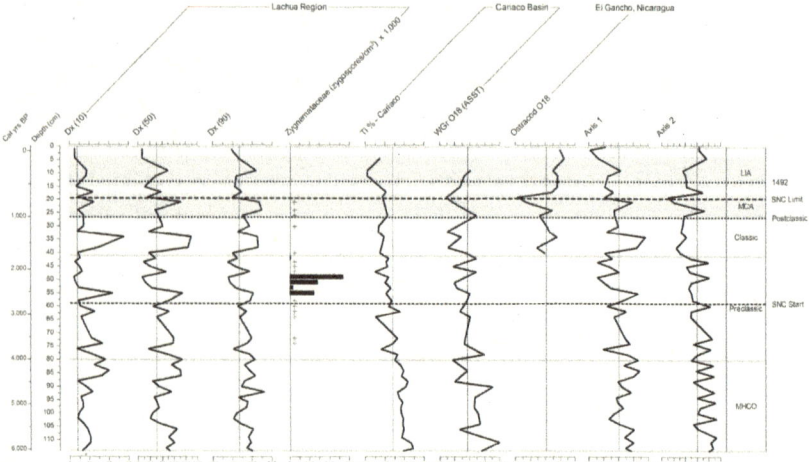

Figure 10.3. PM1 core paleoecological diagram of the last 6022 Cal yrs BP taken from the Puente Mario site next to Lake Lachuá (5 meters from the shore). Particle size D-values are shown as Dx(10), Dx(50), and Dx(90), and baselines indicate 4, 63, and 200 μm. Ti = titanium; WGr = white *Globigerinoides ruber*; ASST = average annual sea surface temperature; O18 = oxygen 18 isotope; Axis 1 and Axis 2 = first two principal components of pollen composition and abundance; LIA = Little Ice Age; MCA = Medieval Climatic Anomaly; MHCO = Mid-Holocene Climatic Optimum; SNC = Salinas de los Nueve Cerros. Ti, WGrO18, and Ostracod O18 baseline indicate average. (Courtesy of Carlos Avendaño.)

The Lachua Region climatology since the Mid-Holocene Climatic Optimum can be partially explained, therefore, by the progressive southern shift of the Inter-Tropical Convergence Zone (Arellano-Torres and Machain-Castillo 2017). This shift would imply that the North American monsoon (Metcalfe et al. 2015), in combination with the Eastern-laden humid Caribbean winds and El Niño Southern Oscillation, plays a more critical role in increasing precipitation values in the Lachua Region (Metcalfe et al. 2015). The Mesoamerican topography exacerbates the precipitation at the Lachua Region, due to horizontal rain orographic processes (Andreani and Gloaguen 2016; Lachniet and Patterson 2009; Xu et al. 2005), which possibly have been historically a prominent feature along the Uxpanapa Arc (see Figure 10.1; Wendt 1989).

The positive temporal correlation between the decreasing Cariaco Basin titanium values with the D-values measurements from the PM1 core (D x 50 Spearman's r = 0.36, $p < 0.05$) during the last 6,000 years suggests opposing climatic scenarios. In the Cariaco Basin, it suggests a decreasing trend of precipitation, and in the Lachua Region it suggests the contrary, as climatic studies in Central America show in recent times (i.e., since 1960; Aguilar et al. 2005). A diminishing particle size trend indicates a reduction in the hydrological regime and, therefore, an increase in the water table and precipitation values. This trend suggests a transition from fluvial to lacustrine conditions or flooded lakeshore environments (see Figure 10.3; An et al. 2012; Vaasma 2008; Warrier et al. 2016). It is very likely that the Mid-Holocene Climatic Optimum in the Lachua Region (ca. 6000 BP) was drier than in the last centuries, as D-values were frequently higher than 200 µm. These findings match the explanation that as lake levels drop during low precipitation periods, the elevational gradient increases and, therefore, also the hydrological regime (i.e., coarser particle size in sediments). The PM1 record suggests that possibly in the current swamp where the PM1 core was collected, there was a river running intermittently (i.e., a ravine) from the Mid-Holocene Climatic Optimum until approximately 750 to 500 years ago. During the last seven to five centuries, the formation of the current stable swamp forested conditions prevailed (i.e., higher water table), according to a change in the Principal Component Analysis Axis 1 trend relative to the zero baseline (see Figure 10.3). A significant increase of particle size around 400 BP (D x 50 = 100) during the middle of the Little Ice Age informs about a dry event (i.e., low water table), which is similar to the climatic records of the Lake El Gancho and Cariaco Basin (see Figure 10.3; Peterson and Haug 2006; Stansell et al. 2013).

The relatively low correlation between D x 50 and titanium values (Spearman $r = 0.36$, $p < 0.05$) indicates how the progressive southern Inter-Tropical Climatic Zone displacement influences the climatic system more at the Cariaco Basin than at the Lachua Region (see Figure 10.3; Haug 2001b). This fact relies on the geographic position of the Lachua Region in northern Central America, as other climatic oscillation systems also intervene, such as the North American monsoon and El Niño Southern Oscillation (Metcalfe et al. 2015). The tropical rainforests in the Lachua Region were configured through the integration of biogeographic and cultural processes beginning with the Mid-Holocene Climatic Optimum (ca. 9000–4000 BP). A diversified composition of dominant Amazonian flora, accompanied by a lesser Andean representation, and even lesser Laurasian one, explains the possible phytogeographic configuration of these lowland forests since the onset of the current interglacial, the Holocene (Avendaño 2012; Gentry 1982; Islebe and Kappelle 1994).

Preclassic (4000–1700 BP): Hydroclimatologic Regimes and Nueve Cerros Occupation

Even though the dry climatic trend of the Mid-Holocene Climatic Optimum persisted nonlinearly through the Preclassic, the D-values show a slightly decreasing trend over the next millennia until current times, as an indication of increasing precipitation in the Lachua Region (correlation with the PM1 age timeline, Spearman's $r = 0.30$ $p < 0.05$; see Figure 10.3). During the Preclassic, there is then an alternating climatology, wet at the Early (i.e., 3770 BP) and Late Preclassic (i.e., 2280–2165 and 1840 BP) and dry in between, approximately during the Middle Preclassic over three periods (i.e., 3650–3530, 2700–2520, and around 2046 BP). The Early Preclassic wet climate at the Lachua Region overlaps observations since 4590 BP at La Mancha coastal lagoon in Veracruz, at the Gulf of Mexico (higher water levels and fluvial discharge; Arellano-Torres et al. 2019), and also observations at Lago Puerto Arturo in El Peten province (Wahl et al. 2014). The first dry period of the Lachua Region during the Middle Preclassic is synchronous with a decreasing precipitation phase recorded at Rio Laguna Biosphere Reserve after approximately 3500 BP (Aragón-Moreno et al. 2012), a drying phase at Lake Peten Itza in between approximately 4500 and 3000 BP (Mueller et al. 2009), and once again to the record at Lago Puerto Arturo (Wahl et al. 2014), but opposite to the temporal climatic trend of high fluvial discharge in the Cariaco Basin (i.e., high precipitation; Tedesco et al. 2007). The first wet and dry periods during the Preclassic in the Lachua Region are evidence of the nonmutually exclusive influence of the Inter-Tropical Convergence Zone, the North American monsoon, and El Niño Southern Oscillation, (among other climatic systems), to the positive and inverse climatic relationships and the historical shifting dominance of such climatic systems (Durán-Quesada et al. 2017).

The first dry period of the Preclassic marks the appearance of the fresh running water adapted Zygnemataceae algal zygospores in the PM1 core, between approximately 3650 and 1631 BP (see Figure 10.3). At around 3770 BP, there is a deep contrast between a high and a low water stand, which is when the Zygnemataceae algae appear. The occurrence of this algae suggests the sudden prevalence of running water into the lake (because of lower lake levels) and warm conditions, which are known to favor zygospores production (Mudie et al. 2011). The highest concentrations of this algae (2500–2160 BP) coincide with the second dry period during the Middle Preclassic (2700–2520 BP). This coincidence matches the findings of fluvial-related algae (i.e., *Concentrycistis*) in paleoenvironments of the Preclassic in the Lagunas de Montebello National Park (Franco-Gaviria et al. 2018). It is then very likely that the Nueve Cerros occupation began under this dry-warm and wet changing climate, which explains the presence of Zygnemataceae algae for approximately 340 years, and also signifies the fulfillment of climatic parameters and habitat conditions at the Lachua Lake shoreline environments that have been unique during the last 6000 BP. The stability of the local climate at 2700 BP during the Middle-Late Preclassic, which probably explains Zygnemataceae high occurrence, was partially a response to regional climatic influences. During this time, the titanium values in the Cariaco Basin exhibited a lesser decreasing trend (i.e., period with more z-scores < 1, over the last 6,000 years), which also means a stable climate in the southern Caribbean. The regional climatic trend is similarly observed in the northern small-shallow lake of Salpeten and large, deep Lake Itza until the Early Classic from dry to wet (Battistel et al. 2018; Rosenmeier et al. 2002). Afterward, the trend registered in both lakes in the Peten District toward drier conditions, unlike the Lachua Region.

The Zygnemataceae reappeared in the record in low concentrations during the Terminal Classic until Nueve Cerros abandonment, which suggests the temporary return of minimum intermittent fluvial conditions at the Lachua Lake shoreline. It is possible that at approximately 780 BP, there was a lateral hydrological displacement, and the PM1 ravine ceased flowing, as this could happen in high stand system tracts (Miall 2014; Wright and Marriott 1993). The PM1 record indicates that lake levels increased significantly at 200 BP, which possibly promoted vertical sedimentation upstream of the ravine (Wright and Marriott 1993). This event could have resulted in minimized water flow and the formation of the current swamp forest.

The pollen record from the L3 core suggests that Maya forest gardens practice took place in Nueve Cerros, at least since 1772 BP, which is synchronous to the Late Preclassic wet period (ca. 1838 BP; Figure 10.4; Avendaño 2012). The pollen evidence suggests that Maya forest gardens were established close to Lachua Lake until the city's abandonment approximately 740 BP during the Late Postclassic. The Nueve Cerros residents may have experienced three main dry periods over the two millennia occupation, according to the PM1 record, at the Early Preclassic (ca. 2700–2521 BP), Early-Middle Classic (ca. 1510–1300 BP), and Late Postclassic (ca. 780 BP). None of these dry periods recorded at the Lachua Region accurately matches other observations in the Mesoamerican region, which indicates the regional geoclimatic diversity (Douglas, Demarest, et al. 2016; Rosenmeier et al. 2002). This asynchronous climatology may suggest that Nueve Cerros's long occupation possibly reflects how its geographic location, at the foot of many mountain ranges, buffers climatic extremes. This finding enriches the discussion about the adaptability of the Nueve Cerros residents to very dynamic climatic conditions. This resilience has been observed historically across different human groups, such as in Copan, Honduras (McNeil et al. 2010), Rapa Nui (Rull 2019), and Angkor (Penny et al. 2019).

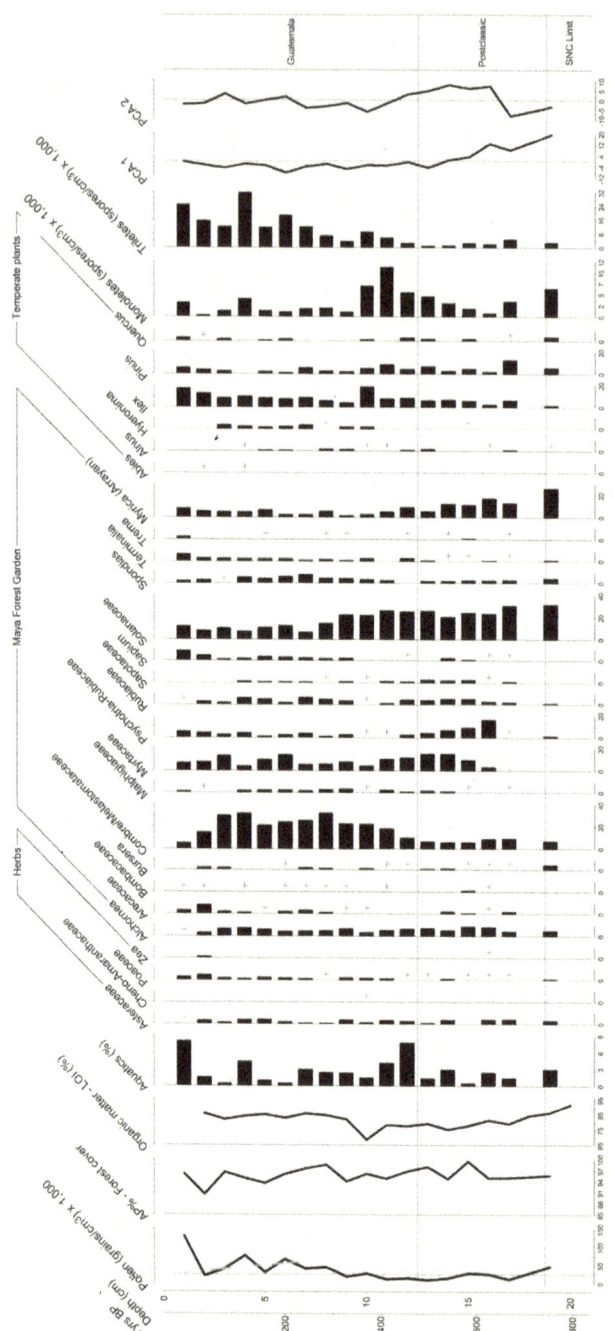

Figure 10.4. L3 core paleoecological diagram of the last 1772 Cal yrs BP taken from a swamp next to Lake Lachuá (5 meters from the shore). AP = arboreal pollen; LOI = loss-on-ignition; PCA 1 and PCA 2 = first two principal components; + = <2% abundance; SNC = Salinas de los Nueve Cerros. Pollen concentration baseline indicates 25,000 pollen grains as a threshold for low to high concentration. (Courtesy of Carlos Avendaño.)

Nueve Cerros Occupation: Chixoy River Floodplain

According to our paleoecological reconstructions of the Lachua Region in the Transversal, the evidence points out cyclic climatic conditions at the Lachua Lake environs since the Mid-Holocene Climatic Optimum. These conditions have alternated between fluvial and lacustrine and flooded at the centennial scale, which possibly affected the local ecological succession and human activities. How does this dynamic climatology relate to the establishment of Nueve Cerros? The answer to this question remains critical to understanding Nueve Cerros geographical permanency for approximately two millennia at the banks of the Chixoy River floodplain.

These cyclic environmental dynamics may have influenced the fluvial geomorphology of the Chixoy River floodplain and thus the spatial configuration of the Nueve Cerros epicenter location, fluvial transportation, and floodplain agricultural activities. The position of recent and ancient oxbow lakes along the nearly 18 km river west-east tract indicates a spatial lateral displacement of the Chixoy River ranging from approximately 800 m to 3 km. The location of the majority of oxbow lakes is on the north side of the floodplain (ca. 20 in the north, and ca. 6 in the south). This pattern could be an indication that the main channel has been migrating southerly, most likely over the last millennia. Among the three main large rivers that flow in the Transversal, the Chixoy has the most extensive floodplain with the largest number of oxbow lakes. In this regard, the striking difference is that the Chixoy floodplain runs west-east (107.93°N), while the Ixcan and Xacbal Rivers run majorly northward (4.92–38.84°N; see Figure 10.2; Duarte et al. 2017). The most likely explanation for this geographic orientation is a geologic fluvial adaptation because the floodplain runs over a westward fault in between four outcropped stratigraphic units, parallel to the Ixcan Fault (Andreani et al. 2014; Estrada 2015). Until our study, the paleofluvial dynamics of this floodplain during the Nueve Cerros occupation had not been addressed. The fluvio-geomorphological configuration during the past millennia may have been highly heterogeneous and different from how it looks currently, as these environments have a fast rate of change (Cardale de Schrimpff et al. 2019; Thompson 2003).

The 1962–2016 analysis shows how, in a relatively short time, there is a significant variation in geomorphic factors. The rapid rate of fluvial change in this period involved the formation of new meanders (six just in 2016), 1.39–11.99 m of lateral displacement, and 60–284 m of river width change (Machuca 2018; Machuca et al. 2019). This variation is not unexpected, since according to the radiocarbon dates retrieved from the Chixoy floodplain cores (Table 10.1; TL4 and core SMS3, 300 BP C14 age at the core bottom of 99.5 cm), the sedimentation rates are 10–20 times faster than lacustrine environments. For future paleoecological studies of the Chixoy floodplain, the collection of sediment cores must aim for many meters of depth and take into account lateral displacements related to neotectonics that can alter stratigraphic sequence (McMichael et al. 1994, 2014).

Table 10.1. Radiocarbon Dates and Calibrated Ranges from Sedimentary Cores Taken Near Salinas de los Nueve Cerros, Alta Verapaz, Guatemala.

Lab. No.[a]	Depth(cm)	$^{13}C/^{12}C$	^{14}C Yrs BP	2σ Calibration Cal AD Age Ranges[b]	2σ Calibration Cal BP Age Ranges[b]
Core PM1					
Beta-407008	35.5	-23.3	1480±30	AD 539 (**586**) 644	1306 (**1364**) 1411
Beta-407007	11.4	-17	5260±30	BC 4083 (**4073**) 3984	5933 (**6022**) 6032
Core TL4[c]					
Beta-410251	108	-24.9	630±30	AD 1337 (**1350**) 1398	552 (**600**) 613
Core L3[c]					
Beta-281242	22.5	-27.8	990±40	AD 986 (**1049**) 1155	796 (**902**) 963
GrA-40111	47.5	---	1835±30	AD 86 (**178**) 245	1704 (**1772**) 1835

Source: Carlos Avendaño.
[a]Cores are associated with these local sites: PM1 = Puente Mario; TL4 = Tres Lagunas; L3 = Lake Lachuá.
[b]Bold numbers in parentheses are the calibrated dates. All radiocarbon-dated material is from bulk samples.
[c]From Avendaño (2012).

Although there are no radiocarbon dates for the soil pits in Santa Marta Salinas and Vista Hermosa villages, chemical measurements at different horizons suggest the existence of possible buried paleosols and past fluvial activity. The evidence relies primarily upon phosphorus (P), magnesium (Mg), iron (Fe), calcium (Ca), and dominant sandy texture (75–96.39%; Figure 10.5; Costantini 2018). The elements P and Fe are chemically bonded in soils and are indicators of past human activity. The three pits in SMS showed different profiles despite their short physical separation (5–10 m)—in particular, their P content, which in SMS3 showed relatively high values from the surface down to 50 cm (40.9–44.59 ppm) and a lower peak at 80–90 cm (18.39–21.62 ppm). The SMS1 pit shows P peaks at 40 cm (12.8 ppm) and 60 cm (17.51 ppm), while in SMS2 P was depleted through the profile except at the surface (28.84 ppm). The findings in these pits are indicative of relatively intermediate to low phosphorus values (Gburek et al. 2000), which suggests that at depths greater than 50 cm, we may be observing paleosols related to agricultural activity in SMS1 and SMS3 (i.e., centennial-timescale). As organic matter depletes below 20 cm across Santa Marta Salinas and Vista Hermosa, we could argue that recent agricultural activity is associated with depths < 50 cm (i.e., decadal timescale; see Figure 10.5; Holdridge and Leigh 2018). Despite these revealing critical results, we need to explore further different locations along the Chixoy floodplain to confirm the observations drawn from these pits.

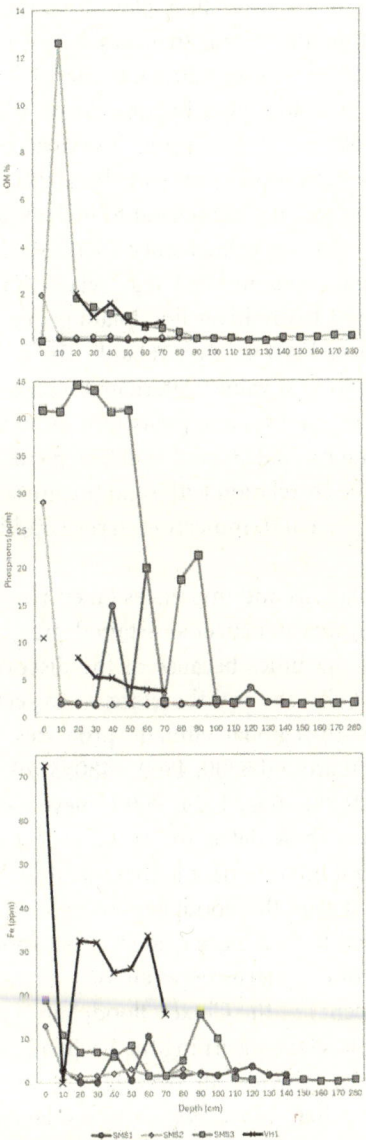

Figure 10.5. Soil pit profiles from Santa Marta Salinas (SMS) and Vista Hermosa (VH) for organic matter (OM), phosphorus, and iron (Fe). (Courtesy of Carlos Avendaño.)

When iron becomes mobile, it reflects together with magnesium, weathering activity in response to increased precipitation and surface runoff (Alnsour 2013; Haldar and Tišljar 2014). In both SMS1 and SMS3 pits, iron values show a positive correlation with potassium (Spearman $r = 0.586$–0.832, $p < 0.05$; P binds to Fe). This correlation may support the existence of past cultural activities in the Chixoy River floodplain because increasing iron suggests higher precipitation and runoff that may have supported a more productive agricultural activity (Alnsour 2013). In the VH1 pit, iron values at the surface (72.5 ppm) are trifold higher in comparison with the SMS pits, and two-fold higher at 20–60 cm (25–33.5 ppm). The surface iron values are most likely pointing to the reactivation of ancient channels (i.e., oxbow lakes) due to flooding in recent times, possibly related to increased precipitation in the Transversal and the Chixoy watershed since 1970 (Machuca 2018). The iron measurements at deeper levels in VH1 may relate to past flooding events, which, according to the Chixoy River floodplain geomorphology, have been more extensive in the northern floodplain bank. The possible high precipitation phases, according to iron values, alternated with dryer ones, as the calcium measurements suggest. Iron and potassium show a negative correlation with calcium (Spearman $r = -0.823$ and $r = -0.878$, $p < 0.05$, respectively), and calcium shows a positive correlation with sand texture (i.e., lower water table; Spearman $r = -0.749$, $p < 0.05$), indicating dryer conditions (i.e., associated with sands).

Among the extrapolations and inferences taken from the PM1 paleoecological reconstructions, we can expect a certain degree of synchronicity with the Chixoy floodplain dynamics because of the discovered correlation between particle size and climate, and therefore we expect spatial contagiousness due to landscape-to-regional climatic processes. High system tracts would have happened at around 5300, 4800, 4480, 3770, 2800 (Nueve Cerros establishment), 2165, 1838, 1631, 1224, 900 (Nueve Cerros abandonment), 538, and 116 BP. During these dates, we would expect an increased density of channel bodies (lateral migration), a higher likelihood of flooding, and the formation of shallow lakes in the floodplain (Wright and Marriott 1993). In future studies, we expect to find more evidence that supports these observations regarding synchronic patterns between long-term sedimentary records (i.e., Pleistocene-Holocene) of the Chixoy floodplain (i.e., high-, transitory-, and low-system fluvial tracts) concerning the Lachua Lake records.

These reconstructions provide an overview of the very complex and changing environment where Maya populations adapted for millennia and most likely developed landscape strategies compatible with natural patterns and cycles (Chase and Scarborough 2014; Demarest et al. 2005; Ford and Emery 2008; McMichael et al. 2014; McNeil et al. 2010) and arguably similar to those promoted in popular culture by Jared Diamond (2011) and others. Residents from Nueve Cerros may have experienced living in a very active floodplain, where different cultural activities, such as agriculture and pisciculture, flourished (see Chapter 3).

NUEVE CERROS LANDSCAPE MANAGEMENT: FORESTS AND FORESTRY
The completion of the Holocene (ca. 12,000–11,000 BP) paleoecology of the Chixoy River floodplain and Lachua Lake shoreline and associated *terra firme* environments is critical to contrast the hypothesis about landscape evolution and the cultural land-use history of the Lachua Region in the context of the Transversal. The paleoecological reconstructions based on L3 and PM1 cores suggest that the Lachua Lake surroundings most likely had a combination of forest stands and Maya forest gardens fields instead of open agricultural land (see Figure 10.4). The retrieval of two pollen grains of *Zea* from L3 over approximately 1300 BP, and of none in PM1, supports such a claim as few grains are not sufficient evidence to state otherwise (Avendaño 2012; Avendaño and Del Cid 2017). According to the Lachua Region landscape geoecological classification (Avendaño et al. 2005), the Chixoy River floodplain would have been a more suitable location for agriculture. Floodplain soils are well developed and deeper than *terra firme* soils, and also alluvial aquifers keep a higher water table annually (i.e., fluvial erosional-depositional flat plains). There is evidence that the Cerro Tortugas dome remained as a salt source known to subsequent Maya groups (e.g., Akalaha and Lakandon), probably until 300 BP (see Chapter 3; also Woodfill et al. 2015; Woodfill 2019). The extracted macrocharcoal from the TL4 core shows a concentration peak during the Late Postclassic around approximately 538 BP (0.73 g/cm^3). During the last 500 years, macrocharcoal dropped below 50%, with an exception between 378–316 BP, which showed a slight increase (0.44 g/cm^3) similar to the one observed approximately 569 BP (0.44 g/cm^3; Figure 10.6). The macrocharcoal found in the Chixoy floodplain core TL4 then suggests that agriculture and salt production activities possibly continued after the main Nueve Cerros abandonment event (see Chapter 8). The retrieval of cores covering longer temporal spans (i.e., > 1,000 years) in the future, will allow us to have a more complete view of the cultural history of the Chixoy floodplain.

The Lachua Lake's diverse shoreline physical settings (Granados et al. 2012) support our differential sediment recovery of cores L3 and PM1. The shorter span of core L3 allowed us to nest its sedimentary record into the 6,000-year recovery time of the PM1 core (see Table 10.1). The calculation of loss on ignition (LOI) from L3 provided evidence of a lakeshore environment with a high-water table and high input of organic matter (> 70%) derived

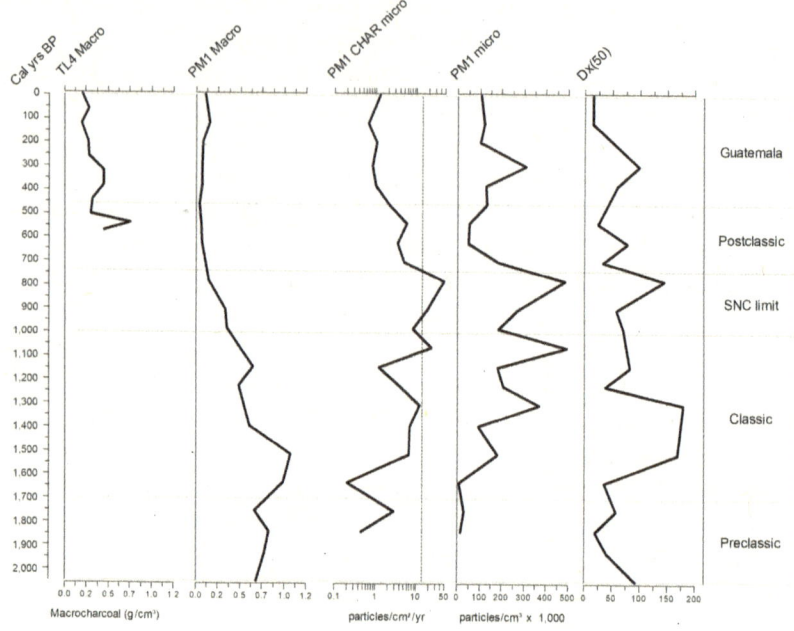

Figure 10.6. Paleoecological diagrams of cores TL4 (108 cm deep, 569 Cal yrs BP) and PM1 (114 cm deep, 6022 Cal yrs BP) showing charcoal records. Macro = macrocharcoal (>53 μm); micro = microcharcoal (5-150 μm); CHAR = Charcoal Accumulated Rate; Dx(50) = D-value from core PM1; SNC = Salinas de los Nueve Cerros. Baseline in CHAR indicates threshold for large fires, according to Vachula et al. (2018). (Courtesy of Carlos Avendaño.)

from an extensive forest cover (> 85%; Avendaño 2012). The reconstructed environment matches the one of a swamp forest where pollen preservation is feasible (e.g., pollen from Cyperaceae aquatic plants present; Faegri et al. 2000; Wilmshurst and McGlone 2005). On the Puente Mario site, pollen preservation in the PM1 core also takes place once a swamp forest becomes established, and a former ravine becomes inactive approximately 800 BP. The preserved pollen record shows the signal of a nearby mature forest (forest cover > 80%), not previously recorded in the core, possibly because of the ravine's poor preservation conditions (Faegri et al. 2000; Traverse 2007). When comparing the temporal overlapped pollen composition of both cores, they have in common the ecological swamp forest conditions (i.e., Cyperaceae pollen in both, ca. 1–9%; Figure 10.7). Both cores suggest a cultural influence, more direct in the L3 location, and more as a background signal in the PM1 one. The L3 and PM1 cores records suggest the influence of spatial heterogeneity and autocorrelation at the landscape scale because their pollen composition reflects, in general, different vegetation succession and geomorphic habitat evolution. In vegetation studies at the landscape scale, these spatial properties have been shown in a previous landscape classification in the Lachua Region (Avendaño et al. 2005; Ávila 2004; Cajas 2009; García 2003), in the Canadian Yukon (Campbell 1999), in New Zealand (Wilmshurst and McGlone 2005) and in England (Tweddle and Edwards 2010). Physiognomically, forests might look alike (i.e., forest cover > 80%), but composition-wise they reflect spatial heterogeneity effects. Forest spatial heterogeneity found nowadays in the Maya region (Ford 2008; Ross 2011) supports, on the one hand, scholars' argument about Maya management strategies adapted to landscape spatial characteristics (Demarest 2004, 2006). On the other hand, this adaptive management allowed the maintenance of high biodiversity levels until the present (Ford and Nigh 2015).

The possible existence of Maya forest gardens at the northeast shore of Lachua Lake until Nueve Cerros abandonment (Avendaño 2012) provides the basis to assess management legacies. For the small trees and shrubs of the Solanaceae family (e.g., chile, tomatoes, and the like) to become ecologically dominant (pollen signal 32–22%), it would have required substantial management. Once Maya forest gardens management halted at the time of Nueve Cerros abandonment, Solanaceae dropped its abundance (15–7%), while late-succession trees, such as Combretaceae-Melastomataceae, became dominant (from ~10 to 22–32%). The similar Solanaceae pollen signal during the last 750 years in both L3 and PM1 cores (5–15%) supports, on the one hand, that such a family is less dominant in unmanaged forests. On the other hand, this similarity would also support the possibly that the environs of the PM1 core were a Maya forest gardens (Table 10.2). The similarity of the Solanaceae modern pollen signal (12–6%; Avendaño 2012; Del Cid 2018; López et al. 2015) to the ones recorded in L3 and PM1 records since Nueve Cerros abandonment could support a Maya forest gardens ancestral signal in different locations of the Lachua Region. This plant abundance pattern, before and after Nueve Cerros abandonment, describes the succession of other pollen taxa from the L3 record, which, like Solanaceae, are culturally beneficial for the Maya, such as Myrtaceae, Sapotaceae, *Spondias*, and *Myrica* (Arrayán). Currently, the location of the L3 core holds a swamp forest where a *Myrica* stand is present (ca. 0.3 ha). The Arrayán is a temperate small tree mostly found in highlands (Ulloa 2001), used as a wax source for manufacturing candles, whose pollen showed up in the record since Late Preclassic times (Avendaño 2012). The existence of this stand supports the hypothesis related to Maya forest gardens practiced by Nueve Cerros inhabitants and poses questions about the how-to of cultural-biological adaptations and domestication across climatic zones (Aguirre-Dugua and González-Rodríguez 2016; Colunga-García and Zizumbo-Villarreal 2004).

Table 10.2. Pollen Types Found on Modern Pollen Calibrations and Fossil Pollen Spectra from Cores Taken Near Salinas de los Nueve Cerros, Alta Verapaz, Guatemala.

Vegetation Belts	Pollen Taxa Genus	Family	Associated Plant Taxon/ Taxa	Uses
Lowlands	Acacia	Fabaceae	Acacia spp.	Medicine, forage, construction
	Alchornea	Euphorbiaceae		
	Anthurium	Araceae		
		Araliaceae	Dendropanax arboreus	Food, ornamental, forage, medicine
		Arecaceae	Acrocomia mexicana	Food
			Attalea cohune	Food, construction, medicine
			Chamaedora spp.	Food
			Cryosophila stauracanhia	Construction, medicine
			Sabal morrisiana	Construction
		Bignoniaceae	Tabebuia rosea	Medicine, timber, ornamental
		Bombacaceae	Ceiba pentandra	Medicine, timber, ritual
			Quararibea	Food
			Pseudobombax	Ritual
		Boraginaceae	Cordia sp.	Food, medicine
	Brosimum	Moraceae	Brosimum alicastram	Food, medicine, forage, ritual, firewood
	Celtis	Ulmaceae	Celtis iguanaea	Food
		Combretaceae	Combretum	
		Melastomataceae	Clidemia	
		Euphorbiaceae	Cnidoscolus aconitifolius	Food
			Manihot esculenta	Food, medicine
		Fabaceae	Lonchocarpus castilloi	Ritual
			Pachyrhizus erosus	Food
			Phaseolus lunatus	Food
		Fabaceae	Mimosa spp.	Medicine, fuel
		Malpighiaceae	Byrsonima crassifolia	Food, medicine, apiculture
		Moraceae	Castilla elastica	Latex
			Pseudolmedia spuria	Food
		Myrsinaceae	Myrsine sp.	
		Myrtaceae	Psidium guayaba	Food
			Pimienta dioica	Food
	Pachira	Bombacaceae	Pachira aquatica	Food, medicine, construction

Vegetation Belts	Pollen Taxa Genus	Family	Associated Plant Taxon/Taxa	Uses
	Piper	Piperaceae	Piper amalago	Medicine
	Psychotria	Rubiaceae	Psychotria chiapensis	Medicine
		Rubiaceae	Alseis yucatanensis	Wood
			Hamelia avillaris	Medicine
	Salvia	Tamiaceae	Saivia coccinea	
	Sapium	Euphorbiaceae		
		Sapotaceae	Crysophyllum mexicanum	Food, medicine
			Manilkara zapota	Food, medicine, latex
			Pouteria campechiena	Food
		Solanaceae	Solanum	Food, medicine, forage, ritual
			Cestrum	Medicine, ornamental
			Capsicum	Food
	Trema	Ulmaceae	Trema micrantha	Food
		Ulmaceae		
Lowland Rainforest (LRF)	Spondias	Anacardiaceae	Spondias mombin	Medicine, construction,
			S. pupurea, S.radikoferi	food
	Bursera	Burseraceae	Bursera simaruba	Medicine, ritual
		Burseraceae	Protium copal	Ritual
LRF–Lower Montaine Rainforest (LMRF)	Cecropia	Cecropiaceae	Cecropia sp.	Medicine, timber
	Terminalia	Combretaceae	Terminalia amazonia	Construction, firewood
	Hedyosmum	Chloranthaceae	Hedyosmum mexicanun	Food
LMRF–Montaine Cloud Forest	Myrica	Myricaceae	Myrica cerifera	Medicine, candle wax
	Quercus	Fagaceae	Quercus sp.	Fuel
Mixed Montaine Forest (MMF)	Abies	Pinaceae	Abies guatemalensis	
MMF–Sub-Alpine Forest	Alnus	Betulaceae	Alnus acuminata, A. jorullensis	
Highlands	Pinus	Pinaceae	Pinus caribaea,	Ritual

Vegetation Belts	Pollen Taxa Genus	Family	Associated Plant Taxon/ Taxa	Uses
Not Associated with Vegetation Belts				
		Amaranthaceae	*Altermanthera sp.*	
		Amaranthaceae	*Amaranthus*	Food
		Chenopodiaceae	*Chenopodium ambrosioides*	Food
		Asteraceae		Medicine
		Cyperaceae	*Cyperus esculentus*	Food
			Eleocharis caribaea	
	Peperomia	Piperaceae		
		Piperaceae		
		Poaceae		Food
	Polygonum	Polygonaceae		Food
	Zea	Poaceae	*Zea mays*	Food
	Trilete spores		Fern	Food
	Monolete spores			

Source: Carlos Avendaño.

Note: Associated plant taxa and uses by ancient Maya populations are shown. Information about vegetation belts and known usage by modern Maya populations is provided. Rare pollen types are shown. Cores are associated with these local sites: Puente Mario, Tres Lagunas, and Lake Lachuá.

After comparing the L3 and PM1 records with modern pollen rain and forest vegetation from different locations in the Lachua Region (Lachua Lake National Park and its Buffer Zone) and village household gardens, we sought to gain evidence about the effects of past cultural management and natural spatial heterogeneity (see Figure 10.7). The gamma (i.e., total) plant diversity of household gardens holds 139 species, including native and exotic taxa (Cajas et al. 2017; Morales 2016). Out of this diversity, 49 species (35.25%) are commonly present in the Lachua Lake National Park forests, such as *Attalea cohune* (Arecaceae) and *Protium copal* (Burseraceae), which are associated with mahogany stands (Ávila 2004; García 2003). Solanaceae plants are not common in the Lachua Lake National Park and are rare in the Buffer Zone forest remnants, but are dominant in household gardens where current Maya populations make use of them (see Figure 10.7; Cajas et al. 2017; Morales

2016). The same argument applies to Myrtaceae and Sapotaceae, both found in household gardens because of their benefits, but the former is rare in the Lachua Lake National Park, and the latter rare in both the Lachua Lake National Park and Buffer Zone (del Cid 2018). When compared, the plant composition of household gardens is more similar to the pollen composition of modern pollen rain from the Lachua Lake National Park and Buffer Zone, the pollen record from PM1 since approximately AD 1492, and the forest stands associated with mahogany, mainly because of the association to contemporary dominant taxa, such as Fabaceae (e.g., beans, Chipilín, Conacaste, Madre Cacao, Paterna, Rosul, and Tamarindo) and Arecaceae (e.g., palms; see Figure 10.7; Morales 2016). To a lesser degree, nevertheless, the household gardens plant composition was similar to the PM1 pollen record at the time after the Nueve Cerros abandonment, because of the abundance of Rubiaceae (e.g., Irayol family, used for firewood). According to these observations, we can speculate the existence of a typology of Maya forest gardens differentiated toward the dominance of particular plants for specific purposes. For example, the household gardens' plant composition, when compared with the pollen signal of the L3 core, differs because the latter suggests a typology centered on the harvesting of Solanaceae. Others could have been focused on differential harvestings, such as Fabaceae, Rubiaceae or Meliaceae (e.g., mahogany), according to their adaptability to landscape heterogeneity (Ford and Nigh 2015).

According to the literature, mahogany is nearly absent in modern pollen calibrations and sedimentary records (Marchant et al. 2002, 2009), and so estimations of its past distribution rely on indirect evidence, speculative associations, or on local knowledge (Toledo 2002, 2009). Pollen grains from *Spondias* (Anacardiaceae), found in the L3 record, which usually preserves in sediments, in this case, could sustain discussions about ancestral forest management because currently it associates with mahogany stands in Buffer Zone forest remnants (Rosales et al. 2017; Steinberg 2005). In this respect, Maya forest rangers in the Lachua Region estimate that the mahogany trees from the Lachua Lake National Park are long-lived (ranging from 200 to 600 years old) and thus possibly anachronic to Nueve Cerros (Rosales et al. 2017). If such anachronism holds certain, the further study of the mahogany tree neighborhood highlights the need to continue studying hypotheses about the spatial ecology of Maya forest gardens. Such an approach has been taken in Belize (Ross 2011; Ross and Rangel 2011).

The mahogany study in the Lachua Region indicates that 51 tree species (e.g., Arecaceae, *Brosimum*, *Bursera*, and Fabaceae found in the PM1 core) arrange in a spatial anisotropic ecological association (135–183°N) around mahogany trees (Rosales et al. 2017). When comparing the Lachua Lake

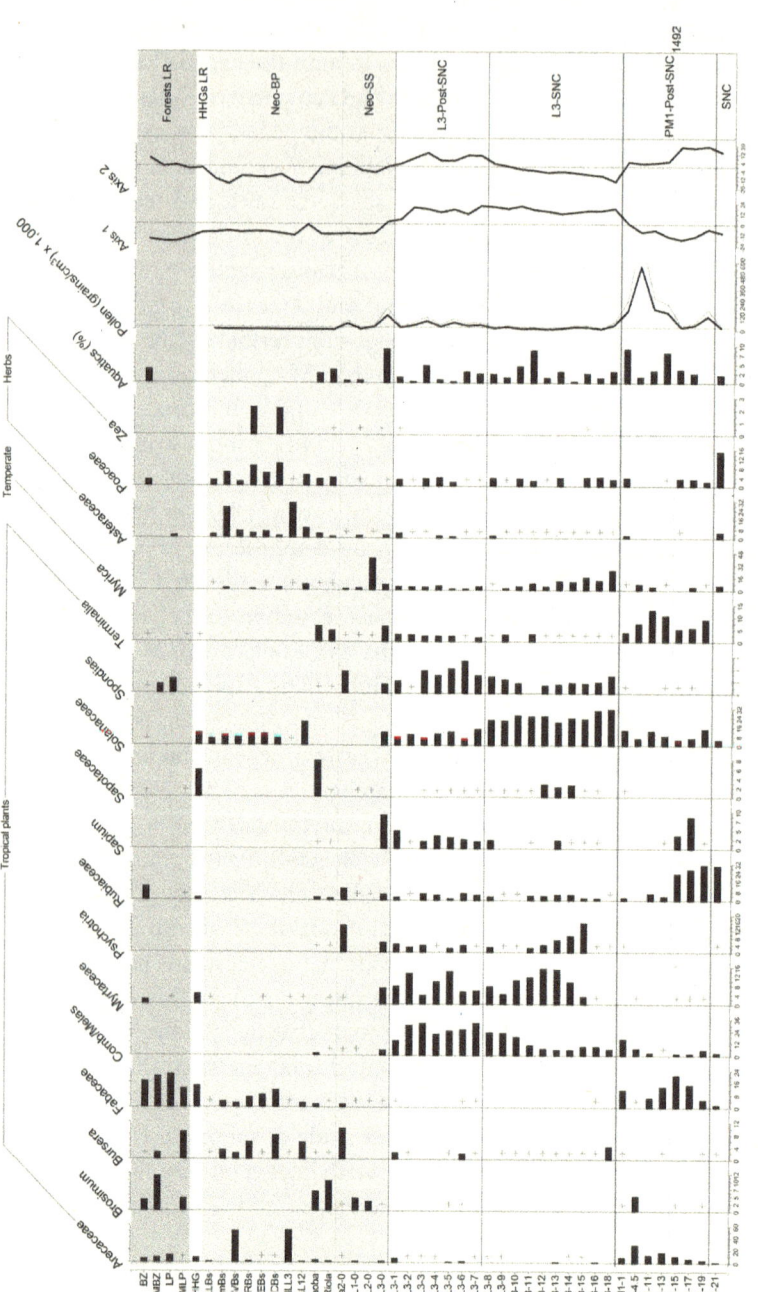

Figure 10.7. PM1 and L3 cores paleoecological and calibration (based on modern pollen data from the Lachua Region) diagram. Axis 1 and Axis 2 = first two principal components; SNC = Salinas de los Nueve Cerros; HHG = household garden; Neo = modern/neoecological; BP = bryophyte polster; SS = surface sediment. + = <2% abundance. Neo-Bp and Neo-SS codes refer to sites from Avendano (2012) and del Cid (2018); Post-SNC = after SNC abandonment. Forests LR (Lachua Region) refer to buffer zone (BZ); SM = *Swietenia macrophylla*; LP = Lachua Lake National Park. (Courtesy of Carlos Avendaño and Carla Paola del Cid López.)

National Park and Buffer Zone spatial circular averages (170.98° and 115.53°, respectively), they are not significantly different (p < 0.05), which could suggest ecological similarities (Figure 10.8). In other words, the segregation of mahogany spatial neighborhoods across the Lachua Region could be responding to community associations at the habitat level, bounded to a phytogeographic origin (i.e., majorly Amazonian; Azaele et al. 2006; Baldeck et al. 2013). Alternatively, the similarity of this spatial tendency could also mean that cultural effects could determine tree neighborhoods and thus explain a link between current land use at the Buffer Zone and historical management at the Lachua Lake National Park (Rosales et al. 2017). All the neighboring mahogany species are known as beneficial to the modern Q'eqchi' Maya populations in the Lachua Region, including uses for construction, firewood, medicine, food, and forage, and for resin and oil production (Avendaño et al. 2018). This fact could signify the historical transmission of knowledge among the Q'eqchi' Maya through the Postclassic in the Verapaces Region. This ethnic group was highly connected through trade, at least until the XVI-XVII centuries, with other Maya groups such as the Xokmo', Lakandon, Ah Xoy, Manche' Ch'ol, Itza, Chontal, and Mopan (Caso Barrera and Aliphat Fernández 2006a, 2006b).

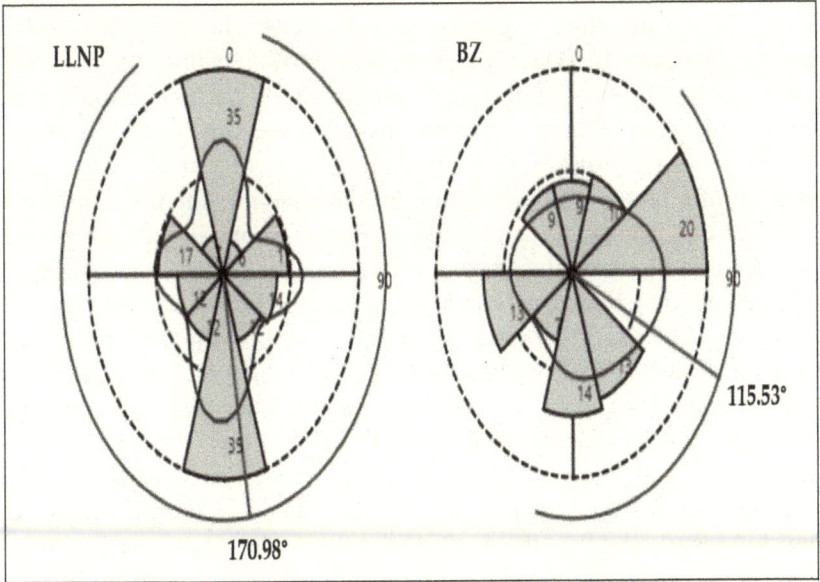

Figure 10.8. Summary rose diagrams of tree neighborhood trees of mahogany stands (10-m radius), in the Lachuá Lake National Park (LLNP) and its buffer zone (BZ). Numbers in polygons indicate frequency of trees in an azimuth direction. Vector with angle measurement indicate circular average. (Courtesy of Carlos Avendaño.)

In terms of vertical structure, vegetation surveys in the Lachua Region village indicate that trees are the main feature in household gardens (54.7%), followed by herbs (34%), and lastly by shrubs (11.3%) while plant uses range from medicinal (34%) to firewood (21.3%) and domestic use (19.1%; Cajas et al. 2017). The most frequent plant across the household gardens is achiote (*Bixa orellana*; see Chapter 8), which is used by the Q'eqchi' Maya for food preparation and is known to be part of the *Triada del chocolate*, or chocolate triad. This triad relates to the ancestral Mesoamerican agrosystem that combined achiote, cacao (*Theobroma cacao* L.), and vanilla (*Vanilla* spp.; see Chapter 8; also Aliphat Fernández 2009; Caso Barrera and Aliphat Fernández 2006a; McNeil 2006b). Historically, through the Spanish conquest and Colonial Period, the Q'eqchi' Maya of Northern Verapaz have kept the inherited knowledge regarding such an agrosystem and recreated it in their household gardens (Caso Barrera and Aliphat Fernández 2012). Due to the colonial and post-1950s Guatemalan sociopolitical reconfiguration, including that the related Civil War, some of these cultural legacies have partially transcended. Possibly because of these sociopolitical issues and other factors, we did not observe the cacao triad in the 15 household gardens that we assessed (Downey 2010; Hurtado 2008).

Based on the literature, finding fossilized cacao remains a challenge, and so we did not find them (e.g., seeds, flowers, pollen) in the Lachua Region sedimentary records (Whitney and Cárdenas 2017). Finding substantial evidence of its cultivation and management in Nueve Cerros remains a goal. Besides the proof of the cultural transmission of the cacao triad to the Q'eqchi' Maya since colonial times, another source of proof would be the demonstration of a center of domestication in Mesoamerica. The origin of cacao is under discussion since it presents a wide geographical distribution (i.e., southeastern Mexico to the Amazon basin; Bletter and Daly 2011; Ogata et al. 2011). According to various authors (Cheesman 1944; Pound 1938; Schultes 1984), cacao had its origin in South America (specifically in the Orinoco and Amazon basins) and was human-dispersed along the Andes in two different ways. These authors suggest human dispersion is likely because cacao seeds lose their viability quickly when removed from the pod and because cacao does not show a particular mechanism of dispersion. Another suggestion by the same authors is the possible migration of two cacao subspecies, one toward Venezuela and the other to Central America. It is also possible that cacao was naturally distributed in Mesoamerica and then domesticated by its inhabitants (Gómez-Pompa et al. 1990).

Another explanation suggests simultaneous origins for cacao (Cuatrecasas 1964), one in South America and another in Central America. Other studies based on morphological diversity from the species found in Central and

South America support this explanation (Cope 1976; Gómez-Pompa et al. 1990; Laurent et al. 1994; Wood and Lass 1985). DNA studies were also used to find a genetic segment that was unique among some cultivars from the Yucatan Peninsula, Lacandon forest, and South American populations (De La Cruz et al. 1995). This proof could support Cuatrecasas's hypothesis, but it is still necessary to gather more information. Some species are area specific, like the Criollo cacao (*Theobroma cacao* spp. cacao), which has been managed by the Maya over the last 1,500 years (Gómez-Pompa et al. 1990). The Forastero group presents diverse origins in South America (Upper Amazon, Lower Amazon, Orinoco, and the Guianas), similar to the Forastero or Trinitario group (a breed between Criollo and Forastero; Motamayor et al. 2002). The subspecies cacao may have originated in Central America and the Lacandon rainforest, where possibly wild trees are present, different from those that came from South America (De La Cruz et al. 1995; Miranda 1962). Nevertheless, Motamayor (2002) found no DNA differences between the Criollo and Forastero groups. The evidence supports the theory that cacao had its origins in South America and that, from there, humans dispersed it to Central America, where it was eventually domesticated (Cheesman 1944; Motamayor et al. 2002; Van Hall 1914).

HISTORICAL CHARCOAL REMAINS: NATURAL OR CULTURAL FIRES?

The cross-correlation of water table levels and macro-charcoal found in the PM1 core suggests natural fires at the centennial scale. Instead, the microcharcoal from PM1 is possibly pointing to a fire signal linked majorly to regional dry macroclimatic conditions and, to a lesser degree, to cultural management at the Nueve Cerros epicenter environs. The PM1 macrocharcoal record of the last 2,046 years suggests a high accumulation of charred material during the Early Classic (1631–1512 BP), which is relatively higher than the average mass ranges of charcoal assessment studies (Crawford and Belcher 2014). In terms of microcharcoal, we observed a gradual decline toward Nueve Cerros abandonment, with a slight event around 116 BP. The pollen composition shows different forest types at the PM1 and L3 sites during the last 740 years. This difference could be because of previous fire regimes around the Puente Mario ravine watershed during the Classic, according to the macrocharcoal retrieval (Froyd 2006). The positive correlation of macrocharcoal with the Zygnemataceae spore record (Spearman $r = 0.496$, $p < 0.05$) supports how the Puente Mario ravine was more susceptible to the intermittent dryer conditions prevalent until 740 BP (Figure 10.9). The geomorphic structure of this ravine could have enhanced the accumulation of vegetation remains that, when exposed to dryer conditions and a lower water table, would act as fuel for fire events, as has been observed elsewhere in tropical and temperate zones (Hokanson et al. 2016; Kelly et al. 2013; Kettridge et al. 2015; Moreno et al. 2018). If these local fires happened, it is feasible that they covered relatively small spaces along the Puente Mario ravine, as macroscopic charcoal dispersal is limited (Duffin et al. 2008). As soon as the establishment of the swamp forest takes place around 740 BP, the PM1 record shows the existence of a mature closed forest (> 80% forest cover). The establishment of this forest is synchronic to the emergence of trilete (e.g., ferns; Spearman $r = -0.521$, $p < 0.05$) and monolete spores (e.g., mosses and liverworts; Spearman $r = -0.49$, $p < 0.05$). These spores may indicate a certain degree of vegetation recovery of damaged spaces by local fires and the onset of wetter conditions (Tuba et al. 2010; Walker and Sharpe 2010).

The macrocharcoal record of PM1 enriched the Lachua Region paleoecological reconstruction with deep insights about habitat scale changes, possibly synchronized to local-regional climatology (Remy et al. 2018). This insight becomes critical when identifying the causes of local fire events. The macrocharcoal record shows a negative correlation to Lake El Gancho δO^{18} measurements (Spearman $r = -0.564$, $p < 0.05$), meaning that registered wet events in southern Central America manifest as the opposite in the Lachua Region (Stansell et al. 2013). Further exploration of the cause behind the fire regimes at the Puente Mario ravine is still needed. The analysis of another sedimentary record 250 m inland of Lake Lachua along the same ravine (core PZ2, 3 m higher in elevation) will provide more certainty in the future about the causes of the local fires.

The microcharcoal found in the PM1 record brings a regional environmental view as its source area, according to various literature, possibly extending to more than 25 km (Clark and Hussey 1996; Vachula et al. 2018; Wu et al. 2019). This area would include the Nueve Cerros epicenter and the Chixoy River floodplain (i.e., northeast to Rubelsanto, 8 km north into Mexico, southwest to Santa Maria Tzejá, southeast to Cuxpemech). The microcharcoal record shows the placement of a subtle cultural forcing against a dominant natural background. During some periods, the microcharcoal shows a distinctive pattern that matches transitions between cultural periods and pulses within them, while for most of the record it correlates with particle size D-values. The calculated microcharcoal concentration correlates slightly differently with $Dx(50)$ values (Spearman $r = 0.506$, $p < 0.05$) than with the CHAR ones (Spearman $r = 0.408$, $p < 0.05$) mainly because of their asynchronous temporal pattern during the Middle Classic and Colonial times (see Figure 10.6). The microcharcoal concentration increases progressively from the Early Classic to the Late Classic, showing three prominent peaks at 1512, 1303, and 1062 BP. These peaks show no correspondence with

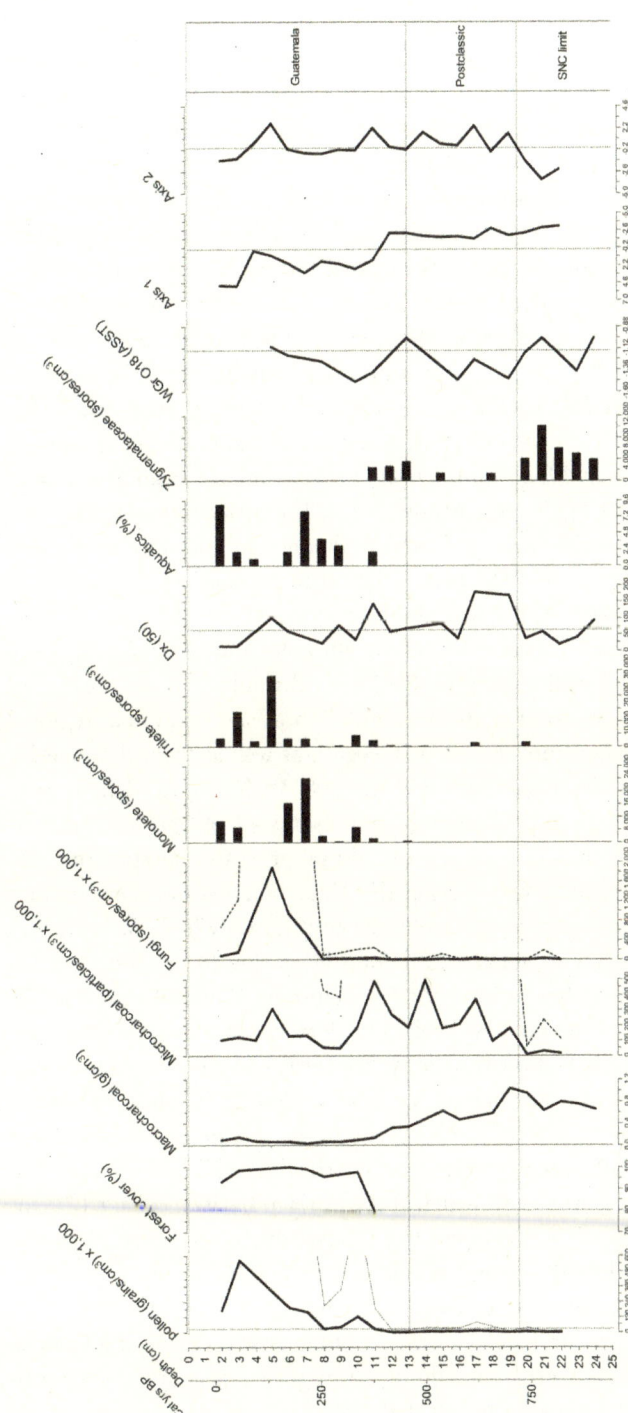

Figure 10.9. PM1 core paleoecological diagram showing the last 2000 Cal yrs BP. AP = arboreal pollen; Axis 1 and Axis 2 = first two principal components; SNC = Salinas de los Nueve Cerros; + = <2% abundance. Particle size D-value is shown as Dx (50) and the baseline indicate 63 μm. WGr = white *Globigerinodes ruber*; ASST = average annual sea surface temperature. Forest cover is based on arboreal pollen content. (Courtesy of Carlos Avendaño.)

Dx(50), but instead a correlation with Poaceae pollen values (Spearman $r = 0.538$, $p < 0.05$). As Poaceae plants are associated with pioneering traits after a fire disturbance, such correlation could support the existence of fire regimes (Armstrong 2011; Linder et al. 2018; McWethy et al. 2017). The microcharcoal peaks during the Classic period are likely to be an indication of cultural fire regimes. These peaks are indicators of an increase in activity, possibly from agriculture at the Chixoy River floodplain and from firewood combustion for salt production. The coincidence of the CHAR second-highest peak with the highest microcharcoal peak at the Late Classic (1062 BP), independent of D-values, strengthens the assumption about cultural forcing as an explanation for the fires during the Classic. Even more, at the highest Dx(50) measurements during the Middle Classic as an indicator of a dry period, and as the microcharcoal record shows no sufficient sensitivity, cultural management of Maya forest gardens and high forest cover seem reasonable as an explanation for it (see Figure 10.9; Nigh and Diemont 2013). The correlation of microcharcoal concentration—with many indicator pollen taxa of Maya forest gardens (i.e., *Alchornea*, Myrtaceae, Rubiaceae, Solanaceae, Sapotaceae, and *Spondias*; Spearman $r = 0.443–0.765$, $p < 0.05$) found in the PM1 record—suggests the practice of cultural activities both at the city epicenter and its outskirts.

The major CHAR peaks from the PM1 record would indicate, instead of relatively large fire occurrence, the accumulation of several annual regional microcharcoal coming from the Lachua Region as well as from different locations along the Transversal (Duffin et al. 2008; Vachula and Richter 2018; Vachula et al. 2018). Each peak probably represents 40–59 years of accumulation, originating from either natural or cultural processes. Despite the possible existence of cultural fires during the Nueve Cerros occupation since at least the Late Preclassic, forest cover was continuously high (i.e., > 80%), which discards arguments related to deforestation due to firewood needed for salt production, as has been suggested before by Woodfill et al. (2015). The synchronicity of the greatest peaks of microscopic charcoal concentration, CHAR and Dx(50), at the time of Nueve Cerros abandonment may suggest the occurrence of a dry period (i.e., the second-driest period reported over a millennium) before the time Puente Mario ravine developed into a swamp forest 780 BP. This dry period in the Transversal could be related to the Medieval Climate Anomaly, which at the Cariaco Basin and Lake El Gancho manifested instead as warm and wet (Haug 2001b; Stansell et al. 2013). We cannot causally link the occurrence of the Medieval Climate Anomaly climatic period with the Nueve Cerros abandonment, as the Maya settlers from this city had already experienced a dryer event, possibly during the Early to Middle Classic. Nueve Cerros abandonment might relate more to socioeconomic and political factors (Woodfill et al. 2015).

During the last 780 BP, the microcharcoal values decreased according to CHAR measurements, suggesting no more large fires occurring in the Lachua Region (see Figure 10.6). Nonetheless, both microcharcoal concentration and Dx(50) showed a pulse approximately 300 BP. This dry climatic pulse in the Lachua Region could be in association with the Little Ice Age, a dry phase that is also observed in the Cariaco Basin and Lake El Gancho (Davis et al. 2019; Haug 2001b; Stansell et al. 2013). This pulse could have led to a fast drop of the water table in the Puente Mario ravine, explaining why pollen identification in the two PM1 levels became difficult (i.e., challenging pollen separation from the sediment matrix). Despite this temporary dryness, the L3 pollen forest signal could indicate that such conditions were not possibly affected locally, even at the Puente Mario ravine. It is interesting to observe a notable increase of fungal spores for the first time in the PM1 record (see Figure 10.9) currently, which suggests the prevalence of warm and humid conditions. The accumulation and stagnation of organic material under a closed canopy (> 80%, providing such humid conditions), could be a possible explanation for high decomposition levels (Talley et al. 2002; van Geel et al. 1995) and therefore a rise in fungal activity. Trilete spores show their highest values in the PM1 core during this dry period (correlated to fungal spores, Spearman $r = 0.712$, $p < 0.05$), which would confirm that somehow humid conditions prevailed under the Puente Mario forest canopy (i.e., at the spatial habitat scale). We know that during this time there was a transition between the Akahala Maya group occupying Nueve Cerros and the Spaniards taking possession, which could be circumstantial to this dry phase (Demarest 2004; Douglas, Demarest, et al. 2016; McNeil et al. 2010) and not causal.

The identification of plants used as firewood is necessary to identify them as well in the pollen or charcoal record. Through the household gardens study, we learned how locals categorize the quality of firewood. Among the high-quality firewood (Morales 2014) there is *Brosimum* (Ramon), *Terminalia* (Canxan), and plants from Fabaceae such as *Dalbergia stenvesonii* (Rosul) and *Gliricidia sepium* (Madre Cacao). Low-quality firewood includes *Cecropia* sp. (Guarumo) and *Vochysia guatemalensis* (San Juan). In future studies, we will be doing the taxonomy of charcoal material collected from archaeological sources (i.e., retrieved through flotation techniques). We will also be looking to match ethnoecological and anthracological (i.e., the study of charred botanical remains) information as a basis to explore Mesoamerican cultural legacies in terms of knowledge, practices, and beliefs.

CONCLUSION

The interdisciplinary contributions from the integration of paleoecological and neoecological methods in this chapter proved advantageous and critical in reconstructing the millennial landscape evolution of the environs of Nueve Cerros at the Lachua Region in the context of the Transversal. The exploration of nearby sedimentary cores allowed us to infer information about spatial heterogeneity at the landscape scale. Both cores L3 and PM1 shed different but congruent information about climatic, ecologic, and cultural processes that otherwise would have led us to generalize one perspective across the Lachua Region. If landscape management took place as our paleoecologic reconstructions are suggesting, Nueve Cerros inhabitants would have done it by following landscape heterogeneity and by choosing preferred locations. For example, forestry would have taken place in the terrain in between the city epicenter and the Lachua Lake (i.e., shallower soils and lower water table) and agriculture most likely along the Chixoy River floodplain (i.e., deepest soils and highest water table). With respect to forestry practices, it is possible that the understanding of the Lachua Region physical geography led the Maya to their differential management allocation; the PM1 location was possibly more susceptible to lowering of the water table and thus not suitable for a Maya forest garden, for example. A swampy location next to the Lachua River (near the main output from the Lachua Lake), however, is more likely because of higher water tables and thus suitable for allocating a Maya forest garden (which L3 pollen evidence suggests). We believe this ancestral differential landscape management left a legacy in the forests of the Lachua Region as seen today in vegetation associations, particularly as it relates to mahogany spatial ecology. More research is needed in this area of forestry.

The congruency from both the L3 and the PM1 cores about a high forest cover (e.g., for at least 1772 and 740 BP, respectively) does not support the neocatastrophist argument about massive and continuous deforestation (e.g., Diamond 2011) and therefore remains unequivocal evidence in support of the hypothesis about ancestral sustainable landscape management (Demarest 2004; Ford and Nigh 2015; McNeil et al. 2010). Despite the possible large-scale usage of firewood for the main economic activity of salt production at Nueve Cerros, our paleoecological evidence supports the argument brought by Woodfill et al. (2015) about sufficient biomass in the Lachua Region that would not have compromised forest cover. The microcharcoal record reflects, possibly, on the one hand, these cultural activities, including salt production and agriculture, as we can observe that a relative drop in charred particle concentration is synchronous with Nueve Cerros abandonment. On the other hand, this record correlates to changes in particle size measured in PM1. This correlation to regional climatic regimes could mean that natural fires possibly took place in the Transversal as a response to regional dry periods. These periods (i.e., droughts) occurred mainly during the Early-Middle Classic, Nueve Cerros abandonment during the Medieval Climate Anomaly (ca. 750

BP), and at the Little Ice Age (ca. 300 BP). Fires related to these dry periods were possibly buffered due to the location of the Lachua Region at the foot of mountain ranges, where humidity is higher due to increased horizontal precipitation. The abandonment of Nueve Cerros is possibly more related to geopolitical factors due to the configuration of new trade networks during the Terminal Classic and less probably related to climatic factors. We believe that these dry periods are likely related to changes in the orbital-forcing factor of obliquity, due to a southern migration of the Inter-Tropical Climatic Zone, in combination with other climatic systems such as the North American monsoon and El Niño southern oscillation.

The socioecological history of Nueve Cerros invites the reflection of how a city remained for nearly two millennia in the same location, irrespective of the highly dynamic temporal environmental regimes experienced across the Lachua Region at least since the Middle Holocene, both in *terra firme* and in the Chixoy River floodplain. As mentioned, the physical geography of the Lachua Region must have been a critical factor in choosing the city location. Along the Northern Transversal Strip, only the Lachua Region has a combination of many distinctive features: the extensive Chixoy floodplain, numerous entrances to the Underworld (i.e., caves), diverse forests, possibly the deepest lake in Central America, a complex fluvial network, and a higher precipitation regime. The most outstanding feature is indeed the salt dome, which is unique in Mesoamerica. There is still further exploration needed to integrate paleoecological and neoecological research, especially in collaboration with the local inhabitants of the Lachua Region. The Q'eqchi' Maya people are living in the land of their ancestors and continue to reproduce a rich millennial cultural legacy in the era of globalization, large-scale monopolies, and geopolitical tensions between international borders, demonstrating their resilience in the face of adversity.

11

Born in Xibalba

Kanek'-Kaweq Lineage History in the Franja Transversal del Norte

RUUD VAN AKKEREN

IN THE MIDDLE of the sixteenth century, when Dominican friars directed their evangelical zeal from Coban and Carcha to the southern lowlands, they found the Ch'olti'-speaking Maya pushed beyond the western banks of the Usumacinta River and squeezed between the upper Pasión River and the highlands. Belize and the central Peten all the way up to the Gulf Coast were, by then, populated by Maya who spoke a language from the Yukatekan family (Itza, Mopan, Kehache, and Yukatek), an area that during the Late Classic was entirely occupied by Ch'ol-speaking Maya (Figure 11.1). What happened?

Archaeologist Juan Pedro Laporte and his Atlas team have shed light on this issue. The Atlas Project focused on the geographical area of the Mopan River basin, a system of major tributaries formed by the Mopan, Chiquibul, and Salsipuedes Rivers, as well as others in Belize. When the Spanish arrived, this region was mostly populated by Mopan Maya (Jones 1998).

In a synthesizing article, the fruit of many years of archaeological reconnaissance, Laporte and Héctor Mejía explain the nature and time frame of the Yucatecan influence in the southeast of Peten (Laporte and Mejía 2002). New architectural features were being incorporated into sites in the Mopan River basin at the end of the Late Classic period. They included elements such as an acropolis, as a seat of power, structures in quadrangular groups, delimitation walls in residential areas, round and semicircular structures, and a number of new construction techniques and sculptural elements that decorated the friezes, corners, and facades of the buildings. The innovations did not appear overnight but came in phases. They identified three waves. The first wave occurred at the end of the Late Classic and saw the introduction of the new

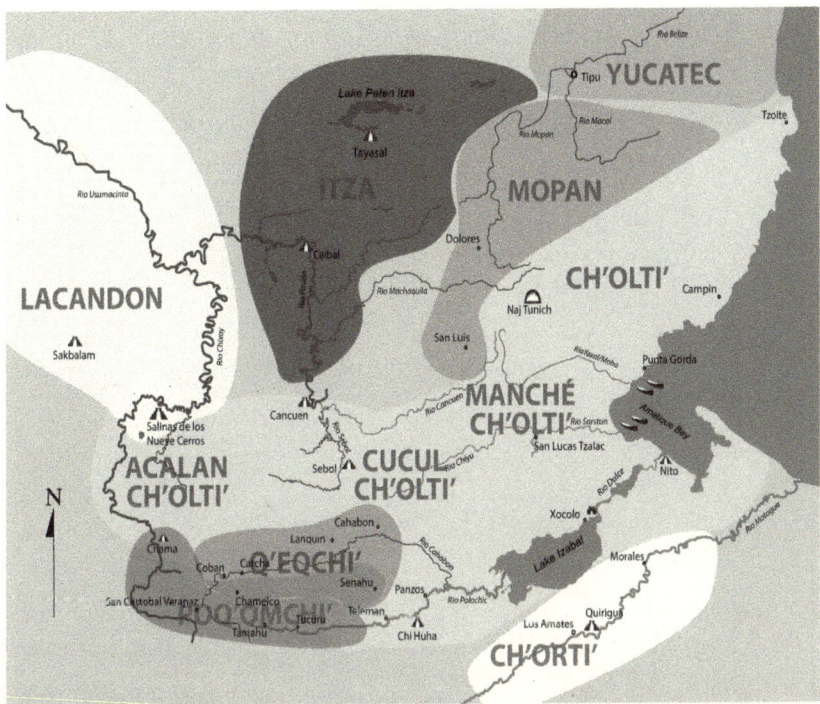

Figure 11.1. Map of the southern Peten, Franja Transversal, and adjacent highlands. (Base map made in Photoshop. Juan Moncada and Ruud van Akkeren)

style at some restricted sites. In the second and broader wave, during the Terminal Classic (AD 800–950), the new architectural features were dispersed throughout the entire area. The third wave started at the end of the ninth century and lasted throughout the tenth century, as demonstrated by the introduction of circular or semicircular platforms (Figure 11.2).

The origin of these architectural innovations lay in northern Yucatan, at centers such as Chichen Itza and Mayapan. Laporte and Mejía also identified the carriers of these changes: the Mopan Maya, speaking a language closely related to Yukatek. They reasoned that at the end of the Classic, large centers such as Tikal, Calakmul, or Caracol began to lose the control they had exercised on trade, resulting in new commercial networks directed from the cities in the north of Yucatan with those in the southeastern Peten.

The trading center of Chichen Itza must have played a pivotal role in these dynamics. After the merchants came the migrants, who were attracted by new resources and prosperity. The first settlers of the Yucatan Peninsula mixed with the Ch'ol-speakers, heirs of the Classical era. Yet in the course of

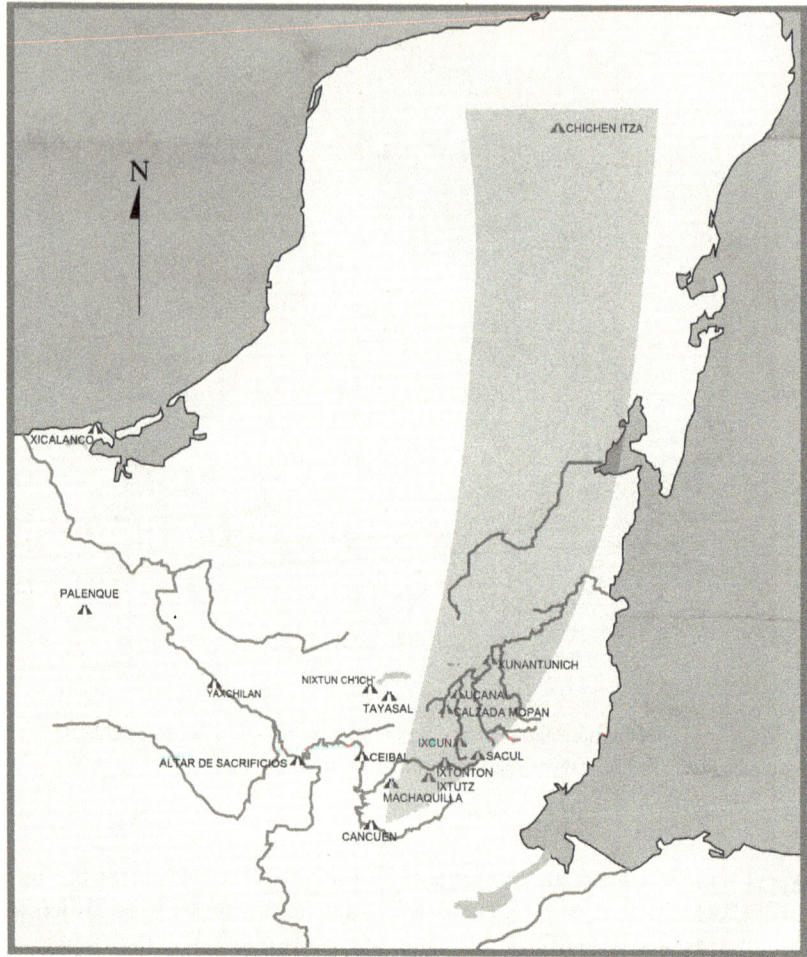

Figure 11.2. Map of Late Classic and Early Postclassic Yukatek migration along the Mopan River tributaries. (Base map made in Photoshop. Juan Moncada and Ruud van Akkeren)

time, immigration reached such a large scale that Yukatek began to dominate the local language: the Ch'ol-speakers were absorbed by the Mopan or left their lands.

A similar process can be identified for the lake area of central Peten—Peten Itza, Sacpuy, Macanche, and Yaxha—where we see the entrance of Itza-speaking people during the Terminal Classic and Early Postclassic (Akkeren 2021:67–71; Boot 2005; Rice and Rice 2004:132, 138). They kept on living in the area until deep into Colonial times, with their seat of power in Tayasal or Ta Itza, and the Kanek' lineage as their rulers (Jones 1998). The Kanek' were one of the dominant lineages acting at the time, cofounders of Chichen Itza, as we may read in the famous quote on the Great and Little Descent in the *Chilam Balam of Chumayel* (Akkeren 2012:21; Boot 2005:96). They were also present in the Terminal Classic sites of the central Maya Lowlands, where their origin lay. In various recent books (Akkeren 2012, 2021; Morán and Akkeren 2016), I argued that the Kanek' lineage was closely connected with, if not the same as, the Kaweq lineage, the highland authors of the *Popol Vuh*.

Indeed, the Kaweq had their origin in the Northern Transversal Strip, where they lived the frantic times of the Terminal Classic, surviving by entering in the neighboring highlands. They later forged the cultural lowland collapse into a literary product, the Xibalba myth, defining themselves as the dwellers of the new epoch. The first man molded from corn dough by Xmukane is B'alam K'itze', founding father of the Kaweq.

In this chapter, I make some claims that might be new, without presenting an elaborate analysis, because of space and previous publications. I also use onomastics—toponyms and patronyms—in my reconstructions, a field that is still novel in Mesoamerican studies. Toponyms, and especially hydronyms, are usually very conservative; they stick to a place, even when everything around them has changed. They belong to the temporality dubbed "geohistory" by Fernand Braudel (1958, 2002), resistant to change, and may serve as a valuable source of historical information. One of the subdivisions of the Department of Economic and Social Affairs of the United Nations is called the United Nations Group of Experts on Geographical Names, which studies toponyms as carriers of cultural heritage. Some 400 countries are members, but unfortunately Guatemala is not, although it has its entire history spread over its landscape (Akkeren 2024).

HISTORICAL XIBALBA

The Northern Transversal Strip in Alta Verapaz has always been a transition area between the Peten Lowlands and the Maya Highlands. Trade passed through this region as early as the Middle Preclassic (Akkeren 2021; Woodfill 2007). Merchants stopped in some of the larger caves, such as the Candelaria caves, to pay homage and leave their offerings. Brent K. S. Woodfill's doctoral work on the cavernous shrines of the Transversal examined ritual and exchange on the ancient trading route (2007). He wrote, "The route from the Salamá Valley down to the Pasión and Usumacinta is one of the easiest ways to transport goods into the lowlands, and for that reason the Maya took advantage of it, not just during the Late Classic, but the 1,700 years preceding it" (Woodfill 2007:182–183). Indeed, the patron deity of commerce, God L, was also the supreme god of the Underworld. This is how the historical Xibalba region came into being. I have shown there is a historically and geographically demonstrable Xibalba, and its location was always there in the text of the *Popol Vuh* itself, but never really recognized by its translators. When describing the ballcourt where One and Seven Jun Ajpuuh are playing, its Kaweq authors locate it in Nim Xol-Karchaj. According to the text, this ballcourt lay on the road toward the entrance of Xibalba (Akkeren 2012).

As it turns out, Karchaj is a reference to San Pedro Carcha, while Nim Xol was the name of a *barrio* of Coban, Santo Tomás Nim Xol. These colonial towns are the outcome of the Spanish effort to congregate Maya people into new settlements, the so-called *reducción*. A historical inquiry into the origin of the peoples that ended up in the *barrios* of both colonial towns, based on the first *Lista de Tributarios* 1570–1572, shows that they were mostly Ch'olti'-speaking Maya from the Transversal, that is, the historical Xibalba. Consequently, colonial and republican papers report that, in several of these *barrios* like Coban or Carcha, they still spoke Ch'olti' up to the mid-nineteenth century (Figure 11.3; Akkeren 2012, 2021).

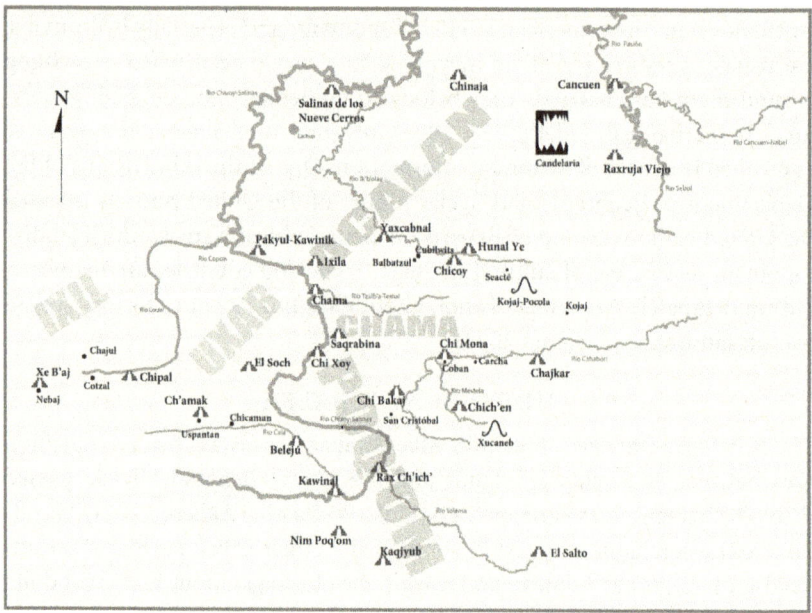

Figure 11.3. Map of the Franja Transversal. (Base map made in Photoshop. Juan Moncada and Ruud van Akkeren)

Unsurprisingly, the historical Xibalba originated in this region. This karstic or limestone area is littered with caves, including the second-largest cavernous system in the Maya area, the Candelaria Caves (Woodfill 2007, 2010). Scrutinizing the geography of this area, other meaningful toponyms and hydronyms have emerged. The Xibalba area appeared to have begun when descending into the plain of Cubilwitz, leaving the rolling mountains and hills of the highlands of Coban. This geographical point is called Balbatzuul, a Q'eqchi' toponym, in which *tzuul* means "mountain," but in the toponymic sense of "place," and *b'alb'a* is the Q'eqchi' term for *xib'alb'a* (Haeserijn 1979:53). Thus, the hamlet of Balbatzuul is the entrance to the geographical Underworld. Interestingly, when travelling to this place, one crosses a river called Temal, probably derived from the Nahua *temalli*, "pus," and a place called Sa Xook' Scorpion Place, near another river. They must be the Pus and Scorpion Rivers mentioned in the *Popol Vuh*, crossed by the Hero Twins when they took the road to Xibalba. In the original manuscript, the river full of pus is called K'ik'ia', Blood River, in the original manuscript of the *Popol Vuh* (folio 14r). It matches the Nahuatl *difrasismo*, *in eztli in temalli*, "blood and pus" (Wimmer 2004).

The Northern Transversal became known to the Maya as the land of the Underworld, the realm of Night and Darkness. The area's western border is the Chixoy River, also known as Río Negro or Black River (see Chapter 3). Black was the epithet that marked the people who lived in this area, regardless of the language they spoke. They were called *ek'* or *ik'* in Ch'olti' or Yukatek, *q'eq* in Q'eqchi', and the language (*chi'*) that they spoke was the Language of Darkness, *q'eqchi'*. Another term found in the Indigenous documents used for the same people is Night People or Aq'aab (Akkeren 2000). Thus, in the course of time, this original, locally developed ethnonym expanded into the neighboring highlands.

These concepts are very old, as shown by the presence of Preclassic and thousands of Early Classic potsherds in, for example, the Candelaria caves (Woodfill 2007, 2010; Woodfill and Andrieu 2012). Accordingly, the tree of the western cardinal direction in the San Bartolo West Wall mural stands on a black, undulating, maybe even watery serpentine path, recalling the black road the Hero Twins selected as the path into Xibalba (Akkeren 2012). These concepts also found their expression in the iconography of one of the Late Classic principal centers in the area, Cancuen (see Chapter 3). The site is characterized by a lack of temple-pyramids (Demarest 2006b). The archaeologists working in Cancuen attribute this distinctive feature to the notion that its habitants did not need pyramids since their focuses of worship were the nearby caves. Thus, on Panel 3 we find lord Tajal Chan Ahk sitting on a personified skull-like Water Throne in a quadrifoliate portal representing the watery Underworld with an elegantly chiseled *ak'bal* or night glyph in the throne's eye (Figure 11.4). The panel once adorned the façade of a temple built on a platform adjoined to the western bench of the main ballcourt—the very game of the Underworld, as attested in the Xibalba myth of the *Popol Vuh*.

Figure 11.4. Panel 3, Cancuen, Guatemala. (Courtesy of Luís Fernando Luin.)

The name Tajal Chan Ahk reveals his position as a lord of the Underworld, as I have argued, comparable to God L, with his carapace. In various writings I have suggested that we need to reconsider the Maya pantheon, as has also been proposed by other scholars (Akkeren 2012, 2018, 2024; Martin 2015). God L and God N are just variations of what all Maya still call Lord Mountain—Valley, Qawa Tzuul-Taq'aa in Q'eqchi'. As his name explains, Chan Ahk is the Sky Turtle, corresponding to the constellation of Orion, which was also perceived as a ballcourt in the nocturnal sky by Mesoamerican people (Akkeren 2012, 2021; Galindo Trejo 2012). In highland Mexico, Sahagún makes mention of the *citlaltlachtli*, or Stellar Ballcourt, without indicating its location. The rectangular constellation has been located in the night sky encompassing the bright stars of Sirius, Procyon, Beltelgeuse and Rigel, which indeed includes Orion (Galindo Trejo 2012).

Tajal Chak Ahk can be compared with and likened to the grandfather figure Xpiyakok, spouse of Xmukane in the *Popol Vuh*. Xpiyakok's name also includes the turtle, though here another term for "turtle," *kok*, is used. Both *ahk* and *kok* are both terms for "turtle" in Ch'olan (Boot 2009:20, 97, 252), as well as in Yukatek (Barrera Vásquez 1991:5, 329). Based on my fieldwork among Kaweq families in Rabinal who preserved this information in their traditional garb, I have argued that the primordial couple Xmukane and Xpiyakok were not K'iche' names but Ch'olan. Both had their celestial counterpart in the constellations Scorpio and Orion—that is, the points where the Milky Way crosses the zodiacal band. Indeed, they are present, as a pair, in the *Paris Codex* (Akkeren 1995, 2000:262, 2003b, 2012, 2021).

The part *taj* in Tajal Chan Ahk, often translated as "torch," is in fact the Classic Maya equivalent of the *xiuhmolpilli*, the bundle of sticks the priests of the Lord of Fire used to light the fire of the Divine Hearth, elegantly portrayed in the *Codex Borbonicus* (folio 34). The same oven features in the Xibalba myth, where the Hero Twins die to be reborn as sun and moon of the new era. Various investigators have identified the quadrifoliate portal on Panel 3 from Cancuen (see Figure 11.4), named in the accompanying hieroglyphic text as the House of Tajal Chan Ahk, as the similar shaped plaza of Machaquila, a city ruled at that time by the same Tajal Chan Ahk. What is less known is that excavations revealed the Machaquila plaza had been the scene of huge bonfires (Lacadena 2005, 2006). I have suggested that Machaquila is the location of the historical hearth on which the authors of the Xibalba myth based their account (Figure 11.5).

In addition, there is a more mundane side to the iconography used by Tajal Chan Ahk. The principal god of the Underworld, God L, was also the patron god of trade and commerce. His Central Mexican counterpart was Xiuhteuctli, Lord of Fire, and supreme god of the combined Pochtecan and Oztomecan merchant guilds, as we may read in *Book 9* of the *Florentine Codex, The Merchants* (Anderson and Dibble 1959). He already had this position in Teotihuacan. The Xiuhteuctli priest oversaw lighting the flames of the New Fire ceremony, which reenacted the birth of the Sun Hero in the Divine Hearth or *teotexcalli*. Again, the torch, or *xiuhmolpilli* in the name of Tajal Chan Ahk, defines him as a priest of Xiuhteuctli or God L, indicating that he belonged to the Mesoamerican organization of merchant guilds (Akkeren 2012, 2021, 2024). He obviously accumulated enough wealth to be able to build the second-largest palace in the Maya area. There is a fine image of a similar Lord of Fire dressed in a carapace on the central columns of the Lower Temple of the Jaguar at the great ballcourt of Chichen Itza, a building almost contemporaneous to the Cancuen ballcourt temple (Figure 11.6). I have suggested that the object in the deity's hands is indeed a torch, while he is surrounded in the corners by the four Fire Snakes, or *Xiuhcoatl*, that borders the Divine Hearth in central Mexican imagery (Akkeren 2012).

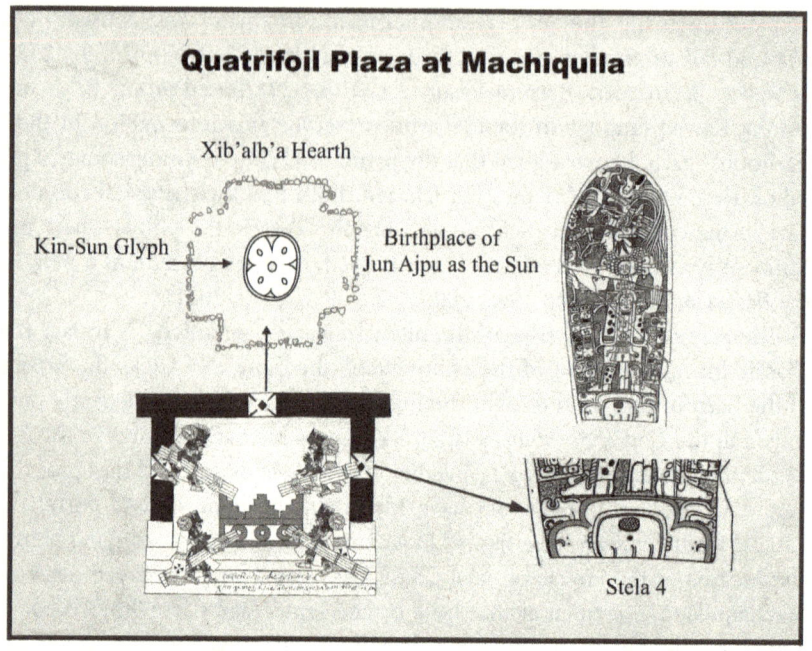

Figure 11.5. Quadrifoliate plaza at Machaquila, Guatemala, is related to the historical hearth of Xibalba. Machaquila's plaza, the quatrefoil design echoed at the bottom of Stela 4, shares connections with the New Fire ceremony and *xiuhmolpilli* (stick bundles) depicted in the *Codex Borbonicus* (Folio 34) as well as *k'in* day glyphs. (Juan Moncada and Ruud van Akkeren)

SALINAS DE LOS NUEVE CERROS

Some 40 miles to the west of Cancuen lies, in the heartland of Xibalba, the site Salinas de los Nueve Cerros (see Chapters 3, 8, and 9). It is located in the very northwestern corner of Alta Verapaz, an area bordered by the Chixoy River or Río Negro, which makes at this point a 90° turn, from a north-south to an east-west direction. It is a site with a long history; recent archaeological research shows the ceramic sequence ran from the Middle Preclassic to the Early Postclassic (Woodfill et al. 2015, 2018).

As the term *salinas* suggests, it earned its name for its salt works, which was, at the same time, the reason for the early occupation of the site. The salt is found deep within a natural hill or dome and is transported by a little brook on the western side of the dome, bringing it onto a plain, or *playa de sal*, where the salt was collected. It is at this side of the hill that the salt production took place, as attested by a series of immense ceramic containers, *vasijones*, in which the brine was stored and boiled down. It is also where elite buildings, covering enormous platforms, containing various tombs, are

Figure 11.6. Lord of Fire or Xiuhteuctli, central column, Lower Temple of the Jaguars, Chichen Itza, Mexico. (Mallary Tiul, adapted from Linda Schele, Schele Drawing Collection, Ancient Americas at Los Angeles County Museum of Art, SD-5045)

concentrated (Woodfill et al. 2015). Salinas de los Nueve Cerros is the only noncoastal salt source in the Maya Lowlands, and it was estimated that the salt production at its peak must have yielded at least 14,500 metric tons, an amount that could cover the needs of over five million people (Woodfill et al. 2015:170; see also Chapter 8). Up until the second half of the last century, salt was still being shipped through the riverine routes of the Chixoy and Pasión Rivers into the Peten heartland, likely copying the prehispanic way of salt distribution (Andrews 1983:99–100; Akkeren 2012).

When explaining the other part of the name Salinas de los Nueve Cerros, scholars in general refer to the supposedly nine hills of the nearby mountain range with a similar name, based on local popular etymology (Woodfill et al. 2015). In a similar way, modern Poqomchi' Maya, upstream from the site on the same Chixoy River, have interpreted their toponym Beleju' or Nine Peaks (Morán and Akkeren 2016). I have stated that toponyms like Nine Peaks belonged to a category of Nine Places, which were, in fact, stops on a merchant route (Akkeren 2003b; Gillespie and Joyce 1998). These Nine Places are the result of an idiosyncratic, mercantile calendar of 9 x 40 days projected on the route they travelled (Vail 2013:182–184, 2022:173). This idea was further elaborated in the study on the Xibalba myth, a myth that originated from the merchant ideology, yet fully cast into a "mercantile model" in my latest book on Kaminaljuyu (Akkeren 2012, 2021, 2024).

At these Nine Places stops, long-distance merchant lineages and their warriors, protecting these caravans, had temples, residences, and storing places. This concept goes at least back to the Early Classic when Mesoamerican trade was directed out of Teotihuacan. In a new interpretation of its iconography, it is demonstrated that one of the longest Techinantitla murals, featuring a serpent representing the road merchants walked, includes a repeating series of nine trees each marked with a toponym glyph; this is in fact a chain of Nine Places on a merchant trade-route (Akkeren 2024). Teotihuacan itself harbored its own toponym Chiconauhtlan, literally Nine Place, which was still in Aztec times the name of the hill and *altepetl* situated at the entrance of the former city and location of a thriving market (Nichols et al. 2009). Kaminaljuyu seems to have been one of the starting points of that trade route. It also carried the title of a Nine Place: modern Chinautla is a corrupted version of Chiconauhtlan. The Poqom, who founded and populated Kaminaljuyu, called it Belej: Nine. We therefore have a series of Nine Places on one of the main Classic routes starting in the Valley of Guatemala—Chinautla—through Baja Verapaz and following the Chixoy River, Beleju, and Salinas de los Nueve Cerros or Bolonte' Witz. We may thus assume that Nueve Cerros was fully integrated in the Mesoamerican trade route. More research is needed for the Usumacinta River, but there was at least another Nine Place toponym at the other end of that river, on the Mexican Gulf

Coast. This is where, according to the *Chilam Balam of Mani*, Tulapan Chiconahthan is linked to the historical trading area of Anahuac Xicalanco (Craine and Reindorp 1979:134, 138). *Chiconah*, then, seems to be a Yukatekan morphological change of the original Nahuatl term Chiconauhtlan (Akkeren 2012).

ACALLAN

Since the Late Classic, the region where Salinas de los Nueve Cerros is located was known as Acallan. Acallan, or Land of the Canoes, was the name of a Mexican province covering parts of the modern states of Tabasco and Campeche on the Gulf Coast, including the port of trade Xicalanco. In his theory about the Putun Maya, Thompson linked the Acallan in Verapaz with the Gulf Coast Acallan; Bernal Díaz del Castillo spoke in this context of *Acalá la chica y la gran Acalá* (Figure 11.7; Saint-Lu 1968:274, note 3; Thompson 1990:25–26, 32–38).

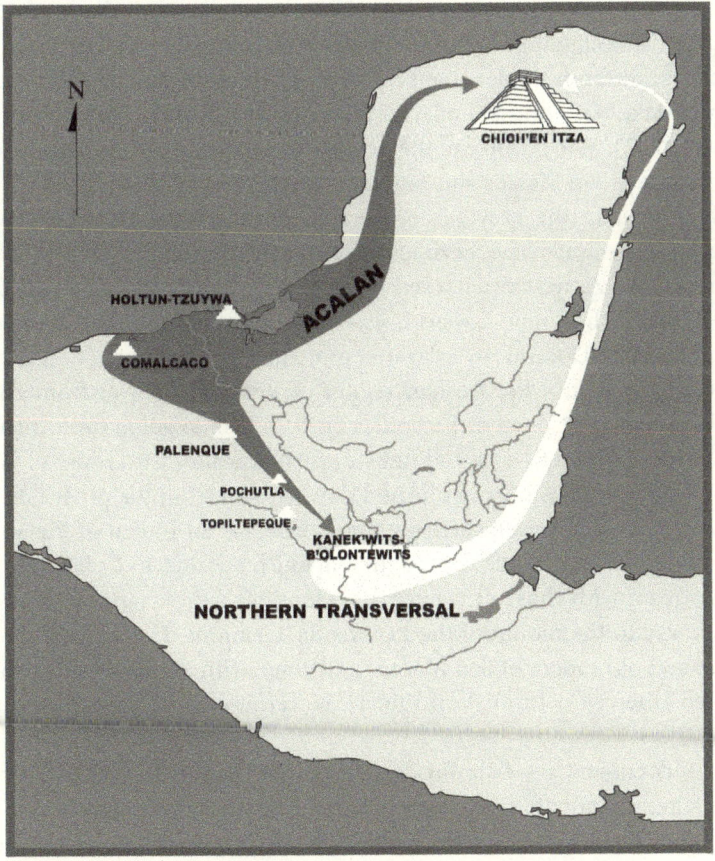

Figure 11.7. Map of Acallan homeland and its expansions. (Base map made in Photoshop. Juan Moncada and Ruud van Akkeren)

The Verapaz Acallan were one of the various examples of the upriver migration of Gulf Coast people along the Usumacinta, Pasión, and Chixoy during the Late Classic. Excavations at Cancuen revealed a *barrio* of people from the Palenque province Bak, and indeed Bac is a common surname in the area (Akkeren 2012:26–27; Forné et al. 2009:212). Colonial documents of the Cucul and Coc Maya, large landowners in Carcha, claim an origin on the Usumacinta (Akkeren 2012, 2021). Other Late Classic groups mentioned in the Indigenous documents were said to have an origin at the Gulf Coast (Akkeren 2012:15–17, 97–103; 2021:56–63). One also imagines that Calakmul may have sent its people to this area when it installed a local vassal in Cancuen (García Capistrán 2012:54–55).

In their homeland, the Postclassic Acallan people spoke Chontal, a language belonging to the Ch'olan branch (Smailus 1975). However, with the arrival of the Dominicans, the Verapaz Acalla had lived for some eight centuries in the Northern Transversal and had assimilated to the local Ch'olti' language, although they had kept the name of their place of origin. Friar Gabriel Salazar, for example, noted in his letters that the language the Acallan people spoke was almost similar to the Ch'olti' of the Manche' people (Feldman 2000:37). Many people of the Acallan area ended up in *barrios* of Coban, still known as San Marcos and San Juan Acala.

As argued in the previous paragraph, the Chixoy-Salinas-Usumacinta corridor had always have been an important trade route, but the historical information that we have, backed by ceramic evidence, dates mostly to the Late Classic. The route, however, was kept in use during the Colonial Period. The same Dominican Salazar commented on the connection between the Gulf Coast and the Acallan region of Verapaz: "Travel from Laguna [de Términos] to Coban or Sacapulas or from Coban going toward Laguna [de Términos] is very easy and links those of Yucatan with those of Guatemala. Going upstream from one and downstream from the other takes less than eight days of travel; certainly this is true, for an Indian of the town of Tixchel [puerto de Acallan] brought a Spanish speaker to Coban. He went downstream with those of Guatemala, identifying these lands and its lakes all the way to the mount of the Laguna de Términos. In the same manner, a wise and old Indian of San Marcos had come with the Spaniards who had entered [the river] from the Laguna [de Términos]" (Salazar in Feldman 2000:53).

In a document by Antonio de León Pinelo (quoted in Boot 2005:101, translation by Woodfill), we learn how the Chixoy-Salinas River was used to connect with Xicalanco on the Gulf Coast starting from Nueve Cerros: "In this year [1625] an attempt was made to discover a route passing through all of these provinces from Verapaz to Xicalango, or Laguna de Términos. [...] They arrived at a stop called Volonteviz, which is the same as nine hills, where they discovered a stream that spills out over some flat plains to form a large salt flat, unique in all of those lands of the Agaitzaes. One league farther down they discovered the navigable river that they sought."

ITZA CONFEDERATION

In 1970 Eric Thompson proposed a theory about the Putun Maya when seeking an explanation for the collapse of the great cities of Peten. He postulated that at the end of the Classic a new power emerged on the Gulf Coast of Mexico, dominated by Putun Maya. The Putun were merchants who used canoes to transport their cargoes and diverted a large part of the commercial network, leaving the routes that crossed the Peten and replacing them with routes that bordered the Yucatan Peninsula. To Thompson, these Putun Maya were the same as the Acallan Maya, the People from the Land of Canoes. One of the main centers of the new power was Chich'en Itza, part of whose population, according to Thompson, descended from these Putun Maya. Nevertheless, there was also a group of Acallan Maya who kept trading along the Usumacinta. The Acallan People in the Northern Transversal were an expression of these commercial contacts, data supported by the Terminal Classic iconography in Ceibal (Thompson 1990).

Thompson's theory has been criticized and, in the course of time, modified. Numerous works have come out on Ceibal's ceramics, epigraphy, and iconography (Boot 2005; Davies 1977; Demarest 2004b; Lacadena 2010; López Austin and López Luján 1999; Pascual Soto and Velásquez García 2012; Ringle et al. 1998; Schele et al. 1998; Tourtellot and González 2004; Vargas 2001). However, the idea of a new class of merchants with its corresponding merchant ideology, yet at a Mesoamerican level, has remained. This new order was characterized by a strong militarism, combined with the promulgation of the ballgame and the cult of the Feathered Serpent or Quetzalcoatl (Ringle et al. 1998). I have suggested that Putun has not been a viable term for these people who were better known as Acallan People, Nonoalco, and Olmeca-Xicalanca. We get an unexpected narrative glimpse of these Canoe People and the way they used their boats in warfare in the Kaqchikel chronicle *Memorial de Sololá*, a fragment of which takes place on the Gulf Coast of Tabasco (Akkeren 2006b). Thompson (1990:Plate 3) himself already indicated a mural of the Canoe People in the Temple of the Warriors in Chich'en Itza. I have suggested that the person portrayed standing in a canoe, in the central scene of the Lower Temple of the Jaguars, must have been other iconographic evidence of Acallan People being part of this new mercantile alliance (Figure 11.8; Akkeren 2012:201).

Figure 11.8. Acalan warrior in canoe, central scene in Lower Temple of the Jaguars, Chichen Itza, Mexico. (Mallary Tiul, adapted from Linda Schele FAMSI, The Linda Schele Drawings Collection Number 7676)

In the aforementioned essay, Thompson drew our attention to a fragment from the *Chilam Balam of Chumayel*, which he thought described the four groups that shaped the Itza confederation and founded Chich'en Itza (Akkeren 2012; Boot 2005; Schele and Mathews 1999:201–204; Thompson 1990:22–24). Various other authors after him have confirmed his idea. In this quote from the chapter on the k'atun-chronicles, the authors write about k'atun 4 Ajaw corresponding with the years AD 711–731 (Boot 2005; Schele and Mathews 1999):

> 4 Ahaw was the *k'atun* when occurred their discovery
> of the mouth of the well of Itzá [Chichen Itza].

There good things came about because of their lords.
Four divisions came forth
four divisions of the land, as they were named.
From some place in the east, K'in Kolah Petén, came one division.
North, from Na' Kokob' emerged one division.
There emerged one division from Holtún Suywá(h),
In the west emerged one division from Kanhek' Witz B'olonte' Witz,
as was the name of the land
[*Chilam Balam of Chumayel*, folio 77, adapted from Boot 2005:96].

Who are the peoples mentioned here? Two of them were Maya groups from northern Yucatan, a third group came from the Gulf Coast of Mexico. They came from Holtun Tzuywa or Xicalanco, the aforementioned Nine Place. They are Thompson's Putun Maya, from the original Acallan area. The fourth group came from Kanhek' Witz-Bolonte' Witz. Bolonte' Witz has long been recognized as an allusion to Salinas de los Nueve Cerros. Here we have, in fact, the triangle of political and economic relations between the Gulf Coast, northern Yucatan, and the Transversal.

Kanhek' Witz is, according to Boot (2005), a reference to the famous Kanek' lineage. They apparently ruled the saltworks in the eighth century. The Kanek' lineage must have been salt traders who subsequently expanded their business to the largest saltworks in Mesoamerica, the northern Coast of Yucatan, as I have suggested. Indeed, Kanek' are present in the foundation of Ek' Balam and are among the cofounders of the city of Chichen Itza (Akkeren 2012:41–44).

YUKATEK SOURCES: XIBALBA IN THE FRANJA TRANSVERSAL AREA

This relation of Northern Yucatan with the Transversal is also expressed in the cosmological realm. It turns out that the only other Maya document outside of the Guatemala highlands naming the term *xibalba* is from Yucatan. Xibalba is mentioned in Landa's *Relación de las Cosas de Yucatan* in his part on the yearbearers, in particular the yearbearer Kawak related to the direction west: "The fourth letter is Cauac: Its year was the portent of the Bacab they call Hozanek, Ekelbacab, Ekbauaktun, Ekxibchac; this marked the part to the west" (Landa 2008 [1556]:folio 28v./70, translation by Woodfill).

Thus, the Bakab associated with this cardinal direction is called Hozanek. Scholars have argued that this appellative is a misspelling by Landa and that it should be Hochanek', derived of the number *ho*, "five" and *chanek'*, the Ch'olan variant of *kanek'* (Bolles 2001). It is further clear that this cardinal direction is connected with the color black: the names of the divinities associated with the west are all prefixed with /ek'/. It corresponds with our finding about several ethnonyms of the people inhabiting the Transversal and surrounding regions like the Q'eqchi' and Aq'aab. Landa then points out that, for the ceremony related to the Kawak years, they made an image of a deity called Wak Mitun Ajaw; *mitun* is one of the Classic Maya terms used for "Underworld" (Tokovinine 2002). Landa (2008 [1556]:folio 32r/77, translation by Woodfill) further adds about the rituals that they "danced some dances among which they danced one called *cazcarientas* [sic], and thus they named it Xibalbaokot, by which they meant the dance of the demon."

Here is the term *xibalba* in the phrase Xibalba Okot, Dance of Xibalba. Intriguingly, one of the dances included the act of *cazcarientas*. Earlier scholars were still struggling with this term (Tozzer 1975:147, nota 723); however, in modern Mexican jargon it means "playing football," as in "*vamos a jugar una cascarita al parque*" or "*ayer cascareamos en el parque*"—it is a reference to the ballgame (Akkeren 2012:170). Of course, the Xibalba myth is specifically associated with the ballgame. Notoriously, the ballcourt at Chichen Itza is one of the largest and most lavishly decorated court in Mesoamerica (Schele and Mathews 1999). Glyphs used to express the term *ballcourt* may vary, yet the one used on the ballcourt rings in Chichen Itza is the same one we find on the ballcourt markers of the main ballcourt at Cancuen. This detail, of course, in itself cannot sustain a relation between both cities, but it is part of the wider set of evidence I am building here (Akkeren 2012:26). We know from the iconography on the columns of the South Temple of the Great Ballcourt of Chichen Itza that the Kanek' lineage was involved in its construction.

Returning to Landa's quote, in the ceremony for the Kawak years, associated with the Kanek'/Chanek' lineage ruling in Salinas de los Nueve Cerros area, we have a festival including a ballgame that was called the Xibalba Dance. These ritual ballgames used to end with a human sacrifice of decapitation. We need to expand on this theme a little bit.

I have developed a set of paradigms that are at the base of all Mesoamerican cosmology and that may be helpful in understanding its mythology, texts, and iconography (Akkeren 2012, 2021, 2024). The paradigms encompass the two main elements of creation: light and food, sun and corn, embodied by the Sun Hero and the Maize Hero. They are complementary: the first one is male, and although the second one is also male, he is obviously linked to the female domain in, for example, his outfit and the social context. They are also related to the complementary colors white and yellow, represented by the Classic couplet K'in and K'an and still omnipresent as prefixes in modern Maya prayers (Akkeren 2012, 2018, 2021).

Both heroes must die in order for the sun and corn to be born. The ballcourt is the place where the Maize Hero finds his demise. Within this paradigm, the ballcourt, in its most profound essence and, therefore, in its shape, represents a furrow on a maize field, and the decapitated head of the Maize Hero, the sown maize kernel. Thus, we find Jun Ajpuuh in the Xibalba myth at one point in the story embodying the Maize Hero, when he loses his head in the Bat House near the ballcourt. However, in Mesoamerican mythology both paradigms sometimes fused in one single hero, and Jun Ajpuuh is a fine example of this fusion. Many scholars may not have realized that Jun Ajpuuh actually dies two times in the Xibalba myth. Indeed, he also represents the Sun Hero, and the second time he perishes in the divine hearth to later become the sun of the new era.

Landa not only refers in the section on the Kawak year of the cardinal direction of the west to the ballgame but also notes that the Yukatek Maya celebrated this period-ending by building a huge arched, wooden shed and filling it with firewood. Various fire priests were handed torches made of bound-together sticks and lit the building. The torches resemble the *xiuhmolpilli*, which was part of the hieroglyphic name of Tajal Chan Ahk. As noted, this lord of Cancuen is presented as a fire priest. The fire ceremony recalls the divine hearth of the Xibalba myth. In addition, archaeological research on the quadripartite plaza of Machaquila has revealed that this space has been the scenery of huge bonfires. I have suggested that it was the historical stage of the Underworld Fireplace, which ended up in the Xibalba myth (Akkeren 2012:28–31). The quadripartite form corresponds with the central Mexican glyph for *xochitl*, a standard symbol in iconography for the birth of the sun, the equivalent of the dayname Jun Ajpuuh.

Thus, in Landa's quote we have summarized the two rituals related to the two paradigms embodied by the Maize Hero and Sun Hero, impersonated by Jun Ajpuuh. We have a Xibalba Ballgame Dance linked with the cardinal direction west and the color black, which in its turn is connected with the Salinas de los Nueve Cerros area, the geographical Xibalba. One wonders how people of northern Yucatan knew about this area.

KANEK' AND KAWEQ

One of the driving forces behind the power changes suggested by Thompson turned out to be the Kanek' lineage, a lineage that was very active during the Terminal Classic. When Lord Watul started the tenth Baktun, the revival of Ceibal, by building a radial temple, he was sent by a Kanek' lord of Ucanal. Among the lords present at the inauguration of the temple were other kinsmen like the Kanek' family member who was lord of Motul de San José, and probably a Kanek' lord from Panhale, near Pomona on the Usumacinta. Thus, with Salinas de los Nueve Cerros, we have at the end of the Classic an interesting network of Kanek' lineages in the southern Peten, extending all the way to the north of Yucatan (Akkeren 2012, 2021; Boot 2005:45; Schele and Mathews 1999).

In other studies (Akkeren 2003b, 2012), I proposed that the Kanek' lineage was related to the Kaweq, the intellectual authors of the *Popol Vuh*. I believe that the latter originated from the former. When it comes to the Postclassic Highland Maya peoples like K'iche', Tz'utujil, or Kaqchikel, scholars used to have an outdated view about their origin, once formulated by Goetz, Morley, and Recinos (1950) and Carmack (1981). In my reconstruction of these Postclassic confederations through a methodology I have called "lineage-history," I found that the origin of the Kaweq lineage lay in the Transversal (Akkeren 2000, 2006a, 2012)

It is clear that, linguistically, *kaweq* cannot be derived from *kanek'*, but it is also clear from many years of investigation that the patronym *kaweq* does not have a meaning of its own and appears to be a constructed lineage name. However, there is plenty of other evidence that connects the two. Both lineages can be traced back to the Transversal, the historical Xibalba. The lineage name Kanek' is written in several ways: with the number "four" (*kan*), the logograms for "sky" (*kan*) or "snake" (*kan*), followed by the logogram for "star" (*ek'*) or with the syllables /e/ and /k'e/ (*ek'e = ek'*). Interestingly, there are also full-figure variants that allow us to understand the meaning of this lineage name: a serpent with its tail enrolled in the glyph for "star." In these pictograms, the opened jaws of the serpent serve as a cavernous entrance to the Underworld (Figure 11.9; Boot 2009).

Kanek' translates as "Serpent Star." The name Serpent Star evokes the concept of a constellation. I suggested that Tajal Chan Ahk also referred to an asterism; another name for that constellation was Ahk Ek' or Turtle Star (Barrera Vásquez 1991:150). This brings us to the ancestral couple, Xmukane and Xpiyakok. I have reasoned that both deities had their projections on the nocturnal sky as Kan Ek' and Ahk Ek', linking them to the constellations of Scorpio and Turtle (Orion; Akkeren 2000, 2012, 2021). Now Xmukane is omnipresent in the Xibalba myth, whereas Xpiyakok is mentioned only in the beginning of the *Popol Vuh* and subsequently erased from the story. Thus, there is good reason to assume that the grandmother goddess Xmukane was the patron deity of the Kaweq-Kanek'. It would fit Mesoamerican schemes, in which salt production is generally related with goddesses, like the Nahua deity Huixtocihuatl or Salt Woman.

As observed, Xmukane is a Ch'olan (or Yukatekan) appellative meaning

Figure 11.9. Pictograph of Kanek' patronym on ceramic plate in the Chocholá Maxcanú style. (Juan Moncada)

Buried Tail, if we take the /a/ simply to be an epithetic vowel. The name refers to the constellation of Scorpio, whose tale is buried in the starry region of the Milky Way. Indeed, of all the Maya zodiacal images of the *Paris Codex*, Scorpio is the only creature that is connected to the Ecliptic Band with its tail, instead of with its beak. Thus, Xmukane is an ophidian or scorpion-like creature whose open jaws lead into a particular dark part in the Milky Way that was perceived as the Underworld. In this case the full figure variant of the lineage name Kanek' represented the same notion as Xmukane. In these versions, we see God N or L peeping out from between these jaws, possibly her spouse Xpiyakok.

Earlier we found that the Kanek' were situated in Bolonte' Witz or Salinas de los Nueve Cerros during the 4 k'atun of AD 711–731. Knowing that the place was also called Kanek' Witz, they must have been there already much longer. From Salinas de los Nueve Cerros, they must have started their commercial expansion toward the largest salt fields of Mesoamerica, to Emal on the northern coast of Yucatan (Figure 11.10). This corresponds with a *hul*–an arrival event often associated with important dynasty changes in 770 of a figure called Ek' Balam in northern Yucatan. Ek' Balam gave his name to this city that became the center of power in northwestern Yucatan before the foundation of Chichen Itza. Also known as Tal(ol) (Lacadena 2003), it lay on the road to the shipping docks on the island Cerritos, where, apparently, the canoes laden with salt came and went. Interestingly, Ek' Balam operated in the name of a lord called Chak Jutuw Kanek'. According to the *Relación Geográfica de Ek' Balam*, this Ek' Balam or Black Jaguar was a historical figure, a fact proposed by Lacadena (2003) and Boot (2009). In 814, Chak Jutuw Kanek' was overseeing another arrival in Ek' Balam.

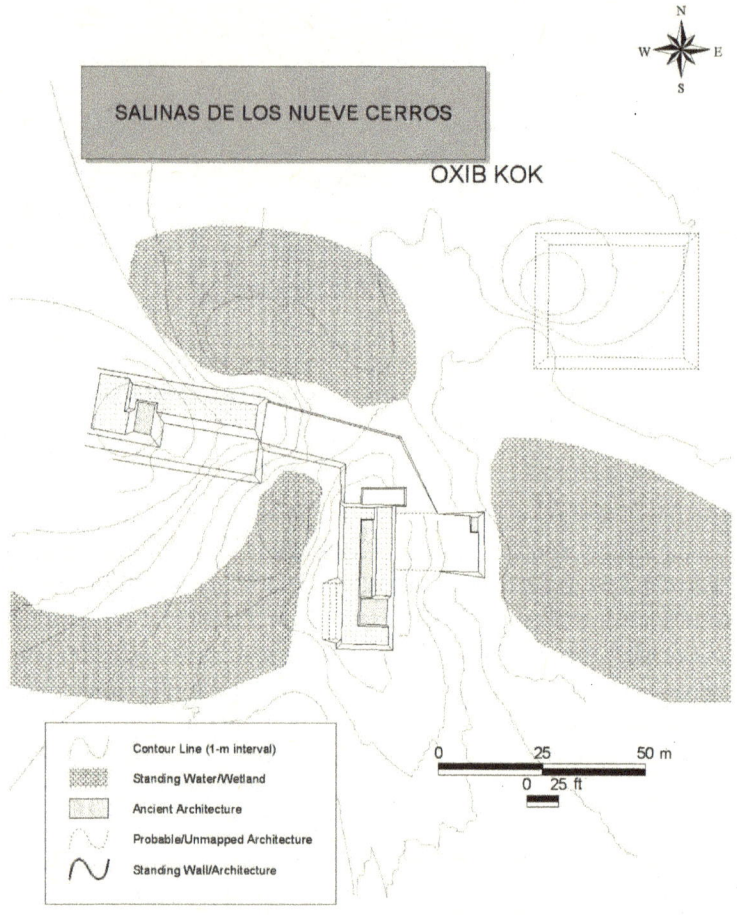

Figure 11.10. Map of the saltworks of northern Yucatan. (Base map made in Photoshop. Juan Moncada and Ruud van Akkeren)

It is possible that Ek' Balam came from Salinas de los Nueve Cerros, as we may infer from Stela 1, one of the few remaining monuments of this city. Unfortunately, it is without a date, but it features a Maya lord with a layered headdress atop a frontal jaguar face. At the top of the headdress sits the glyphic collocation Ik' Ajaw or Lord of the Darkness (Figure 11.11; Erik Boot, personal communication 2011). We know that Salinas de los Nueve Cerros belonged to the historical Xibalba, an area typified by the color black, where we found names of the people, lineages, and toponyms including the term "black." Recently, some Early Postclassic tombs were discovered on the ancient road between San Cristóbal Verapaz and Chama, in a village where the people still recall their origin in Chama. The tombs contained a great number of very fine Tohil Plumbate pottery. The Indigenous name of this village is Pan Amaq' Ik'i—that is, Place of the Peoples of the Darkness, again marking the people of this part of the Franja Transversal as denizens of the night (Morán and Akkeren 2016).

Figure 11.11. Ik' Ajaw glyphs on jaguar headdress, Stela 1, Salinas de los Nueve Cerros, Alta Verapaz, Guatemala. Berlin State Museums, Ethnological Museum, IV Ca 29782. (Ruud van Akkeren)

With this observation, we have come upon another connection with the Kaweq. I have compared this historical figure Ek' Balam with one of the four founding fathers mentioned in the *Popol Vuh*: Ik'i Balam. Interestingly, in the *Relación Geográfica de Ek' Balam* the city is called Tiquibalon, which reads as Ta Ik'i Balam. Ik'i Balam remains a shadowy figure in the *Popol Vuh*; in several other chronicles, he is considered an ancestor without offspring. It seems as if there has been an effort to erase Ik'i Balam from the K'iche' annals. The early history in the *Popol Vuh* is clearly deformed. Its Kaweq authors claim that their ancestral father was Balam K'itze', who they say was also the founder of the K'iche' confederation. Carmack already suggested that the real founders were not the Kaweq but the Ajaw K'iche' lineage, and I have taken up his idea (Akkeren 2000, 2002; Carmack 1981). Scrutinizing research of the Indigenous texts has proven that Ik'i Balam once was the ancestor of the Kaweq, as I show in my book on the Xibalba myth (Akkeren 2012:43).

It should further be recalled that an outstanding architectural feature of Ek' Balam is the raised temple with the open jaws visible from far away in the flat countryside of northern Yucatan. Admittedly, temples featuring a monster-maw entrance are a common feature in the Chenes-Puuc architectonical styles. Yet the Serpent Maw entrance of Ek' Balam exhibits some interesting additional features: the lower jaw, which is the floor of the entrance, rests on a platform with skull figures, similar to the Watery Throne of Cancuen. The spaces between the skulls are adorned with images of fish sucking on water lilies, as we find in Tajal Chan Ahk's headdress on Cancuen's Panel 3 (see Figure 11.4). Between the larger fangs of the lower jaw, there are symbols that may be *ak'bal* glyphs (Figure 11.12). These are all elements associated with Xibalba iconography.

The Ik'i Balam, or Black Jaguar, figure is but another name of the Xbalam Q'e hero in the *Popol Vuh*. Translators of this text and many modern K'iche', for that matter, have missed that the term *xbalam q'e* is not K'iche' but Q'eqchi', meaning Hidden Sun. There is an entire complex of Q'eqchi' mythology about the Moon Goddess Qana Po, in which Balam Q'e features as the protagonist, which is the standard creation myth of the Verapaz and Northern Transversal Strip (Akkeren 2012; Braakhuis 2010). In these stories, Balam Q'e may be coupled with or become Saq Q'e. Saq Q'e and Balam Q'e are but two aspects of the sun warrior: the Sun of the Day and the Sun of the Night. It is for this reason that Jun Ajpuuh, the Sun of the Day in the Xibalba myth, suffers in the Underworld, while his brother, Xb'alam Q'e, for whom the Underworld is his natural habitat, helps him out every time. Ik'i Balam or Xb'alam Q'e are also equivalents of the Classic Jaguar God of the Underworld or Night Sun. As previously mentioned, Balam Q'e is very much alive among modern

Figure 11.12. Photograph of huge jaws as temple entrance. Note the skulls and ak'bal signs on the jaws. Stucco façade, Ek' Balam acropolis, Mexico. (Ruud van Akkeren)

Q'eqchi', who still see a jaguar figure on the face of a full moon—that is, the Sun of the Night (Akkeren 2012:128).

How the name Kaweq originated, apparently void of a direct meaning, remains unclear and needs to be studied. I have argued that the Kanek' of Salinas de los Nueve Cerros and Xibalba were strongly related with the cardinal direction west and the day sign Kawak that Kanek' and Kawak blended into Kaweq—that is, in the Highland Maya variant of the dayname Kawak—which was, and still is, Kawoq in K'iche' and Kawuq in Q'eqchi'. In Poqom it was Kahoq/Kohoq, and indeed one of the ancestral leaders of neighboring Chama was a Kohoq (Akkeren 2012; Morán and Akkeren 2016).

CHAMA

Up to the present, excavations at Salinas de los Nueve Cerros have hardly generated new iconography that could help in identifying the presence of the Xmukane figure, like the personified cave with jaws and entrance to the Underworld. However, farther upstream on the Chixoy River, we have the richly decorated ceramics of Chama. Chama lay on the trade route of Nine Places, of which the famous God L vase K593 is an apt expression. If we are reconstructing a possible path for the Kanek' to have joined the Highland Poqom confederation during the Late Classic and Early Postclassic, and in the process to have become the Kaweq, it might have been along this trade route. Indeed, Kaweq is a surname found in many Poqomchi' towns (Akkeren 2000, 2003a, 2012, 2021), which I believe can be traced back to the founding population of Kaminaljuyu before it splintered into Poqom and Poqomchi' in the Early Postclassic (Akkeren 2019, 2024). It is a historical fact thatPoqom people constituted a part of Chama's population; in the sixteenth century, they were congregated by a Dominican friar in the town of San Cristóbal Verapaz. They produced a chronicle, *Título del Barrio de Santa Ana* (1565), in which they described their origin in Chama. The people of Chama still perform a Merchant Dance that recalls the scene on the famous Chama vessel K593, named Tzama Q'eq. It is even possible that Poqom lineages had already settled in Salinas de los Nueve Cerros and were present in Cancuen (Akkeren 2024; Morán and Akkeren 2016).

As for other Chama ceramics, the enormous personified upper jaws on the vases K5944 and K7602 are fine examples of the Xmukane concept of the entrance of a cave. They include *ak'bal* signs on the antenna of the monster's maw. As mentioned, one of the ancestors named in the *Título del Barrio de Santa Ana* was a Kohoq. It is by no means a coincidence that, when the people of Chama merged their prehispanic patron deity with Catholic saints, they picked Santa Ana, another grandmother figure (Akkeren 2012, 2021; Morán and Akkeren 2016).

Like in Salinas de los Nueve Cerros, we have in Chama various indications of a connection with the Yucatan Peninsula. There is, for example, the toponym Chama. It is derived from a Late Classic lineage of rulers belonging to a certain warrior class called *Gato de Monte*, or Fox. As I have shown, there is ample evidence that the anthropomorphic personages on Chama pottery are actually historical references to lineages (Akkeren 2000, 2012, 2018, 2021). There are several copies of an anthropomorphic figure in the position of a ruler, with a human body but with the head of a fox (*Urocyon cinero-argenteus fraterculus*; Figure 11.13). In Poqomchi' or Q'eqchi', this animal is called *yak*; however, in lowland languages like Ch'olti' or Yukatek, the same animal is called *ch'amak*. According to the books of *Chilam Balam* of Yucatan, there was a military lineage with that name, one of the various military lineages represented by totemic animals, as already suggested by Ralph Roys (1967). This group was also mentioned at an earlier date in Tikal; members from the Ch'amak lineage raised the well-known Marcador in AD 416 in honor of Spearthrower Owl and their captain Siyah K'aahk'. In Chama, they must have become the ruling lineage, giving its name to the prehispanic site, much as the Kanek' gave its name to Kanek' Witz or Salinas de los Nueve Cerros. These Fox warriors are mentioned in the *Chilam Balam* books with other military lineages, such as the Kinkayou and Weasel (the Weasel lineage is discussed below). Kinkayou is *ch'okoj*, a common surname in the Northern Transversal and adjacent Maya Highlands, and is also connected to the Kaweq lineage. There was at least one Kinkayou lineage branch at the Palenque court of K'inich Ahkal Mo' Naab III (Akkeren 2003a, 2021:59–60, 150). Finally, Chama ceramics include hieroglyphic texts, and epigraphic analysis has shown that the artists were using a Yukatek Yearbearer system (Muluk, K'an, Kawak, and Ix), which strengthens our Kawak hypothesis (Akkeren 2000:439; Boot 2003).

CONNECTIONS TO THE PACIFIC COAST

The Xibalba area of Cancuen, Salinas de los Nueve Cerros, and Chama was just a chain in a Mesoamerican network of trade. Apparently merchants, protected by warriors, crossed the Maya Highlands to the Pacific Coast of Guatemala. The road passed through Uspantan, where we have a site contemporary to Chama. It is still called Chamac, likely once Ch'amak. John W. Fox (1987:117–120) has drawn the attention to the similarities of Chamac to Chichen Itza in its architecture as well as in its ceramics. From Uspantan, merchants would then traverse the Sajkabaja and Quiche region, the archaeological sites of which all yielded Chama-style ceramics (Ichon 1992; Wauchope 1975).

From there it ran all the way to the Pacific Coast, to Cotzumalguapa. Chama-style ceramics are one of the main "foreign" ceramics at that site (Chinchilla et al. 2005). It is important to stress this connection because

Figure 11.13. Anthropomorphic images of fox associated with Ch'amak lineage on Chama-style vases. (Mallary Tiul and Juan Moncada)

specialists of both sites, Chichen Itza and Cotzumalguapa, are in accordance that there are strong similarities in their respective iconography (Chinchilla 2016; Schmidt 1998). The Transversal may have served as a bridge between both centers that saw their apogee at similar moments in time, during the Late and Terminal Classic.

There is little knowledge about the northern lowland Maya traveling to, or having connections with, the Pacific Coast. It is likely that they did, given its economic importance, the abundance of cacao, cotton, or indigo-dye plantations, and the various classes of shells. The ceramic materials and similar styles suggest contact. We know about Ch'ol speakers on the coast from the *Memorial de Sololá* (Memorial de Sololá 1550s–1600). The following quote is set during the Late Classic, and Sukitan is the site known as Chocola on the Middle Nahuala River (proper spelling "Xoq'ola"), the equivalent of the Nahua Sukitan, Mud Place (River): "They then descended to Ch'ol Amaq' and to Sukitan. Their tongue was truly difficult. Only the animals knew it! They showed it to the animals Loxpin and Ch'upichin. They told them when they arrived: 'Waya waya, ela opa!' They were immediately startled. So, we spoke their language to the Ch'ol Amaq' and they were startled as well. They had good words with us when we arrived" (Memorial de Sololá 1550s–1600:folio 7:§15, translation by Woodfill). Ch'ol Amaq' indicates a group of Ch'ol speakers. The animals Loxpin and Ch'upichin are references to their leaders' names.

Returning to Cotzumalguapa and its connection with Chichen Itza, both cities harbored at least one group in common, the aforementioned Weasel lineage. The Weasel warriors, *saqb'im* in highland languages, *sab'im* in Yukatek, even lent their name to Cotzumalguapa, derived from *cozamatl*, "weasel." Its Maya name was Saqb'im Ya or Weasel River, in Nahua Cotzumalguapan.

Earlier I noted that the historical Ek' Balam, who helped found the place of Ek' Balam, was connected to Salinas de los Nueve Cerros. As the hieroglyphic text reveals, he acted on behalf of a higher lord, called Chak Jutuuw Kanek'. The origin of this Kanek' lord is not quite clear. Yet he appears with an emblem glyph in the texts of Ek' Balam. Some epigraphers have suggested that the main sign in the emblem glyph is a weasel (Lacadena 2003). This proposition would connect Chichen Itza with Cotzumalguapa, Nueve Cerros and Chama, the historical Xibalba region, being the intermediate.

There may be an iconographic rendering of the name Kanek' in Cotzumalguapa. Several monuments feature a lord with a balloon headdress, similar to those portrayed on Chama pottery, which sports a series of four serpents with split tongues. See, for example, Bilbao Monuments 9, 20 and El Baúl Monument 7. The number four, as well as the snakes, would read as *kan*; still, the *ek'* or "star" part of its name would be lacking (Figure 11.14).

Figure 11.14. Pictograph of Kanek' patronym with four snakes on a balloon headdress, Bilbao Monument 20, Cotzumalguapa, Guatemala. (Courtesy of Oswaldo Chinchilla Mazariegos.)

A colonial document proves it is possible that a Kanek' person was in the area. Franciscan friar Francisco Vázquez (1938) writes the following in his *Crónica de la Provincia del Santísimo Nombre de Jesús de Guatemala*: "Let the declaration of Juan Zakbín, Indian of the leaders of the town of Patinamit stand, that shortly after Governor Don Pedro de Alvarado conquered this kingdom of Guatemala, P. Fr. Toribio, friar of S. Francisco, arrived with other friars, and they baptized him and gave him the name Juan, while before he was named Kanec Zakb'in" (XV Tomo II:160, translation by Woodfill). Here we have a lord from Patinamit, which is the Kaqchikel capital Iximche', with a lineage name Saqb'im or Weasel, who further carries the lineage name Kanek'.

I have identified the Classic Maya cities of the Pacific Coast as being one of the main pools of elite lineages for the Postclassic confederations like Tz'utujil, K'iche', Kaqchikel, and so on (Akkeren 2000, 2005, 2008, 2009, 2016, 2024). The Weasel lineage exists among all these Maya polities up until today, where Saqb'im is still a common surname. The Weasel warriors are mentioned in the *Memorial de Sololá* as well. They are spies and are employed as such by the head of the K'iche' Winaq when they are about to conquer the Poqom capital Nim Poqom in the Valley of Rabinal. It is the very moment when the Kaweq-Kanek' surrender and become part of the K'iche' confederation (Akkeren 2000, 2012, 2021). The Saqb'im must have been descendants of the various lineages of the special reconnoitering forces known as the *Nawaloztomeca*. They included the warriors of the Coyote warriors (Xajil) as well, the lineage that produced the *Memorial de Sololá*.

CONCLUSIONS

In a recent article about Salinas de los Nueve Cerros, Woodfill and coauthors are keen to prove that the town played an important role in trade within the entire Maya area: "Despite the fact that pioneering work at the site was carried out in 1975—four decades ago—Nueve Cerros has not been adequately incorporated into our understanding of Classic Maya interregional interactions and trade" (Woodfill et al. 2015:164). Indeed, there is ample evidence of a connection between Salinas de los Nueve Cerros, the only saltworks in the central Maya Lowlands, and the northern Yucatan, another important region of the salt industry. There is also a connection with the Pacific Coast of Cotzumalguapa.

Salinas de los Nueve Cerros is an exceptional site, according to Woodfill and coauthors, because it offers a unique case study of an elite group conducting the salt production, since they lived literally on top of it. Instead of abstract questions related to symbolic control that might have been exercised by distant urban elites over the hamlets and villages directly responsible for their extraction, the site contains the actual imprints the elites left on the saltworking area to show that the economic activities performed there happened under their auspices (Woodfill et al. 2015:175).

With this, we have very likely identified one of the major players that controlled the salt-production: the Kanek' lineage. It therefore came as a surprise to read the following conclusions reached: Andrews and Mock and McKillop (Andrews and Mock 2002; McKillop 1995, 2002) state that "the southern Maya Lowlands have very little evidence of sustained trade with northern Yucatan, and multiple saltworks have been identified along the Belizean coast," and Woodfill and coauthors state that "there is little direct evidence of interaction and exchange between the southern lowlands and the saltworking sites of Yucatan. Nueve Cerros alone would have been able to produce sufficient salt to meet the conceivable demands of much of the Classic Maya economy" (Woodfill et al. 2015:167). I understand the authors are trying to promote their site, showing that it was the main source of salt for the central lowlands and that it is worthy of being taken into account as an important trading partner on the Chixoy-Usumacinta River, when it has long been ignored in or not connected to the lowland literature until very recently. Yet by being focused only on salt production and some ceramic evidence, they have not made use of the comprehensive set of available archaeological, ethnohistorical, and epigraphical evidence that supports their claims.

As my investigations suggest, there are promising conclusions to be made about the role of the Transversal and its ruling lineages. First, contrary to what the authors of the Salinas de los Nueve Cerros article purport, there is sufficient evidence for a connection between this site and northern Yucatan, and for a good reason: the expansion of the salt trade. We actually have a unique case, an important trading agent, the Kanek'—a lineage dominant throughout the Late and Terminal Classic and beyond. Because of its many caves, the Northern Transversal was the home of the historical and geographical Xibalba, seat of the gods of trade and commerce, and that was known as far as northern Yucatan, as Landa and the Chilam Balam books prove. One can even claim that Kanek's very lineage name originated as the reptilian entrance to this Underworld.

Kanek' is further closely related to the Kaweq, whose patron goddess Xmukane represented the same ophidian deity. The Kaweq produced an unparalleled account of the Maya Underworld because, just like the Kanek', they originated in the Xibalba area. This should integrate the Highland Maya into the rest of the Maya world, the political dynamics that have often been denied by Classic Maya scholars (Akkeren 2021). We hinted at a connection with Cotzumalguapa, which Kanek'-Kaweq needed to have crossed the highlands. The Chama-style pottery found along that route may be an indication of these dynamics.

After these first contacts, perhaps set off by the Kanek' salt merchants, the path was paved for the intrusion of more groups of Yukatek people, finally resulting in a complete "yucatecanization" of the Maya Lowlands. The Atlas team headed by Laporte has shown that this process started at the end of the Classic period. By the time the Spanish arrived, this immigration had changed the linguistic map of the Peten. This massive influx into the central area is hardly taken into account when discussing the Classic Maya collapse, which is an oversight.

Bibliography

Adams, Richard, E. W.
1971   *The Ceramics of Altar de Sacrificios.* Papers of the Peabody Museum of Archaeology and Ethnology, Harvard University, Vol. 63, No. 1. Peabody Museum Press, Cambridge, Massachusetts.
1978   Routes of Communication in Mesoamerica: The Northern Guatemalan Highlands and the Petén. In *Mesoamerican Communication Routes and Cultural Contacts*, edited by Thomas A. Lee Jr. and Carlos Navarrete, pp. 27–36. Papers of the New World Archaeological Foundation, No. 40. New World Archaeological Foundation, Brigham Young University, Provo, Utah.

Aguilar, Enric, T. C. Peterson, Paula Ramírez Obando, R. Frutos, J. A. Retana, M. Solera, J. Soley, et al.
2005   Changes in Precipitation and Temperature Extremes in Central America and Northern South America, 1961–2003. *Journal of Geophysical Research* 110:1–15.

Aguirre-Dugua, Xitlali, and Antonio González-Rodríguez
2016   Phylogeographical Approaches to the Study of Plant Domestication, with Special Emphasis on Perennial Plants. In *Ethnobotany of Mexico*, edited by Rafael Lira, Alejandro Casas, and José Blancas, pp. 319–366. Springer, New York.

Akkeren, Ruud van
1995   The Scorpion and the Turtle. Texas Notes on Precolumbian Art, Writing, and Culture, Vol. 73 (June). University of Texas, Austin.
2000   *Place of the Lord's Daughter: Rab'inal, Its History, Its Dance-Drama.* Center for Non-Western Studies (CNWS) Publications, Vol. 91. Research School of Asian, African, and Amerindian Studies, Leiden University, Leiden.
2002   El Lugar en Donde Salió el Primer Sol para los K'iche': Jakawits, su Nueva Ubicación. In *XV Simposio de Investigaciones Arqueológicas en Guatemala, 2001*, edited by Juan Pedro Laporte, Héctor Escobedo, and Bárbara Arroyo, pp. 1–12. Museo Nacional de Arqueología y Etnología, Guatemala City.
2003a Kawinal or Forty Place: Stop on an Ancient Trade Route. In *Misceláneas . . . En honor a Alain Ichon*, edited by Marie-Charlotte Arnauld, Alain Breton, Marie-France Fauvet-Berthelot, and Juan Antonio Valdés, pp. 115–139. Caudal, Guatemala City.
2003b Authors of the Popol Wuj. *Ancient Mesoamerica* 14(2):237–256.
2005   Conociendo a los Pipiles de la Costa Pacífica de Guatemala. Un Estudio

Etnohistórico de Documentos Indígenas y Documentos del AGCA. In *XVIII Simposio de Investigaciones Arqueológicas en Guatemala, 2004*, edited by Juan Pedro Laporte, Bárbara Arroyo, and Héctor Mejía, pp. 1000–1014. Museo Nacional de Arqueología y Etnología, Guatemala City.

2006a   El Chinamit y la Plaza Postclásica. La Arqueología y la Etnohistoria en Búsqueda del Papel de la Casa del Consejo. In *XIX Simposio de Investigaciones Arqueológicas en Guatemala, 2005*, edited by Juan Pedro Laporte, Bárbara Arroyo, Héctor Mejía, pp. 223–234. Museo Nacional de Arqueología y Etnología, Guatemala City.

2006b   Tzuywa: Place of the Gourd. *Ancient America* 9:36–73. Boundary End Archaeology Research Center, Barnardsville, North Carolina.

2008   Título de los Señores de Sacapulas. In *Crónicas Mesoamericanas I*, edited by Horacio Cabezas Carcache, pp. 59–92. Universidad Mesoamericana, Guatemala City.

2009   Título de los Indios de Santa Clara la Laguna. In *Crónicas Mesoamericanas II*, edited by Horacio Cabezas Carcache, pp. 69–86. Universidad Mesoamericana, Guatemala City.

2010   Fray Domingo de Vico: Maestro de autores indígenas. *Revista de Estudios Mayas* 2(7):1–61.

2012   *Xib'alb'a y el Nacimiento del Nuevo Sol: Una Visión Posclásica del Colapso Aya*. Editorial Piedra Santa, Guatemala City.

2016   Tojil Cult in Classic Cotzumalguapa: Origin of Postclassic Confederations on the Pacific Coast. In *Archaeology and Identity in Southeastern Mesoamerica*, edited by Claudia Garcia-Des Lauriers and Michael Love, pp. 142–171. University of Utah Press, Salt Lake City.

2018   *Maya Studies with the Maya*. Self-published manuscript.

2019   Cerro de Maguey, el Nombre Original de Kaminal Juyu. In *Culturas Visuales Indígenas y las Prácticas Estéticas en las Américas Desde la Antigüedad Hasta el Presente*, edited by Sanja Savkić, pp. 51–81. Estudios Indiana, No. 13. Gebr. Mann Verlag, Berlin.

2021   *Los Mayas Nunca se Fueron. Hoy Hablan Q'eqchi'. Alta Verapaz y El Petén—Tres Mil Años de Historia*. Editorial Piedra Santa, Guatemala City.

2025   Cerro de Maguey—Lugar Donde Nació el Tiempo. Un Estudio Etnohistórico de Kaminal Juyu—Capital del Pueblo Poq'om (3 Volumes). Self-published volumes.

Alexander, Edward P., and Mary Alexander

1996   *Museums in Motion: An Introduction to the History and Functions of Museums*. AltaMira Press, Lanham, Maryland.

Aliphat Fernández, Mario

2009   Huertos y Cacaotales Mayas: Un Análisis Agroecosistémico. In *XXII Simposio de Investigaciones Arqueológicas en Guatemala, 2008*, edited by Juan Pedro Laporte, Bárbara Arroyo, and Héctor Mejía, pp. 267–275. Museo Nacional de Arqueología y Etnología, Guatemala City.

Alnsour, Najwa

2013   Organic Matter in Holocene Paleosols at the Farwell Site. MSc thesis, Department of Soil Science, Iowa State University, Aimes.

Alvarado, Carlos
2004 Excavaciones en el Puerto Principal de Cancuén: Temporada 2003. In *Proyecto Arqueológico Cancuen, Informe No. 5, Temporada 2003*, edited by Arthur A. Demarest, Tomás Barrientos, Brigitte Kovacevich, Michael Callaghan, Brent K. S. Woodfill, and Luis F. Luin, pp. 345–364. Department of Anthropology, Vanderbilt University, Nashville, Tennessee.

Alvarado, Carlos, Carrie Anne Berryman, Anna Novotny, and Kristen Demarest
2006 Investigaciones en el Puerto Principal de Cancuén. In *Proyecto Arqueológico Cancuén, Informe No. 6, Temporada 2004–2005, Volumen II*, edited by Tomás Barrientos, Arthur A. Demarest, Luis F. Luin, and Brent K. S. Woodfill, pp. 435–452. Department of Anthropology, Vanderbilt University, Nashville, Tennessee.

Alvarado, Pedro de
1924 [1525] *An Account of the Conquest of Guatemala in 1524*, edited by S. J. Mackie. Cortes Society, New York.

Alvarado, Silvia Najarro
2013 Manejo hidráulico durante el Clásico Tardío en Cancuen, Petén, Guatemala. *Contributions in New World Archaeology* 5:125–149.

Alvarado, Silvia, and Elisa Mencos
2008 CAN 48: Excavaciones en la Cisterna o Reserva de Agua Norte. In *Proyecto Arqueológico Cancuén, Informe Final No. 8, Temporada 2007*, edited by Horacio Martínez Paiz, Arthur A. Demarest, Mélanie Forné, and Luis F. Luin, pp. 79–113. Department of Anthropology, Vanderbilt University, Nashville, Tennessee.

An, FuYuan, HaiZhou Ma, HaiCheng Wei, and ZhongPing Lai
2012 Distinguishing Aeolian Signature from Lacustrine Sediments of the Qaidam Basin in Northeastern Qinghai-Tibetan Plateau and its Palaeoclimatic Implications. *Aeolian Research* 4:17–30.

Anderson, Arthur J. O., and Charles E. Dibble
1959 *Florentine Codex: General History of the Things of New Spain; Book 9: The Merchants*. Monographs of the School of American Research and the Museum of New Mexico Number 14, Part X. School of American Research and University of Utah, Santa Fe, New Mexico.

Andreani, Louis, and Richard Gloaguen
2016 Geomorphic Analysis of Transient Landscapes in the Sierra Madre de Chiapas and Maya Mountains (Northern Central America): Implications for the North American-Caribbean-Cocos Plate Boundary. *Earth Surface Dynamics* 4(1):71–102.

Andreani, Louis, Klaus Stanek, Richard Gloaguen, Ottomar Krentz, and Leomaris Domínguez-González
2014 DEM-Based Analysis of Interactions between Tectonics and Landscapes in the Ore Mountains and Eger Rift (East Germany and NW Czech Republic). *Remote Sensing* 6(9):7971–8001.

Andrews, Anthony
1980 Salt-Making, Merchants, and Markets: The Role of a Critical Resource in the Development of Maya Civilization. PhD dissertation, Department of Anthropology, University of Arizona, Tucson.

1983   *Maya Salt Production and Trade*. University of Arizona Press, Tucson.
1984   A Survey of Maya Salt Sources. *National Geographic Society Research Reports* 16:43–61.
1998   El Comercio Prehispánico Maya de la Sal: Nuevos Datos, Nuevas Perspectivas. In *La Sal en México II*, edited by Juan Carlos Reyes, pp. 1–28. Universidad de Colima, Colima, Mexico.

Andrews, Anthony, and Shirley Mock
2002   New Perspectives on the Prehispanic Maya Salt Trade. In *Ancient Maya Political Economies*, edited by Marilyn Masson and David Freidel, pp. 307–34. AltaMira Press, Walnut Creek, California.

Andrews V, E. Wyllys
1990   Early Ceramic History of the Lowland Maya. In *Vision and Revision in Maya Studies*, edited by Flora Clancy and Peter Harrison, pp. 1–19. University of New Mexico Press, Albuquerque.

Andrews, George F.
1975   *Maya Cities: Placemaking and Urbanization*. University of Oklahoma Press, Norman.

Andrieu, Chloé
2009   Outils Mayas: Distribution et Production du Silex et de L'obsidienne Dans les Basses Terres Mayas. PhD dissertation, Département Ethnologie et Préhistoire, Université Paris Ouest Nanterre, Paris.

Andrieu, Chloé, and Mélanie Forné
2010   Producción y Distribución del Jade en el Mundo Maya: Talleres, Fuentes y Rutas del Intercambio en su Contexto Interregional: Vista desde Cancuén. In *XXIII Simposio de Investigaciones Arqueológicas en Guatemala, 2009*, edited by Bárbara Arroyo, Adriana Linares Palma, and Lorena Paiz Aragón, pp. 946–955. Museo Nacional de Arqueología y Etnología, Guatemala City.

Andrieu, Chloé, Melanie Forné, and Arthur A. Demarest
2012   El Valor del ade: Producción y Distribución del Jade en el Sitio de Cancuén. In *El Jade y Otras Piedras Verdes: Perspectivas Interdisciplinarias e Interculturales*, edited by Walburga Wiesheu and Gabriela Guzzy, pp. 145–180. Colección Científica, Instituto Nacional de Arqueología e Historia, Mexico City.

Andrieu, Chloé, Olaf Jaime Riverón, María Dolores Tenorio, Thomas Calligaro, Juan Carlos Cruz Ocampo, Melania Jiménez, and Mikhail Ostrooumov
2011   Últimos Datos sobre la Producción de Artefactos de Jade en Cancuén. In *XXIV Simposio de Investigaciones Arqueológicas de Guatemala, 2010*, edited by Bárbara Arroyo, Adriana Linares Palma, and Lorena Paiz Aragón, pp. 1012–1021. Museo Nacional de Arqueología y Etnología, Guatemala City.

Andrieu, Chloé, and Douglas Quiñónez
2011   Análisis Lítico. In *Proyecto Arqueológico Cancuen, Informe Final No. 10, Temporada 2010*, edited by Arthur A. Demarest and Horacio Martínez Paiz, pp. 201–224. Department of Anthropology, Vanderbilt University, Nashville, Tennessee, and Universidad de San Carlos de Guatemala, Dirección General del Patrimonio Cultural y Natural, Guatemala City.

Andrieu, Chloé, Edna Rodas, and Luis F. Luin
2014 The Values of Classic Maya Jade: A Reanalysis of Cancuen's Jade Workshop. *Ancient Mesoamerica* 25(1):141–164.

Andrieu, Chloé, and Julien Sion
2017 Presentación del Sub-proyecto Regional Raxruha Viejo. In *Proyecto Arqueológico Cancuen, Informe Final No. 16, Temporada de Campo 2016: Tomo II—Proyecto Arqueológico Regional Raxruha Viejo*, edited by Julien Sion, Chloé Andrieu, Paola Torres, and Arthur A. Demarest, pp. 449–454. Ministerio de Cultura y Deportes de Guatemala, Guatemala City.

2018 Presentación de la Temporada 2017 del Sub-proyecto Regional Raxruha Viejo. In *Proyecto Arqueológico Regional Cancuen, Informe Final No 17, Temporada de Campo 2017: Tomo II—Proyecto Arqueológico Regional Raxruha Viejo*, edited by Julien Sion, Chloé Andrieu, Paola Torres, and Arthur A. Demarest, pp. 279–288. Ministerio de Cultura y Deportes de Guatemala, Guatemala City.

2019 Presentación de la Temporada 2018 del Sub-proyecto Arqueológico Regional Raxruha Viejo. In *Proyecto Arqueológico Regional Cancuen, Informe Final No. 18, Temporada 2018: Tomo II—Proyecto Arqueológico Regional Raxruha Viejo*, edited by Julien Sion, Chloé Andrieu, Paola Torres, and Arthur A. Demarest, pp. 193–199. Ministerio de Cultura y Deportes de Guatemala, Guatemala City.

2020 Presentación de la Temporada 2019 del Sub-proyecto Arqueológico Regional Raxruha Viejo. In *Proyecto Arqueológico Regional Cancuen, Informe Final No. 19, Temporada 2019: Tomo II—Proyecto Arqueológico Regional Raxruha Viejo*, edited by Julien Sion, Paola Torres, Chloé Andrieu, and Arthur A. Demarest, pp. 193–201. Ministerio de Cultura y Deportes de Guatemala, Guatemala City.

Annereau-Fulbert, Marie
2012 Intermediate Settlement Units in Late Postclassic Maya Sites in the Highlands: An Assessment from Archaeology and Ethnohistory. In *The Neighborhood as a Social and Spatial Unit in Mesoamerican Cities*, edited by Marie-Charlotte Arnauld, Linda R. Manzanilla, and Michael E. Smith, pp. 261–285. University of Arizona Press, Tucson.

Appadurai, Arjun (editor)
1988 *The Social Life of Things: Commodities in Cultural Perspective*. Cambridge University Press, Cambridge.

Aragón-Moreno, Alejandro A., Gerald A. Islebe, and Nuria Torrescano-Valle
2012 A ~3800-yr, High-Resolution Record of Vegetation and Climate Change on the North Coast of the Yucatán Peninsula. *Review of Palaeobotany and Palynology* 178:35–42.

Arellano-Torres, Elsa, Alexander Correa-Metrio, Diego López-Dávila, Jaime Escobar, Jason H. Curtis, and María Cecilia Cordero-Oviedo
2019 Mid to Late Holocene Hydrological and Sea-Level Change Reconstructions from La Mancha Coastal Lagoon, Veracruz, Mexico. *Palaeogeography, Palaeoclimatology, Palaeoecology* 520:150–162.

Arellano-Torres, Elsa, and María L. Machain-Castillo
2017 Late Pleistocene-Holocene Variability in the Southern Gulf of Mexico

Surface Waters Based on Planktonic Foraminiferal Assemblages. *Marine Micropaleontology* 131:44–58.

Armstrong, Graeme
2011 Evidence for the Equal Resilience of *Triodia* spp. (Poaceae), from Different Functional Groups, to Frequent Fire Dating Back to the Late Pleistocene. *Heredity* 107:558–564.

Arnauld, Marie-Charlotte
1985 La Céramique de la Structure A-7 de la Lagunita. In *Le Protoclassique à La Lagunita, El Quiché, Guatemala,* edited by Alain Ichon and Marie-Charlotte Arnauld, pp. 105–193. Centre National de la Recherche Scientifique, Paris.
1986 *Archéologie de L'habitat en Alta Verapaz (Guatemala).* Collection Études Mésoaméricaines, No. 10. Centre d'Études Mésoaméricaines et Centraméricaines, Mexico City.
1987 Regional Ceramic Development in the Northern Highlands, Alta Verapaz, Guatemala: Classic and Postclassic Material. In *Maya Ceramics: Papers from the 1985 Maya Ceramic Conference, Part II,* edited by Prudence M. Rice and Robert J. Sharer, pp. 307–328. BAR International Series 345. British Archaeological Reports, Oxford.
1990 El comercio clásico de obsidiana: Rutas entre tierras altas y tierras bajas en el área Maya. *Latin American Antiquity* 1(4):347–367.

Arnauld, Marie-Charlotte, Christopher Beekman, and Grégory Pereira (editors)
2021 *Mobility and Migration in Ancient Mesoamerican Cities.* University Press of Colorado, Boulder.

Arnold, Dean, Hector Neff, and Ronald L. Bishop
1991 Compositional Analysis and "Sources" of Pottery: An Ethnoarchaeological Approach. *American Anthropologist* 93(1):70–90.

Arroyo, Bárbara
1993 *Informe Final, Proyecto Nueve Cerros.* Manuscript on file in the Departamento de Monumentos Prehispánicos, Ministerio de Cultura y Deportes, Guatemala City.
1994 El Proyecto Nueve Cerros, un Ejemplo de la Arqueología de Rescate: Ventajas y Desventajas. In *VII Simposio de Investigaciones Arqueológicas en Guatemala, 1993,* edited by Juan Pedro Laporte and Héctor Escobedo, pp. 188–198. Museo Nacional de Arqueología y Etnología, Guatemala City.

Arruda, Daniel M., Carlos E. G. R. Schaefer, Rúbia S. Fonseca, Ricardo R. C. Solar, and Elpídio I. Fernandes-Filho
2018 Vegetation Cover of Brazil in the Last 21 ka: New Insights into the Amazonian Refugia and Pleistocenic Arc Hypotheses. *Global Ecology and Biogeography* 27(1):47–56.

Ashmore, Wendy
1991 Site-Planning Principles and Concepts of Directionality among the Ancient Maya. *Latin American Antiquity* 2(3):199–226.

Ashmore, Wendy (editor)
1981 *Lowland Maya Settlement Patterns.* University of New Mexico Press, Albuquerque.

Ashmore, Wendy, and A. Bernard Knapp (editors)
1999 *Archaeologies of Landscape: Contemporary Perspectives*. Blackwell, Malden, Massachusetts.

Avendaño, Carlos
1999 Utilización de un Método Geoestadístico para Estimar Distancias Mínimas de Trampeo y Patrones Espaciales en Scarabaeinae (Coleoptera: Scarabaeidae). Licenciatura thesis, Escuela de Biología, Universidad de San Carlos, Guatemala City.
2001 Caracterización de la Avifauna del Parque Nacional Laguna Lachuá y su Zona de Influencia Cobán, Alta Verapaz, Guatemala. Licenciatura thesis, Escuela de Biología, Universidad de San Carlos, Guatemala City.
2007 The Petén Basin Final: Gathering the Pieces of a Foreland Model in Guatemala. Manuscript on file from graduate course GLG431, Department of Geography, University of Toronto, Toronto.
2012 Natural and Cultural Landscape Evolution during the Late Holocene in North Central Guatemalan Lowlands and Highlands. PhD dissertation, Department of Geography, University of Toronto, Toronto.

Avendaño, Carlos, and Carla del Cid
2017 Exploración Inicial del Paleoambiente Vecino del Holocen Medio de la Ciudad Maya de Salinas de los Nueve Cerros. In *XXX Simposio de Investigaciones Arqueológicas en Guatemala, 2016*, edited by Bárbara Arroyo, Luis Méndez Salinas, and Gloria Ajú Álvarez, pp. 621–625. Museo Nacional de Arqueología y Etnología, Guatemala City.

Avendaño, Carlos, Sharon A. Cowling, Sarah Finkelstein, and Juan Carlos Berrio
2012 Landscape Reconstruction at the Lachuá Region of the Last ~2000 yrs: Maya Environmental Management Implications in Salinas de los Nueve Cerros, Guatemala. *Japanese Journal of Palynology* 58 (Special):7–8.

Avendaño, Carlos, Claudia L. Morales-Flores, Carla Del Cid, Nora Machuca, Silvia Duarte, Dolores Piperno, and Juan Carlos Berrio
2019 Resiliencia Histórica en Mesoamérica: Dinámica Paisajística Milenaria de Salinas Nueve Cerros. In *XXXII Simposio de Investigaciones Arqueológicas en Guatemala, 2018*, edited by Bárbara Arroyo and Héctor Mejía, pp. 263–282. Museo Nacional de Arqueología y Etnología, Guatemala City.

Avendaño, Carlos, Rosa Sunum, Claudia L. Morales-Flores, Carla del Cid, Mónica Cajas, Dolores Piperno, Juan Carlos Berrio, María José Hernández, and Carolina Rosales de Zea
2018 ¿Cómo Fue el Ambiente Antes del Establecimiento y Después del Abandono de la Ciudad Maya de Salinas Nueve Cerros? Legado Moderno de Diversidad Biológica y Cultural en la Ecoregión Lachuá, Franja Transversal del Norte. In *XXXI Simposio de Investigaciones Arqueológicas en Guatemala, 2017*, edited by Bárbara Arroyo, Luis Méndez, and Gloria Ajú Álvarez, pp. 1027–1032. Museo Nacional de Arqueología y Etnología, Guatemala City.

Avendaño-Mendoza, Carlos, Alejando Morón-Ríos, Enio B. Cano, and Jorge L. León-Cortés
2005 Dung Beetle Community (Coleoptera: Scarabaeidae: Scarabaeinae) in a

Tropical Landscape at the Lachuá Region, Guatemala. *Biodiversity and Conservation* 14(4):801–822.

Avendaño, Claudia E., Carlos Avendaño, Ana Carías, Manolo García, Mónica Cajas, Kristian De León, and Roberto Garnica
2005   *Dinámica del Uso de la Tierra y Conservación de los Recursos Naturales de la Eco-región Lachuá*. Consejo Nacional de Ciencias y Tecnología, Escuela de Biología, CCQQFar, Universidad de San Carlos, Guatemala City.

Aveni, Anthony F., Susan Milbrath, and C. Peraza Lope
2004   Chichen Itza's Legacy in the Astronomically Oriented Architecture of Mayapan. *RES: Anthropology and Aesthetics* 45:123–143.

Ávila, Rafael C.
2004   Estudio Base para el Programa de Monitoreo de la Vegetación en la Zona de Influencia del Parque Nacional Laguna Lachuá. Licenciatura thesis, Escuela de Biología, Universidad de San Carlos, Guatemala City.

Azaele, Sandro, Simone Pigolotti, Jayanth R. Banavar, and Amos Maritan
2006   Dynamical Evolution of Ecosystems. *Nature* 444(7121):926–928.

Babcock, Thomas F.
2012   *Utatlán: The Constituted Community of the K'iche' Maya of Q'umarkaj*. University Press of Colorado, Boulder.

Baker, Matthew E., and Ryan S. King
2010   A New Method for Detecting and Interpreting Biodiversity and Ecological Community Thresholds: Threshold Indicator Taxa Analysis (TITAN). *Methods in Ecology and Evolution* 1(1):25–37.

Baldeck, Claire A., Steven W. Kembel, Kyle E. Harms, Joseph B. Yavitt, Robert John, Benjamin L. Turner, George B. Chuyong, et al.
2013   A Taxonomic Comparison of Local Habitat Niches of Tropical Trees. *Oecologia* 173(4):1491–1498.

Barrera-Bassols, Narciso, and Victor M. Toledo
2005   Ethnoecology of the Yucatec Maya: Symbolism, Knowledge and Management of Natural Resources. *Journal of Latin American Geography* 4(1):9–41.

Barrera Vásquez, Alfredo
1991   *Diccionario Maya*. Editorial Porrua, Mexico City.

Barrientos, Mónica E.
2006   Atlas Palinológico de las Especies Más Abundantes de la Sucesión Vegetal en la Zona de Influencia de la Ecorregión Lachuá. Licenciatura thesis, Escuela de Biología, Universidad de San Carlos, Guatemala City.

Barrientos, Tomás J.
2008   *Hydraulic Systems in Central Cancuén: Ritual, Reservoir, and/or Drainage?* Report #05082 submitted to the Foundation for the Advancement of Mesoamerican Studies (FAMSI; website), July 18, 2006, accessed June 27, 2024.
2014   The Royal Palace of Cancuen: The Structure of Lowland Maya Architecture and Politics at the End of the Late Classic Period. PhD dissertation, Department of Anthropology, Vanderbilt University, Nashville, Tennessee.

Barrientos, Tomás, Brigitte Kovacevich, Michael Callaghan, and Lucía Morán
2001   Investigaciones en el Área Residencial Sur y Suroeste de Cancuén. In *Proyecto Arqueológico Cancuen, Informe No. 2, Temporada 2000*, edited by

Arthur A. Demarest and Tomás Barrientos, pp. 99–160. Instituto de Antropología e Historia, Guatemala.

Barthel, Stephan, and Christian Isendahl
2013   Urban Gardens, Agriculture, and Water Management: Sources of resilience for long-term food security in cities. *Ecological Economics* 86:224–234.

Barthes, Roland
1979   Literature According to Minou Drouet. In *The Eiffel Tower and Other Mythologies*, translated by Richard Howard, pp. 111–118. Hill and Wang, New York.
1997   Eiffel Tower. n *Rethinking Architecture*, edited by Neil Leach, pp. 172–180. Routledge, New York.

Bassie-Sweet, Karen, Nicholas A. Hopkins, and Robert M. Laughlin
2015   History and Conquest of the Pre-Columbian Ch'ol and Lacandon Ch'ol. In *The Ch'ol Maya of Chiapas*, edited by Karen Bassie-Sweet, pp. 3–28. University of Oklahoma Press, Norman.

Batres, Lucrecia de, Carlos Batres, Ramiro Martínez, and Luis Rosada
2002   Pintura rupestre entre las fronteras este y oeste de Guatemala. *Identidad* 7:29–31.

Batschelet, Edward
1981   *Circular Statistics in Biology: Mathematics in Biology*. Academic Press, London.

Battistel, Dario, Marco Roman, Andrea Marchetti, Natalie M. Kehrwald, Marta Radaelli, Eleonora Balliana, Giuseppa Toscano, and Carlo Barbante
2018   Anthropogenic Impact in the Maya Lowlands of Petén, Guatemala, during the last 5500 Years. *Journal of Quaternary Science* 33(2):166–176.

Baumgarten, Amrei
2000   Características Poblacionales y Uso de Hábitat del Mono Aullador Negro (Alouatta pigra) en la Zona de Influencia del Parque Nacional Laguna Lachuá, Alta Verapaz. Licenciatura thesis, Escuela de Biología, Universidad de San Carlos, Guatemala City.

Beaudry, P. Marilyn
1991   The New World Paste Compositional Investigations. In *The Ceramic Legacy of Anna O. Shepard*, edited by Ronald L. Bishop and Frederick W. Lange, pp. 224–256. University Press of Colorado, Boulder.

Becker, Marshall J.
1971   The Identification of a Second Plaza Plan at Tikal, Guatemala and Its Implications for Ancient Maya Social Complexity. PhD dissertation, University of Pennsylvania, Philadelphia.

Becquelin, Pierre, Alain Breton, and Véronique Gervais
2001   *Arqueología de la Región de Nebaj, Guatemala*. Cuadernos de Estudios Guatemaltecos 5. Centre d'Études Mexicaines et Centraméricaines, Mexico City.

Becquelin, Pierre, and Claude Baudez
1979   *Toniná, Une Cité Maya du Chiapas, Tome I*. Mission Archéologique et Ethnologique Française au Mexique, Collection Études Mésoaméricaines 6-1. Editions Recherche sur les civilisations, Paris.
1982   *Toniná, Une Cité Maya du Chiapas, Tome III*. Mission Archéologique et Ethnologique Française au Mexique, Collection Études Mésoaméricaines 6-3. Editions Recherche sur les civilisations, Paris.

Bergmann, John F.
1969 The Distribution of Cacao Cultivation in Pre-Columbian America. *Annals of the Association of American Geographers* 59(1):85–96.

Bill, Cassandra, and Michael Callaghan
2002 Frecuencias Relativas de los Tipos y Modos Cerámicos en Cancuén. In *Proyecto Arqueológico Cancuen, Informe Final No. 3, Temporada 2001*, edited by Arthur A. Demarest and Tomás Barrientos, pp. 251–266. Department of Anthropology, Vanderbilt University, Nashville, Tennessee.

Bishop, Ronald L.
1980 Aspects of Ceramic Compositional Modeling. In *Models and Methods in Regional Exchange*, edited by Robert E. Fry, pp. 47–66. SAA Papers No. 1. Society for American Archaeology, Washington, DC.
2003 Five Decades of Maya Fine Orange Ceramic Investigation by INAA. In *Patterns and Process. A Festschrift in Honor of Dr. Edward V. Sayre*, edited by Lambertus van Zelst, pp. 81–92. Smithsonian Center for Material Research and Education, Suitland, Maryland.

Bishop, Ronald L., Jacqueline S. Olin, and Michael J. Blackman
1984 SARCAR: A New Archaeometric Resource. *ICOM: 7th Triennial Meeting, Preprints*, pp. 84.8.1–84.8.2. Smithsonian Institution, Washington, DC.

Bishop, Ronald L., Erin L. Sears, and Michael J. Blackman
2005 A través del rio cambio. *Estudios de Cultura Maya* 26:7–40.

Blake, Michael
2010 *Colonization, Warfare, and Exchange at the Postclassic Maya Site of Canajasté, Chiapas, Mexico*. Papers of the New World Archaeological Foundation, No. 70. New World Archaeological Foundation, Brigham Young University, Provo, Utah.

Blake, Michael, Douglas Donne Bryant, Thomas A. Lee Jr., Pierre Agrinier, and Susanna M. Ekholm
2005 Late Classic Ceramics. In *Ceramic Sequence of the Upper Grijalva Region, Chiapas, Mexico, Part 2*, edited by Douglas Donne Bryant, John E. Clark, and David Cheetham, pp. 415–547. Papers of the New World Archaeological Foundation, No. 67. New World Archaeological Foundation, Brigham Young University, Provo, Utah.

Bletter, Nathaniel, and Douglas Daly
2011 Cacao and Its Relatives in South America. In *Chocolate in Mesoamerica: A Cultural History of Cacao*, edited by Cameron McNeil, pp. 1–48. University Press of Florida, Gainesville.

Blom, Frans, and Gertrude Duby
1957 *La Selva Lacandona, Andanzas Arqueológicas*. Editorial Cultura, Mexico City.

Bogotá, Raúl G., Mirella H. M. Groot, Henry Hooghiemstra, Lucas J. Lourens, Marjolein Van der Linden, and Juan Carlos Berrio
2011 Rapid Climate Change from North Andean Lake Fúquene Pollen Records Driven by Obliquity: Implications for a Basin-Wide Biostratigraphic Zonation for the Last 284 ka. *Quaternary Science Reviews* 30(23–24):3321–3337.

Bolles, David
2001 *Combined Dictionary—Concordance of the Yucatecan Mayan Language*.

Report #96072 submitted to the Foundation for the Advancement of Mesoamerican Studies (FAMSI; website) on May 1, 1998.

Bonnafoux, Patrice
2008   Étude Iconographique des Céramiques du Classique Ancien Dans les Basses Terres Mayas. PhD dissertation, Université Paris I, Paris.

Boot, Erik
2003   An Overview of Classic Maya Ceramics Containing Sequences of Day Signs. Mesoweb (website), June 19, 2003, accessed June 25, 2024.

2005   *Continuity and Change in Text and Image at Chichén Itzá, Yucatan, Mexico: A Study of the Inscriptions, Iconography, and Architecture at a Late Classic to Early Postclassic Maya Site.* Center for Non-Western Studies (CNWS) Publications, Vol. 135. Research School of Asian, African, and Amerindian Studies, Leiden University, Leiden.

2009   The Theonym Chanek'/Kanek': A Short Exploration of Classic Maya Inscriptions and Iconography. Manuscript circulated by the author, November 18, 2009.

Borrelli, Natalia, Margarita Osterrieth, Asunción Romanelli, María F. Alvarez, José L. Cionchi, and Héctor Massone
2012   Biogenic Silica in Wetlands and Their Relationship with Soil and Groundwater Biogeochemistry in the Southeastern of Buenos Aires Province, Argentina. *Environmental Earth Sciences* 65:469–480.

Bove, Frederick J.
1989   *Formative Settlement Patterns on the Pacific Coast of Guatemala: A Spatial Analysis of Complex Societal Evolution.* BAR International Series 493. British Archaeological Reports, Oxford.

Bowes, Anne L., and David G. Allen
1969   Biology and Conservation of the Quetzal. *Biological Conservation* 1(4):297–306.

Braakhuis, Edwin
2010   Xbalanque's Marriage. A Commentary on the Q'eqchi' Myth of Sun and Moon. PhD dissertation, Faculty of Social and Behavioural Sciences, Leiden University, Leiden, Netherlands.

Brady, James E.
1989   An Investigation of Maya Ritual Cave Usage with Special Reference to Naj Tunich, Petén, Guatemala. PhD dissertation, Department of Archaeology, University of California, Los Angeles.

Brady, James E. (editor)
2009   *Exploring Highland Maya Ritual Cave Use—Archaeology and Ethnography in Huehuetenango, Guatemala.* AMCS Bulletin 20. Association for Mexican Cave Studies, Austin, Texas.

Brady, James E., Joseph W. Ball, Ronald L. Bishop, Duncan C. Spring, Norman Hammond, and Rupert A. Housley
1998   The Lowland Maya "Protoclassic": A Reconsideration of Its Nature and Significance. *Ancient Mesoamerica* 9(1):17–38.

Brady, James E., and Keith M. Prufer (editors)
2005   *In the Maw of the Earth Monster: Mesoamerican Ritual Cave Use.* University of Texas Press, Austin.

Brady, James E., and George Veni
1992   Man-Made and Pseudo-Karst Caves: The Implications of Subsurface Features within Maya Centers. *Geoarchaeology* 7(2):49–67.

Braswell, Geoffrey E. (editor)
2004   *The Maya and Teotihuacan: Reinterpreting Early Classic Interaction*. University of Texas Press, Austin.

Braswell, Geoffrey E.
1996   A Maya Obsidian Source: The Geoarchaeology, Settlement History, and Ancient Economy of San Martín Jilotepeque, Guatemala. PhD dissertation, Department of Anthropology, Tulane University, New Orleans, Louisiana.
1998   La arqueologia de San Martín Jilotepeque. *Mesoamerica* 35:117–135.
2002   Praise the Gods and Pass the Obsidian? The Organization of Ancient Economy in San Martín Jilotepeque, Guatemala. In *Ancient Maya Political Economies*, edited by Marilyn Masson and David Freidel, pp. 285–306. AltaMira Press, Lanham, Maryland.
2003   Obsidian Exchange Spheres. In *The Postclassic Mesoamerican World*, edited by Michael E. Smith and Francis Berdan, pp.131–158. University of Utah Press, Salt Lake City.

Braswell Geoffrey E., John E. Clark, Kazuo Aoyama, Heather I. McKillop, and Michael Glascock
2000   Determining the Geological Provenance of Obsidian Artifacts from the Maya Region: A Test of Efficacy of Visual Sourcing. *Latin American Antiquity* 11(3):269–282.

Braswell, Geoffrey E., Iken Paap, and Michael D. Glascock
2011   The Obsidian and Ceramics of the Puuc Region: Chronology, Lithic Procurement, and Production at Xkipche, Yucatan, Mexico. *Ancient Mesoamerica* 22(1):135–154.

Braudel, Fernand
1958   Histoire et Sciences Sociales: La Longue Durée. In *Annales. Économies, Sociétés, Civilisations* 13(4):725–753.
2002   La Larga Duración. In *Las ambiciones de la historia*, edited by Fernand Braudel, pp. 147–177. Editorial Crítica, Barcelona.

Breschi, Stefano, and Franco Malerba (editors)
2007   *Clusters, Networks and Innovation*. Oxford University Press, Oxford.

Brett, Roddy
2007   *Una Guerra sin Batallas: Del Odio, la Violencia y el Miedo en el Ixcán y el Ixil, 1972–1983*. F & G Editores, Guatemala City.

Bricker, Harvey M., and Victoria R. Bricker
1999   Astronomical Orientation of the Skyband Bench at Copán. *Journal of Field Archaeology* 26:435–442.

Bricker, Victoria Reifler
1981   *The Indian Christ, the Indian King*. University of Texas Press, Austin.

Brown, Kenneth L.
1980   Archaeology in the Quiche Basin, Guatemala. *Mexicon* 2(5):72–73.

Brown, Linda A.
2005   Planting the Bones: Hunting Ceremonialism at Contemporary and

Nineteenth-Century Shrines in the Guatemalan Highlands. *Latin American Antiquity* 16(2):131–146.

Bryant, Douglas Donne, John E. Clark, and David Cheetham (editors)
2005 *Ceramic Sequence of the Upper Grijalva Region, Chiapas, Mexico, Part 1 and 2.* Papers of the New World Archaeological Foundation, No. 67. New World Archaeological Foundation, Brigham Young University, Provo, Utah.

Bryant, Douglas Donne, Thomas A. Lee Jr., and Mary E. Pye
2020 Discussion. In *Postclassic and Colonial Sites of the Upper Grijalva River Basin in Chiapas, Mexico: Los Encuentros, Coapa, and Coneta*, edited by Douglas Donne Bryant and Thomas A. Lee Jr., pp. 289–328. Papers of the New World Archaeological Foundation, No. 86. New World Archaeological Foundation, Brigham Young University, Provo, Utah.

Buenaflor, Erika
2018 *Cleansing Rites of Curanderismo: Limpias Espirituales of Ancient Mesoamerican Shamans.* Simon and Schuster, New York.

Burkitt, Robert
1924 A Journey in Northern Guatemala. *Museum Journal* 15(2):115–145.

Buma, Brian, Brian J. Harvey, Daniel G. Gavin, Ryan Kelly, Tatiana Loboda, Brenden E. McNeil, Jennifer R. Marlon, et al.
2019 The Value of Linking Paleoecological and Neoecological Perspectives to Understand Spatially-Explicit Ecosystem Resilience. *Landscape Ecology* 34(1):17–33.

Butler, Mary
1962 A Pottery Sequence from the Alta Verapaz, Guatemala. In *The Maya and Their Neighbors*, edited by Clarence L. Hay, Ralph L. Linton, Samuel K. Lothrop, Harry L. Shapiro, and George C. Vaillant, pp. 250–267. University of Utah Press, Salt Lake City.

Cajas, Mónica
2009 Análisis de la Heterogeneidad Geoecológica y la Diversidad Biológica en el Parque Nacional Laguna Lachuá Cobán, Alta Verapaz. Licenciatura thesis, Escuela de Biología, Universidad de San Carlos, Guatemala City.

Cajas, Mónica, Carlos Avendaño, and Claudia L. Morales-Flores
2017 Estudio de Caso de los Huertos Familiares Q'eqchi'es de Santa Lucía Lachuá, Cobán, Alta Verapaz. Consejo Nacional de Ciencias y Tecnología, Escuela de Biología, CCQQFar, Universidad de San Carlos, Guatemala City.

Cambranes, Rafael
2019 Reconocimiento y Mapeo en el Sitio Arqueológico Sebol, Grupo Sebolito. In *Proyecto Arqueológico Regional Cancuen, Informe Final No. 18, Temporada de Campo 2018: Tomo I—Proyecto Arqueológico Regional Cancuen*, edited by Arthur A. Demarest, Paola Torres, Julien Sion, Chloé Andrieu, and Carlos Fidel Tuyuc, pp. 5–14. Ministerio de Cultura y Deportes de Guatemala, Guatemala City.

Campbell, David G., Anabel Ford, Karen S. Lowell, Jay Walker, Jeffrey K. Lake, Constanza Ocamporaeder, Andrew Townesmith, and Michael Balick
2006 The Feral Forests of the Eastern Petén. In *Time and Complexity in Historical Ecology: Studies in the Neotropical Lowlands*, edited by William L. Balee and Clark I. Erickson, pp. 21–55. Columbia University Press, New York.

Campbell, Ian D.
1999 Quaternary Pollen Taphonomy: Examples of Differential Redeposition and Differential Preservation. *Palaeogeography, Palaeoclimatology, Palaeoecology* 149(1–4):245–256.

Cano, Enio B., Jack C. Schuster, and Juan Morrone
2018 Phylogenetics of *Ogyges* Kaup and the Biogeography of Nuclear Central America (Coleoptera, Passalidae). *ZooKeys* 737:81–111.

Canter, Ronald
2021 Travel Times Versus Transport Costs on Maya Rivers. In *Caravans in Global Perspective: Contexts and Boundaries*, edited by Persis B. Clarkson and Calogero M. Santoro, pp. 17–31. Routledge, London.

Canuto, Marcello A., and Tomás Barrientos
2013 The Importance of La Corona. *La Corona Notes* 1(1):1–5.

Canuto, Marcello A., Francisco Estrada-Belli, Thomas G. Garrison, Stephen D. Houston, Mary Jane Acuña, Milan Kováč, Damien Marken, et al.
2018 Ancient Lowland Maya Complexity as Revealed by Airborne Laser Scanning of Northern Guatemala. *Science* 361(6409):1355–1371.

Cardale de Schrimpff, Marianne, Juan Carlos Berrio, Ana M. Groot, Pedro Botero, and Neil Duncan
2019 Culture and the Environment on the Floodplain of the River Cauca in Southwestern Colombia: Reconstructing the Evidence from the Late Pleistocene to the Late Holocene. *Quaternary International* 505:34–54.

Cardoso, Pedro, François Rigal, Simone Fattorini, Sofia Terzopoulou, and Paulo A. V. Borges
2013 Integrating Landscape Disturbance and Indicator Species in Conservation Studies. *PLoS ONE* 8(5):e63294.

Carmack, Robert M.
1977 Ethnohistory of the Central Quiche: The Community of Utatlan. In *Archaeology and Ethnohistory of the Central Quiche*, edited by Dwight T. Wallace and Robert M. Carmack, pp. 1–19. Publication 1. Institute for Mesoamerican Studies, State University of New York, Albany.
1981 *The Quiché Mayas of Utatlan: The Evolution of a Highland Guatemala Kingdom*. University of Oklahoma Press, Norman.

Carmack, Robert M., and John M. Weeks
1981 The Archaeology and Ethnohistory of Utatlan: A Conjunctive Approach. *American Antiquity* 46:323–341.

Carneiro, Robert
1970 *A Theory on the Origin of the State*. Macmillan Publishing, New York.

Carot, Patricia
1987 Archéologie des Grottes du Nord de l'Alta Verapaz. Master's thesis, Department of Anthropology, Université Paris I.
1989 *Arqueología de las Cuevas del Norte de Alta Verapaz*. Cuadernos de Estudios Guatemaltecos I. Centre d'Études Mexicaines et Centraméricaines, Mexico City.

Carpio Rezzio, Edgar H.
2016 Estudio comparativo de artefactos de obsidiana en algunos sitios de las

tierras altas de Guatemala: producción, intercambio y consumo. *Antropología e Historia de Guatemala*, III Época (15):119–140.

Caso Barrera, Laura, and Mario Aliphat Fernández

2006a Cacao, Vanilla and Annatto: Three Production and Exchange Systems in the Southern Maya Lowlands, XVI-XVII Centuries. *Journal of Latin American Geography* 5(2):29–52.

2006b The Itza Maya Control Over Cacao: Politics, Commerce, and War in the Sixteenth and Seventeenth Centuries. In *Chocolate in Mesoamerica: A Cultural History of Cacao*, edited by Cameron McNeil, pp. 289–306. University Press of Florida, Gainesville.

2012 Mejores son Huertos de Cacao y Achiote Que Minas de Oro y Plata: Huertos Especializados de los Choles del Manche y de los K'ekchi'es. *Latin American Antiquity* 23(3):282–99.

Castañeda, César

1997 Estudio Florístico en el Parque Nacional Laguna Lachuá, Alta Verapaz, Guatemala. Agronomic Engineering thesis, Facultad de Agronomía, Universidad de San Carlos, Guatemala City.

Castro Dorado, Antonio

1989 *Petrografía Básica. Texturas, Clasificación y Nomenclatura de Rocas*. Editorial Paraninfo, S. A., Madrid.

Castillo, Victor

2013 El Sitio Arqueológico Chaculá. In *Proyecto Arqueológico de la Región de Chaculá, Reporte de las Actividades de Campo de la Temporada 2013*, edited by Victor Castillo and Ulrich Wölfel, pp. 57–76. Report presented to the Instituto de Antropología e Historia de Guatemala, Guatemala City.

CEH (Comisión para el Esclarecimiento Histórico)

1999 *Guatemala Memoria del Silencio: Casos Presentados*. Vols. 8–9. Oficina de Servicios para Proyectos de las Naciones Unidas (UNOPS), Guatemala City.

Chase, Arlen F., and Diane Z. Chase

1998 Scale and Intensity in Classic Period Maya Agriculture: Terracing and Settlement at the "Garden City" of Caracol, Belize. *Culture and Agriculture* 20(2–3):60–77.

2012 Belize Red Ceramics and Their Implications for Trade and Exchange in the Eastern Maya Lowlands. *Research Reports in Belizean Archaeology* 9:3–14.

Chase, Arlen F., Diane Z. Chase, Christopher T. Fischer, Stephen J. Leisz, and John F. Weishampel

2012 Geospatial Revolution and Remote Sensing LiDAR in Mesoamerican Archaeology. *Proceeding of the National Academy of Science* 190(32):12916–12921.

Chase, Arlen F., and Vernon Scarborough

2014 Diversity, Resiliency, and IHOPE-Maya: Using the Past to Inform the Present. *Archaeological Papers of the American Anthropological Association* 24(1):1–10.

Cheesman, Ernest E.

1944 Notes on the Nomenclature, Classification and Possible Relationships of Cocoa Populations. *Tropical Agriculture* 21:144–159.

Cheong, Kong F.
2012 A Description of the Ceramic Musical Instruments Excavated from the North Group of Pacbitun, Belize. In *Pacbitun Regional Archaeological Project (PRAP): Report on the 2011 Field Season*, edited by Terry G. Powis, pp. 15–29. Kennesaw State University, Kennesaw, Georgia.
2013 Archaeological Investigations of the North Group at Pacbitun, Belize: The Function, Status and Chronology of an Ancient Maya Epicenter Residential Group. Master's thesis, Department of Anthropology, Trent University, Peterborough, Ontario, Canada.
2020 Music, Performance, Rituals, and Ceramic Musical Instrument Production at Pacbitun, Belize. In *An Archaeological Reconstruction of Ancient Maya Life at Pacbitun, Belize*, edited by Terry G. Powis, Sheldon Skaggs, and George J. Micheletti, pp. 91–102. Archaeology of the Maya, Vol. 4. BAR International Series 2970. British Archaeological Reports, Oxford.

Cheong, Kong F., Roger Blench, Paul F. Healy, and Terry G. Powis
2014 Ancient Maya Musical Encore: Analysis of Ceramic Musical Instruments from Pacbitun, Belize and the Maya Subarea. In *Flower World: Music Archaeology of the Americas*, edited by Mattias Stöckli and M. Howell, pp. 123–40. Vol 3. Ekho Verlag, Berlin.

Child, Mark B.
2007 Ritual Purification and the Ancient Maya Sweatbath at Palenque. In *Palenque: Recent Investigations at the Classic Maya Center*, edited by Damien Marken, pp. 233–262. AltaMira Press, Lanham, Maryland.

Chinchilla Mazariegos, Oswaldo
1998 Pipiles y Cakchiqueles en Cotzumalguapa: La Evidencia Etnohistórica y Arqueológica. In *Anales de la Academia de Geografía e Historia de Guatemala* LXXIII, edited by Jorge Luján Muñoz, pp. 143–184. Academia de Geografía e Historia de Guatemala, Guatemala City.
2011 *Imágenes de la Mitología Maya*. Museo Popol Vuh, Universidad Francisco Marroquín, Guatemala City.
2016 Yearning for the Ancestors: Identity in Cotzumalhuapa Sculpture. In *Archaeology and Identity in Southeastern Mesoamerica*, edited by Claudia Garcia-Des Lauriers and Michael Love, pp. 104–125. University of Utah Press, Salt Lake City.
2017 *Art and Myth of the Ancient Maya*. Yale University Press, New Haven.

Chinchilla Mazariegos, Oswaldo, Ronald L. Bishop, M. James Blackman, Erin L. Sears, José Vicente Genovez, and Regina Moraga
2005 Intercambio de Cerámica a Larga Distancia en Cotzumalguapa: Resultados del Análisis por Activación de Neutrones. In *XVIII Simposio de Investigaciones Arqueológicas en Guatemala 2004*, edited by Juan Pedro Laporte, Héctor Escobedo, and Bárbara Arroyo, pp. 983–991. Museo Nacional de Arqueología y Etnología, Guatemala City.

Chocano Alfaro, Guillermo Alejandro
2012 Investigaciones Etnoarqueológicas en la Región Tujaal, Sacapulas, Quiché. In *XXV Simposio de Investigaciones Arqueológicas en Guatemala, 2011*, edited by Bárbara Arroyo, Lorena Paiz, and Héctor Mejía, pp. 486–494. Museo Nacional de Arqueología y Etnología, Guatemala City.

Claringbould, Johan S., Britney B. Hyden, J. Frederick Sarg, and Bruce D. Trudgill
2013   Structural Evolution of a Salt-Cored, Domed, Reactivated Fault Complex, Jebel Madar, Oman. *Journal of Structural Geology* 51:118–131.

Clark, James S., and Tristram C. Hussey
1996   Estimating the Mass Flux of Charcoal from Sedimentary Records: Effects of Particle Size, Morphology, and Orientation. *The Holocene* 6(2):129–144.

Clark, John
1981   Guatemalan Obsidian Sources and Quarries: Additional Notes. *Journal of New World Archaeology* 4(3):1–15.
2003   A Review of Twentieth-Century Mesoamerican Obsidian Studies. In *Mesoamerican Lithic Technology: Experimentation and Interpretation*, edited by Kenneth G. Hirth, pp. 15–54. University of Utah Press, Salt Lake City.

Clark, John E., Thomas A. Lee Jr., and Tamara Salcedo
1989   The Distribution of Obsidian. In *Ancient Trade and Tribute: Economies of the Soconusco Region of Mesoamerica*, edited by Barbara Voorhies, pp. 268–284. University of Utah Press, Salt Lake City.

Cleaves, Cecilia
2001   Etnobotánica Médica Participativa en Siete Comunidades de la Zona de Influencia del Parque Nacional Laguna Lachuá, Cobán, Alta Verapaz, Guatemala. Licenciatura thesis, Escuela de Biología, Universidad de San Carlos, Guatemala City.

Cochrane, Mark A.
2009   Fire in the Tropics. In *Tropical Fire Ecology: Climate Change, Land Use, and Ecosystem Dynamics*, edited by Mark A. Cochrane, pp. 1–23. Springer, Berlin.

Cochrane, Mark A., and Kevin C. Ryan
2009   Fire and Fire Ecology: Concepts and Principles. In *Tropical Fire Ecology: Climate Change, Land Use, and Ecosystem Dynamics*, edited by Mark A. Cochrane, pp. 25–62. Springer, Berlin.

Coe, Michael D.
1973   *The Maya Scribe and His World*. The Grolier Club, New York.

Colunga-García Marín, Patricia, and Daniel Zizumbo-Villarreal
2004   Domestication of Plants in Maya Lowlands. *Economic Botany* 58:S101–S110.

Cook, Duncan E., Brigitte Kovacevich, Timothy Beach, and Ronald Bishop
2006   Deciphering the Inorganic Chemical Record of Ancient Human Activity Using ICP-MS: A Reconnaissance Study of Late Classic Soil Floors at Cancuén, Guatemala. *Journal of Archaeological Science* 33(5):628–640.

Cope, Francis W.
1976   Cacao. *Theobroma cacao* L. (Sterculiaceae). In *Evolution of Crop Plants*, edited by Norman W. Simmonds, pp. 207–213. Longman, London.

Córdoba-Avalos, Victor, Miguel Sánchez Hernández, Nestor Estrella Chulim, Alfonso Macias Láylle, Engleberto Sandoval Castro, Tomás Martínez Saldaña, and Carlos Fredy Ortiz-García
2001   Factores que afectan la producción de cacao (*Theobroma cacao* L.) en el ejido Francisco 1, Madero del Plan Chontalpa, Tabasco, México. *Universidad y Ciencia* 17(34):93–100.

Correa-Metrio, Alex, M. B. Bush, Kenneth R. Cabrera, Shannon Sully, Mark Brenner, David A. Hodell, Jaime Escobar, and Tom Guilderson

2012   Rapid Climate Change and No-Analog Vegetation in Lowland Central America during the Last 86,000 Years. *Quaternary Science Reviews* 38:63–75.

Correa-Metrio, Alex, M. B. Bush, David A. Hodell, Mark Brenner, Jaime Escobar, and Tom Guilderson

2012   The Influence of Abrupt Climate Change on the Ice-Age Vegetation of the Central American Lowlands: Abrupt Climate Change in Ice-Age Central America. *Journal of Biogeography* 39(3):497–509.

Costantini, Edoardo A. C.

2018   Paleosols and Pedostratigraphy. *Applied Soil Ecology* 123:597–600.

Cowan, Robin, and Nicolas Jonard

2004   Network Structure and the Diffusion of Knowledge. *Journal of Economic Dynamics and Control* 28(8):1557–1575.

Craggs, Simon, Dave Keighley, John W. F. Waldron, and Adrian Park

2017   Salt Tectonics in an Intracontinental Transform Setting: Cumberland and Sackville Basins, Southern New Brunswick, Canada. *Basin Research* 29(3):266–283.

Craine, Eugene R., and Reginald C. Reindorp

1979   *The Codex Pérez and the Book of Chilam Balam of Maní*. University of Oklahoma Press, Norman.

Crandall, Lee S.

1939   Notes on Plumage Changes in the Quetzal. *Zoologica: Scientific Contributions of the New York Zoological Society* 24:61–64.

Crawford, Alaistar J., and Claire M. Belcher

2014   Charcoal Morphometry for Paleoecological Analysis: The Effects of Fuel Type and Transportation on Morphological Parameters. *Applications in Plant Sciences* 2(8):1400004.

Cuatrecasas, José

1964   Cacao and Its Allies: A Taxonomic Revision of the Genus *Theobroma*. *Contribution to the US Herbarium* 35:379–614.

Culbert, T. Patrick, and Don S. Rice (editors)

1990   *Precolumbian Population History in the Maya Lowlands*. University of New Mexico Press, Albuquerque.

Daniels, James T., Jr., and Geoffrey E. Braswell

2014   Procurement, Production, and Distribution of Obsidian in the Southern Belize Region. *Research Reports in Belizean Archaeology* 11:289–296.

Danien, Elin C.

1998   The Chama Polychrome Ceramic Cylinders. PhD dissertation, Department of Anthropology, University of Pennsylvania, Philadelphia.

2009   Painted Metaphors: Pottery and Politics of the Ancient Maya. *Expedition* 51(1):42–56.

Danien, Elin C. (editor)

2005   *Maya Folktales from the Alta Verapaz*. Museum of Archaeology and Anthropology, University of Pennsylvania, Philadelphia.

Das, Tushar K., and Teng Bing-Sheng

1998   Between Trust and Control: Developing Confidence in Partner Cooperation in Alliances. *Academy of Management Review* 23(3):491–512.

2001   Trust, Control, and Risk in Strategic Alliances: An Integrative Framework. *Organizational Studies* 22(2):251–283.

Davies, Gavin, and María de los Ángeles Corado
2023   "The Mountain Trails Are Well Traveled": Routes and Economic Organization in the Lake Atitlan Basin. In *Routes, Interaction and Exchange in the Southern Maya Area*, edited by Eugenia Robinson and Gavin Davies, pp. 163–199. Routledge, New York.

Davies, Nigel
1977   *The Toltecs: Until the Fall of Tula*. Civilization of American Indian Series. University of Oklahoma Press, Norman.

Davis, Ashley N., Catherine V. Davis, Robert C. Thunell, Emily B. Osborne, David E. Black, and Claudia R. Benitez-Nelson
2019   Reconstructing 800 Years of Carbonate Ion Concentration in the Cariaco Basin Using the Area Density of Planktonic Foraminifera Shells. *Paleoceanography and Paleoclimatology* 34(12):2129–2140.

Davis, Jason P.
2016   The Group Dynamics of Interorganizational Relationships: Collaborating with Multiple Partners in Innovation Ecosystems. *Administrative Science Quarterly* 61(4):621–661.

De La Cruz, Marlene, Richard Whitkus, Arturo Gómez-Pompa, and Luis Mota-Bravo
1995   Origins of Cacao Cultivation. *Nature* 375(6532):542–543.

de Montmollin, Olivier
1988   Tenam Rosario—A Political Microcosm. *American Antiquity* 53(2):351–370.
1995   *Settlement and Politics in Three Classic Maya Polities*. Monographs in World Archaeology, No 24. Prehistory Press, Madison, Wisconsin.
1997   A Regional Study of Classic Maya Ballcourts from the Upper Grijalva Basin, Chiapas, Mexico. *Ancient Mesoamerica* 8(1):23–41.

Del Cid, Carla
2018   Ensamble Polínico Moderno Como Indicador de la Composición Vegetal y Cobertura Boscosa en los Paisajes de la Sección Norte de la Ecoregión Lachuá, Cobán, Alta Verapaz. Licenciatura thesis, Escuela de Biología, Universidad de San Carlos, Guatemala City.

Del Cid, Carla, and Carlos Avendaño
2015   Ensamble Polínico Moderno Indicador de la Composición Vegetal y Cobertura Paisajística, Sección Norte Eco-región Lachuá, Alta Verapaz: Calibración Paleoecológica. In *XXVIII Simposio de Investigaciones Arqueológicas en Guatemala, 2014*, edited by Bárbara Arroyo and Héctor Mejía. Museo Nacional de Arqueología y Etnología, Guatemala City.

Demarest, Arthur A.
1989   The Olmec and the Rise of Civilization in Eastern Mesoamerica. In *The Olmec and the Development of Formative Mesoamerican Civilization*, edited by Robert Sharer and David Grove, pp. 323–344. Cambridge University Press, Cambridge.
2004a   *Ancient Maya: The Rise and Fall of a Rainforest Civilization*. Cambridge University Press, Cambridge.

2004b After the Maelstrom: Collapse of the Classic Maya Kingdoms and the Terminal Classic in Western Petén. In *The Terminal Classic in the Maya Lowlands: Collapse, Transition, and Transformation*, edited by Arthur A. Demarest, Prudence M. Rice, and Don S. Rice, pp. 102–124. University Press of Colorado, Boulder.
2006a *The Petexbatun Regional Archaeological Project: A Multidisciplinary Study of the Maya Collapse.* Vanderbilt University Press, Nashville, Tennessee.
2006b Sacred and Profane Mountains of the Pasión: Contrasting Architectural Paths to Power. In *Palaces and Power in the Americas: From Peru to the Northwest Coast*, edited by Jessica Joyce Christie and Patricia Joan Sarro, pp. 117–140. University of Texas Press, Austin.
2009 Maya Archaeology for the Twenty-First Century: The Progress, the Perils, and the Promise. *Ancient Mesoamerica* 20(2):253–263.
2011 The Political, Economic, and Cultural Correlates of Late PreClassic Southern Highland Material Culture: Evidence, Analysis, and Controversies. In *The Southern Maya in the Late Preclassic: The Rise and Fall of an Early Mesoamerica Civilization*, edited by Michael Love and Jonathan Kaplan, pp. 345–386. University Press of Colorado, Boulder.
2013 Ideological Pathways to Economic Exchange: Religion, Economy, and Legitimation at the Classic Maya Royal Capital of Cancuén. *Latin American Antiquity* 24(4):371–402.
2014 The Royal Port of Cancuen and the Role of Long-Distance Exchange in the Apogee of Maya Civilization. In *The Maya and Their Central American Neighbors: Settlement Patterns, Architecture, Hieroglyphic Texts, and Ceramics*, edited by Geoffrey E. Braswell, pp. 201–222. Routledge, London.

Demarest, Arthur A., Chloé Andrieu, Paola Torres, Mélanie Forné, Tomás Barrientos, and Marc Wolf
2014 Economy, Exchange, and Power: New Evidence from the Late Classic Maya Port City of Cancuen. *Ancient Mesoamerica* 25(1):187–219.

Demarest, Arthur A., Chloé Andrieu, Paola Torres, and Julien Sion
2019 Conclusiones Temporada 2018. In *Proyecto Arqueológico Regional Cancuen, Informe Final No. 18, Temporada de Campo 2018: Tomo II—Proyecto Arqueológico Regional Raxruha Viejo*, edited by Julien Sion, Chloé Andrieu, Paola Torres, and Arthur A. Demarest, pp. 332–358. Ministerio de Cultura y Deportes de Guatemala, Guatemala City.

Demarest, Arthur A., Chloé Andrieu, Bart Victor, and Paola Torres
2021 Monumental Landscapes as Instruments of Radical Economic Change: The Rise and Fall of a Maya Economic Network. In *Monumental Landscapes: How the Maya Shaped Their World*, edited by Brett Houk, Bárbara Arroyo, and Terry G. Powis, pp. 242–267. University Press of Florida, Gainesville.

Demarest, Arthur A., Chloé Andrieu, Bart Victor, Paola Torres, and Mélanie Forné
2017 La Producción e Intercambio de Mercancías en le Siglo Octavo en las Tierras Bajas Mayas: Nuevos Datos, Conceptos e Interpretaciones. In *XXX Simposio de Investigaciones Arqueológicas en Guatemala, 2016*, edited by Bárbara Arroyo, Luis Méndez Salinas and Gloria Ajú Álvarez, pp. 937–948. Museo Nacional de Arqueología y Etnología, Guatemala City.

Demarest, Arthur A., and Tomás Barrientos
1999   Proyecto Cancuén: Introducción a la Primera Temporada, 1999. *Proyecto Arqueológico Cancuen, Informe Preliminar No. 1, Temporada 1999*, edited by Arthur A. Demarest and Tomás Barrientos, pp. 5–16. Department of Anthropology, Vanderbilt University, Nashville, Tennessee.
2001   Conclusiones de la Temporada de Campo de 2000, Proyecto Arqueológico Cancuen. In *Proyecto Arqueológico Cancuen, Informe Preliminar No.2, Temporada 2000*, edited by Arthur A. Demarest and Tomás Barrientos, pp. 289–292. Department of Anthropology, Vanderbilt University, Nashville, Tennessee.
2004   Proyecto Arqueológico Cancuén, Temporada 2003: Antecedentes y Resumen de Actividades. In *Proyecto Arqueológico Cancuén, Informe Final No. 5, Temporada 2003*, edited by Arthur A. Demarest, Tomás Barrientos, Brigitte Kovacevich, Michael Callaghan, Brent K. S. Woodfill, and Luis F. Luin, pp. 1–18. Department of Anthropology, Vanderbilt University, Nashville, Tennessee.

Demarest, Arthur A., and Tomás Barrientos (editors)
2002   *Proyecto Arqueológico Cancuen, Informe No. 3, Temporada 2001*. Instituto de Antropología e Historia de Guatemala, Guatemala City.

Demarest, Arthur A., Tomás Barrientos, and Federico Fahsen
2006   El Apogeo y el Colapso del Reinado de Cancuén: Resultados e Interpretaciones del Proyecto Cancuén, 2004–2005. In *XIX Simposio de Investigaciones Arqueológicas en Guatemala, 2005*, edited by Juan Pedro Laporte, Bárbara Arroyo, and Héctor Mejía, pp. 757–768. Museo Nacional de Arqueología y Etnología, Guatemala City.

Demarest, Arthur A., and Geoffrey W. Conrad (editors)
1992   *Ideology and Pre-Columbian Civilizations*. School of American Research, Advanced Seminar Series, Santa Fe, New Mexico.

Demarest, Arthur A., and Horacio Martínez Paiz
2015   Síntesis de la Temporada 2014 del Proyecto Arqueológico Cancuen. In *Proyecto Arqueológico Cancuen, Informe Final No. 14, Temporada 2014*, edited by Arthur A. Demarest and Horacio Marínez Paiz, pp. 297–302. Department of Anthropology, Vanderbilt University, Nashville, Tennessee.

Demarest, Arthur A., Prudence M. Rice, and Don S. Rice
2004   The Terminal Classic in the Maya Lowlands: Assessing Collapses, Terminations, and Transformations. In *The Terminal Classic in the Maya Lowlands: Collapse, Transition, and Transformation*, edited by Arthur A. Demarest, Prudence M. Rice, and Don S. Rice, pp. 545–572. University Press of Colorado, Boulder.

Demarest, Arthur A., Prudence M. Rice, and Don S. Rice (editors)
2005   *The Terminal Classic in the Maya Lowlands: Collapse, Transition, and Transformation*. University Press of Colorado, Boulder.

Demarest, Arthur A., and Robert J. Sharer
1986   Late Classic Ceramic Spheres, Culture Areas and Cultural Evolution in the Southern Highlands of Mesoamerica. In *The Southeast Maya Periphery*, edited by Patricia A. Urban and Edward M. Schortman, pp. 194–223. University of Texas Press, Austin.

Demarest, Arthur A., Paola Torres, Horacio Martínez Paiz, Miryam Saravia, Juan Fransisco Saravia, Carlos Fidel Tuyuc, Susana Sánchez, Chloé Andrieu, Marc Wolf, and Luis F. Luin
2016   Los Reyes de Ríos y Valles: Cancuen, Raxruha Viejo, Sebol, Sesakkar y el Control de las Fronteras y las Rutas Mayas. In *XXIX Simposio de Investigaciones Arqueológicas en Guatemala, 2015*, edited by Bárbara Arroyo, Luis Méndez Salinas, and Gloria Ajú Álvarez, pp. 49–62. Museo Nacional de Arqueología y Etnología, Guatemala City.

Demarest, Arthur A., Paola Torres, Julien Sion, Chloé Andrieu, and Carlos Fidel Tuyuc (editors)
2019   *Proyecto Arqueológico Regional Cancuen, Informe Final No. 18, Temporada de Campo 2018: Tomo I—Proyecto Arqueológico Regional Cancuen*. Ministerio de Cultura y Deportes de Guatemala, Guatemala City.

Demarest, Arthur A., Paola Torres, Julien Sion, and Chloé Andrieu (editors)
2020   *Proyecto Arqueológico Regional Cancuen, Informe Final No. 19, Temporada de Campo 2019: Tomo I—Proyecto Arqueológico Regional Cancuen*. Ministerio de Cultura y Deportes de Guatemala, Guatemala City.

Demarest, Arthur A., Juan Antonio Valdés, Héctor Escobedo, Federico Fahsen, Tomás Barrientos, and Horacio Martínez Paiz
2012   25 Años de Proyectos Regionales en el Valle del Río La Pasión: Una Visión General de las Investigaciones, Resultados y Perspectivas Sobre los Últimos Siglos de una Gran Ruta Maya. In *XXV Simposio de Investigaciones Arqueológicas en Guatemala, 2011*, edited by Bárbara Arroyo, Lorena Paiz, and Héctor Mejía, pp. 93–107. Ministerio de Cultura y Deportes, Instituto de Antropología e Historia y Asociación Tikal, Guatemala City.

Demarest, Arthur A., and Bart Victor
2022   Constructing Policy to Confront Collapse: Ancient Experience and Modern Risk. *Academy of Management Perspectives* 36(2):768–800.

Demarest, Arthur A., Bart Victor, Chloé Andrieu, and Paola Torres
2020   A New Direction in the Study of Ancient Maya Economics: Language, Logic, and Models from Strategic Management Studies. In *The Real Business of Ancient Maya Economies: From Farmers' Fields to Rulers' Realms*, edited by Marilyn A. Masson, David A. Freidel, and Arthur A. Demarest, pp. 28–56. University Press of Florida, Gainesville.

Diamond, Jared
2011   *Collapse: How Societies Choose to Fail or Succeed*. Rev. ed. Penguin, New York.

Dieseldorff, Erwin P.
1894   A Pottery Vase with Figure Painting from a Grave in Chama. US Bureau of American Ethnology Bulletin 28:639–644.
1904   Extracto del libro antiguo que conserva la cofradía de Carcha. *Proceedings of the International Congress of Americanists* 14:399–402.

Dillon, Brian D.
1975   Notes on Trade in Ancient Mesoamerica. *Contributions of the University of California Archaeological Research Facility* 24:79–135.
1977   Salinas de los Nueve Cerros, Guatemala. *Studies in Mesoamerican Art,*

Archaeology, and Ethnohistory, No. 2, edited by John A. Graham. Ballena Press, Socorro, New Mexico.
1979 The Archaeological Ceramics of Salinas de los Nueve Cerros, Alta Verapaz, Guatemala. PhD dissertation, Department of Anthropology, University of California, Berkeley.
1981 Camelá Lagoon: Preliminary Investigations at a Lowland Maya Site in El Quiché, Guatemala. *Journal of New World Archaeology* 4(3):55–81.
1988 Meatless Maya? Ethnoarchaeological Implications for Ancient Subsistence. *Journal of New World Archaeology* 7(2/3):59–70.
1990 *Salinas de los Nueve Cerros, Alta Verapaz, Proyecto de Rescate de los Vasijones: Informe Final.* Report submitted to the Departamento de Monumentos Prehispánicos, Ministerio de Cultura y Deportes, Guatemala City.

Dillon, Brian D., Kevin Pope, and Michael Love
1988 An Ancient Extractive Industry: Maya Saltmaking at Salinas de los Nueve Cerros, Guatemala. *Journal of New World Archaeology* 7(2/3):37–58.

Donkin, Robin A.
1974 Bixa Orellana: "The Eternal Shrub." *Anthropos* 69:33–56.

Dormann, Carsten F., Stanislaus J. Schymanski, Juliano Cabral, Isabelle Chuine, Catherine Graham, Florian Hartig, Michael Kearney, et al.
2012 Correlation and Process in Species Distribution Models: Bridging a Dichotomy. *Journal of Biogeography* 39(12):2119–2131.

Douglas, Peter M. J., Mark Brenner, and Jason H. Curtis
2016 Methods and Future Directions for Paleoclimatology in the Maya Lowlands. *Global and Planetary Change* 138:3–24.

Douglas, Peter M. J., Arthur A. Demarest, Mark Brenner, and Marcelo A. Canuto
2016 Impacts of Climate Change on the Collapse of Lowland Maya Civilization. *Annual Review of Earth and Planetary Sciences* 44(1):613–645.

Downey, Sean S.
2010 Q'eqchi' Maya Swidden Agriculture, Settlement History, and Colonial Enterprise in Modern Belize. *Ethnohistory* 57(3):389–414.

Doyle, James
2016 Vessel, Throne Scene, Maya late 7th–8th c. The Metropolitan Museum of Art, accession #1999.484.2, accessed September 25, 2018.

Doz, Yves L.
1996 The Evolution of Cooperation in Strategic Alliances: Initial Conditions or Learning Processes. *Strategic Management Journal* 17(S1):55–83.

Dreux, Daniel
1968 *La Espeleología en Guatemala.* Expediciones Espeleológicas Francesas en Guatemala, Guatemala City.

Dreiss, Meredith L., and Sharon E. Greenhill
2008 *Chocolate: Pathway to the Gods.* University of Arizona Press, Tucson.

Duarte, Silvia, Carlos Avendaño, and Nora Machuca
2017 *Geomorfología del Rio Xacbal y Su Relación con Procesos Geológicos y de Uso del Suelo Actual en las Tierras Bajas de la Cuenca Sedimentaria Chapayal, El Quiché, Guatemala.* Report submitted to the Escuela de Biología. Universidad de San Carlos, Guatemala City.

Duarte, Silvia, Carlos Avendaño, and Nora Machuca
In Prep Exploración de la Relación Entre la Distribución de Meandros Hidrológicos y la Deformación Tectónica y Litológica en Tres Ríos de la Cuenca Sedimentaria de Chapayal (Petén-Sur). Guatemala.

Duffin, Kristina I., Lindsey Gillson, and Katherine J. Willis
2008 Testing the Sensitivity of Charcoal as an Indicator of Fire Events in Savanna Environments: Quantitative Predictions of Fire Proximity, Area and Intensity. *The Holocene* 18(2):279–291.

Dunning, Nicholas P., Vernon L. Scarborough, Fred Valdez Jr., Sheryl Luzzadder-Beach, Timothy P. Beach, and John G. Jones
1999 Temple Mountain, Sacred Lakes, and Fertile Fields: Ancient Maya Landscapes in Northwestern Belize. *Antiquity* 73(281):650–660.

Dunning, Nicholas P., Eric Weaver, Michael P. Smyth, and David Ortegón Zapata
2014 Xcoch: Home of Ancient Maya Rain Gods and Water Managers. In *The Archaeology of Yucatán: New Directions and Data*, edited by Travis W. Stanton, pp. 65–78. Archaeopress, Oxford.

Durand-Forest, Jacqueline
1967 El cacao entre los Aztecas. *Estudios de Cultura Nahuatl* VII:155–81.

Durán-Quesada, Ana M., Luis Gimeno, and Jorge Amador
2017 Role of Moisture Transport for Central American Precipitation. *Earth System Dynamics* 8(1):147–161.

Earley, Caitlin
2008 Ritual Deposits and Sculpted Stones: The Construction of Identity at Late Preclassic Chiapa de Corzo. Master's thesis, Department of Art History, University of Texas, Austin.
2015 At the Edge of the Maya World: Power, Politics, and Identity in Monuments from the Comitán Valley, Chiapas, Mexico. PhD dissertation, Department of Art History, University of Texas, Austin.
2020 "A Place So Far Removed": Dynasty and Ritual in Monuments from Chinkultic, Chiapas, Mexico. *Ancient Mesoamerica* 31(2):287–307.
2023 *The Comitán Valley: Sculpture and Identity on the Maya Frontier*. University of Texas Press, Austin.

Eberl, Markus
2014 *Community and Difference: Change in Late Classic Maya Villages of the Petexbatun Region*. Vanderbilt Institute of Mesoamerican Archaeology Series, Vol. 8. Vanderbilt University Press, Nashville, Tennessee.

Eisermann, Knut, and Carlos Avendaño
2006 Diversidad de Aves en Guatemala, con una Lista Bibliográfica. *Biodiversidad de Guatemala*, Vol. 1, edited by Enio B. Cano, pp. 525–623. Universidad del Valle de Guatemala, Guatemala City.
2009 Important Bird Areas of the Neotropics: Guatemala. *Neotropical Birding* 5:4–11.

Ericastilla Godoy, Sergio
2004 Investigando "El Encanto." *Utz'ib* 3(6):12–21.

Escobar, Friar Alonso de
1841 Account of the Province of Vera Paz, in Guatemala, and of the Indian

Settlements or Pueblos Established Therein. *Journal of the Royal Geographical Society of London* 11:89–97.

Estrada, Beatríz
2015 Application of Drainage Analysis to Infer "Hidden" Regional or Local Tectonic Deformation. *Bulletin of Engineering Geology and the Environment* 74(2):493–506.

Faegri, Knut, Johs Iversen, Peter E. Kaland, and Knut Krzywinski
2000 *Textbook of Pollen Analysis*. Blackburn Press, Caldwell, New Jersey.

Fahsen, Federico
2000 La Cronología de las Dinastías de Cancuén y Machaquilá. In *Proyecto Epigráfico Cancuén, Informe Preliminar No. 2*, edited by Arthur A. Demarest and Tomás Barrientos. Vanderbilt University, Nashville, Tennessee, and the Universidad del Valle, Guatemala City.

Fahsen, Federico, and Tomás Barrientos
2006 Los Monumentos de Taj Chan Ahk y Kan Maax. In *Proyecto Arqueológico Cancuén, Informe Final, No. 6, Temporada 2004–2005*, edited by Tomás Barrientos, Arthur A. Demarest, Luis F. Luin, and Brent K. S. Woodfill, pp. 35–56. Department of Anthropology, Vanderbilt University, Nashville, Tennessee.

Fahsen, Federico, and Arthur A. Demarest
2001 El Papel del Reino de Cancuen en la Historia de las Tierras Bajas Mayas: Nuevos Datos Epigráficos. In *XIV Simposio de Investigaciones Arqueológicas en Guatemala, 2000*, edited by Juan Pedro Laporte, Ana Claudia de Suasnávar, and Bárbara Arroyo, pp. 858–874. Museo Nacional de Arqueología y Etnología, Guatemala City.

Fahsen, Federico, Arthur A. Demarest, and Luis F. Luin
2003 Sesenta Años de Historia en la Escalinata Jeroglífica de Cancuen. In *XVI Simposio de Investigaciones Arqueológicas en Guatemala, 2002*, edited by Juan Pedro Laporte, Bárbara Arroyo, Héctor Escobedo, and Héctor Mejía, pp.703–713. Museo Nacional de Arqueología y Etnología, Guatemala City.

Falla, Ricardo
1992 *Masacres de la Selva: Ixcán, Guatemala (1975–1982)*. Editorial Universitaria, Guatemala City.

Fash, Barbara W.
2011 *The Copan Sculpture Museum*. Peabody Museum Press, Harvard University, Cambridge, Massachusetts.

Fash, Barbara, William Fash, Sheree Lane, Rudy Larios, Linda Schele, Jeffrey Stomper, and David Stuart
1992 Investigations of a Classic Maya Council House at Copan, Honduras. *Journal of Field Archaeology* 19(4):419–442.

Fash, William L.
1991 *Scribes, Warriors, and Kings: The City of Copán and the Ancient Maya*. Thames and Hudson, London.

Fedick, Scott L. (editor)
1996 *The Managed Mosaic: Ancient Maya Agriculture and Resources Use*. University of Utah Press, Salt Lake City.

Feinman, Gary M.
1988   Mesoamerican Temples. In *Temple in Society*, edited by Michael V. Fox, pp. 67–82. Eisenbrauns, Winona Lake, Indiana.

Feldman, Lawrence H.
1978   Los Choles Entre los Kekchies. In *Anales de la Sociedad de Geografía e Historia de Guatemala*, Vol. LI, edited by Luis Luján Muñoz, pp. 79–112. Sociedad de Geografía e Historia de Guatemala, Guatemala City.
1985   *A Tumpline Economy: Production and Distribution Systems in Sixteenth-Century Eastern Guatemala*. Labyrinthos, Culver City, California.
2000   *Lost Shores, Forgotten Peoples: Spanish Explorations of the South East Maya Lowlands*. Duke University Press, Durham, North Carolina.

Feller, Jacob
2016   A 5200 Year Record of Precipitation Changes in West-Central Guatemala Inferred from Lacustrine Carbonate-Based Stable Isotopes. Master's thesis, Department of Geology and Environmental Geosciences, Northern Illinois University, De Kalb.

Fialko, Vilma
1982   El Pataxte, Izabal, Guatemala: Una Aproximación a Su Contexto Socio-Cultural. Licenciatura thesis, Escuela de Historia, Universidad de San Carlos, Guatemala City.

Fitzsimmons, James L.
2010   *Death and the Classic Maya Kings*. University of Texas Press, Austin.

Ford, Anabel
2008   Dominant Plants of the Maya Forest and Gardens of El Pilar: Implications for Paleoenvironmental Reconstructions. *Journal of Ethnobiology* 28(2):179–199.

Ford, Anabel, and Kitty Emery
2008   Exploring the Legacy of the Maya Forest. *Journal of Ethnobiology* 28(2):147–153.

Ford, Anabel, and Ronald Nigh
2009   Origins of the Maya Forest Garden: Maya Resource Management. *Journal of Ethnobiology* 29(2):213–236.
2015   *The Maya Forest Garden: Eight Millennia of Sustainable Cultivation of the Tropical Woodlands*. Routledge, New York.

Ford, Anabel, Fred Stross, Frank Asaro, and Helen V. Michel
1997   Obsidian Procurement and Distribution in the Tikal-Yaxha Intersite Area of the Central Maya Lowlands. *Ancient Mesoamerica* 8(1):101–110.

Formica, Piero
2017   Why Innovators Should Study the Rise and Fall of Venetian Empire. *Harvard Business Review* (website), January 17, 2017, accessed March 12, 2024.

Forné, Mélanie, Silvia Alvarado, Paola Torres, and Diana Belches
2009   Análisis Cerámico en Cancuén y Su Región: Perspectivas Cronológica y Cultural. In *Proyecto Arqueológico Cancuén, Informe Final No. 9, Temporada 2008*, edited by Arthur A. Demarest, Horacio Martínez Paiz, Mélanie Forné, Claudia Quintanilla, and Luis F. Luin, pp. 139–185. Vanderbilt University, Nashville, Tennessee, and the Universidad de San Carlos, Guatemala City.

Forné, Mélanie, Silvia Alvarado, and Paola Torres
2011   Cronología cerámica en Cancuén: historia de una ciudad del Clásico Tardío. *Estudios de Cultura Maya* XXXVIII:11–39.
Forné, Mélanie, Chloé Andrieu, Arthur A. Demarest, Paola Torres, Claudia Quintanilla, Ronald L. Bishop, and Olaf Jaime Riverón
2013   Crisis y Cambios en el Clásico Tardío: Los Retos Económicos de una Ciudad Entre las Tierras Altas y las Tierras Bajas Mayas. In *Millenary Maya Societies: Past Crises and Resilience*, edited by Marie-Charlotte Arnauld and Alain Breton, pp. 49–61. Mesoweb (website).
Fourcade, Eric, Luis Piccioni, José Escriba, and Eduardo Rosselo
1999   Cretaceous Stratigraphy and Palaeoenvironments of the Southern Petén Basin, Guatemala. *Cretaceous Research* 20:793–811.
Fox, John G.
1996   Playing with Power: Ballcourts and Political Ritual in Southern Mesoamerica. *Current Anthropology* 37(3):483–503.
Fox, John W.
1978   *Quiché Conquest: Centralism and Regionalism in Highland Guatemalan State Development*. University of New Mexico Press, Albuquerque.
1981   The Late Postclassic Eastern Frontier of Mesoamerica: Cultural Innovation along the Periphery. *Current Anthropology* 22(4):321–346.
1987   *Maya Postclassic State Formation*. Cambridge University Press, Cambridge.
Franco-Gaviria, Felipe, Alexander Correa-Metrio, Cecilia Cordero-Oviedo, Minera I. López-Pérez, Guaria M. Cárdenes-Sandí, and Francisco M. Romero
2018   Effects of Late Holocene Climate Variability and Anthropogenic Stressors on the Vegetation of the Maya Highlands. *Quaternary Science Reviews* 189:76–90.
Freeman, John H., Glen R. Carroll, and Michael T. Hannan
1983   The Liability of Newness: Age Dependence in Organizational Death Rates. *American Sociological Association* 48(5):692–710.
Freestone, Ian
1991   Extending Ceramic Petrology. In *Recent Developments in Ceramic Petrology*, edited by Andrew Middleton and Ian Freestone, pp. 399–410. Occasional Paper 89. British Museum, London.
Freidel, David A., Marilyn Masson, and Michelle Rich
2016   Imagining a Complex Maya Political Economy: Counting, Tokens, and Currencies in Image, Text, and the Archaeological Record. *Cambridge Archaeological Journal* 27(1):29–54.
Freidel, David A., and F. Kent Reilly III
2010   The Flesh of the Gods: Cosmology, Food, and the Origins of Political Power in Ancient Southeastern Mesoamerica. In *Pre-Columbian Foodways: Interdisciplinary Approaches to Food, Culture, and Markets in Mesoamerica*, edited by John E. Staller and Michael Carrasco, pp. 635–680. Springer, New York City.
Freidel, David, Linda Schele, and Joy Parker
1995   *Maya Cosmos: Three Thousand Years on the Shaman's Path*. William and Morrow, New York.

Freiwald, Carolyn, Brent K. S. Woodfill, and Ryan Mills
2019   Chemical Signatures of Salt Sources in the Maya World: Implications for Isotopic Signals in Ancient Consumers. *Journal of Archaeological Science Reports* 27:1–8.

French, Matthew, Sergio Garza, Serinah Alexandri, Christian Christensen, and Torben Redder
2009   Death and Identity at Quen Santo, Huehuetenango, Guatemala: Analysis of a Newly Discovered Burial in the Ritual Fissure. *TempleHunter.DK* (website), April 24, 2009, accessed March 12, 2024.

Froyd, Cynthia A.
2006   Holocene Fire in the Scottish Highlands: Evidence from Macroscopic Charcoal Records. *The Holocene* 16(2):235–249.

Gage, Thomas
1958   *Thomas Gage's Travels in the New World*. Edited by J. Eric S. Thompson. University of Oklahoma Press, Norman.

Galindo Trejo, Jesús
2012   *Arqueoastronomía en la América Antigua*. Equipo Sirius, Madrid.

Gall, Francis
2001   *Diccionario Geográfico de Guatemala*. Vol. II. Instituto Geográfico Nacional, Guatemala.

Gallego, Francisco
2000   The Rediscovery of the Manché Chol, 1676. In *Lost Shores, Forgotten Peoples: Spanish Explorations of the South East Maya Lowlands*, edited and translated by Lawrence H. Feldman, pp. 170–180. Duke University Press, Durham, North Carolina.

García, Dora
2016   Análisis de Cerámica. In *Proyecto Arqueológico de la Región de Chaculá, Reporte de las Actividades de Campo de la Temporada 2015*, edited by Ulrich Wölfel and Byron Hernández, pp. 167–312. Report presented to the Instituto de Antropología e Historia, Guatemala City.
2017   Análisis de Cerámica. In *Proyecto Arqueológico de la Región de Chaculá, Reporte de las Actividades de Campo de la Temporada 2016*, edited by Ulrich Wölfel and Byron Hernández, pp. 93–159. Report presented to the Instituto de Antropología e Historia, Guatemala City.

García, Manolo
2003   Estructura y Composición Florística de los Estratos Arbustivo y Arbóreo en la Zona de Influencia del Parque Nacional Laguna Lachuá, Entre las Comunidades Santa Lucía Lachuá y Río Tzetoc, Cobán, A. V. In *Diversidad de Flora y Sus Usos en Paisajes no Protegidos de la Región Lachuá, Guatemala. Fase I: Ecología Integrada de la Vegetación*, edited by Carlos Avendaño, Julio Morales Can, Rafael Ávila, Manolo García, and Roberto Garnica. Escuela de Biología, Fideicomiso para la Conservación en Guatemala, Guatemala City.
2006   Caracterización de la Dieta y el Hábitat del Tapir (Tapirus bairdii Gill, 1865) en Ecosistemas Ribereños del Parque Nacional Laguna Lachuá, Cobán, Alta Verapaz, Guatemala. Licenciatura thesis, Escuela de Biología, Universidad de San Carlos, Guatemala City.

García Capistrán, Hugo
2012   El reino de la serpiente bajo la mirada de sus aliados. *Contributions in New World Archaeology* 4:39–55.
Garrido López, Jose Luis
2008   Las Figurillas de Salinas de los Nueve Cerros, Cobán, Alta Verapaz: Un Estudio Descriptivo e Interpretativo sobre Su Función. Licenciatura thesis, Escuela de Historia, Universidad de San Carlos, Guatemala City.
2012   *Proyecto Arqueológico de Rescate Caserío Ixquisis, San Mateo Ixtatán, Huehuetenango, Informe Final*. Report presented to the Dirección General de Patrimonio Cultural y Natural de Guatemala and the Departamento de Monumentos Prehispánicos y Coloniales, Guatemala City.
Gasco, Janine
1996   Cacao and Economic Inequality in Colonial Soconusco, Chiapas, Mexico. *Journal of Anthropological Research* 52(4):385–409.
Gburek, William J., Andrew N. Sharpley, Louise Heathwaite, and Gordan J. Folmar
2000   Phosphorus Management at the Watershed Scale: A Modification of the Phosphorus Index. *Journal of Environmental Quality* 29(1):130–144.
Gentry, Alwyn H.
1982   Neotropical Floristic Diversity: Phytogeographical Connections between Central and South America, Pleistocene Climatic Fluctuations, or an Accident of the Andean Orogeny? *Annals of the Missouri Botanical Garden* 69(3):557–593.
Geopetrol, S. A.
2005   *Estudio de Impacto Ambiental, Área de Contrato 7–2005*. Report submitted to Petrolatina, Guatemala City. Manuscript in the possession of the Guatemalan Ministry of Culture and Sports, Guatemala City.
Gillespie, Susan D., and Rosemary A. Joyce
1998   Deity Relationships in Mesoamerican Cosmologies: The Case of the Maya God L. *Ancient Mesoamerica* 9(2):279–296.
Gillson, Lindsey
2015a   Ecosystem Services: Lessons from the Past for a Sustainable Future. In *Biodiversity Conservation and Environmental Change*, edited by Lindsey Gillson, pp. 116–138. Oxford University Press, Oxford.
2015b   Past, Present, and Future Climate Change: Can Palaeoecology Help Manage a Warming World? In *Biodiversity Conservation and Environmental Change*, edited by Lindsey Gillson, pp. 87–115. Oxford University Press, Oxford.
Goetz, Delia, and Sylvanus G. Morley
1950   *Popol Vuh: The Sacred Book of the Ancient Quiché Maya*. Translated by Adrián Recinos. University of Oklahoma Press, Norman.
Golden, Charles, and Andrew Scherer
2013   Territory, Trust, Growth, and Collapse in Classic Period Maya Kingdoms. *Current Anthropology* 54(4):397–435.
Golitko, Mark, James Meierhoff, Gary M. Feinman, and Patrick R. Williams
2012   Complexities of Collapse: The Evidence of Maya Obsidian as Revealed by Social Network Graphical Analysis. *Antiquity* 86(332):507–523.
Golitko, Mark, and Gary M. Feinman

2015   Procurement and Distribution of Pre-Hispanic Mesoamerican Obsidian 900 BC–AD 1520: A Social Network Analysis. *Journal of Archaeological Method and Theory* 22:206–247.

Gómez-Pompa, Arturo, José Salavdor Flores, and Mario Aliphat Fernández
1990   The Sacred Cacao Groves of the Maya. *Latin American Antiquity* 1(3):247–257.

Graham, Alan
1999   The Tertiary History of the Northern Temperate Element in the Northern Latin American Biota. *American Journal of Botany* 86(1):32–38.
2003   The Concepts of Deep-Time Floras and Paleobotanical Hot-Spots. *Systematic Botany* 28(2):461–464.
2011   The Age and Diversification of Terrestrial New World Ecosystems through Cretaceous and Cenozoic Time. *American Journal of Botany* 98(3):336–351.

Graham, Ian
1965   *Tres Islas*. Report submitted to the Ministerio de Cultura y Deportes, Guatemala City.

Granados-Dieseldorff, Pablo, Mäds F. Christensen, and P. Herman Kihn-Pineda
2012   Fishes from Lachuá Lake, Upper Usumacinta Basin, Guatemala. *Check List* 8(1):95–101.

Granovetter, Mark
1985   Economic Action and Social Structure: The Problem of Embeddedness. *American Journal of Sociology* 91(3):481–510.

Green, Judith S.
2010   Feasting with Foam: Ceremonial Drinks of Cacao, Maize, and Pataxte Cacao. In *Pre-Columbian Foodways: Interdisciplinary Approaches to Food, Culture, and Markets in Ancient Mesoamerica*, edited by John E. Staller and Michael D. Carrasco, pp. 315–343. Springer, Berlin.

Groark, Kevin P.
1997   To Warm the Blood, to Warm the Flesh: The Role of the Steambath in Highland Maya (Tzeltal-Tzotzil) Ethnomedicine. *Journal of Latin American Lore* 20(1):3–96.

Grogan, James, Stephen B. Jennings, R. Matthew Landis, Mark Schulze, Anadilza M. V. Baima, José Do Carmo Alves Lopes, Julian M. Norghauer, L. Rogério Oliveira, Frank Pantoja, Diane Pinto, et al.
2008   What Loggers Leave Behind: Impacts on Big-Leaf Mahogany (*Swietenia macrophylla*) Commercial Populations and Potential for Post-Logging Recovery in the Brazilian Amazon. *Forest Ecology and Management* 255(2):269–281.

Gronemeyer, Sven
2020   Descripción y Análisis Epigráfico Preliminar de la Escalinata Jeroglífica de La Linterna, Chisec, Alta Verapaz. In *Proyecto Arqueológico Regional Cancuen, Informe Final No. 19, Temporada de Campo 2019: Tomo I—Proyecto Arqueológico Regional Cancuen*, edited by Arthur A. Demarest, Paola Torres, Julien Sion, and Chloé Andrieu, pp. 168–179. Ministerio de Cultura y Deportes de Guatemala, Guatemala City.

Groot, Mirella H. M., Henry Hooghiemstra, Juan Carlos Berrio, and Catalina Giraldo
2013   North Andean Environmental and Climatic Change at Orbital to

Submillennial Time-Scales: Vegetation, Water Levels and Sedimentary Regimes from Lake Fúquene 130–27ka. *Review of Palaeobotany and Palynology* 197:186–204.

Grube, Nikolai
2002 Stela Fragment from Chinkultic, Chiapas. *Mexicon* 24(4):65–66.

Guderjan, Thomas H.
2007 *The Nature of an Ancient Maya City: Resources, Interaction, and Power at Blue Creek, Belize.* University of Alabama Press, Tuscaloosa.

Guerra Ruiz, Jenny, and James E. Brady
2009 A Restudy of Cave 1 at Quen Santo. In *Exploring Highland Maya Ritual Cave Use: Archaeology and Ethnography in Huehuetenango, Guatemala*, edited by James E. Brady, pp. 27–40. AMCS Bulletin 20. Association for Mexican Cave Studies, Austin, Texas.

Gutiérrez-García, Tania A., and Ella Vázquez-Domínguez
2013 Consensus between Genes and Stones in the Biogeographic and Evolutionary History of Central America. *Quaternary Research* 79(3):311–324.

Habel, Simeon
1878 *The Sculptures of Santa Lucia Cosumalwhuapa in Guatemala, with an Account of Travels in Central American and on the Western Coast of South America.* Smithsonian Contributions to Knowledge, No. 269. Smithsonian Institution, Washington, DC.

Haeserijn, Esteban
1979 *Diccionario K'ekchi' Español.* Editorial Piedra Santa, Guatemala City.

Hagen, Victor Wolfgang von
1946 *Jungle in the Clouds: A Naturalist's Explorations in the Republic of Honduras.* Duell, Sloan and Pearce, New York.

Haines, Helen R., and Michael D. Glascock
2012 *Intra-Site Obsidian Distribution and Consumption Patterns in Northern Belize and the North-Eastern Petén.* BAR International Series 2326. British Archaeological Reports, Oxford.

Haldar, Swapan K., and Josip Tišljar
2014 Sedimentary Rocks. In *Introduction to Mineralogy and Petrology*, edited by Swapan K. Haldar, pp. 121–212. Elsevier, Waltham, Massachusetts.

Hammond, Norman
1972 Obsidian Trade in the Mayan Area. *Science* 178:1092–1093.
1973 Models for Maya Trade. In *The Explanation of Culture Change: Models in Prehistory*, edited by Colin Renfrew, pp. 600–607. Duckworth, Liverpool.
1986 New Light on the Most Ancient Maya. *Man, Second Series* 21(3):399–413.

Hammond, Norman (editor)
1977 *Social Process in Maya Prehistory: Studies in Honour of Sir Eric Thompson.* Academic Press, New York.

Hammond, Norman, and Jeremy R. Bauer
2001 A Preclassic Maya Sweatbath at Cuello, Belize. *Antiquity* 75(290):683–684.

Hammond, Norman, Mary D. Neivens, and Garman Harbottle
1984 Trace Element Analysis of Obsidian Artifacts from a Classic Maya Residential Group at Nohmul, Belize. *American Antiquity* 49(4):815–820.

Hastenrath, Stefan
2002 The Intertropical Convergence Zone of the Eastern Pacific Revisited. *International Journal of Climatology* 22(3):347–356.

Hatch, Marion P.
1982 La Céramique de Los Encuentros. In *Archéologie de sauvetage dans la vallée du Río Chixoy, 4: Los Encuentros*, edited by Alain Ichon and Marion P. Hatch, pp. 97–150. RCP 500. Centre National de la Recherche Scientifique, Institut D'Ethnologie, Paris.

Haug, Gerald H.
2001a *Cariaco Basin Trace Metal Data* (Data Contribution Series No. #2001-071). GBP PAGES/World Data Center A for Paleoclimatology, Boulder, Colorado.
2001b Southward Migration of the Intertropical Convergence Zone through the Holocene. *Science* 293(5533):1304–1308.

Haviland, William A.
1971 Entombment, Authority, and Descent at Altar de Sacrificios, Guatemala. *American Antiquity* 36(1):102–105.

Helmke, Christophe
2006 Recent Investigations into Ancient Maya Domestic and Ritual Activities at Pook's Hill, Belize. *Papers from the Institute of Archaeology* 17:77–85.

Henderson, Lucia R., and Brent K. S. Woodfill
2024 Missing Persons: Animate Landscapes and Non-Human Personhood in the Maya Ritual Economy. In *"Peopling" the Americas: Animate Landscapes and the Archaeology of the Western Hemisphere*, edited by Brent K. S. Woodfill and Lucia R. Henderson. University Press of Florida, Gainesville.

Hermes, Bernard A.
1981 La Cerámica Arqueológica de Pataxte, Izabal: Un Análisis. Licenciatura thesis, Escuela de Historia, Universidad de San Carlos, Guatemala City.

Hernández, Byron, and Marlen Garnica
2019a Análisis de Cerámica. In *Proyecto Arqueológico de la Región de Chacula, Reporte de las Actividades de Campo de la Temporada 2018*, edited by Ulrich Wölfel and Byron Hernández, pp. 91–132. Report presented to the Instituto de Antropología e Historia de Guatemala, Guatemala City.
2019b Análisis de Otros Materiales. In *Proyecto Arqueológico de la Región de Chacula, Reporte de las Actividades de Campo de la Temporada 2018*, edited by Ulrich Wölfel and Byron Hernández, pp. 133–166. Report presented to the Instituto de Antropología e Historia de Guatemala, Guatemala City.

Hernández, Byron, Fernando Morales, Dora García, and Ulrich Wölfel
2017 Excavaciones de Pozos de Sondeo en los Grupos A y B del Sitio Arqueológico Pueblo Viejo Quen Santo. In *Proyecto Arqueológico de la Región de Chacula, Reporte de las Actividades de Campo de la Temporada 2016*, edited by Ulrich Wölfel and Byron Hernández, pp. 71–91. Report presented to the Instituto de Antropología e Historia de Guatemala, Guatemala City.

Hewitt, William P., Marcus C. Winter, and David A. Patterson
1987 Salt Production at Hierve El Agua, Oaxaca. *American Antiquity* 52(4):799–816.

Hightower, Jessica N., A. Christine Butterfield, and John F. Weishampel

2014   Quantifying Ancient Maya Land Use Legacy Effects on Contemporary Rainforest Canopy Structure. *Remote Sensing* 6(11):10716–10732.

Hill II, Robert M.
1982   Ancient Maya Houses at Cauinal and Pueblo Viejo Chixoy, El Quiché, Guatemala. *Penn Museum Expedition Magazine* 24(2):40–48.

Hill II, Robert M., and John Monaghan
1987   *Continuities in Highland Maya Social Organization: Ethnohistory in Sacapulas, Guatemala.* University of Pennsylvania Press, Philadelphia.

Hokanson, Kelly J., Max C. Lukenbach, Kevin J. Devito, Nicholas Kettridge, Richard M. Petrone, and James Michael Waddington
2016   Groundwater Connectivity Controls Peat Burn Severity in the Boreal Plains. *Ecohydrology* 9(4):574–584.

Holdridge, Genevieve, and David S. Leigh
2018   Stable Carbon Analysis of Alluvial Paleosols in the Mixteca Alta, Oaxaca, Mexico. *Quaternary International* 490:60–73.

Hooghiemstra, Henry, and Thomas Van der Hammen
2004   Quaternary Ice-Age Dynamics in the Colombian Andes: Developing an Understanding of Our Legacy. *Philosophical Transactions of the Royal Society of London, Series B: Biological Sciences* 359(1442):173–181.

Houston, Stephen D.
2012   Heavenly Bodies. In *Maya Decipherment: Ideas on Ancient Maya Writing and Iconography* (blog), July 16, 2012, accessed April 13, 2022.
2018   Essential Luxuries: On Pleasing and Powerful Things among the Maya. In *Golden Kingdoms: Luxury Arts in the Ancient Americas*, edited by Joanne Pillsbury, Timothy Potts, and Kim N. Richter, pp. 91–98. Getty Research Institute, Los Angeles, California.

Houston, Stephen D., Charles Golden, and Andrew Scherer
2017   Information Storage and the Classic Maya. In *Maya Decipherment: Ideas on Ancient Maya Writing and Iconography* (blog), May 19, 2017, accessed August 27, 2018.

Hubbard, Raymond, Brian Douglas Haig, and Rahul A. Parsa
2019   The Limited Role of Formal Statistical Inference in Scientific Inference. *American Statistician* 73(sup1):91–98.

Hull, Kerry
2010   An Epigraphic Analysis of Classic-Period Maya Foodstuffs. In *Pre-Columbian Foodways: Interdisciplinary Approaches to Food, Culture, and Markets in Ancient Mesoamerica*, edited by John E. Staller and Michael D. Carrasco, pp. 235–256. Springer, New York.

Hurst, W. Jeffrey, Stanley M. Tarka Jr., Terry G. Powis, Fred Valdez Jr., and Thomas R. Hester
2002   Archaeology: Cacao Usage by the Earliest Maya Civilization. *Nature* 418:289–290.

Hurtado, Laura
2008   *Dinámicas Agrarias y Reproducción Campesina en la Globalización: El Caso de Alta Verapaz, 1970–2007.* F & G Editores, Guatemala City.

Hutson, Scott R.

2017   Introduction: The Long Road to Maya Markets. In *Ancient Maya Commerce: Multidisciplinary Research at Chunchucmil*, edited by Scott R. Hutson, pp. 3–26. University Press of Colorado, Boulder.

Hutson, Scott R., Bruce H. Dahlin, and Daniel Mazeau

2010   Commerce and Cooperation among the Classic Maya: The Chunchucmil Case. In *Cooperation in Economy and Society*, edited by Robert C. Marshall, pp. 81–103. AltaMira Press, Lanham, Maryland.

Ichon, Alain

1977   *Les Sculptures de La Lagunita, El Quiché, Guatemala*. RCP 294. Centre National de la Recherche Scientifique, Institut D'Ethnologie, Paris

1979   Le Peuplement de la Vallée Moyenne du Rio Chixoy à L'époque Préhispanique. In *Rabinal et la Vallée Moyenne du Rio Chixoy: Baja Verapaz—Guatemala*, edited by Alain Ichon, Pierre Usselmann, Nicole Percheron, Michel Bertrand, Alain Breton, and Denise Douzant-Rosenfeld, pp. 27–57. Cahiers de la RCP 500, Vol. 1. Centre National de la Recherche Scientifique (CNRS), Institut D'Ethnologie, Paris.

1982   Pueblo Viejo-Chixoy: La Fouille du Site Postclassique (Groupe G). In *Rabinal et la Vallée Moyenne du Rio Chixoy: Baja Verapaz—Guatemala*, edited by Alain Ichon, Nicole Percheron, Michel Bertrand, and Alain Breton, pp. 79–103. Cahiers de la RCP 500, Vol. 4. Centre National de la Recherche Scientifique (CNRS), Institut D'Ethnologie, Paris.

1987   Regional Ceramic Development in El Quiche and Baja Verapaz, Guatemala. In *Maya Ceramics, Part II: Papers from the 1985 Maya Ceramic Conference*, edited by Prudence M. Rice and Robert J. Sharer, pp. 277–306. British Archaeological Reports, Oxford.

1992   *Los Cerritos-Chijoj: La Transición Epiclásica en las Tierras Altas de Guatemala*. Centro de Estudios Mexicanos y Centroamericanos (CEMCA), Mexico.

1996   El Poblamiento Prehispánico. In *La Cuenca Media del Río Chixoy, Guatemala*, edited by Alain Ichon, Denise Douzant-Rosenfeld, and Pierre Usselmann, pp. 43–170. Cuadernos de Estudios Guatemaltecos, No. 3. Centro de Estudios Mexicanos y Centroamericanos (CEMCA), Mexico.

Ichon, Alain, and Marie-Charlotte Arnauld

1985   *Le Protoclassique à La Lagunita: El Quiché, Guatemala*. RCP 294 et 500. Centre National de la Recherche Scientifique, Institut D'Ethnologie, Paris.

Ichon, Alain, Denise Douzant-Rosenfeld, and Pierre Usselmann (editors)

1996   *La Cuenca Media del Río Chixoy (Guatemala)*. Cuadernos de Estudios Guatemaltecos, No. 3. Centro de Estudios Mexicanos y Centroamericanos (CEMCA), Mexico.

Ichon, Alain, Marie-France Fauvet-Berthelot, Christine Plocieniak, Robert Hill II, Rebecca Gonzalez Lauck, and Marco-Antonio Bailey (editors)

1980   *Rescate Arqueológico en la Cuenca del Río Chixoy 2: Cauinal*. Cahiers de la RCP 500. Centre National de la Recherche Scientifique, Institut D'Ethnologie, Paris.

Ichon, Alain, and Marion P. Hatch

1982   *Archéologie de Sauvetage Dans la Vallée du Río Chixoy 4: Los Encuentros*. RCP 500. Centre National de la Recherche Scientifique, Institut D'Ethnologie, Paris.

Ingram, Jeans S., and B. J. Francis
1969   The Annatto Tree (*Bixa orellana* L.)—A Guide to its Occurrence, Cultivation, Preparation, and Uses. *Tropical Science* 11(2):97–102.

Inomata, Takeshi, Daniela Triadan, Kazuo Aoyama, Victor Castillo, and Hitoshi Yonenobu
2013   Early Ceremonial Constructions at Ceibal, Guatemala and the Origins of Lowland Maya Civilization. *Science* 340(6131):467–471.

Inomata, Takeshi, and Kenichiro Tsukamoto
2014   Gathering in an Open Space: Introduction to Mesoamerican Plazas. In *Mesoamerican Plazas: Arenas of Community and Power*, edited by Kenichiro Tsukamoto and Takeshi Inomata, pp. 3–16. University of Arizona Press, Tucson.

Inomata, Takeshi, Daniela Triadan, Verónica A. Vázquez López, Juan Carlos Fernandez-Diaz, Takayuki Omori, María Belén Méndez Bauer, Melina García Hernández, et al.
2020   Monumental Architecture at Aguada Fénix and the Rise of Maya Civilization. *Nature* 582:530–533.

Isendahl, Christian
2012   Agro-Urban Landscapes: The Example of Maya Lowland Cities. *Antiquity* 86 (334):1112–1125.

Islebe, Gerald A., and Maarten Kappelle
1994   A Phytogeographical Comparison between Subalpine Forests of Guatemala and Costa Rica. *Feddes Repertorium* 105(1–2):73–87.

Jackson, Sarah E.
2013   *Politics of the Maya Court: Hierarchy and Change in the Late Classic Period.* University of Oklahoma Press, Norman.

James, Keith
2007   Structural Geology: From Local Elements to Regional Synthesis. In *Central America: Geology, Resources, and Hazards*, edited by Jochen Bundschuh and Guillermo Alvarado, pp. 277–321. Balkema, Rotterdam.

Jaramillo, Carlos
2006   Cenozoic Plant Diversity in the Neotropics. *Science* 311(5769):1893–1896.

Jiménez Álvarez, Socorro, and Luis Obando Acuña
2022   Estudio Petrográfico en la Cerámica de Salinas de los Nueve Cerros: Informe Técnico de Láminas Delgadas. In *Proyecto Salinas de los Nueve Cerros, Informe Final, Temporadas 2020 y 2021*, edited by Brent K. S. Woodfill, Judith Valle, and Carlos Efrain Tox Tiul, pp. 54–134. Department of Sociology, Criminology, and Anthropology, Winthrop University, Rock Hill, South Carolina.

Joaquin, Eddy, Miryam Saravia, Carlos Fidel Tuyuc, and Paola Torres
2019   Operación SEB3: Excavaciones en el Grupo Sebolito, Sitio Arqueológico Sebol, Fray Bartolomé de las Casas, Alta Verapaz. In *Proyecto Arqueológico Regional Cancuen, Informe Final No. 18, Temporada 2018: Tomo I—Proyecto Arqueológico Regional Cancuen*, edited by Arthur A. Demarest, Paola Torres, Julien Sion, Chloé Andrieu, and Carlos Fidel Tuyuc, pp. 15–54. Ministerio de Cultura y Deportes de Guatemala, Guatemala City.

Johnsgard, Paul A.
2000   *Trogons and Quetzals of the World*. Smithsonian Institution Press, Washington, DC.

Johnson, Jay K.
1996   Lithic Analysis and Questions of Cultural Complexity. In *Stone Tools: Theoretical Insight into Human Prehistory*, edited by George H. Odell, pp. 159–179. Interdisciplinary Contributions to Archaeology (IDCA). Plenum Press, New York.

Jones, Grant D.
1989   *Maya Resistance to Spanish Rule: Time and History on a Colonial Frontier*. University of New Mexico Press, Albuquerque.
1998   *The Conquest of the Last Maya Kingdom*. Stanford University Press, Stanford, California.

Katz, Hayah
2012   "He Shall Bathe in Water; Then He Shall Be Pure": Ancient Immersion Practice in the Light of Archaeological Evidence. *Vetus Testamentum* 62(3):369–380.

Kelly, Ryan, Melissa L. Chipman, Philip E. Higuera, Ivanka Stefanova, Linda B. Brubaker, and Feng Sheng Hu
2013   Recent Burning of Boreal Forests Exceeds Fire Regime Limits of the Past 10,000 Years. *Proceedings of the National Academy of Sciences of the United States of America* 110(32):13055–13060.

Keppie, J. Duncan
2004   Terranes of Mexico Revisited: A 1.3 Billion Year Odyssey. *International Geology Review* 46(9):765–794.

Keppie, J. Duncan, J. Brendan Murphy, R. Damian Nance, and Jaroslav Dostal
2012   Mesoproterozoic Oaxaquia-Type Basement in Peri-Gondwanan Terranes of Mexico, the Appalachians, and Europe: TDM Age Constraints on Extent and Significance. *International Geology Review* 54(3):313–324.

Kerr, Paul, F.
1965   *Mineralogía Óptica*. Translated by José Huidobro, technical revision by Agustin Navarro. McGraw-Hill, New York.

Kertzer, David L.
1989   *Ritual, Politics, and Power*. Yale University Press, New Haven, Connecticut.

Kettridge, Nicholas, Merritt R. Turetsky, James H. Sherwood, Dan K. Thompson, Courtney A. Miller, Brian W. Benscoter, Mike Flannigan, Mike Wotton, and James Michael Waddington
2015   Moderate Drop in Water Table Increases Peatland Vulnerability to Post-Fire Regime Shift. *Scientific Reports* 5(8063):1–4.

Kettunen, Harri, and Christophe Helmke
2010   *La Escritura Jeroglífica Maya*. Instituto Iberoamericano de Finlandia, Helsinki.

Kidder, Alfred V.
1959   *The Art of the Maya*. Crowell Press, New York.

Kidder, Alfred V., Jesse D. Jennings, and Edwin M. Shook
1946   *Excavations at Kaminaljuyu*. Carnegie Institution of Washington Publication, No. 561. Carnegie Institution of Washington, Washington, DC.

King, Arden R.
1974 *Coban and the Verapaz: History and Cultural Process in Northern Guatemala.* Middle American Research Institute Publications, No. 37. Middle American Research Institute, Tulane University, New Orleans, Louisiana.

Kinkella, Andrew James
2009 Draw of the Sacred Water: An Archaeological Survey of the Ancient Maya Settlement at the Cara Blanca Pools, Belize. PhD dissertation, Department of Anthropology, University of California, Riverside

Kopytoff, Igor
1988 The Cultural Biography of Things: Commoditization as a Process. In *The Social Life of Things*, edited by Arjun Appadurai, pp. 64–91. Cambridge University Press, Cambridge.

Kovacevich, Brigitte
2006 Reconstructing Classic Maya Economic Systems: Production and Exchange at Cancuen. PhD dissertation, Department of Anthropology, Vanderbilt University, Nashville, Tennessee.
2011 The Organization of Jade Production at Cancuen, Guatemala. In *The Technology of Maya Civilization: Political Economy and Beyond in Lithic Studies*, edited by Zachary X. Hruby, Geoffrey E. Braswell, and Oswaldo Chinchilla Mazariegos, pp. 151–163. Equinox Publishing, London
2013 Craft Production and Distribution in the Maya Lowlands: A Jade Case Study. In *Merchants, Markets, and Exchange in the Pre-Columbian World*, edited by Kenneth Hirth and Joanne Pillsbury, pp. 255–282. Dumbarton Oaks Research Library and Collection, Washington, DC.

Kovacevich, Brigitte, and Michael G. Callaghan
2019 Fifty Shades of Green: Interpreting Maya Jade Production, Circulation, Consumption, and Value. *Ancient Mesoamerica* 30(3):457–472.

Kramer, Gerhardt, and Salo K. Lowe
1940 *Archaeological Sites in the Maya Area.* Middle American Research Institute, Tulane University, New Orleans, Louisiana.

Krupp, Edwin C.
1989 The Cosmic Temples of Old Beijing. In *World Archaeoastronomy*, edited by Anthony F. Aveni, pp. 65–75. Cambridge University Press, Cambridge.

Lacadena García-Gallo, Alfonso
2003 *El Corpus Glífico de Ek' Balam, Yucatán, México.* Report submitted to the Foundation for the Advancement of Mesoamerican Studies (FAMSI), March 6, 2003, accessed June 28, 2024.
2005 Excavaciones en Machaquilá, Poptún: Estudio Epigráfico Realizado durante la Temporada 2004. In *Reporte 19, Atlas Arqueológico de Guatemala*, pp. 235–247. Dirección General del Patrimonio Cultural y Natural, Ministerio de Cultura y Deportes, Guatemala City.
2006 Excavaciones en Machaquilá, Temporada 2005: El Recinto Cuadrilobulado de la Plaza A. In *Reporte 20, Atlas Arqueológico de Guatemala*, pp. 74–123. Dirección General del Patrimonio Cultural y Natural, Ministerio de Cultura y Deporte, Guatemala City.
2010 Highland Mexican and Maya Intellectual Exchange in the Late Postclassic:

Some Thoughts on the Origin of Shared Elements and Methods of Interaction. In *Astronomers, Scribes, and Priests: Intellectual Interchange between the Northern Maya Lowlands and Highland Mexico in the Late Postclassic Period*, edited by Gabrielle Vail and Christine Hernández, pp. 383–406. Dumbarton Oaks Research Library and Collection, Washington, DC.

Lachniet, Matthew S., and William P. Patterson
2009 Oxygen Isotope Values of Precipitation and Surface Waters in Northern Central America (Belize and Guatemala) Are Dominated by Temperature and Amount Effects. *Earth and Planetary Science Letters* 284(3–4):435–446.

Landa, Diego de
2008 [1566] *Relación de las Cosas de Yucatán*. European Association of Mayanists Wayeb Resources (website), accessed March 12, 2024.
2013 *Yucatán at the Time of the Spanish Conquest/Relación de las Cosas de Yucatán*. Translated and edited by Luis E. V. Nevaer. Hispanic Economics, Coral Gables, Florida.

Laporte, Juan Pedro, Jesús Adánez, and Héctor H. Mejía
2008 Entre Cayucos y Caites: Una Ruta de Interacción Entre el Mar Caribe y el Río Pasión. In *XXI Simposio de Investigaciones Arqueológicas de Guatemala, 2007*, edited by Juan Pedro Laporte, Bárbara Arroyo, and Héctor Mejía, pp.744–769. Museo Nacional de Arqueología y Etnología, Guatemala City.

Laporte, Juan Pedro, and Héctor E. Mejía
2002 Tras la Huella del Mopan: Arquitectura del Clásico Terminal y del Postclásico en el Sureste de Petén. In *XV Simposio de Investigaciones Arqueológicas en Guatemala, 2001*, edited by Juan Pedro Laporte, Héctor Escobedo, and Bárbara Arroyo, pp. 59–88. Museo Nacional de Arqueología y Etnología, Guatemala City.

Laskar, Jacques, Philippe Robutel, Frederic Joutel, Mickaël Gastineau, Alexandre C. M. Correia, and Benjamin Levrard
2004 A Long-Term Numerical Solution for the Insolation Quantities of the Earth. *Astronomy and Astrophysics* 428(1):261–285.

Las Casas, Bartolomé de
1951 *Apologética Historia de las Indias*. Edited by Manuel Serrano y Sanz. Bailly Bailiére é hijos, Madrid.

Laurent, Valerie, Ange-Marie Risterucci, and Claire Lanaud
1994 Genetic Diversity in Cocoa Revealed by cDNA Probes. *Theoretical Applied Genetics* 88(2):193–198.

Leal, Marco Antonio
2006 *Proyecto de Exploración Arqueológica en el Área de Nueve Cerros*. Report submitted to Petrolatina Corporation, Guatemala City.

Lee Jr., Thomas A.
2001 El Camino Real de Chiapas a Guatemala—Un Enlace Entre Dos Pueblos. *Arqueología Mexicana* IX(50):50–55.

Lee, Thomas A., Jr., and Carlos Navarrete (editors)
1978 *Mesoamerican Communication Routes and Cultural Contacts*. Papers of the New World Archaeological Foundation, No. 40. New World Archaeological Foundation, Brigham Young University, Provo, Utah.

Legendre, Pierre
1993 Spatial Autocorrelation: Trouble or New Paradigm? *Ecology* 74(6):1659–1673.
Legendre, Pierre, and Louis Legendre
1998 *Numerical Ecology*. Elsevier, Amsterdam.
Leight, Megan E.
2018 Excavaciones en el Grupo de las Ofrendas, Temporada 2017 (Operaciones SNC52B a G). In *Proyecto Arqueológico, Salinas de los Nueve Cerros, Informe Final, Temporada 2017*, edited by Judith Valle, Brent K. S. Woodfill, and Carlos Efraín Tox Tiul, pp. 9–51. Nueva Guatemala de la Asunción, Guatemala City.
2020 Examinando el Puerto Comercial Fluvial en Salinas de los Nueve Cerros, Alta Verapaz, Guatemala. In *XXXIII Simposio de Investigaciones Arqueológicas en Guatemala, 2019*, edited by Bárbara Arroyo and Héctor Mejía, pp. 1009–1020. Museo Nacional de Arqueología y Etnología, Guatemala City.
Leight, Megan E., and Brent K. S. Woodfill
2017 Excavaciones en el Grupo de las Ofrendas. In *Proyecto Arqueológico Salinas de los Nueve Cerros, Informe Final, Temporada 2016*, edited by Brent K. S. Woodfill and Judith Valle, pp. 48–71. Dirección General del Patrimonio Cultural y Natural, Guatemala City.
Lemus, Byron R., and Efraín Peralta
1996 *Hallazgo de Site Piedras Calizas Talladas Esculpidas en Bjo Relieve (Glivos)*. Report submitted to the Department of Prehispanic and Colonial Monuments, Guatemala City.
Lentz, David L., Brian Lane, and Kim Thompson
2014 Food, Farming, and Forest Management at Aguateca. In *Life and Politics at the Royal Court of Aguateca: Artifacts, Analytical Data, and Synthesis*, edited by Takeshi Inomata and Daniela Triadan, pp. 201–215. Monograph of the Aguateca Archaeological Project First Phase, Vol. 3. University of Utah Press, Salt Lake City.
Levi, Laura J., Christian Sheumaker, and Sarah Boudreaux
2019 Technologies of Movement at Wari Camp, Belize. *Mexicon* 41(4):105–111
Lin, Hui-Ling, Larry C. Peterson, Jonathan T. Overpeck, Susan E. Trumbore, David W. Murray
1997 Late Quaternary Climate Change from $\delta^{18}O$ Records of Multiple Species of Planktonic Foraminifera: High-Resolution Records from the Anoxic Cariaco Basin, Venezuela. *Paleoceanography* 12(3):415–427.
2001 Cariaco Basin Stable Isotope Data. IGBP PAGES/World Data Center for Paleoclimatology Data Contribution Series #2001-075. NOAA/NGDC Paleoclimatology Program, Boulder, Colorado.
Linder, H. Peter, Caroline E. R. Lehmann, Sally Archibald, Colin P. Osborne, and David M. Richardson
2018 Global Grass (Poaceae) Success Underpinned by Traits Facilitating Colonization, Persistence and Habitat Transformation. *Biological Reviews* 93:1125–1144.
Liu, Yi, Li Lo, Zhengguo Shi, Kuo-Yen Wei, Chien-Ju Chou, Yi-Chi Chen, Chih-Kai Chuang, et al.

2015　Obliquity Pacing of the Western Pacific Intertropical Convergence Zone over the Past 282,000 Years. *Nature Communications* 6(10018):1–7.

Lockley, Timothy James
2009　*Maroon Communities in South Carolina: A Documentary Record*. University of South Carolina Press, Columbia.

López, Rolando, Maura Liseth Quezada, Carlos Avendaño, Rosa Sunum, and Carla Del Cid
2015　*Evaluación Contemporánea del Paisaje de la Ecorregión Lachuá y Su Correspondencia con la Composición de Esporo-Polen: Fundamentos para Estudios de Cambio Climático y Manejo de Recursos Naturales*. Consejo Nacional de Ciencia y Tecnología, Escuela de Biología, CCQQFar, Universidad de San Carlos, Guatemala City.

López Austin, Alfredo, and Leonardo López Luján
1999　*Mito y Realidad de Zuyuá: Serpiente Emplumada y las Transformaciones Mesoamericanas del Clásico al Posclásico*. El Colegio de México, Fideicomiso Historia de las Américas y Fondo de Cultura Económica, Mexico City.

López-Pérez, M.
2015　*Métodos en la Reconstrucción de Incendios*. Laboratorio de Palinología y Paleoecología, Instituto de Geología, Universidad Nacional Autónoma de México, Mexico City.

Los Angeles County Museum of Art (LACMA)
2022　Carved Door Lintel with Female in Moon Cartouche, Guatemala or Mexico, Petén or Chiapas, Usumacinta River Valley, nearby Yaxchilan, Maya 750–850 CE. Electronics collection record from LACMA #AC1992.76.1.

Lowe, Gareth W., Thomas A. Lee Jr., and Eduardo Martínez Espinosa
1982　*Izapa: An Introduction to the Ruins and Monuments*. Papers of the New World Archaeological Foundation, No. 31. New World Archaeological Foundation, Brigham Young University, Provo, Utah.

Lucero, Lisa J.
2003　*Water and Ritual: The Rise and Fall of Classic Maya Rulers*. University of Texas Press, Austin.
2018　A Cosmology of Conservation in the Ancient Maya World. *Journal of Anthropological Research* 74(3):327–359.

Lucero, Lisa J., and Barbara W. Fash
2006　*Precolumbian Water Management: Ideology, Ritual, and Power*. University of Arizona Press, Tucson.

Lucero, Lisa J., and Andrew Kinkella
2015　Pilgrimage to the Edge of the Watery Underworld: An Ancient Maya Water Temple at Cara Blanca, Belize. *Cambridge Archaeological Journal* 25(1):163–185.

Lucero, Lisa J., Jean T. Larmon, and Aimée E. Carbaugh
2017　The Ancient Maya Ceremonial Circuit of Cara Blanca, Belize. *Research Reports in Belizean Archaeology* 14:249–259.

Maca, Allan L.
2002　Spatio-Temporal Boundaries in Classic Maya Settlement Systems: Copan's Urban Foothills and the Excavations at Group 9J-5. PhD

dissertation, Department of Anthropology, Harvard University, Cambridge, Massachusetts.

Macario, Raquel
2012   La Configuración Especial en Q'umarkaj Intramuros Analizada a Través de la Arqueología y la Etnohistoria, 1225–1524, d.C. Licenciatura thesis, Escuela de Historia, Universidad de San Carlos, Guatemala City.

Macario, Raquel, Yvonne Putzeys, Marie Fulbert, Edgar Telón, Edgar Ortega, Jorge Cáceres, Juan Manuel Palomo, et al.
2007   Proyecto Etnoarqueológico Q'um'arkaaj, Quiché, Guatemala, 2003–2006. In *XX Simposio de Investigaciones Arqueológicas en Guatemala, 2006*, edited by Juan Pedro Laporte, Bárbara Arroyo, and Héctor Mejía, pp. 971–986. Museo Nacional de Arqueología y Etnología, Guatemala City.

Machuca, Nora
2018   Relación Histórica de la Variabilidad Climática y Actividad Antrópica en la Planicie Aluvial de la Cuenca Baja del Río Chixoy en la Sección Norte de la Ecoregión Lachuá. Licenciatura thesis, Escuela de Biología, Universidad de San Carlos, Guatemala City.

Machuca, Nora, Silvia Duarte, and Carlos Avendaño
2019   *Relación Histórica del Cambio Ambiental y Actividad Antrópica en la Planicie Aluvial en la Cuenca Baja del Río Chixoy: Línea Base para Planes de Mitigación y Prevención de Inundaciones en la Sección Norte de la Ecoregión Lachuá*. Consejo Nacional de Ciencia y Tecnología. Escuela de Biología, CCQQFar, Universidad de San Carlos, Guatemala City, Guatemala.

MacKinnon, J. Jefferson, and Susan Kepecs
1991   Prehispanic Salt-Making in Belize: A Reply to Valdez and Mock and to Marcus. *American Antiquity* 56(2):528–30.

MacLeod, Murdo
2008   *Spanish Central America: A Socioeconomic History, 1520–1720*. 2nd ed. University of Texas Press, Austin.

Maler, Teobert
1908   *Explorations of the Upper Usumatsintla and Adjacent Region: Altar de Sacrificios; Seibal; Itsimté-Sácluk; Cankuen*. Memoirs of the Peabody Museum of American Archaeology and Ethnology, Harvard University, Vol. 4, No. 1 and 2. Peabody Museum, Cambridge, Massachusetts.

Mannikka, Eleanor
1996   *Angkor Wat: Time, Space, and Kingship*. University of Hawaii Press, Honolulu.

Manz, Béatriz
2005   *Paradise in Ashes: A Guatemalan Journey of Courage, Terror, and Hope*. University of California Press, Berkeley.

Marchant, Rob A., Antoine Cleef, Sandy P. Harrison, Henry Hooghiemstra, Vera Markgraf, John Van Boxel, Thomas A. Ager, et al.
2009   Pollen-Based Biome Reconstruction for Latin America at 0, 6000 and 18000 Radiocarbon Years Ago. *Climate of the Past* 5(4):725–767.

Marchant, Rob A., Lucia Almeida, Hermann Behling, Juan Carlos Berrio, Mark Bush, Antoine Cleef, Joost Duivenvoorden, et al.
2002   Distribution and Ecology of Parent Taxa of Pollen Lodged within the Latin

American Pollen Database. *Review of Palaeobotany and Palynology* 121(1):1–75.

Marcus, Joyce
1984 Reply to Hammond and Andrews. *American Antiquity* 49(4):829–33.
1991 Another Pinch of Salt: A Comment on MacKinnon and Kepecs. *American Antiquity* 56(3):526–527.

Márquez Morfín, Lourdes (editor)
1982 *Playa del Carmen: Una Población de la Costa Oriental en el Posclásico (un Estudio Osteológico)*. Colección científica—Antropología Física, No. 119. Instituto Nacional de Antropología e Historia, Mexico City.

Martin, Simon
2006 Cacao in Ancient Maya Religion: First Fruit from the Maize Tree and Other Tales from the Underworld. In *Chocolate in Mesoamerica: A Cultural History of Cacao*, edited by Cameron McNeil, pp. 154–183. University Press of Florida, Gainesville.
2012 Hieroglyphs from the Painted Pyramid: The Epigraphy of Chiik Nahb Structure Sub 1–4, Calakmul, Mexico. In *Maya Archaeology 2*, edited by Charles Golden, Stephen D. Houston, and Joel Skidmore, pp. 60–81. Precolumbia Mesoweb Press, San Francisco.
2015 Old Man of the Maya Universe: A Unitary Dimension within Ancient Maya Religion. In *Maya Archaeology 3*, edited by Charles Golden, Stephen D. Houston, and Joel Skidmore, pp.186–227. Precolumbia Mesoweb Press, San Francisco.

Martin, Simon, and Nikolai Grube
2008 *Chronicle of the Maya Kings and Queens: Deciphering the Dynasties of the Ancient Maya*. 2nd ed. Thames and Hudson, London.

Martínez Paiz, Horacio, Arthur A. Demarest, Chloé Andrieu, Paola Torres, and Mélanie Forné
2017 Cancuén: una ciudad portuaria en el río de La Pasión. *Estudios de Cultura Maya* 49:11–37.

Martinez, Maria M., Erin L. Sears, and Lauren Sieg (editors)
2022 *Contextualizing Museum Collections at the Smithsonian Institution: The Relevance of Collections-Based Research in the Twenty-First Century*. Smithsonian Contributions to Anthropology, No. 54. Smithsonian Institution Scholarly Press, Washington, DC.

Masson, Marilyn A., David A. Freidel, and Arthur A. Demarest (editors)
2020 *The Real Business of Ancient Maya Economies: From Farmers' Fields to Rulers' Realms*. University Press of Florida, Gainesville.

Math, Rudrayya G., G. Ramesh, Allani Nagender, and Satyanarayana Akula
2016 Design and Development of Annatto (*Bixa Orellana* L.) Seed Separator Machine. *Journal of Food Science Technology* 53(1):703–11.

Mathews, Jennifer P., and James F. Garber
2004 Models of Cosmic Order: Physical Expression of Sacred Space among the Ancient Maya. *Ancient Mesoamerica* 15(1):49–59.

Matthews, Peter
1977 The Inscription on the Back of Stela 8, Dos Pilas. Paper presented at Yale University, New Haven, Connecticut.

Maudslay, Ann C., and Alfred P. Maudslay
1899 *A Glimpse at Guatemala, and Some Notes on the Ancient Monuments of Central America*. John Murray, London.
Mays, Larry W., and Andreas N. Angelakis
2019 Ancient Gods and Goddesses of Water. In *Evolution of Water Supply through the Millennia*, edited by Andreas N. Angelaskis, Larry W. Mays, Demetris Koutsoyiannis, and Nikos Mamassis, pp.1–17. IWA Publishing, London.
McAnany, Patricia A.
1995 *Living with the Ancestors: Kinship and Kingship in Ancient Maya Society*. University of Texas Press, Austin.
2010 *Ancestral Maya Economies in Archaeological Perspective*. Cambridge University Press, Cambridge.
McBryde, Felix Webster
1933 *Sololá: A Guatemalan Town and Cakchiquel Market-Center*. Studies in Middle America, No. 5. Department of Middle American Research, Tulane University, New Orleans, Louisiana.
1971 *Cultural and Historical Geography of Southwest Guatemala*. Greenwood Press, Westport, Connecticut.
McCampbell, Kathleen G.
2010 Highland Maya Effigy Funerary Urns: A Study of Genre, Iconography, and Function. Master's thesis, Department of Art History, Florida State University, Tallahassee.
McCluskey, Stephen C.
2007 Calendrical Cycles, the Eighth Day of the World, and the Orientation of English Churches. In *Skywatching in the Ancient World: New Perspectives in Cultural Astronomy*, edited by Clive Ruggles and Gary Urton, pp. 331–353. University Press of Colorado, Boulder.
McGlue, Michael M., Geoffrey S. Ellis, and Andrew S. Cohen
2015 The Modern Muds of Laguna Mar Chiquita (Argentina): Particle Size and Geochemical Trends from a Large Saline Lake in the "Thick-Skinned" Andean Foreland. *Geological Society of America Special Papers* 515:1–18.
McKillop, Heather
2002 *Salt: White Gold of the Ancient Maya*. University Press of Florida, Gainesville.
2005 Finds in Belize Document Late Classic Maya Salt Making and Canoe Transport. *Proceedings of the National Academy of Sciences of the United States of America* 102(15):5630–5634.
2019 *Maya Salt Works*. University Press of Florida, Gainesville.
McMichael, Crystal N. H., Michael W. Palace, Mark B. Bush, Rob Braswell, Stephen Hagen, Eduardo G. Neves, Miles R. Silman, Eduardo Kazuo Tamanaha, and Christina Czarnecki
2014 Predicting Pre-Columbian Anthropogenic Soils in Amazonia. *Proceedings of the Royal Society B: Biological Sciences* 281(1777):1–9.
McMichael, Crystal N. H., Frazer Matthews-Bird, William Farfan-Rios, and Kenneth J. Feeley
2017 Ancient Human Disturbances May Be Skewing Our Understanding of Amazonian Forests. *Proceedings of the National Academy of Sciences of the United*

States of America 114(3):522–527.

McNeil, Cameron L.

2006a Introduction: The Biology, Antiquity, and Modern Uses of the Chocolate Tree (*Theobroma cacao* L.). In *Chocolate in Mesoamerica: A Cultural History of Cacao*, edited by Cameron L. McNeil, pp. 1–28. University Press of Florida, Gainesville.

2006b Traditional Cacao Use in Modern Mesoamerica. In *Chocolate in Mesoamerica: A Cultural History of Cacao*, edited by Cameron L. McNeil, pp. 341–366. University Press of Florida, Gainesville.

McNeil, Cameron (editor)

2006c *Chocolate in Mesoamerica: A Cultural History of Cacao*. University Press of Florida, Gainesville.

McNeil, Cameron, David A. Burney, and Lida Pigott Burney

2010 Evidence Disputing Deforestation as the Cause for the Collapse of the Ancient Maya Polity of Copán, Honduras. *Proceedings of the National Academy of Sciences of the United States of America* 107(3):1017–1022.

McWethy, David B., Simon G. Haberle, Felicitas Hopf, and David M. J. S. Bowman

2017 Aboriginal Impacts on Fire and Vegetation on a Tasmanian Island. *Journal of Biogeography* 44:1319–1330.

Memorial de Sololá

1500s–1600 Manuscrito Cakchiquel ó Sea Memorial de Tecpán-Atitlán (Sololá): Historia del Antiguo Reino del Cakchiquel, Dicho de Guatemala. Colección Lingüística Berendt-Brinton of the Library of the University of Pennsylvania, Philadelphia. Ms. Coll. 700, Item 221.

Metcalfe, Sarah E., John A. Barron, and Sarah J. Davies

2015 The Holocene History of the North American Monsoon: "Known Knowns" and "Known Unknowns" in Understanding Its Spatial and Temporal Complexity. *Quaternary Science Reviews* 120:1–27.

Meunier, Jean Dominique, Fabrice Colin, and Charles Alarcon

1999 Biogenic Silica Storage in Soils. *Geology* 27(9):835–838.

Miall, Andrew

2014 *Fluvial Depositional Systems*. Springer, New York.

Mijangos, Blanca

2014 Las Piedras y Manos para Moler del Sitio Salinas de los Nueve Cerros, Implementos Utilizados en el Refinamiento de Sal. Licenciatura thesis, Escuela de Historia, Universidad de San Carlos, Guatemala City.

Miksicek, Charles H., Kathryn J. Elsesser, Ingrid A. Wuebber, Karen Olsen Bruhns, and Norman Hammond

1981 Rethinking Ramón: A Comment on Reina and Hill's Lowland Maya Subsistence. *American Antiquity* 46(4):916–919.

Milbrath, Susan

1999 *Star Gods of the Maya: Astronomy in Art, Folklore, and Calendars*. University of Texas Press, Austin.

Millan, René F.

1955 When Money Grew on Trees: A Study of Cacao in Ancient Mesoamerica. PhD dissertation, Department of Political Science, Columbia University, New York.

Miller, Catherine Annalisa
2013 Earth. Water. Sky. The Liminal Landscape of the Maya Sweatbath. PhD dissertation, Architecture and Design Research, Virginia Tech, Blacksburg.

Miller, Mary E.
1997 Imaging Maya Art. *Archaeology* 50(3):34–40.
1999 *Maya Art and Architecture.* Thames and Hudson, New York.

Miller, Mary E., and Simon Martin (editors)
2004 *Courtly Art of the Ancient Maya.* Thames and Hudson, New York.

Miller, Mary E., and Karl A. Taube
1993 *The Gods and Symbols of Ancient Mexico and the Maya: An Illustrated Dictionary of Mesoamerican Religion.* Thames and Hudson, New York.
1997 *An Illustrated Dictionary of the Gods and Symbols of Ancient Mexico and the Maya.* Thames and Hudson, New York.

Miranda, Fr. Francisco Montero de
1953–1954 Descripción de la Provincia de la Verapaz, Relación del Siglo XVI, Año de 1574. In *Anales de la Sociedad de Geografía e Historia de Guatemala* XXVII, No. 1–4, edited by Ricardo Castañeda Paganini, pp. 342–335. Sociedad de Geografía e Historia de Guatemala, Guatemala City.

Miranda, Faustino
1962 Wild Cacao in the Lacandona Forest, Chiapas, Mexico. *CACAO—Inter-American Institute of Agricultural Sciences, Cacao Center* 7(4):8.

Mock, Shirley
1994 The Northern River Lagoon Site (NRL): Late to Terminal Classic Maya Settlement, Saltmaking, and Survival on the Northern Belize Coast. PhD dissertation, University of Texas, Austin.

Moga, Iulian
2009 Salt Extraction and Imagery in the Ancient Near East. *Journal for Interdisciplinary Research on Religion and Science* 4:175–213.

Moholy-Nagy, Hattula
2003 Source Attribution and the Utilization of Obsidian in the Maya Area. *Latin American Antiquity* 14(3):301–310.

Moholy-Nagy Hattula, Frank Assaro, and Fred H. Stross
1984 Tikal Obsidian: Sources and Typology. *American Antiquity* 49(1):104–117.

Molins Fábrega, N.
1956 *El Códice Mendocino y la Economía de Tenochtitlán.* Libro-Mex, Mexico City.

Monterroso, Mirza
2006 El Sitio Arqueológico La Lima, Chisec, Alta Verapaz durante el Clásico Tardío (600–900 d.C.). Licenciatura thesis, Escuela de Historia, Universidad de San Carlos de Guatemala, Guatemala City.

Monterroso, Mirza, and Brent Woodfill
2005 Investigaciones en el Sitio Arqueológico La Lima: Temporadas 2004 y 2005. In *Proyecto Arqueológico Regional Cancuén, Informe No. 6, Temporada 2004—5, Volumen III*, edited by Tomás Barrientos, Arthur A. Demarest, Luis F. Luin, and Brent Woodfill, pp. 697–724. Ministerio de Cultura y Deportes de Guatemala, Guatemala City.

Montes, Camilo, Agustín Cardona, Carlos Jaramillo, Andrés Pardo-Trujillo,

Juan-Carlos Silva, Victor A. Valencia, Caroline Ayala, Lina C. Pérez-Angel, Luis A. Rodriguez-Parra, Victor Ramirez, Helga Niño.
2015 Middle Miocene Closure of the Central American Seaway. *Science* 348(6231):226–229.

Montoya, Julia
2023 La Relevancia de Chich'en dentro del Contexto Regional de Cobán, Alta Verapaz. In *Tejiendo Imágenes: Homenaje a Victòria Solanilla Demestre*, edited by Catalina Simmons Caldas and Marina Valls i García, pp. 198–209. Zea Books, Lincoln, Nebraska.

Monzón Miranda, Rovoham Mardoqueo
1999 Estudio General de los Recursos Agua, Suelo y Uso de la Tierra de Parque Nacional Laguna Lachuá y Su Zona de Influencia, Cobán, Alta Verapaz. Licenciatura thesis, Facultad de Agronomía, Universidad de San Carlos, Guatemala City.

Morales, Claudia
2014 Etnobotánica de la Madera de Uso Doméstico para Leña en la Comunidad de Santa Lucía Lachuá, Alta Verapaz, Guatemala. Ejercicio Profesional Supervisado, Escuela de Biología, Universidad de San Carlos, Guatemala City.
2016 Relación de la Diversidad Vegetal en Huertos Familiares Maya Q'eqchi' con Aspectos Socioculturales en la Comunidad Santa Lucía Lachuá, Alta Verapaz, Guatemala. Licenciatura thesis, Escuela de Biología, Universidad de San Carlos, Guatemala City.

Morán Ical, Humberto, and Ruud van Akkeren
2016 *Tras las Huellas del Puma: La Historia Antigua del Pueblo Poq'omchi' San Cristóbal Verapaz*. Serviprensa, Guatemala City.

Morán Giracca, Lucia
2003 Evidencia de Actividad Ceremonial en Grupo L6 de Cancuén, Petén. Licenciatura thesis, Departmento de Anthropologia, Universidad del Valle de Guatemala, Guatemala.

Moreno, Patricio I., Isabel Vilanova, Rodrigo P. Villa-Martínez, and Jean P. Francois
2018 Modulation of Fire Regimes by Vegetation and Site Type in Southwestern Patagonia since 13 ka. *Frontiers in Ecology and Evolution* 6(34):1–10.

Morley, Sylvanus G.
1915 Archeology. In *Carnegie Institution of Washington Year Book*, No. 14, pp. 343–346. Carnegie Institution of Washington, Press of Gibson Brothers, Washington, DC.

Motamayor, Juan Carlos, Ange-Marie Risterucci, Procopio Alejandro López, Carlos F. Ortiz, Argelio Moreno, and Claire Lanaud
2002 Cacao Domestication I: The Origin of the Cacao Cultivated by the Mayas. *Heredity* 89(5):380–386.

Mudie, Petra J., Suzanne A. G. Leroy, Fabienne Marret, Natalia P. Gerasimenko, Susan E. A. Kholeif, Tatiana Sapelko, and Mariana V. Filipova-Marinova
2011 Nonpollen Palynomorphs: Indicators of Salinity and Environmental Change in the Caspian–Black Sea–Mediterranean Corridor. *Geological Society of America, Special Papers* 473:89–115.

Mueller, Andreas D., Gerald A. Islebe, Michael B. Hillesheim, Dustin A. Grzesik, Flavio S. Anselmetti, Daniel Ariztegui, Mark Brenner, Jason H. Curtis, David A. Hodell, and Kathryn A. Venz
2009 Climate Drying and Associated Forest Decline in the Lowlands of Northern Guatemala During the Late Holocene. *Quaternary Research* 71:133–141.

Munson, Jessica L., Andrés G. Mejía Ramón, and Lorena Paiz Aragón
2019 Mapeo de Asentamientos en Alta Resolución con Sistemas Aéreos No Tripulados en Altar de Sacrificios, Guatemala. In *XXXII Simposio de Investigaciones Arqueológicas en Guatemala, 2018*, edited by Bárbara Arroyo, Luis Méndez Salinas, and Gloria Ajú Álvarez, pp. 637–648. Museo Nacional de Arqueología y Etnología, Guatemala City.

Navarrete, Carlos
1978 The Pre-Hispanic System of Communications Between Chiapas and Tabasco (Preliminary Report). In *Mesoamerican Communication Routes and Cultural Contacts*, edited by Thomas A. Lee Jr. and Carlos Navarrete, pp. 75–106. Papers of the New World Archaeological Foundation, No. 40. New World Archaeological Foundation, Brigham Young University, Provo, Utah.
1979 *Las Esculturas de Chaculá, Huehuetenango, Guatemala*. Serie Antropológica, No. 31. Instituto de Investigaciones Antropológicas, Universidad Nacional Autónoma de México, México City.
1981 Las Rutas de Comunicación Prehispánica en los Altos Cuchumatanes: Un Proyecto Arqueológico y Etnohistórico. In *Los Legítimos Hombres: Aproximación antropológica al grupo tojolabal*, Vol. I, edited by Mario Humberto Ruz, pp. 75–88. Instituto de Investigaciones Filológicas, Universidad Nacional Autónoma de México, Mexico City.
1990 Chinkultic, un Sitio Puerta Intermedio Entre los Altos de Guatemala y el Occidente de Chiapas. In *La Época Clásica: Nuevos Hallazgos, Nuevas Ideas*, edited by Amalia Cardós de Méndez, pp. 447–453. Instituto Nacional de Antropología e Historia, Mexico City.

Nelson, Fred W.
1985 Summary of the Results of Analysis of Obsidian Artifacts from the Maya Lowlands. *Scanning Electron Microscopy* 2(15):631–649.
1994 Redes de Intercambio de Obsidiana en Mesoamérica. In *Cristales y Obsidiana Prehispánicos*, edited by Mari Carmen Serra Puche and Michel Zabé, pp. 53–70. Siglo Veintiuno Editores, México City.
2004 El Intercambio de Obsidiana en las Tierras Bajas Mayas. In *XVII Simposio de Investigaciones Arqueológicas en Guatemala, 2003*, edited by Juan Pedro Laporte, Bárbara Arroyo, Héctor Escobedo, and Héctor Mejía, pp.925–935. Museo Nacional de Arqueología y Etnología, Guatemala City.

Nelson, Fred W., and John E. Clark
1989 Rutas de Intercambio de Obsidiana en el Norte de la Península de Yucatán. In *La Obsidiana en Mesoamérica*, edited by Margarita Gaxiola and John E. Clark, pp. 343–363. Instituto Nacional de Antropología e Historia, Mexico City.
1990 The Determination of Exchange Patterns in Prehistoric Mesoamerica. In *Nuevos Enfoques en el Estudio de la Lítica*, edited by María de los Dolores

Soto de Arechaveleta, pp. 153–175. Instituto de Investigaciones Antropológicas, Universidad Nacional Autónoma de México, Mexico City.
1998   Obsidian Production and Exchange in Eastern Mesoamerica. In *Rutas de intercambio en Mesoamérica*, edited by Evelyn Rattray, pp. 277–333.Instituto de Investigaciones Antropológicas, Universidad Nacional Autónoma de México, Mexico City.

Nichols, Deborah L., Christina Elson, Leslie G. Cecil, Nina Neivens de Estrada, Michael D. Glascock, and Paula Mikkelsen
2009   Chiconautla, Mexico: A Crossroads of Aztec Trade and Politics. *Latin American Antiquity* 20(3):443–472.

Nigh, Ronald, and Stewart A. W. Diemont
2013   The Maya Milpa: Fire and the Legacy of Living Soil. *Frontiers in Ecology and the Environment* 11(Online Issue 1):e45–e54.

O'Dea, Aaron O., Harilaos A. Lessios, Anthony G. Coates, Ron I. Eytan, Sergio A. Restrepo-Moreno, Alberto L. Cione, Laurel S. Collins, et al.
2016   Formation of the Isthmus of Panama. *Science Advances* 2(8):1–12.

ODHAG (Oficina de Derechos Humanos del Arzobispado de Guatemala)
1998   *Guatemala Nunca Más*. Tomo I and II. Arzobispado de Guatemala, Guatemala City.

Ogata, Nisao, Arturo Gómez-Pompa, and Karl Taube
2011   The Domestication and Distribution of *Theobroma cacao* L. in the Neotropics. In *Chocolate in Mesoamerica: A Cultural History of Cacao*, edited by Cameron L. McNeil, pp. 69–89. University Press of Florida, Gainesville.

Oliver, Christine
1996   The Institutional Embeddedness of Economic Activity. In *The Embeddedness of Strategy: Advances in Strategic Management*, Vol. 13, edited by Joel A. C. Baum and Jane E. Dutton, pp 163–186. JAI Press, Stamford, Connecticut.

Ortiz, Jorge Mario
2022   Resultados Generales del Análisis Cerámico del Proyecto Arqueológico Salinas de los Nueve Cerros. In *Proyecto Salinas de los Nueve Cerros, Informe Final, Temporadas 2020 y 2021*, edited by Brent K. S. Woodfill, Judith Valle, and Carlos Efrain Tox Tiul, pp. 7–53. Department of Sociology, Criminology, and Anthropology, Winthrop University, Rock Hill, South Carolina.

Ortíz, Jorge Mario, Claudia Estela Arriaza, and Diana Patricia Méndez
2017   El Juego de Pelota y el Grupo 7 Ahau Como Evidencia de un Predominio Poblacional Local durante el Clásico Tardío en Salinas de los Nueve Cerros a Través del Estudio de Su Cerámica. In *XXX Simposio de Investigaciones Arqueológicas en Guatemala, 2016*, edited by Bárbara Arroyo, Luis Méndez Salinas, and Gloria Ajú Álvarez, pp. 805–814. Museo Nacional de Arqueología y Etnología, Guatemala City.

Ortíz, Jorge Mario, Mónica Urquizú, Sheryl Carcuz, and Claudia Arriaza
2015   Salinas de los Nueve Cerros, Actualización de Su Inventario Cerámico: La Relación entre Tierras Altas y Tierras Bajas. In *XXVIII Simposio de Investigaciones Arqueológicas en Guatemala, 2014*, edited by Bárbara Arroyo, Luis Méndez Salinas, and Lorena Paiz, pp. 799–808. Museo Nacional de Arqueología y Etnología, Guatemala City.

Paez Betancor, Alonso, and Fr. Pedro de Arboleda
1964   Relación de Santiago Atitlán—Año de 1585. In *Anales de la Sociedad de Geografía e Historia de Guatemala* XXXVII, No. 1–4, edited by Francis Gall, pp. 87–106. Sociedad de Geografía e Historia de Guatemala, Guatemala City.
1965   Para la Estancia de Sanct Bartolome, Subjecto a Atitlan. In *Anales de la Sociedad de Geografía e Historia de Guatemala* XXXVIII, No. 1–4, edited by Francis Gall, pp. 265–276. Sociedad de Geografía e Historia de Guatemala, Guatemala City.

Pascual Soto, Arturo, and Erik Velásquez García
2012   Relaciones y Estrategias Políticas entre El Tajín y Diversas Entidades Mayas durante el Siglo IX D.dC. *Contributions in New World Archaeology* 4:205–227.

Patch, Robert W.
2002   *Maya Revolt and Revolution in the Eighteenth Century.* M. E. Sharpe, New York.

Pellecer, José M., Julio R. Morales, and Sergio G. Pérez
2019   Noteworthy Records of the Northern Naked-Tailed Armadillo, *Cabassous centralis* (Cingulata: Chlamyphoridae), in Guatemala, Central America. *Edentata* 20:17–21.

Penny, Dan, Tegan Hall, Damian Evans, and Martin Polkinghorne
2019   Geoarchaeological Evidence from Angkor, Cambodia, Reveals a Gradual Decline Rather Than a Catastrophic 15th-Century Collapse. *Proceedings of the National Academy of Sciences of the United States of America* 116(11):4871–4876.

Pérez Consuergra, Sergio G., and Ella Vázquez-Domínguez
2015   Mitochondrial Diversification of the *Peromyscus mexicanus* Species Group in Nuclear Central America: Biogeographic and Taxonomic Implications. *Zoological Systematics and Evolutionary Research* 53(4):300–311.

Pérez Romero, Alberto, and Rafael Cobos P.
1990   Una nota arqueológica respecto a la preferencia de *Theobroma cacao* en las Tierras Bajas Mayas. *Boletín de la Escuela de Ciencias Antropológicas de la Universidad de Yucatán* 17(102):33–66.

Perkins, Dexter, and Kevin R. Henke
2002   *Minerales en Lámina Delgada.* Translated by Manuel Pozo Rodríguez. Prentice Hall, Madrid.

Peterson, Amy A., and A. Townsend Peterson
1992   Aztec Exploitation of Cloud Forests: Tributes of Liquidambar Resin and Quetzal Feathers. *Global Ecology and Biogeography Letters* 2(5):165–173.

Peterson, Larry C., and Gerald H. Haug
2006   Variability in the Mean Latitude of the Atlantic Intertropical Convergence Zone as Recorded by Riverine Input of Sediments to the Cariaco Basin (Venezuela). *Palaeogeography, Palaeoclimatology, Palaeoecology* 234(1):97–113.

Pineda, Juan de
1925   Descripción de la Provincia de Guatemala—Año 1549. In *Anales de la Sociedad de Geografía e Historia*, Vol. I, No. 4, edited by J. Antonio Villacorta C. and José Matos, pp. 327–363. Sociedad de Geografía e Historia de

Guatemala, Guatemala City.

Piperno, Dolores R.
2006   Quaternary Environmental History and Agricultural Impact on Vegetation in Central America. *Annals of the Missouri Botanical Garden* 93(2):274–296.

Piperno, Dolores R., Crystal McMichael, and Mark B. Bush
2015   Amazonia and the Anthropocene: What Was the Spatial Extent and Intensity of Human Landscape Modification in the Amazon Basin at the End of Prehistory? *The Holocene* 25(10):1588–1597.

Piperno, Dolores R., J. Enrique Moreno, Jose Iriarte, Irene Holst, Matthew S. Lachniet, John G. Jones, Anthony J. Ranere, and R. Castanzo
2007   Late Pleistocene and Holocene Environmental History of the Iguala Valley, Central Balsas Watershed of Mexico. *Proceedings of the National Academy of Sciences of the United States of America* 104(29):11874–11881.

Pohl, Mary
1985   An Ethnohistorical Perspective on Ancient Maya Wetland Fields and Other Cultivation Systems in the Lowlands. In *Prehistoric Lowland Maya Environment and Subsistence Economy*, edited by Mary Pohl, pp. 35–45. Papers of the Peabody Museum of Archaeology and Ethnology, Harvard University, Vol. 77. Harvard University Press, Cambridge, Massachusetts.

Pope, Kevin, and Malcolm Sibberenson
1981   In Search of Tzultacaj: Cave Explorations in the Maya Lowlands of Alta Verapaz, Guatemala. *Journal of New World Archaeology* 4(3):16–54.

Poppema, Margriet
2009   Guatemala, the Peace Accords and Education: A Post-Conflict Struggle for Equal Opportunities, Cultural Recognition and Participation in Education. *Globalisation, Societies and Education* 7(4):383–408.

Pound, Frederick J.
1938   Cacao and Witchbroom Disease (*Marasmius perniciosus*) of South America with Notes on Other Species of Theobroma. *Archives of Cocoa Research* 1:20–72.

Price, T. Douglas, and Gary M. Feinman
2008   *Images of the Past*. 5th ed. McGraw Hill, Boston, Massachusetts.

Puga, Diego, and Daniel Trefler
2012   International Trade and Institutional Change: Medieval Venice's Response to Globalization. Working Papers No. 18288. National Bureau of Economic Research, Washington, DC.

Pugh, Timothy
2006   Cacao, Gender, and the Northern Lacandon God House. In *Chocolate in Mesoamerica: A Cultural History of Cacao*, edited by Cameron McNeil, pp. 367–383. University Press of Florida, Gainesville.

Puleston, Dennis E.
1977   The Art and Archaeology of Hydraulic Agriculture in the Maya Lowlands. In *Social Process in Maya Prehistory: Studies in Honor of Sir Eric Thompson*, edited by Norman Hammond, pp. 449–467. Academic Press, New York.

Putzeys, Yvonne, Cindy Flores, and Edgar Telón
2008   Primer Reconocimiento Arqueológico en la Sierra Chinaja, Chisec, Alta

Verapaz. In *XXI Simposio de Investigaciones Arqueológicas en Guatemala, 2007*, edited by Juan Pedro Laporte, Bárbara Arroyo, and Héctor Mejía, pp. 280–299. Museo Nacional de Arqueología y Etnología, Guatemala City.

Pye, Mary E., John E. Clark, and Michael Blake
2016 Conclusions. In *Upper Grijalva River Basin Survey*, edited by Michael Blake, Thomas A. Lee Jr., Mary E. Pye, and John E. Clark, pp. 423–460. Papers of the New World Archaeological Foundation, No. 79. New World Archaeological Foundation, Brigham Young University, Provo, Utah.

Quezada, Maura Liseth, Victor Arroyo-Rodríguez, Evangelina Pérez-Silva, and T. Mitchell Aide
2014 Land Cover Changes in the Lachuá Region, Guatemala: Patterns, Proximate Causes, and Underlying Driving Forces over the Last 50 Years. *Regional Environmental Change* 14(3):1139–1149.

Quintanilla González, Claudia María
2013 Estudio y Análisis de los Enterramientos Humanos del Sitio Arqueológico Cancuen. Licenciatura thesis, Escuela de Historia, Universidad de San Carlos de Guatemala, Guatemala City.

Rands, Robert L.
1969 Relationship of Monumental Stone Sculpture of Copán with the Maya Lowlands. In *Verhandlungen des XXXVIII Internationalen Amerikanistenkongresses, 12 bis 18 August 1968*, Vol. I, pp. 517–529. Klaus Renner Verlag, München.

Rands, Robert L., and Monica Bargielski Weimar
1992 Integrative Approaches in the Compositional Characterization of Ceramic Pastes. In *Chemical Characterization of Ceramic Pastes in Archaeology*, edited by Hector Neff, pp. 31–58. Monographs in World Archaeology, No. 7. Prehistory Press, Madison, Wisconsin.

Rands, Robert L., and Ronald L. Bishop
2003 The Dish-Plate Tradition at Palenque: Continuity and Change. In *Patterns and Processes: A Festschrift in Honor of Dr. Edward V. Sayre*, edited by Lambertus van Zelst, pp. 109–134. Smithsonian Center for Materials Research and Education, Washington, DC.

Rands, Robert L., and Barbara C. Rands
1959 The Incensario Complex of Palenque, Chiapas. *American Antiquity* 25(2):225–236.

Rapp, George
2009 *Archaeomineralogy*. Springer, Heidelberg.

Rathje, William L.
1971 The Origin and Development of Lowland Classic Maya Civilization. *American Antiquity* 36(3):275–285.

Ravelo, Ana Christina, and Claude Hillaire Marcel
2007 The Use of Oxygen and Carbon Isotopes of Foraminifera in Paleoceanography. *Developments in Marine Geology* 1:735–764.

Reents-Budet, Dorie
1994 *Painting the Maya Universe: Royal Ceramics of the Classic Period*. Duke University Press, Durham, North Carolina.

2006   The Social Context of *Kakaw* Drinking among the Ancient Maya. In *Chocolate in Mesoamerica: A Cultural History of Cacao*, edited by Cameron McNeil, pp. 202–223. University Press of Florida, Gainesville.

Reimer, Paula J., Edouard Bard, Alex Bayliss, J. Warren Beck, Paul G. Blackwell, Christopher Bronk Ramsey, Caitlin E. Buck, et al.
2013   IntCal13 and Marine13 Radiocarbon Age Calibration Curves 0–50,000 Years cal BP. *Radiocarbon* 55(4):1869–1887.

de Remesal, Fr. Antonio
1932   *Historia General de las Indias Occidentales, y Particular de la Gobernación de Chiapa y Guatemala.* Sociedad de Geografía e Historia, Vol. V, Tomo II. Biblioteca "Goathemala," Guatemala City.

Remy, Cécile C., Cécile Fouquemberg, Hugo Asselin, Benjamin Andrieux, Gabriel Magnan, Benoît Brossier, Pierre Grondine, et al.
2018   Guidelines for the Use and Interpretation of Palaeofire Reconstructions Based on Various Archives and Proxies. *Quaternary Science Reviews* 193:312–322.

Rice, Prudence M.
1984   Obsidian Procurement in the Central Petén Lakes Region, Guatemala. *Journal of Field Archaeology* 11(2):181–194.
1987   *Pottery Analysis: A Sourcebook.* University of Chicago Press, Chicago, Illinois.
2018   Maya Crocodilians: Intersections of Myth and the Natural World at Early Nixtun-Ch'ich', Petén, Guatemala. *Journal of Archaeological Method and Theory* 25:705–738.

Rice, Prudence M., Helen V. Michel, Frank Asaro, and Fred Stross
1985   Provenience Analysis of Obsidians from the Central Petén Lakes Region, Guatemala. *American Antiquity* 50(3):591–604.

Rice, Prudence M., and Don S. Rice
2004   Late Classic to Postclassic Transformations in the Petén Lakes Region, Guatemala. In *The Terminal Classic in the Maya Lowlands: Collapse, Transition, and Transformation*, edited by Arthur A. Demarest, Prudence M. Rice, and Don S. Rice, pp. 125–139. University Press of Colorado, Boulder.

Rich, Michelle, and David Freidel
2010   Assemblage of Figurines from the Tomb of an Unknown Ruler (AD 550–650), El Perú-Waka', Guatemala. In *Fiery Pool: The Maya and the Mythic Sea*, edited by Daniel Finamore and Stephen D. Houston, pp. 284–287. Yale University Press, New Haven, Connecticut.

Rich, Michelle, and Varinia Matute
2014   The Power of the Past: Crafting Meaning at a Royal Funerary Pyramid. In *The Archaeology at El Perú-Waka': Ancient Maya Performances of Ritual, Memory, and Power*, edited by Olivia C. Navarro-Farr and Michelle Rich, pp. 66–84. University of Arizona Press, Tucson.

Riederer, James
2004   Thin Section Microscopy Applied to the Study of Archaeological Ceramics. *Hyperfine Interactions* 154:143–158.

Ringle, William M., Tomás Gallareta Negrón, and George J. Bey III
1998   The Return of Quetzalcoatl: Evidence for the Spread of a World Religion during the Epiclassic Period. *Ancient Mesoamerica* 9(2):183–232.

Rivero Torres, Sonia E.
1992　*Laguna Miramar, Chiapas, México: Una Aproximación Histórica-Arqueológica de los Lacandones desde el Clásico Temprano.* Serie Antropología, No. 4. Gobierno del Estado de Chiapas, Consejo Estatal de Fomento a la Investigación y Difusión de la Cultura, DIF-Chiapas/Instituto Chiapaneco de Cultura e Instituto Nacional de Antropología e Historia, Tuxtla Gutiérrez.

Robertson, G. Philip
1987　Geostatistics in Ecology: Interpolating with Known Variance. *Ecology* 68(3):744–748.

Rochette, Erick
2014　Out of Control? Rethinking Assumptions about Wealth Goods Production and the Classic Maya. *Ancient Mesoamerica* 25(1):165–185.

Röhrs, Stefan, Caroline Vibert, and Stefan Simon
2020　*μ-XRF Study of Obsidian Blades.* Technical Report 37_052119. Rathgen-Forschungslabor, Staatliche Museen zu Berlin, Berlin.

Romano Pacheco, Arturo, Josefina Bautista Martínez, and María Teresa Jaén Esquivel
2011　*Análisis Craneano de los Restos de la Cueva Las Banquetas, Chiapas.* Colección Científica—Antropología Física, No. 575. Instituto Nacional de Antropología e Historia, Mexico City.

Romero, Luis
1999　La Organización Social del Sitio La Reforma en el Motagua Medio, Zacapa (300 a.C.-900 d.C.): Análisis del patrón de asentamiento y áreas de actividad. Licenciatura thesis, Escuela de Historia, Universidad de San Carlos, Guatemala City.

Rosales de Zea, Carolina, Carlos Avendaño, Rosa Sunum, and María José Hernández
2017　*Aportes para el Manejo Contemporáneo de la Caoba en la Ecoregión Lachuá: Un Legado de la Forestería Ancestral Maya de Nueve Cerros.* Proyecto FODECYT No. 25-2013. Consejo Nacional de Ciencia y Tecnología, Jardín Botánico, Escuela de Biología, CCQQFar, Universidad de San Carlos, Guatemala City.

Rosenmeier, Michael F., David A. Hodell, Mark Brenner, Jason H. Curtis, and Thomas P. Guilderson
2002　A 4000-Year Lacustrine Record of Environmental Change in the Southern Maya Lowlands, Petén, Guatemala. *Quaternary Research* 57(2):183–190.

Ross, Nanci J.
2011　Modern Tree Species Composition Reflects Ancient Maya "Forest Gardens" in Northwest Belize. *Ecological Applications* 21(1):75–84.

Ross, Nanci J., and Thiago F. Rangel
2011　Ancient Maya Agroforestry Echoing through Spatial Relationships in the Extant Forest of NW Belize. *Biotropica* 43(2):141–148.

Rovner, Irwin, and Suzanne Lewenstein
1997　*Maya Stone Tools of Dzibilchaltún, Yucatán, and Becán and Chicanná, Campeche.* Middle American Research Institute Publications, No. 65. Middle American Research Institute, Tulane University, New Orleans, Louisiana.

Roys, Ralph L.
1939 *The Titles of Ebtun*. Carnegie Institute of Washington Publication, No. 505. Carnegie Institution of Washington, Washington, DC.
1967 [1933] *The Book of Chilam Balam of Chumayel*. University of Oklahoma Press, Norman.

Ruane, Jonathan
2019 Archaeological Recording of Ancient Maya Water Management Features. Paper presented at the 84th Annual Meeting of the Society for American Archaeology, Albuquerque, New Mexico.

Rull, Valentí
2019 Drought, Freshwater Availability and Cultural Resilience on Easter Island (SE Pacific) during the Little Ice Age. *The Holocene* 30(5):774–780.

Rybak, Christopher J., Carol Lakota Eastin, and Irma Robbins
2004 Native American Healing Practices and Counseling. *The Journal of Humanistic Counseling, Education and Development* 43(1):25–32.

Sacor Quiché, Hugo Fidel
2007 El Cacao: Producción y comercio durante las épocas Prehispánica y Hispánica en Guatemala. Anuario de la Dirección General del Patrimonio Cultural y Natural, Instituto de Antropología e Historia. *Antropología e Historia de Guatemala* 3(6):97–125.

de Sahagún, Bernardino
1955 *Historia General de las Cosas de Nueva España*. Vol. II. Edición Alfa, Mexico City.
1963 *Florentine Codex: General History of the Things of New Spain; Book 11: Earthly Things*. Translated by Charles E. Dibble and Arthur J. O. Anderson. Monographs of The School of American Research, Number 14, Part XII. University of Utah Press, Salt Lake City.

Saint-Lu, André
1968 *La Vera Paz, Esprit Évangélique et Colonisation*. Centre de Recherches Hispaniques, Paris.

Salazar, Gabriel
2000 Geography of the Lowlands: Gabriel Salazar, 1620. In *Lost Shores, Forgotten Peoples: Spanish Explorations of the South East Maya Lowlands*, edited and translated by Lawrence H. Feldman, pp. 21–54. Duke University Press, Durham, North Carolina.

Sánchez de Aguilar, Pedro
1937 *Informe Contra Idolorum Cultores del Obispado de Yucatán (1555–1648)*. E. G. Riay e Hijos, Mérida, Yucatán, México.

Sanford, Victoria
2003 *Buried Secrets: Truth and Human Rights in Guatemala*. Palgrave Macmillan, New York.

Sapper, Karl
1985 *The Verapaz in the Sixteenth and Seventeenth Centuries: A Contribution to the Historical Geography and Ethnography of Northeastern Guatemala*. Translated by Theodore Gutman. Institute of Archaeology, Occasional Paper No. 13. University of California, Los Angeles.

Saravia, Juan Francisco
2014 Los Monumentos de Raxruha Viejo. In *Proyecto Arqueológico Cancuen, Informe Final No. 13, Temporada 2013*, edited by Arthur A. Demarest and Horacio Martínez Paiz, pp. 71–102. Ministerio de Cultura y Deportes de Guatemala, Guatemala City.
2016 Registro de Estelas y Altares de Sesakkar. In *Proyecto Arqueológico Regional Cancuen, Informe Final No. 15, Temporada 2015*, edited by Arthur A. Demarest, and Horacio Martínez Paiz. Ministerio de Cultura y Deportes de Guatemala, Guatemala City.

Saravia, Miryam
2018 Resultados del Análisis Cerámico de las Operaciones Sessakar 1 y Sessakar 2: Muestra Cerámica Procedente del Sitio Arqueológico Sessakar. In *Proyecto Arqueológico Regional Cancuen, Informe Final No. 17, Temporada 2017: Tomo I—Proyecto Arqueológico Regional Cancuen*, edited by Arthur A. Demarest, Paola Torres, Julien Sion, and Chloé Andrieu, pp. 196–214. Ministerio de Cultura y Deportes de Guatemala, Guatemala City.

Sarmiento, Gustavo, Sergio Gaviria, Henry Hooghiemstra, Juan Carlos Berrio, and Thomas Van der Hammen
2008 Landscape Evolution and Origin of Lake Fúquene (Colombia): Tectonics, Erosion and Sedimentation Processes during the Pleistocene. *Geomorphology* 100(3–4):563–575.

Scarborough, Vernon L.
1998 Ecology and Ritual: Water Management and the Maya. *Latin American Antiquity* 9(2):135–159.
2003 *The Flow of Power: Ancient Water Systems and Landscapes*. SAR Press, Santa Fe, New Mexico.

Scarborough, Vernon L., and David R. Wilcox (editors)
1991 *The Mesoamerican Ballgame*. University of Arizona Press, Tucson.

Schele, Linda, and David Freidel
1990 *A Forest of Kings: The Untold Story of the Ancient Maya*. William Morrow, New York.

Schele, Linda, Nikolai Grube, and Erik Boot
1998 Some Suggestions on the K'atun Prophecies in the Books of Chilam Balam in Light of Classic-Period History. In *Memorias del Tercer Congreso Internacional de Mayistas* (July 9–15, 1995), Vol. 1, pp. 399–432. Instituto de Investigaciones Filológicas, Centro de Estudios Mayas, Universidad Nacional Autónoma de México, Mexico City.

Schele, Linda, and Julia Guernsey Kappelman
2001 What the Heck's Coatépec? The Formative Roots of an Enduring Mythology. In *Landscape and Power in Ancient Mesoamerica*, edited by Rex Koontz, Kathryn Reese-Taylor, and Annabeth Headrick, pp. 29–54. Routledge, New York.

Schele, Linda, and Peter Mathews
1999 *The Code of Kings: The Language of Seven Sacred Maya Temples and Tombs*. Simon and Schuster, New York.

Schele, Linda, and Jefferey Miller
1983 The Mirror, the Rabbit, and the Bundle: "Accession" Expressions from the

Classic Maya Inscriptions. *Studies in Pre-Columbian Art and Archaeology,* Vol. 25. Dumbarton Oaks Research Library and Collection, Washington, DC.

Schmidt, Hans Joachim
1979 Steinskulpturen vom Lago Miramar, Chiapas, Mexiko. *Mexicon* 1(5):62–64.

Schmidt, Peter
1998 Contacts with Central Mexico and the Transition to the Postclassic: Chichén Itzá in Central Yucatán. In *Maya*, edited by Peter Schmidt, Mercedes de la Garza, and Enrique Nalda, pp. 426–449. Rizzoli, New York.

Scholes, France V., and Ralph L. Roys
1968 *The Maya Chontal Indians of Acalan-Tixchel: A Contribution to the History and Ethnography of the Yucatan Peninsula.* 2nd ed. University of Oklahoma Press, Norman.

Schortman, Edward M., and Wendy Ashmore
2012 History, Networks, and the Quest for Power: Ancient Political Competition in the Lower Motagua Valley, Guatemala. *Journal of the Royal Anthropological Institute* 18(1):1–21.

Schortman, Edward M., and Patricia A. Urban
1994 Living on the Edge: Core/Periphery Relations in Ancient Southeastern Mesoamerica. *Current Anthropology* 35(4):401–430.
2011 *Networks of Power: Political Relations in the Late Postclassic Naco Valley.* University Press of Colorado, Boulder.

Schultes, Richard E.
1984 Amazonian Cultigens and Their Northward and Westward Migrations in Pre-Columbian Times. In *Pre-Columbian Plant Migration*, edited by Doris Stone, pp. 69–83. Papers of the Peabody Museum of Archaeology and Ethnology, Vol. 76. Harvard University Press, Cambridge, Massachusetts.

Schuster, Jack C., and Enio B. Cano
2006 What Can Scarabaeoidea Contribute to the Knowledge of the Biogeography of Guatemala? *Coleopterists Society Monograph* 5:57–70.

Schwab, Gregory T.
2013 Maya Cave Art Survey at Nueve Cerros, Alta Verapaz, Guatemala. Master's thesis, Department of Anthropology, St. Cloud State University, St. Cloud, Minnesota.

Schwab, Gregory T., Mark Lentz, Seleste Sanchez, Brent K. S. Woodfill, Mirza Monterroso, and Judith Valle
2012 Espeleoarqueología, Etnohistoria y Etnografía en la Región Nueve Cerros. In *XXV Simposio de Investigaciones Arqueológicas en Guatemala, 2011*, edited by Bárbara Arroyo, Lorena Paiz, and Héctor Mejía, pp. 580–589. Ministerio de Cultura y Deportes, Instituto de Antropología e Historia y Asociación Tikal, Guatemala City.

Sears, Erin L.
2009 Maya Figurines Along the Water Trails of the Chixoy and Pasión. Presented at the 27th Annual Maya Weekend, University of Pennsylvania Museum, Philadelphia.
2016 A Reflection of Maya Representation, Distribution, and Interaction: Ceramic Figurines from the Late Classic Site of Cancuén, Petén Department of

Guatemala. PhD dissertation, Department of Anthropology, University of Kentucky, Lexington.
2017   Mesoamerica—Maya. In *Prehistoric Figurines*, edited by Timothy Insoll, pp. 221–244. Oxford University Press, Oxford.

Sears, Erin L., Nikolai Grube, Alejandro Garay, Brent K. S. Woodfill, and Alexander E. Rivas
2021   A Story of Awe and Clay: Mold-Made Hieroglyphs from Alta Verapaz, Guatemala. *Ancient Mesoamerica* 33(3):417–431.

Sedat, David W., and Robert J. Sharer
1972   Archaeological Investigations in the Northern Maya Highlands: New Data on the Maya Preclassic. In *Studies in the Archaeology of Mexico and Guatemala*, No. 16, edited by John A. Graham, pp. 23–35. University of California Archaeological Research Facility, Department of Anthropology, University of California, Berkeley.

Seler, Eduard
1901   *Die Alten Ansiedlungen von Chaculá im Distrikte Nenton des Departements Huehuetenango der Republik Guatemala*. Dietrich Reimer, Berlin.
1908   Vierter Abschnitt: Archäologisches und Anderes aus den Maya-Ländern. In *Gesammelte Abhandlungen zur Amerikanischen Sprach und Alterthumskunde*, Vol. 3, by Eduard Seler, pp. 561–640. Behrend, Berlin.
1993   Antiquities from the Alta Vera Paz. In *Collected Works in Mesoamerican Linguistics and Archaeology*, Vol. 4, edited by J. Eric S. Thompson and Francis Richardson, pp. 326–337. Labyrinthos, Culver City, California.

Shafer, Harry J., and Thomas R. Hester
1991   The Puleston Axe: A Late Preclassic Maya Hafted Tool from Northern Belize. In *Ancient Maya Wetland Agriculture: Excavations on Albion Island, Northern Belize*, edited by Mary D. Pohl, pp. 279–294. Westview Press, Boulder, Colorado.

Sharer, Robert J.
1983   Interdisciplinary Approaches to the Study of Mesoamerican Highland-Lowland Interaction: A Summary View. In *Highland-Lowland Interaction in Mesoamerican: Interdisciplinary Approaches*, edited by Arthur G. Miller, pp. 241–263. Dumbarton Oaks Research Library and Collection, Washington, DC.
2006   *The Ancient Maya*. 6th ed. Stanford University Press, Stanford, California.

Sharer, Robert J., and David C. Grove (editors)
1989   *Regional Perspectives on the Olmec*. Cambridge University Press, Cambridge.

Sharer, Robert J., and David W. Sedat
1987   *Archaeological Investigations in the Northern Maya Highlands, Guatemala: Interaction and the Development of Maya Civilization*. University Museum Monograph, No. 59. University of Pennsylvania Museum, Philadelphia.

Sidrys, Raymond
1976   Classic Maya Obsidian Trade. *American Antiquity* 41(4):449–464.

Sills, Elizabeth C., and Heather McKillop
2013   Underwater Excavations of Classic Period Salt Works, Paynes Creek National Park, Belize. *Research Reports in Belizean Archaeology, Papers of the 2012 Belize Archaeology Symposium*, Vol. 11, edited by John Morris, Jaime Awe,

Melissa Badillo, and George Thompson, pp. 281–288. Institute of Archaeology, National Institute of Culture and History, Belmopan, Belize.

Sion, Julien, Chloé Andrieu, Paola Torres, and Arthur A. Demarest (editors)
2017 *Proyecto Arqueológico Regional Cancuen, Informe Final No. 16, Temporada de Campo 2016: Tomo II—Proyecto Arqueológico Regional Raxruha Viejo*. Department of Anthropology, Vanderbilt University, Nashville, Tennessee.
2018 *Proyecto Arqueológico Regional Cancuen, Informe Final No. 17, Temporada 2017: Tomo II—Proyecto Arqueológico Regional Raxruha Viejo*. Ministerio de Cultura y Deportes de Guatemala, Guatemala City.

Skidmore, Joel
2010 Royal Tomb Discovered in the Diablo Group at El Zotz, Guatemala. *Mesoweb* (website), accessed April 13, 2022.

Smailus, Ortwin
1975 *El Maya-Chontal de Acalan*. Centro de Estudios Mayas, Cuaderno 9. Universidad Nacional Autónoma de Mexico, Mexico City.

Smith, A. Ledyard
1955 *Archaeological Reconnaissance in Central Guatemala*. Carnegie Institution of Washington Publication, No. 608. Carnegie Institution of Washington, Washington, DC.
1972 *Excavations at Altar de Sacrificios: Architecture, Settlement, Burials, and Caches*. Papers of the Peabody Museum of Archaeology and Ethnology, Harvard University, Vol. 62, No. 2. Peabody Museum, Cambridge, Massachusetts.

Smith, Robert E.
1952 *Pottery from Chipoc, Alta Verapaz, Guatemala*. Carnegie Institution of Washington Publication, No. 596. Carnegie Institution of Washington, Washington, DC.

Snitker, Grant
2018 Identifying Natural and Anthropogenic Drivers of Prehistoric Fire Regimes through Simulated Charcoal Records. *Journal of Archaeological Science* 95:1–15.

Solari, Luigi A., Antonio García-Casco, Uwe Martens, James K. W. Lee, and Amabel Ortega-Rivera
2013 Late Cretaceous Subduction of the Continental Basement of the Maya Block (Rabinal Granite, Central Guatemala): Tectonic Implications for the Geodynamic Evolution of Central America. *Geological Society of America Bulletin* 125(3–4):625–639.

Somerville, Andrew D., Ben A. Nelson, and Kelly J. Knudson
2010 Isotopic Investigation of pre-Hispanic Macaw Breeding in Northwest Mexico. *Journal of Anthropological Archaeology* 29(1):125–135.

Sosa, John R.
1985 Maya Sky, Maya World: A Symbolic Analysis of Yucatec Maya Cosmology. PhD dissertation, Department of Anthropology, State University of New York, Albany.

Stansell, Nathan D., Byron A. Steinman, Mark B. Abbott, Michael Rubinov, and Manuel Roman-Lacayo
2013 Lacustrine Stable Isotope Record of Precipitation Changes in Nicaragua

during the Little Ice Age and Medieval Climate Anomaly. *Geology* 41(2):151–154.

Stansell, Nathan D., Byron A. Steinman, Matthew S. Lachniet, Jacob Feller, William Harvey, Alejandro Fernandez, Christopher J. Shea, et al.

2020 A Lake Sediment Stable Isotope Record of Late-Middle to Late Holocene Hydroclimate Variability in the Western Guatemala Highlands. *Earth and Planetary Science Letters* 542:116327.

Stark, Barbara L., and Alanna Ossa

2007 Ancient Settlement, Urban Gardening, and Environment in the Gulf Lowlands of Mexico. *Latin American Antiquity* 18(4):385–406.

Steinberg, Michael K.

2005 Mahogany (*Swietenia macrophylla*) in the Maya Lowlands: Implications for Past Land Use and Environmental Change? *Journal of Latin American Geography* 4(1):127–134.

Steinbrenner, Larry

2006 Cacao in the Greater Nicoya: Ethnohistory and a Unique Tradition. In *Chocolate in Mesoamerica: A Cultural History of Cacao*, edited by Cameron McNeil, pp. 253–270. University Press of Florida, Gainesville.

Stephens, John L.

1841 *Incidents of Travel in Central America, Chiapas, and Yucatan*. Harper and Brothers, New York.

Stoltman, James B.

1991 Ceramic Petrography as a Technique for Documenting Cultural Interaction: An Example from the Upper Mississippi Valley. *American Antiquity* 56(1):103–120..

Stone, Andrea, and Marc Zender

2011 *Reading Maya Art: A Hieroglyphic Guide to Ancient Maya Painting and Sculpture*. Thames and Hudson, New York.

Storey, Rebecca

1992 *Life and Death in the Ancient City of Teotihuacan: A Modern Paleodemographic Synthesis*. University of Alabama Press, Tuscaloosa.

Stuart, David

2006a The Language of Chocolate: References to Cacao on Classic Maya Drinking Vessels. In *Chocolate in Mesoamerica: A Cultural History of Cacao*, edited by Cameron L. McNeil, pp. 184–201. University Press of Florida, Gainesville.

2006b Jade and Chocolate: Bundles of Wealth in Classic Maya Economics and Ritual. In *Sacred Bundles: Ritual Acts of Wrapping and Binding in Mesoamerica*, edited by Julia Guernsey and F. Kent Reilly, pp 127–144. Ancient America Special Publication, No. 1. Boundary End Archaeology Research Center, Barnardsville, North Carolina.

2012 More on the Paddler Gods. *Maya Decipherment: Ideas on Ancient Maya Writing and Iconography* (blog), July 28 ,2016, accessed April 13, 2022.

Stuiver, Minze, Paula J. Reimer, and Ron W Reimer

2019 CALIB Radiocarbon calibration, revision 7.1.

Suasnávar, José, Alan Robinson, Heidy Quezada, Oscar Ixpatá, Guillermo Vásquez, and Patricia Ixcot

2007   Investigación Antropológico Forense de la Aguada Sur del Sitio Arqueológico Cancuén, Operación 42. *Report on the Proyecto Arqueológico Cancuen, Guatemala*. Fundación de Antropología Forense de Guatemala, Guatemala City.

Sugiyama, Saburo
2005   *Human Sacrifice, Militarism, and Rulership: Materialization of State Ideology at the Feathered Serpent Pyramid, Teotihuacan*. Cambridge University Press, Cambridge.

Sytch, Maxim, Adam Tatarynowicz, and Ranjay Gulati
2012   Toward a Theory of Extended Contact: The Incentives and Opportunities for Bridging Across Network Communities. *Organization Science* 23(6):1658–1681.

Talley, Sharon M., Phyllis D. Coley, and Thomas A. Kursar
2002   The Effects of Weather on Fungal Abundance and Richness among 25 Communities in the Intermountain West. *BMC Ecology* 2(7):1–11.

Tatarynowicz, Adam, Maxim Sytch, and Ranjay Gulati
2016   Environmental Demands and the Emergence of Social Structure: Technological Dynamism and Interorganizational Network Forms. *Administrative Science Quarterly* 61(1):52–86.

Taube, Karl A.
1992   *The Major Gods of Ancient Yucatan*. Studies in Pre-Columbian Art and Archaeology, No. 32. Dumbarton Oaks Research Library and Collection, Washington, DC.
1995   *Aztec and Maya Myths*. University of Texas Press, Austin.

Tedesco, Kathy, Robert Thunell, Yrene Astor, and Frank Muller-Karger
2007   The Oxygen Isotope Composition of Planktonic Foraminifera from the Cariaco Basin, Venezuela: Seasonal and Interannual Variations. *Marine Micropaleontology* 62(3):180–193.

Tedlock, Dennis
1996   *Popol Vuh: The Definitive Edition of the Mayan Book of the Dawn of Life and the Glory of Gods and Kings*. Touchstone, New York.

Tejada Bouscayrol, Mario, and Thomas A. Lee Jr.
2019   *El Camino Real de los Altos de Chiapas a Guatemala*. Dirección General del Diario de Centro América, Tipografía Nacional, Guatemala City.

Thompson, Douglas M.
2003   A Geomorphic Explanation for a Meander Cutoff Following Channel Relocation of a Coarse-Bedded River. *Environmental Management* 31(3):385–400.

Thompson, J. Eric S.
1956   Notes on the Use of Cacao in Middle America. *Notes on Middle American Archaeology and Ethnology* 128(5):95–116.
1985   *Maya Hieroglyphic Writing: An Introduction*. 7th ed. University of Oklahoma Press, Norman.
1990   *Maya History and Religion*. University of Oklahoma Press, Norman.

Thornton, Erin Kennedy, and Arthur A. Demarest
2019   At Water's Edge: Ritual Maya Animal Use in Aquatic Contexts at Cancuen, Guatemala. *Ancient Mesoamérica* 30(3):473–491.

Tiesler, Vera
2012   *Transformarse en Maya: El Modelado Cefálico entre los Mayas Prehispánicos y Coloniales*. Universidad Nacional Autónoma de México, Instituto de Investigaciones Antropológicas y Universidad Autónoma de Yucatán, Mexico City and Mérida.

Tiesler, Vera, and Alfonso Lacadena
2018   Head Shapes and Group Identity on the Fringes of the Maya Lowlands. In *Social Skins of the Head: Body Beliefs and Ritual in Ancient Mesoamerica and the Andes*, edited by Vera Tiesler and María Cecilia Lozada, pp. 37–58. University of New Mexico Press, Albuquerque.

Tokovinine, Alexandre
2002   Divine Patrons of the Maya Ballgame. Mesoweb (website), accessed March 9, 2024.
2012   Writing Color: Words and Images of Colors in Classic Maya Inscriptions. *RES: Anthropology and Aesthetics* 61/62:283–299.

Tokovinine, Alexandre, and Cameron L. McNeil
2012   Colored Things, Chromatic Stories: Searching for the Pigments of the Past. *RES: Anthropology and Aesthetics* 61/62:279–282.

Toledo, Víctor M.
2002   Ethnoecology: A Conceptual Framework for the Study of Indigenous Knowledge of Nature. In *Ethnobiology and Biocultural Diversity: Proceedings of the Seventh International Congress of Ethnobiology*, edited by John R. Stepp, Felice S. Wyndham, and Rebecca K. Zarger, pp. 511–522. University of Georgia Press, Athens.
2009   ¿Por qué los pueblos indígenas son la memoria de la especie? *Papeles de relaciones ecosociales y cambio global* 107:27–38.

Torres, Paola
2011   Los Juegos de Pelota como Evidencia de un Sitio Fronterizo: El Caso de Cancuén. Licenciatura thesis, Escuela de Historia, Universidad de San Carlos, Guatemala City.

Torres, Paola, Arthur A. Demarest, Horacio Martínez Paiz, Juan Francisco Saravia, Miryam Saravia, and Carlos Fidel Tuyuc
2018a Geografía Sagrada, Monumentos e Interacción Política y Económica en la Red Transversal hacia El Caribe: Nuevos datos del epicentro de Sesakkar, Alta Verapaz. In *XXXI Simposio de Investigaciones Arqueológicas en Guatemala, 2017*, edited by Bárbara Arroyo, Luis Méndez Salinas, and Gloria Ajú Álvarez, pp. 689–704. Museo Nacional de Arqueología y Etnología, Guatemala City.

Torres, Paola, Melanie Forné, Carlos Fidel Tuyuc, Miryam Saravia, and Juan Francisco Saravia
2018b Tipología Cerámica de Cancuen: Evidencias de la Relación con los Vecinos Cercanos y Distantes. In *XXXI Simposio de Investigaciones Arqueológicas en Guatemala, 2017*, edited by Bárbara Arroyo, Luis Méndez Salinas, and Gloria Ajú Álvarez, pp. 169–182. Museo Nacional de Arqueología y Etnología, Guatemala City.

Torres, Paola, Miryam Saravia, Juan Francisco Saravia, and Carlos Fidel Tuyuc

2014   Resultados Cerámicos del Sitio de Cancuen y Raxruha Viejo: Perspectivas Generales. In *Proyecto Arqueológico Cancuen, Informe Final No. 13, Temporada 2013*, edited by Arthur A. Demarest and Horacio Martínez Paiz, pp. 187–239. Department of Anthropology, Vanderbilt University, Nashville, Tennessee.

Torres, Paola, Miryam Saravia, Juan Francisco Saravia, and Carlos Fidel Tuyuc
2016   Análisis y Re-análisis de Contextos Especiales Asociados a Pastas Finas dentro del Sitio Arqueológico de Cancuen. In *Proyecto Arqueológico Cancuen, Informe Final No. 15, Temporada 2015*, edited by Arthur A. Demarest and Horacio Martínez Paiz, pp. 293–376. Ministerio de Cultura y Deportes de Guatemala, Guatemala City.

Torres, Paola, and Carlos Fidel Tuyuc
2020   Lin 2: Excavaciones en el grupo "C" del Sitio La Linterna, Chisec, Alta Verapaz. In *Proyecto Arqueológico Regional Cancuen, Informe Final No. 19, Temporada de Campo 2019: Tomo I—Proyecto Arqueológico Regional Cancuen*, edited by Arthur A. Demarest, Paola Torres, Julien Sion, and Chloé Andrieu, pp. 148–167. Ministerio de Cultura y Deportes de Guatemala, Guatemala City.

Torres, Vladimir, Jef Vandenberghe, and Henry Hooghiemstra
2005   An Environmental Reconstruction of the Sediment Infill of the Bogotá Basin (Colombia) During the Last 3 Million Years from Abiotic and Biotic Proxies. *Palaeogeography, Palaeoclimatology, Palaeoecology* 226(1–2):127–148.

Tourtellot, Gair, III, and Jason J. González
2004   The Last Hurrah: Continuity and Transformation at Seibal. In *The Terminal Classic in the Maya Lowlands: Collapse, Transition, and Transformation*, edited by Arthur A. Demarest, Prudence M. Rice, and Don S. Rice, pp. 60–82. University Press of Colorado, Boulder.

Tourtellot, Gair, III, Jeremy A. Sabloff, and Robert Sharick
1978   *Excavations at Seibal, Department of Petén, Guatemala: A Reconnaissance of Cancuen*. Memoirs of the Peabody Museum of Archaeology and Ethnography, Harvard University, Vol. 14, No. 2. Peabody Museum, Cambridge, Massachusetts.

Tourtellot, Gair, III, Marc Wolf, Francisco Estrada Belli, and Norman Hammond
2000   Discovery of Two Predicted Maya Sites in Belize. *Antiquity* 74(285):481–482.

Tovilla, Martín Alfonso
1960   *Relación Histórica Descriptiva de las Provincias de la Verapaz y del Manché Escrita por el Capitán don Martín Alfonso Tovilla ~ Año de 1635*. Edited by France V. Scholes and Eleanor B. Adams. Editorial Universitaria, Guatemala.

2000a   Borderlands: Martin Tovilla, 1635. In *Lost Shores, Forgotten Peoples: Spanish Explorations of the South East Maya Lowlands*, edited and translated by Lawrence H. Feldman, pp. 85–115. Duke University Press, Durham, North Carolina.

2000b   Coming of the Soldiers: Martin Tovilla, 1635. In *Lost Shores, Forgotten Peoples: Spanish Explorations of the South East Maya Lowlands*, edited and translated by Lawrence H. Feldman, pp. 116–150. Duke University Press, Durham, North Carolina.

Tozzer, Alfred M.
1907 *A Comparative Study of the Mayas and the Lacandones.* Macmillan, New York.
Tozzer, Alfred M. (editor)
1941 *Landa's Relación de las Cosas de Yucatan: A Translation.* Edited with notes by Alfred M. Tozzer. Papers of the Peabody Museum of American Archaeology and Ethnology, Harvard University, Vol. 18. Peabody Museum Press, Cambridge, Massachusetts.
1975 *Landa's Relación de las Cosas de Yucatán.* Translated by Alfred M. Tozzer. Reprinted. Kraus Reprint Company, Millwood, New York. Originally published 1941, Papers of the Peabody Museum of Archaeology and Ethnology, Harvard University, Vol. 18. Peabody Museum Press, Cambridge, Massachusetts.
Traverse, Alfed
2007 *Paleopalynology.* Springer, Dordrecht.
Tremain, Cara Grace
2016 Birds of a Feather: Exploring the Acquisition of Resplendent Quetzal (*Pharomachrus mocinno*) Tail Coverts in Pre-Columbian Mesoamerica. *Human Ecology* 44:399–408.
Trik, Aubrey S.
1963 The Splendid Tomb of Temple I at Tikal, Guatemala. *Expedition* 6(1):2–19. University of Pennsylvania Museum of Archaeology and Anthropology (website), accessed March 12, 2024.
Tuba, Zoltán, Nancy G. Slack, and Lloyd R. Stark
2011 *Bryophyte Ecology and Climate Change.* Cambridge University Press, Cambridge.
Tweddle, John C., and Kevin J. Edwards
2010 Pollen Preservation Zones as an Interpretative Tool in Holocene Palynology. *Review of Palaeobotany and Palynology* 161(1–2):59–76.
Ulloa, Carmen Ulloa
2001 Myricaceae. In *Flora de Nicaragua*, edited by Warren Douglas Stevens, Carmen Ulloa Ulloa, Amy Pool, and Olga M. Montiel, pp. 1541–1542. Monographs in Systematic Botany from the Missouri Botanical Garden, Vol. 85. Missouri Botanical Garden Press, St. Louis.
Uzzi, Brian
1996 The Sources and Consequences of Embeddedness for the Economic Performance of Organizations: The Networks Effect. *American Sociological Review* 61(4):674–698.
Vaasma, Tiit
2008 Grain-Size Analysis of Lacustrine Sediments: A Comparison of Pre-Treatment Methods. *Estonian Journal of Ecology* 57(4):231–243.
Vachula, Richard S., and Nora Richter
2018 Informing Sedimentary Charcoal-Based Fire Reconstructions with a Kinematic Transport Model. *The Holocene* 28(1):173–178.
Vachula, Richard S., James M. Russell, Yongsong Huang, and Nora Richter
2018 Assessing the Spatial Fidelity of Sedimentary Charcoal Size Fractions as Fire History Proxies with a High-Resolution Sediment Record and Historical Data. *Palaeogeography, Palaeoclimatology, Palaeoecology* 508:166–175.

Vail, Gabrielle
2009　Cacao Use in Yucatán Among the Pre-Hispanic Maya. In *Chocolate: History, Culture, and Heritage*, edited by Louis Evan Grivetti and Howard-Yana Shapiro, pp. 3–15. John Wiley and Sons, Hoboken, New Jersey.
2013　*Códice de Madrid*. Publicaciones Mesoamericanas, Universidad Mesoamericana, Guatemala City.
2022　*Códice de Dresde: Introducción y Comentarios*. Publicaciones Mesoamericanas, Universidad Mesoamericana, Guatemala City.

Vail, Gabrielle, and Christine Hernández
2013　*Re-Creating Primordial Time: Foundation Rituals and Mythology in the Postclassic Maya Codices*. University Press of Colorado, Boulder.

Valdez, Fred, Jr., and Shirley Mock
1991　Additional Considerations for Prehispanic Salt-Making in Belize. *American Antiquity* 56(3):520–525.

Valle, Judith, Brent K. S. Woodfill, and Carlos Efrain Tox (editors)
2017　*Proyecto Arqueologico Salinas de los Nueve Cerros, Informe Final de Temporada 2017*. Department of Anthropology, Georgia State University, Atlanta.

van Geel, Bas, Jan Peter Pals, Guido B. A. van Reenen, and Ko Van Huissteden
1995　The Indicator Value of Fossil Fungal Remains, Illustrated by a Palaeoecological Record of a Late Eemian/Early Weichselian Deposit in the Netherlands. *Mededelingen Rijks Geologische Dienst* 52:297–315.

Van Hall, Constant Johan Jacob
1914　*Cocoa*. Macmillan, London.

Vannucchi, Paola, Simone Galeotti, Peter D. Clift, César R. Ranero, and Roland von Huene
2004　Long-Term Subduction-Erosion along the Guatemalan Margin of the Middle America Trench. *Geology* 32(7):617–620.

Vargas Pacheco, Ernesto
2001　*Itzamkanac y Acalan: Tiempos de Crisis Anticipado el Futuro*. Instituto de Investigaciones Antropológicas, Universidad Nacional Autónoma de México, Mexico City.

Vázquez, Fr. Francisco
1938　*Crónica de la Provincia del Santísimo Nombre de Jesús de Guatemala*. Sociedad de Geografía e Historia Vol. XV, Tomo II. Biblioteca "Goathemala", Guatemala City.

Vázquez de Ágredos Pascual, María Luisa, Antonio Fernando Batista dos Santos, and Dolores Julia Yusá Marco
2010　Annatto in America and Europe: Tradition, Treatises and Elaboration of an Ancient Colour. *Arché: Publicación del Instituto Universitario de Restauración del Patrimonio de la UPV* (4/5):97–102.

Velásquez Muñoz, Juan Luis
1995　Nuevas Evidencias de la Ocupación del Lago de Izabal-Río Dulce y Este del Río Polochic. Licenciatura thesis, Escuela de Historia, Universidad de San Carlos de Guatemala, Guatemala City.

de Viana, Francisco, Lucas Gallego, and Guillén Cadena
1982　Relación de la Provincia y Tierra de la Verapaz (1574). In *Relaciones*

geográficas del siglo XVI: Guatemala, edited by René Acuña, pp. 204–22. Universidad Nacional Autónoma de México, Mexico City.

Villagutierre Soto-Mayor, Juan de
1983   *History of the Conquest of the Province of the Itza*. Translated by Robert D. Wood, and edited by Frank E. Comparato. Labyrinthos, Culver City, California.

Vogt, Evon Z.
1969   *Zinacantan: A Maya Community in the Highlands of Chiapas*. Belknap Press of Harvard University, Cambridge, Massachusetts.

Wahl, David, Roger Byrne, and Lysanna Anderson
2014   An 8700 Year Paleoclimate Reconstruction from the Southern Maya Lowlands. *Quaternary Science Reviews* 103:19–25.

Wahl, David, Roger Byrne, Thomas Schreiner, and Richard Hansen
2007   Palaeolimnological Evidence of Late-Holocene Settlement and Abandonment in the Mirador Basin, Petén, Guatemala. *The Holocene* 17(6):813–820.

Walker, Lawrence R., and Joanne M. Sharpe
2010   Ferns, Disturbance and Succession. In *Fern Ecology*, edited by Klaus Mehltreter, Lawrence R. Walker, and Joanne M. Sharpe, pp. 177–219. Cambridge University Press, Cambridge.

Wallace, Dwight T.
1977   An Intra-Site Locational Analysis of Utatlán: The Structure of an Urban Site. In *Archaeology and Ethnohistory of the Central Quiché*, edited by Dwight T. Wallace and Robert M. Carmack, pp. 20–54. Institute for Mesoamerican Studies, Publication No. 1. State University of New York, Albany.

Warrier, Anish Kumar, Hermant Pednekar, Badanal S. Mahesh, Rahul Mohan, and Sahina Gazi
2016   Sediment Grain Size and Surface Textural Observations of Quartz Grains in Late Quaternary Lacustrine Sediments from Schirmacher Oasis, East Antarctica: Paleoenvironmental Significance. *Polar Science* 10(1):89–100.

Watanabe, John M.
1990   From Saints to Shibboleths: Image, Structure, and Identity in Maya Religious Syncretism. *American Ethnologist* 17(1):131–150.

Wauchope, Robert
1975   *Zacualpa, El Quiche, Guatemala: An Ancient Provincial Center of the Highland Maya*. Middle American Research Institute Publications, No. 39. Middle American Research Institute, Tulane University, New Orleans, Louisiana.

Webster, David, Barbara Fash, Randolph Widmer, and Scott Zeleznik
1998   The Skyband Group: Investigation of a Classic Maya Elite Residential Complex at Copán, Honduras. *Journal of Field Archaeology* 25(3):319–343.

Weeks, John M.
1983   Chisalin: Una Comnunidad Ilocab Quiché del Siglo XVI. In *Nuevas Perspectivas Sobre el Popol Vuh*, edited by Robert M. Carmack and Francisco Morales, pp. 255–269. Piedra Santa, Guatemala.

Wells, E. Christian, and Karla L. Davis-Salazar (editors)
2007   *Mesoamerican Ritual Economy: Archaeological and Ethnological Perspectives*. University Press of Colorado, Boulder.

Wendt, Tom
1989 Las selvas de Uxpanapa, Veracruz-Oaxaca, México: Evidencia de refugios florísticos cenozoicos. *Anales del Instituto de Biología, Universidad Nacional Autónoma de México, Serie Botánica* 58:29–54.

White, Christine D., Paul F. Healey, and Henry P. Schwarcz
1993 Intensive Agriculture, Social Status, and Maya Diet at Pacbitun, Belize. *Journal of Anthropological Research* 49(4):347–375.

Whitney, Bronwen S., and Macarena L. Cárdenas
2017 Legacies of Pre-Columbian Land Use on Latin American Ecosystem Composition and Diversity: A Case for Paleoecology. *Past Global Changes Magazine* 25(2):84–85.

Whittington, Kjersten Bunker, Jason Owen-Smith, and Walter W. Powell
2009 Networks, Propinquity, and Innovation in Knowledge-Intensive Industries. *Administrative Science Quarterly* 54(1):90–122.

Willey, Gordon R.
1953 *Prehistoric Settlement Patterns in the Virú Valley, Perú.* Bureau of American Ethnology Bulletin, No. 155. Smithsonian Institution, Washington, DC.
1973 *The Altar de Sacrificios Excavations: General Summary and Conclusions.* Papers of the Peabody Museum of Archaeology and Ethnology, Harvard University, Vol. 64, No. 3. Peabody Museum Press, Cambridge, Massachusetts.
1990 *Excavations at Seibal, Department of Petén, Guatemala: General Summary and Conclusions.* Memoirs of the Peabody Museum of Archaeology and Ethnology, Harvard University, Vol. 17, No. 4. Peabody Museum Press, Cambridge, Massachusetts.

Willey, Gordon R., A. Ledyard Smith, William R. Bullard, and John A. Graham
1960 Altar de Sacrificios, A Prehistoric Maya Crossroads. *Archaeology* 13(2):110–117.

Wilmshurst, Janet M., and Matt S. McGlone
2005 Corroded Pollen and Spores as Indicators of Changing Lake Sediment Sources and Catchment Disturbance. *Journal of Paleolimnology* 34(4):503–517.

Wilson, Richard
1999 *Maya Resurgence in Guatemala: Q'eqchi' Experiences.* University of Oklahoma Press, Norman.

Wimmer, Alexis
2004 Dictionnaire de la langue Nahuatl classique. Malinal.net (website)accessed March 5, 2024.

Wölfel, Ulrich
2015 Reconocimiento Arqueológico en la Región de Chaculá. In *Proyecto Arqueológico de la Región de Chaculá, Reporte de las Actividades de Campo de la Temporada 2014*, edited by Ulrich Wölfel and Paola Torres, pp. 7–46. Report presented to the Instituto de Antropología e Historia de Guatemala, Guatemala City.
2019 Reconocimiento Arqueológico en la Región de Chacula. In *Proyecto Arqueológico de la Región de Chacula, Reporte de las Actividades de Campo de la Temporada 2018*, edited by Ulrich Wölfel and Byron Hernández, pp. 7–24.

Report presented to the Instituto de Antropología e Historia de Guatemala, Guatemala City.

2022 *Contextualización del Reconocimiento Arqueológico de Eduard Seler en la Región de Chaculá, Departamento de Huehuetenango, Guatemala.* Archaeopress Pre-Columbian Archaeology, No. 16. Archaeopress, Oxford.

Wölfel, Ulrich, and Elisabeth Wagner

2010 In the Realm of the Chan Ajaw. Paper presented at the 15th European Maya Conference, Madrid, Spain.

Wood, G. A. R., and R. Antony Lass

1985 *Cocoa.* Tropical Agriculture Series. 4th ed. Longman, London.

Woodfill, Brent K. S.

2007 Shrines of the Pasión-Verapaz Region, Guatemala: Ritual and Exchange along an Ancient Trade Route. PhD dissertation, Department of Anthropology, Vanderbilt University, Nashville, Tennessee.

2010 *Ritual and Trade in the Pasión-Verapaz Region, Guatemala.* Vanderbilt Institute of Mesoamerican Archaeology Series, Vol. 6. Vanderbilt University Press, Nashville, Tennessee.

2011a The Central Role of Cave Archaeology in the Reconstruction of Classic Maya Culture History and Highland-Lowland Interaction. *Ancient Mesoamerica* 22(2):213–227.

2011b Introducción a la Temporada 2011. In *Proyecto Salinas de los Nueve Cerros, Informe Preliminar No. 2, Temporada 2011,* edited by Brent Woodfill, Mirza Monterroso, Blanca Mijangos, Judith Valle, and Carlos Efraín Tox Tiul, pp. 1–9. University of Louisiana at Lafayette.

2014 Three Previously Unrecorded Cave Features in the Western Highlands of Guatemala. *Mexicon* 36(4):114–120.

2019a *War in the Land of True Peace: The Fight for Maya Sacred Places.* University of Oklahoma Press, Norman.

2019b *Improved Understanding of Regional Trade and Development from the Emergency Salvage of a Late Classic Site.* National Science Foundation (NSF) Rapid Final Report, NSF# 1840898.

2020 Large-Scale Production of Basic Commodities at Salinas de los Nueve Cerros, Guatemala: Implications for Ancient Maya Political Economy. In *The Real Business of Ancient Maya Economies: From Farmers' Fields to Rulers' Realms,* edited by Marilyn A. Masson, David A. Freidel, and Arthur A. Demarest, pp. 172–183. University Press of Florida, Gainesville.

Woodfill, Brent K. S., and Chloé Andrieu

2012 Tikal's Early Classic Domination of the Great Western Trade Route: Ceramic, Lithic, and Iconographic Evidence. *Ancient Mesoamerica* 23(2):189–209.

Woodfill, Brent K. S., Brian D. Dillon, Marc Wolf, Carlos Avendaño, and Ronald Canter

2015 Salinas de los Nueve Cerros, Guatemala: A Major Economic Center in the Southern Maya Lowlands. *Latin American Antiquity* 26(2):162–179.

Woodfill, Brent K. S., Stanley Guenter, and Mirza Monterroso

2012 Changing Patterns of Ritual Activity in an Unlooted Cave in Central Guatemala. *Latin American Antiquity* 23(1):93–119.

Woodfill, Brent K. S., Nicolas Miller, Margaret Tarpley, and Amalia Kenward
2003   Investigaciones Subterráneas y de Superficie en Chisec, Alta Verapaz y La Caoba, Sayaxché, Petén. In *Proyecto Arqueológico Cancuen, Informe No. 4, Temporada 2002*, edited by Arthur A. Demarest, Tomás Barrientos, Brigitte Kovacevich, Michael Callaghan, and Luis F. Luin, pp. 373–414. Department of Anthropology, Vanderbilt University, Nashville, Tennessee, and Instituto de Antropología e Historia, Guatemala.

Woodfill, Brent K. S., Mirza Monterroso, Erin L. Sears, Donaldo Castillo, and José Luis Garrido López
2011   Proyecto Salinas de los Nueve Cerros: Resultados de la Primera Temporada de Campo, 2010. In *XXIV Simposio de Investigaciones Arqueológicas en Guatemala, 2010*, edited by Bárbara Arroyo, Lorena Paiz Aragón, Adriana Linares Palma, and Ana Lucía Arroyave, pp. 126–137. Museo Nacional de Arqueología y Etnología, Guatemala City.

Woodfill, Brent K. S., Alexander E. Rivas, Judith Valle, and Carlos Efraín Tox Tiul
2017   Investigaciones Regionales, Espeleología y Trabajo Comunitario de Salinas de los Nueve Cerros: La Importancia de Acercamientos Comunitarios en la Arqueología Guatemalteca. In *XXX Simposio de Investigaciones Arqueológicas en Guatemala, 2016*, edited by Bárbara Arroyo, Luis Méndez Salinas, and Gloria Ajú Álvarez, pp. 393–400. Museo Nacional de Arqueología y Etnología, Guatemala City.

Woodfill, Brent K. S., and Judith Valle
2016   El Papel Económico de Salinas de los Nueve Cerros y Sus Vecinos a Través de la Historia. In *XXIX Simposio de Investigaciones Arqueológicas en Guatemala, 2015*, edited by Bárbara Arroyo, Luis Méndez Salinas, and Gloria Ajú Álvarez, pp. 205–214. Museo Nacional de Arqueología y Etnología, Guatemala City.

Woodfill, Brent K. S., Judith Valle, Edgar H. Carpio Rezzio, Socorro Jiménez de Pilar, Megan E. Leight, Katerín Molina, William Odum, Alexander E. Rivas, and Carlos Efraín Tox Tiul
2018   Salinas de los Nueve Cerros: Nuevos Datos, Nuevas Interpretaciones. In *XXXI Simposio de Investigaciones Arqueológicas en Guatemala, 2017*, edited by Bárbara Arroyo, Luis Méndez Salinas, and Gloria Ajú Álvarez, pp. 183–192. Museo Nacional de Arqueología y Etnología, Guatemala City.

Woodfill, Brent K. S., Judith Valle, Blanca Mijangos, Walter Burgos, and Leslie Clements
2013   Salinas de los Nueve Cerros: Un Centro de Producción e Intercambio entre Fronteras. In *XXVI Simposio de Investigaciones Arqueológicas en Guatemala, 2012*, edited by Bárbara Arroyo and Luis Méndez Salinas, pp. 235–246. Museo Nacional de Arqueología y Etnología, Guatemala City.

Wright, V. Paul, and Susan B. Marriott
1993   The Sequence Stratigraphy of Fluvial Depositional Systems: The Role of Floodplain Sediment Storage. *Sedimentary Geology* 86(3–4):203–210.

Wu, Li, Linying Li, Hui Zhou, Xinyuan Wang, and Guangsheng Zhang
2019   Holocene Fire in Relation to Environmental Change and Human Activity Reconstructed from Sedimentary Charcoal of Chaohu Lake, East China. *Quaternary International* 507:62–73.

Ximénez, Fr. Francisco
ca. 1710 Empiezan las Historias del Origen de los Indios de esta Provincia de Guatemala. Facsímile manuscript, Ayer MS 1515., Newberry Library, Chicago, Illinois.
1929–31 *Historia de la Provincia de San Vicente de Chiapa y Guatemala de la Orden de los Predicadores*. Sociedad de Geografía e Historia, Tomos I-III. Biblioteca "Goathemala," Guatemala City.

Xu, Haiming, Shang-Ping Xie, Yuqing Wang, and R. Justin Small
2005 Effects of Central American Mountains on the Eastern Pacific Winter ITCZ and Moisture Transport. *Journal of Climate* 18(18):3856–3873.

Ziyad, Elias R.
2014 Relationship between Tectonic Activity, Fluvial System and River Morphology in the Dohuk Catchment, Iraqi Kurdistan. *Géomorphologie: Relief, Processus, Environment* 20(1):91–100.

Zucker, Lynne G.
1986 Production of Trust: Institutional Sources of Economic Structure, 1840–1920. In *Research in Organizational Behavior*, Vol. 8, edited by Barry M. Staw and L. L. Cummings, pp. 53–111. Working Paper Series, No. 82. JAI Press, Greenwich, Connecticut.

Contributors

Chloé Andrieu is a researcher for the French National Centre for Scientific Research and Université Paris 1 Panthéon-Sorbonne.

Claudia Arriaza is the director of the Proyecto Arqueológico de Rescate Antigua Guatemala Finca Desengaño 1.

Carlos Avendaño is the research coordinator of the Earth Sciences and Local Sovereignty Group and a sessional lecturer at University of San Carlos of Guatemala, the University of Toronto, and George Brown College in Canada.

Juan Carlos Berrio is a biologist, researcher, and lecturer at School of Geography, Geology and Environment, University of Leicester, United Kingdom.

Mónica María Cajas Castillo is a biologist with the University of San Carlos of Guatemala.

Edgar H. Carpio Rezzio is a professor of anthropology in the history department at the University of San Carlos of Guatemala. He is the author of *La Relación Kaminaljuyu/Teotihuacan* and *El Estudio Arqueológico de la Obsidiana en Guatemala*.

Sharon A. Cowling is an associate professor in the Department of Earth Sciences at the University of Toronto.

Carla Paola del Cid López is a biologist and professor of sciences with the faculty of humanities at the University of San Carlos of Guatemala.

Arthur A. Demarest is the Ingram Professor of Anthropology and director of the Vanderbilt Institute of Mesoamerican Archaeology at Vanderbilt University. He is the author of *The Petexbatun Regional Archaeological Project: A Multidisciplinary Study of the Maya Collapse* and *Ancient Maya: The Rise* *and Fall of a Rainforest Civilization* and is coeditor of *The Terminal Classic in the Maya Lowlands: Collapse, Transition, and Transformation* and *The Real Business of Ancient Maya Economies: From Farmers' Fields to Rulers' Realms*, among other works.

Silvia Carolina Duarte Morales is a faculty member in the School of Biology at the University of San Carlos of Guatemala.

Caitlin Earley is an assistant professor of art history at the University of Washington. She is the author of *The Comitán Valley: Sculpture and Identity on the Maya Frontier*.

Sarah Finkelstein is professor and chair of the Department of Earth Sciences at the University of Toronto.

Socorro Jiménez Álvarez is a research professor in the archaeology program at the Autonomous University of the Yucatan. She is the coeditor of *Diálogo Entre Saberes: Estudios Interdisciplinarios en Arqueología*.

Megan E. Leight is a teaching assistant professor of art history in the School of Art and Design at West Virginia University.

Mark W. Lentz is an associate professor of history at Utah Valley University. He is the author of *Murder in Mérida, 1792: Violence, Factions, and the Law* and the coeditor of *City Indians in Spain's American Empire: Urban Indigenous Society in Colonial Mesoamerica and Andean South America, 1530–1810*.

Nora Machuca Mejía is a biologist from the University of San Carlos of Guatemala and the University of Costa Rica specializing in the comprehensive management of water resources.

Diana Méndez Lee is a PhD student in the Department of Anthropology at the University of California, Riverside.

Claudia L. M. Morales-Flores is a biologist, cofounder of Biosfera GT, and research associate in the Center for Conservation Studies at the University of San Carlos of Guatemala.

Jorge Mario Ortíz de León is a field archaeologist for the Tayasal Archaeological Project and ceramicist for the Salinas de los Nueve Cerros project in Guatemala.

Alexander E. Rivas is an anthropologist working as a senior user experience researcher at Ventera in Florida.

Oscar A. Rojas-Castillo is a postdoctoral fellow studying freshwater biology in the Department of Biology at the University of Copenhagen, Denmark.

Carolina Rosales de Zea is the director of the botanical garden at the University of San Carlos of Guatemala, where she also teaches classes as part of the Faculty of Chemical Sciences and Pharmacology.

Juan Francisco Saravia is a field archaeologist and ceramic analyst at the Cancuen and Raxruha Viejo Regional Archaeological Project.

Miryam Saravia is a field archaeologist and ceramic analyst at the Cancuen and Raxruha Viejo Regional Archaeological Project.

Erin L. Sears is a research associate at the Department of Anthropology, National Museum of Natural History, Smithsonian Institution, Washington, DC. She is the coeditor of *Contextualizing Museum Collections at the Smithsonian Institution: The Relevance of Collections-Based Research in the Twenty-First Century*.

Rosa Delfina Sunum Orellana is the head biologist of the Climate Change Department at the National Forest Institute of Guatemala. She is the author of *Hongos Comestibles del Corredor Biológico del Bosque Nuboso y de la Reserva de Biósfera Maya: Recetas Tradicionales* and *Líquenes de Guatemala: Historia Natural y Lista Actualizada*.

Paola Torres is the codirector and ceramicist of the Cancuen Regional Archaeological Project and professor in the School of History of the University of San Carlos of Guatemala.

Ramiro Tox was auxiliary mayor of the Laguna Ecoregion, Guatemala, and the president of the NGO Q'eqchi' Maya heritage organization, the Asociación No Lucrativo Aj Waklisenel Franja Transversal del Norte (ADAWA). He served as the community liaison for the Salinas de los Nueve Cerros Project for many years before his untimely and tragic death in 2020 from COVID-19.

Carlos Fidel Tuyuc Nij is a ceramicist and laboratory director for the Cancuen Regional Archaeological Project and professor at the University of San Carlos of Guatemala.

Ruud van Akkeren is an associate researcher in the Centro de Investigaciones, Arqueológicas y Antropológicas at the Universidad del Valle in Guatemala. He is the author of numerous books, among them *Maya Studies with the Maya* and *Los Mayas Nunca se Fueron, Hoy Hablan Q'eqchi'*.

Marc Wolf is a GIS specialist working as an archeologist in the Conecuh Ranger District of the National Forests in Alabama with the US Forest Service.

Ulrich Wölfel is a researcher affiliated with the Department of Ancient American Studies at the University of Bonn. He is the author of *Contextualización del Reconocimiento Arqueológico de Eduard Seler en la Región de Chaculá, Departamento de Huehuetenango, Guatemala*.

Brent K. S. Woodfill is professor of anthropology at Winthrop University. He is the author of *War in the Land of True Peace: The Fight for Maya Sacred Places* and *Ritual and Trade in the Pasión-Verapaz Region, Guatemala* and is the coeditor of *Archaeology in a Living Landscape: Envisioning Nonhuman Persons in the Indigenous Americas*.

Index

Page numbers in italics refer to illustrations.

Acallan, Verapaz, 257, 258, 259
Acallan Maya: Acallan homeland and expansions, map of, *257*, 259; Chontal speaking, 258; narrative in *Memorial de Sololá*, 259
accelerator mass spectrometry (AMS), 214
achiote (*Bixa orellana L.*): bloodletting ritual, *Codex Tro-Cortesianus* (*Madrid Codex*), *155*; exportation of, 159; in household gardens, 238; trade of, 170; *Triada del chocolate* (achiote, cacao, and vanilla), 238; use as red colorant, 105, 155, 158
Adams, Richard, E. W., 15–16
Aguada Fenix, 14
aguada (water reservoir), 52, 138–139; figurines recovered from, 125, 128
Aguateca, 24
Ah Q'anil and Ah Toltekat *chinamits* (lineage groups), 70
Ah Xoy Maya, 237
Ajaw K'iche' lineage, founding of K'iche' confederation, 268
ajaw (lord), 166. See also *kaloomte* (high king); *k'uhul ajaw* (holy lord); *yajaw* (subordinate noble)
Akalaha Ch'ol, 163–164, 243
alcalde mayor, Colonial Period magistrate, 174
alfardas (balustrades), 95
Altar de Sacrificios: Altar Vase, Maya Late Classic period, polychrome ceramic, Tomb 96, *80*; ceramic exchange with Chama Valley, 67, 79, 86; at confluence of Salinas and Pasión Rivers, 85; Harvard project, 79; and Northern Transversal Strip, 1; tombs with Verapaz-style ceramics and figurines from larger exchange network, 67
Alta Verapaz ceramics: "Altar Verapaz" style figurines as musical ocarinas, 82; Coban 2 complex, 110; depictions of God L, *133*, 135; Jaguar-Way figurines from Chama and Nueve Cerros, *131, 133*, 134; polychrome ceramics, 97, 116, 132, 134; porous paste, 55
Alta Verapaz Region: central Peten interactions with, 109; differing ecological and cultural zones, 178; Fray Bartolomé de las Casas (municipality), 107; material culture, 50; ritual ceremonies in large cave systems, 121. See also Hun Nal Ye stone coffer
Alvarado, Pedro, 69
Andrews, Anthony, 70, 159, 275
Angkor, 223
Annals of the Cakchiquels, 68
Aq'aab (Night People), 262
Aragón, 81–83, 128–129, 171
Arnauld, Marie-Charlotte, 16, 72, 73
Arrayán tree, 231
Arroyo, Bárbara, 148

Index

Atitlan, Lake and Basin, 21, 72, 73
Atz'am K'em, 96
axis-mundi, 193–194
Aztec Empire, 25, 156, 170–172, 186, 195–196, 197, 256. *See also* Tenochtitlan

bajos (swamps), 52
bakab' (Sky deities), 100, 261. *See also* Hozanek, cardinal direction; *k'uhul bakab'*
B'alam K'itze', founding father of the Kaweq, 249
Balam Q'e, 268, 270. *See also* Ik'i Balam
Balbatzuul, Q'eqchi' toponym, 251
ballcourts: Cancuen, 46, 48, 53, 61, *61*, 114, 182, 251, 253, 262; Chich'en, Coban Plateau, 81; Chichen Itza Great Ballcourt, 253, 262; Chinkultic, Chiapas, Mexico, 100; Chitomax 1, 77; Chuitinamit, 70; *citlaltlachtli* (Stellar Ballcourt), 252; El Jocote, 76; as figurative entrance to Underworld, 154, *154*, 158; Grijalva Basin, 95; Guayabal (half), 95; I-shaped, 78, 96; *Popol Vuh*, 250, 251; Quen Santo Group B, 93, *94*, *95*, 99–100; Q'umarkaj, 69; role in religious-political performances, 100; Sakajut, 81; Salinas de los Nueve Cerros, sacred directionality, 200, *202*, 203–205; as shape of furrow on maize field, 263; of Tajal Chan Ahk, 184; Toniná, 100; Verapaz/Quiche style feasting ballcourt, 61, *61*; Yalambojoch, 92
ballgame, *47*, 139, 259, 262–263
barrios (neighborhoods): Cancuen, 258; Salinas de los Nueve Cerros, 211; Santo Tomás Nim Xol, Coban, 250, 258
Barthes, Roland, 177, 199
Barton Ramie, Belize, 191
Battz, Cristóbal, 175–176
Becker, Marshall J., 191
Belize, 156, 159–160, 168, 179, 195
Bentham, Jeremy, 177
Bilbao, Guatemala, 273, *273*

Biotopo del quetzal, Verapaz, 17
Bishop, Ronald, 114
Blake, Michael, 101
Bolonte' Witz. *See* Salinas de los Nueve Cerros
Bonampak, 132, 172
Books of Chilam Balam, 271, 275; of Chumayel, 249, 259, 261; of Mani, 257; of Yucatan, 271
Boot, Eric, 261, 265, 266
Brady, James E., 87, 99
Braswell, Geoffrey, 145, 150
Braudel, Fernand, 249
breakaway networks, 42–43. *See also* Cancuen/Transversal breakaway network
Bryant, Douglas Donne, 90, 101
bundles, 166, 172, 253, *254*, 263
Burkitt, Robert, 79, 134, 135

cacao (*Theobroma cacao* or *pataxte*): agricultural commodity in Northern Transversal Strip, 4, 8, 105, 152–153, 159; association with Underworld and birth of Maize God, 154; bundled for trade, 172; combined with addition of achiote and chile to make drink resembling blood, 158; Criollo cacao (*Theobroma cacao* spp. cacao), 239; Forastero cacao, 239; grown in seventeenth century, 172–173; illicit trade among Maya and Spaniards, 172–175; importance to sacred and utilitarian economy, 181–182; Late Classic polychrome vessel scene with, 154, *154*, 158; origins, discussions of, 238–239; primary and secondary cacao growing regions, *153*, 156; production before and after Spanish conquest, 156, 158; production from pods and seeds ("beans"), 154; in scenes of abundance, 158; as tribute item, medicine, ritual offering, and form of currency and exchange, 158, 172; Trinitario cacao, 239; wild cacao growth in microclimates, 156
Cahabon, Verapaz, 165

Cahaboneros, 173
Calakmul, 167, 247, 258
Camela, Guatemala, 84–85
camino real (royal road), 98
Cancuen, ceramics, 105, 107, 109, *110*; evidence of exchange, 114–116, 118; figurines, 82, *127*, 128, *133*, 134–136, 138–139; history, 4, 6, 26, 57, 258; interregional and "international" styles, modes, and pastes, 27, 36, 105, 107, 143; jade, 6, 22, 27–28, 29, 57, 60–63, 82; location, 26, 177; Nueve Cerros-Chinaha ceramic sphere, 7–8, 37, *117*, 118, 143, 171; obsidian, 27, 29, 57, 143, 145–151, *147*; production, 30–31; sacred urban landscape, 53, 61, 82, 106, 178–190, *180*, *183*, *189*; settlement patterns, 53, 82, 106, 178, 179, 181, 184, 187, 251; Water Throne, 251–252, *252*, 268

Cancuen/Transversal breakaway network: ballcourts, 61, *61*; innovative interregional economic networks, 26, 29, 31–36, *33*, 43–48, *56*, 57–58, 118, 252; jade exchange, 4, 6, 12, 28–30, 57, 60–63, 82, 105; network failure, 6, 41, 43, 56; Nueve Cerros-Chipoc-Cancuen ceramic network in 750 to 800 period, 37, 171; obsidian production and exportation, 28–30, 57, 143, 145–151, *147*; salt, 115; sites involved, 27, 48–56, 58–60, 63–64. *See also* Cancuen, ceramics

Candelaria Caves, 2, 5, 115, 116, 178, 249, 250–251
Caracol, Belize, 15, 168, 247
Carcha: Ch'olti'-speaking population, 250; Cucul and Coc Maya landowners, 258; evangelized, 246; Q'eqchi' lords of, 163, 166
cardamom, 181
Cariaco Basin, 219, 220, 221, 222; dry period, 242–243
Caribbean: climatology, 219–220, 223; salt sources, 18, 159–160. *See also* Belize

Carmack, Robert, 68, 264, 268
Carot, Patricia, 2
Castillo, Bernal Díaz del, 257
caves: La Lagunita, El Quiche, Guatemala, ceramic vessels, 73, *74*, 86; Quen Santo Cave III, 92; ritual pilgrimage and cave use, 5, 6–7, 18, 90, 107, 121; speleothems carved with faces, 99. *See also* Candelaria Caves; Hun Nal Ye cave; Hun Nal Ye stone coffer
Ceibal, Guatemala, 14, 24, 259, 263
cenotes, 91, 156, 199
ceramic pastes, 108; porous, 55, 110–111, 117
ceramic petrography, 107–108
ceramic spheres, 55; Altar-style, 79, *80*; Alta Verapaz, 97, 116, 132, 134; Chamán complex, 55, 57, 107, 115–116; Charas (Kaminaljuyu), 72; Chixoy Basin, 77; Chuacús, 117; Conchas (Pacific Coast), 72; Cuchumatanes, 117; eastern highland Providencia, 72; map of, Maya Lowlands, Transversal, and northern Maya Highlands, *106*; Nueve Cerros-Chinaha (proposed), 7–8, *117*, 118, 143, 171; Tepeu, 26, 55, 59, 110, 117; Tepeu II, 109, 117, 118; Tepeu III, 117
ceramic types/group: Atzam Red, 160, *161*; Cambio Unslipped, 55, *109*, 110, *112*, 113; Camenac Red, *109*, 111, *112*; Campamento Fine Orange, 27, 57, 60; Cebada Porous, 55, 110; Chablekal Fine Grey, 27, 56–57; Chablekal Group, 115; Chachalaca Red, 96; Chaquiste Impressed, 55, 110; Chichicaste Brown, 110, 116; Chichicuil Washed, 55; Chinaja Impressed, 55, 110; Cubuc Fluted, 114; Encanto Striated, 55, 110; Fine Greys, 27, 56–57, 116; Fine Orange, 82, 97, 116; Hinojo Negative, *110*, 115; Infierno Black, *109*, *112*, 113; Jekcha Red, 96; Kaleb'aal Incised, 116; Kanalkan Gouged, *110*, 115; Kanalkan Gouged-Incised, 50–51; La Isla Orange,

50, 55, 111; Nichel Red, 96; Nitro Incised, *110*, 115–116; Olola Orange, 113; polychrome, *80*, 97, 116; Sebastián Fluted, 55, 111; Sendero Black, 114, 116; Subin, *112*; Subin Red, *109*, 113; Tasajo Red, 96; Tigrán Red, 55; Tinaja Red, 55, 110; Tohil Plumbate, 77; Tres Micos Impressed, 113; Unnamed Red-on-Cream, *110*; Volcancito Composite, 115; Xelub Dichrome, *110*, 115, 116; Yerba Buena Fine, 96

Chacula Region, Northwestern Huehuetenango: architecture and settlement patterns, 92–96; art and writing, 98–99; Atz'am K'em, 96; ballcourts, 93–96, *94, 95*; delimitations of, 88; differences in archaeological record of eastern and western portions of, 101–102; El Cimarrón, 93; ethnolinguistic affiliation, 100–101; faces in sculptures and rock art, 6, 99; Laguna Mirabel, 96; material culture and trade, 96–98; obsidian objects, 96–97; paleoclimate, 91; political organization, 99–100; Rancho Viejo, 93; sites, 7, 87–88, *88*, 102; Tres Lagunas, 93, 94; Uaxac Canal, 90; Unin Witz, 88, 90; unsurveyed areas, 102; Yalambojoch, 88; Yal Tzimin, 96; Yuxquén, 96. *See also* Quen Santo

Chak Jutuw Kanek', ruler of Ek' Balam, 265, 273

Chama, Guatemala, site, 65, 79–83; active into Colonial Period, 4; "at the Xoy" (*Chi Xoy*), 79; Ch'amak lineage, 271; connection with Yucatan peninsula, 271; location on Chixoy River, 82; Poqom people in, 270

Chama ceramics: exchange of figurines, 167, 271–272; exchange with Altar de Sacrificios, 67, 79, 86, 134; hieroglyphic texts on, 271; Jaguar-Way figurines, *131, 133*, 134; lords with balloon headdress, 273; personified jaws on, 270; vases with fox associated with Ch'amak lineage, 271, *272*

Chama Mountains, 206, 208

Chamelco, Verapaz, 165, 166

Chapayal Basin, 84, 207–208

charcoal records, macro- and microscopic, 207, 215, 217–218, 229, *230*, 239, 240, 242, 244

Chenes-Puuc architectural styles, 268

Chi, Gaspar Antonio, 156

Chich'en, Coban Plateau, reconstruction of, *81*

Chichen Itza, 9, 26; architectural innovations, 247; Chama-style ceramics, 271–272; Cotzumalguapa connection, 272–274; Great Ballcourt of, 253, 262; Kanek' lineage as cofounders of, 248–249, 261, 262; and migration of Mopan Maya to Yucatan, 247–248; Putun Maya (Acallan People), 259–261; relationship with Tula, 26; Temple of the Jaguars (Lower), 253, *255*, 259, *260*; Temple of the Owls, 156, *157*; Temple of the Warriors, 195

Chichicastennango, 65, 68

Chiconah, 257

Chicruz, Middle Chixoy Basin settlement, 73

Chinaja Range (Sierra de Chinaja), 46, 58, 60, 206

chinamit (lineage group), 70

Chinkultic, Chiapas, Mexico, 91; ballcourt and acropolis, 100; Chan Ajaw emblem glyph, 100; "gateway site" *(sitio-puerta)*, 98; sculptural corpus, 98, 100

Chipoc, 80

Chiquibul River, 246

Chirramos, 73

Chitomax 1 and 2, 77

Chixoy River, 65, 67, 70, *211*, 251, 254, 258–259

Chixoy River Basin, 1, 7, 16, 65, *66*, 67, 178, 258; ceramics, 21, 85–86; Chama Valley and Coban Plateau, 79–83; effects of cyclic climate on floodplain, 225–226; fertility of soil, 152; iron values, 228;

Lower Chixoy, 83–85; Middle Chixoy, 72–79; oxbow lakes, 214, 225; satellite image of, *215*, 217, 225
Ch'ol: Ch'olan language, 258, 262, 264; language/speakers, 174, 246, 247, 248, 272; people, 164, 237
Ch'ol Amaq', 272
Ch'olti Maya: language, 246, 250, 251, 258, 271; people, 168, 169, 246, 250, 258
Chontal: language, 256; people, 237
Chontalpa, Tabascan Gulf Coast, 156
Chuchun, Sacapulas, 69–70
Chuitinamit, near Sacapulas, Guatemala, 70
Chutixtiox, 70; reconstruction of, *71*
citlaltlachtli (Stellar Ballcourt), 252
Coateca *chinamit*, Chutixtiox, 70
Cobaneros, 169–170
Coban Plateau, *81*, 81–83, 128–129; exchange networks with Transversal and highlands, 16, 22, 67, 71, 77; oil production, 84; quetzal feathers, 80
codices, 172; *Codex Borbonicus*, 253, *254*; *Codex Mendoza*, 172; *Codex Tro-Cortesianus* (*Madrid Codex*), *155*, 156; *Florentine Codex*, 253; *Paris Codex*, 253, 265
Comitán Valley, Chiapas, 87, 96, 98
Concordia River, 181–182
Copalar, 97
copal (*Bursera* spp.), 97, 165
Copan, 12, 133–134, 140, 141, 166, 223; Skyband Bench from, 125, *126*, 129, 139, 141
corbeled vault, 70, 92
"core vs. periphery" models, 23
corn, 262–263; corn dough, 249; cornfields/ maize fields (fincas), 83, 263
Cotzumalguapa: Chama-style ceramics, 271–272, 275; connection to Chichen Itza, 272–275; Kanek' patronym, Bilbao Monument 20, 273, *273*
cranial modification, 101
Cruz, Martín de la, 155
Cuatrecasas, José, 238–239
Cubilwitz plain, 251

Cuchumatanes Mountains, 87, 98, 102, 117, 206, 207, 208
Cueva de las Murciélagos, Grijalva Basin, 101

deer, 134, 139, 195
de Montmollin, Olivier, 95
Dieseldorff, Erwin P., 166
Dillon, Brian D., 2, 17, 49, 83, 84, *133*, 134, 137, 211
Dolores, Lakandon settlement (later Sak Balam), 164, 165
Dos Pilas: Cancuen, 25–26; hegemony, 24–26; INAA studies, 25, 128; investigations at, 24–25; military garrisons, 6; resource control, 45; Stela, 8, 134
dwarf, 139

Earley, Caitlin, 7, 87, 98
ecliptic, 204, 265
economics, models of, 16–17, 22–23, 25–27, 28–30, 36, 56–58, 274–275
Ek' Balam (city), 261, 265, 268, *269*
Ek' Balam (person), 265–266, 268, 272–273
El Aguacate (modern), Chacula, 96
El Chayal obsidian, 18, 21, 97, 151
El Gancho Lake, 216, 219, 221, 242–243
El Jocote, 74, 76, 77
El Mesak, Retalhuleu, 14
El Mirador, Peten, Guatemala, 15
El Niño Southern Oscillation, 219, 222, 245
El Raudal, 45, 117, 179
emblem glyph, 46, 60, 100, 141, 273
epigraphy, 6, 19, 24, 26, 168, 271. *See also* hieroglyphs
Esmeralda Lake, 91
ethnonyms, 251, 262

Feathered Serpent, 69, 259
feathers: alo, 165; appliqued, 135; bundles of, 166, *169*, 171; with cacao in art, 168–169; exotic, 152, 165; jungle animals, 6; Muan, 135; quetzals, 6, 8,

17, 80, 84, 105, *153*, *157*, 165–166, 168–171, *169*; traps, 166; as tribute, 168, 170–171; working of, 166
Feldman, Lawrence H., 170, 172
finca (large plantation or landholding), 107
Fire Snakes, 253
firewood, 243
fish, dried salted industry, 152; distribution of salt cakes for, 6; fish descalers, obsidian, *161*, 162–163; fishing grounds of Chixoy, 162; fishing weights recovered near Chixoy, 162
foredeep, Sepur formation, 208
Foucault, Michel, 177
Freidel, David A., 62, 171, 191

Gallego, Francisco, 173
García de Monzabal, Captain Francisco Joseph, 175
God L: association with cacao, 158; ceramic figurines from Cancuen and Roknima, *133*, 134–135; ceramic whistle box from Chajcar, 135; God of the Underworld, 134–135, 249, 252–253; imagery on polychrome ceramics, 132, 134–135; and Lunar Maize God and rabbit-transformed Moon Goddess, 123–124, *124*, 132; and Muan owl bird, *133*, 135; patron deity of commerce, 249, 253; variation of Lord Mountain-Valley (Qawa Tzuul-Taq'aa), 252
Graham, Ian, 24
Grijalva Basin, Chiapas: ballcourts, 95; ceramic types, 96; Cueva de las Banquetas, 101; Cueva de las Murciélagos, 101; "Grijalva system" *(camino real)*, 98; independence, 100; population surge during Late Classic, 7, 89, 101; Upper region trade routes, 98
Grijalva River: Upper Tributaries of, 89–90; west-southwest river flow, 91
Grube, Nikolai, 32, 140
Guatemalan Civil War, 2, 3, 19, 67, 120, 187–188, 210, 238

Guatemalan Peace Accords, 1996, 2
Guayabal, Chacula, 95
Gulf Coast: architectural patterns, 14; ceramic traditions of, 82, 107, 109, 118; connections with Cancuen, 6, 47, 57–58; Mexico, Great Western Trade Route, 57–58, 178, 259; Putun Maya and, 259; Tabasco, cacao-producing region, 156, 259; Yucatan, salt-production, 159, 168; Yukatek Maya-speaking, 246, 257–258, 261

Habel, Simeon, 83
halites, 207–208, 213
halotectonics, 213
Hatch, Marion, 72, 75
head shaping, 101
Helmke, Christophe, 185
Hero Twins, 203, 251, 253
hieroglyphs: Aragon mold-made plaque, 129; Chama ceramics with hieroglyphic texts using Yukatek, 271; Ek' Balam acting as Chak Jutuw Kanek', 265, 273; hieroglyphic staircase, Cancuen, 53; hieroglyphic staircase, La Linterna, 58–60; Hun Nal Ye stone coffer, 121, 123, 130, 135, 140–141; lack of in Chacula, 98–99; lack of in Northern Transversal Strip, 1, 4; Panel 3, Cancuen, *252*, 253, 263; on polychrome vessels, 168; Stela 8 in Dos Pilas, 134; taxes/payment details from Maya polities, 185; on Yalambojoch ceramic vessel, 98. *See also* epigraphy
highlands. *See* northern highlands
Holtun Tzuywa or Xicalanco, Nine Place, 261
Houston, Stephen D., 24, 121
Hozanek, cardinal direction, 261–262
Huixtocihuatl (Salt Woman), 264
Hunahpu, 158. *See also* Jun Ahpuuh
Hun Nal Ye cave: ceramic styles, 80; exploration of cave, 121; transformation to ritual center used by merchants and

travelers, 5. *See also* Hun Nal Ye stone coffer
Hun Nal Ye stone coffer: calcified tapir bone within, 121; connections with other regional influences, 125–129, *136*, 137, 138, 142; hieroglyphs, 121, 123, 130, 135, 140–141; interior of coffer containing raised bump at center, *139*, 139–140; lid, 122–125, *126*, 128, 129, 139, 141; potential paper codex within, 121–122; Side 1 and 3, 121–122, *122*, 130–135, *131*, *133*, 138–139; Side 2 and 4, 135–138, *136*; Transversal variants of characters, *133*, 133–135, 138–139; from unlooted cave, Alta Verapaz Region, Central Guatemala, 120, 142; Woodfill's discovery and interpretation of, 80, 121, 123, 130, 135, 138, 140–141
hydronyms, 249, 250

Ichon, Alain, 67, 72–76, 77, 79
ichon gesture, 137–138
Ik' Ajaw (Lord of Darkness), on Stela 1, Salinas de los Nueve Cerros, 266, *267*
Ik'i Balam (Black Jaquar), ancestor of Kaweq, 268. *See also* Balam Q'e
ik (wind) sign, 130, 185
instrumental neutron activation analysis (INAA), 25, 27, 107–108, 114–116
Inter-Tropical Convergence Zone, 219–220, 222, 245
Isla Cerritos, 265
Itza, Lake, 223
Itza people: conflict with Manche' Ch'ol, 173; conquest of, 156; and Q'eqchi', 237; tributes paid to K'iche Empire, 169
Ixcan Fault, *211*, 213, 225
Ixcan River, *211*, 217, 225
Ixil (people), near Nebaj, Guatemala, 71
Ixil Triangle, 71, 79
Ixtepeque, obsidian source, 22, 144–145, 168
Izabal, Lake and Basin, 55, 56, 74, 107, 156, 159, 168; Province, 207, 209
Izapa, 13

jade: beads, 77, 137; boulders, 60, 62; *camahuiles* inside a jaguar *incensario*, Chitomax 1, 77; celts, 62; commodity, 170; control of sources, 22–23; cultural biography of, 62–63; debris, 29–30; long-distance exchange, 4, 6, 12, 18, 28–30, 32, 44, 57, 60–63, 77, 82, 84, 105, 146, 168; mass production of, 29, 114; Motagua source, 18, 22; outcrops and source in eastern Quiche and Verapaces, 17, 60, 62; preforms, 57, 61; raw, 5, 6; "social jade," 97; Tikal workshops using El Chayal obsidian and highland jade, 5, 17–18, 97; trade through "biotopo del quetzal," Verapaz, 17; workshops, 30–31, 52, 53, 57, 61, 114
jaguar: art of, 69, 70, 266, *267*; figurines, 134; *incensario*, 77; Lower Temple of the Jaguars, Chichen Itza, 253, 254; and moon, 270; Olmec motif, 14; pelt cushion, 135; *way/wayhel* figures, 133, 134–135; were-jaguar clefts, 199; whistle box, 135. *See also* Chichen Itza, Lower Temple of the Jaguars; Ek' Balam; Jaguar God of the Underworld (JGU); Paddler Gods
Jaguar God of the Underworld (JGU), 130, 268
Jakawitz, early K'iche' capital, 68
Jasaw Chan K'awiil, ruler of Tikal, *169*
Jun Ajpuuh, Sun of the Day in Xibalba myth, 250, 263, 268. *See also* Hunahpu

kaloomte (high king), 100. See also *ajaw*; *k'uhul ajaw* (holy lord); *yajaw* (subordinate noble)
Kaminaljuyu, 12, 13, 18, 19, 21, 72–73, 75, 270
K'anan Nichal, 92, 95, 97
Kanek'-Kaweq connection, 249, 263–270; blend of Kanek' and Kaweq, 270; origins

of both in historical Xibalba, 264, 275; patron deity of, 264; surrender to K'iche' Federation, 274. *See also* Kanek' lineage; Kaweq lineage

Kanek' lineage: cofounders of Chichen Itza, 248–249, 261, 262; foundation of Ek' Balam, 261; network in southern Peten to northern Yucatan, 264; origin in central Maya Lowlands, 249; patronym, 264, *265*, 273, *273*; relation to west, 270; as salt traders, 261, 262, 265, 275; "Serpent Star," 264; and Xibalba Dance, 262, 263

Kanek' Witz or Bolonte' Witz, allusion to Salinas de los Nueve Cerros, 256, 261, 265, 271

Kan Maa'x, Cancuen ruler, 115–116

Kaqchikel Maya, 259, 264, 274

karst hills, 46, *49*, 54–55, 60, 200, 251

k'atun (20 year period), 260, 265

Kaweq lineage, 68, 77, 249–250, 253, 264, 268, 270–271, 274–275

K'awiil, God, association with cacao, 156, *157*, 158

Kawinal, 75; characteristics of highland sites, 77–78; double temple, 79; site plan, *78*

K'iche' Federation, 68, 69, 77, 79, 268, 274; dependence on Sacapultec salt, 71; and Itza Confederation, 169; origins, 264, 274; and Poqom and Poqomchi', 79, 169, 274; receipt of tributes of cacao, salt, gourds, and quetzal feathers, 169, 171

Kinkayou lineage, 271

k'uhul ajaw (holy lord), 31, 36, 46, 48, 60. See also *ajaw; kaloomte* (high king); *yajaw* (subordinate noble)

k'uhul bakab' (holy/divine head of the land), 100

k'uk'umatz (feathered serpent), 69. *See also* Quetzalcoatl, cult of (Feathered Serpent)

Lacadena, Alfonso, 101, 265

Lacandon Forest or Selva Lacandona, 98, 102, 239

Lacandon Region, 156

Lacantun River, 85, 178–179

Lachua Region, paleoecology, 206, 209–210, 213–222, 225, 229–239, 245; Lachua Lake National Park and buffer zone, 209–210, 216, 218, 234, 235, 237; mahogany, 234, 235, *237*; Maya forest gardens, 212–213, 218, 223, 229–239

ladinos (people of mixed European and Indigenous ancestry), 84

Lagartero, 95

Lagunas de Montebello National Park, 222

Lakandon Maya (people), 155, 164, 229, 237

La Lagunita, El Quiche, Guatemala, 73, *73*, *74*, 86

La Lima, Chisec, Guatemala, 116

La Linterna, Chisec, Guatemala, 46–48, 58–60

La Mancha, Veracruz, 222

Landa, Bishop Diego de, 155, 156, 261–263, 275

Laporte, Juan Pedro, 246, 247, 276

Las Casas, Bartolomé de, 163

La Trinidad I, Chacula Region, 100

La Venta, Gulf Coast, Mexico, 14

Léger, George, 81

LiDAR, 14, 19, 21

liquidambar, 165

Lista de Tributarios 1570-1572, 250

Little Ice Age, 243, 245

Los Cerritos-Chijoj, 76–77, 80

Los Encuentros: history, 72, 76; material culture, 73, 75; settlement patterns, *75*, 76

Los Laureles complex, ceramics, 55, 107, 115

Lower Chixoy, 83–85

Lunar Moon Maize God: dressed in ballplayer costume, 132, 139; photograph depicting Moon Goddess and her celestial court, 123–*124*; photograph depicting narrative of, 123–*124*

Lycopodium spores, 214

Macanche, central Peten, 248
Machaquila, Guatemala: location, 46, 117; lords of, 46, *47*; quadrifoliate plaza, related to hearth of Xibalba, 253, *254*, 263
macrocharcoal. *See* charcoal records, macro- and microscopic
Madrid Codex (*Codex Tro-Cortesianus*), *155*, 156
mahogany trees, 234, 235, *237*
Maize God: association with cacao, 154, 158; on Hun Nal Ye stone coffer, lid, 123, 128, 139; and Moon Goddess in piggyback form, 125–126, *127*, 128; and rabbit-transformed Moon Goddess, 123–124, *124*, 132, 139
Maler, Teobert, 184–185
Manche' Ch'ol, 159, 169–170, 173, 176, 237
mano ("overhang") with associated metate, *161*, 162, 163
marine mollusks, objects made of, 97
maroon communities, 175
Martin, Simon, 32, 140, 154, 158
Matal B'atz, Don Juan, Q'eqchi' lord of Carcha, 163
Matthews, Peter, 24, 134
Maya archaeology, 13–14, 19, 53; approaches, 12–15, 18, 23–24; little-investigated or ignored sectors, 12, 18–19, 22; myths of Classic Maya cities, 22, 23
Maya forest gardens, 212–213, 218, 223, 229–239
Mayapan, 247
Maya people: Acallan, 257–259; Ah Xoy, 237; Chontal, 237; Coc Maya, 258; Cucul Maya, 258; Itza, 156, 169, 173–174, 237, 246, 248, 260; Kanek', 69, 248–249, 261–265, 270–271, 274–275; Kaqchikel, 259, 264, 274; Kaweq, 68, 77, 253, 264, 268, 270–271, 274–275; K'iche', 68–69, 71, 77, 79, 169, 171, 253, 264, 268, 270, 274; Lakandon, 164, 229, 237; Manche' Ch'ol, 159, 169–170, 173, 176, 237; Mopan, 237, 246–248; Poqom, 270, 274; Poqomchi', 258, 270, 271; Putun, 257, 259, 261; Q'eqchi', 81, 83, 107, 163–164, 169, 171, 173–175, 203, 218, 237–238, 245, 251–252, 262, 268, 270–271; Tz'utujil, 264, 274; Xokmo', 173, 175, 237
Maya sacred worldview: in architecture and iconography, 191–192, 194, 196; ballcourt as entrance to Underworld, 154, *154*, 158, 183; cosmology, 179, 191; myth of time and creation, 195; paradigms, 262–263; realm of creation, 183; thresholds or gateways, 199; Underworld plane, 199; water associated with world creation, 194–195, 196. *See also* Underworld; water
Maya World Tree, 184
McKillop, Heather, 275
Medieval Climate Anomaly, 242, 244–245
Mejía, Héctor, 246, 247
Memorial de Sololá, 259, 272, 274
merchants: and Aztec Empire, 170, 172; "bad" cacao, 172; and Candelaria Caves, 5, 249; elite or high-ranking, 31, 57; fairs and exchange, 169–170; and God L, 135, 158; at Kawinal, 77; and Putun Maya, 259; quetzal feathers, 170; road, 256, 271; salt, 163, 276; settlers of Yucatan Peninsula, 247; trade routes, 271
microcharcoal. *See* charcoal records, macro- and microscopic
middens (trash pits), 114, 115
Middle Chixoy: Epiclassic and Postclassic occupation, 77–79; Late Classic ceramics, 76; Late Classic through Postclassic, 76–77; Preclassic and Early Classic occupation, 72–75
Milky Way, 253, 265
milpas, 94
Mirador Basin, Peten, Guatemala, 12
Mirador Lake, 96
Momostenango, Guatemala, 73

moon, 123, 125, 132, 204, 253, 270
Moon Goddess, 125–126, *127*, 128, 139
Mopan Maya, 237, 246–248
Mopan River Basin: map of, *247*; migration through, 246–248, *248*; sites in, 246–247
Morán, Friar Francisco, 159, 164
Morley, Sylvanus G., 264
Myrica, 231, *233*
Myrtaceae, 231, *232*, 235, 242

Nahua, 251, 264, 272
Nahuala, early K'iche' capital, 68
Nahuala River, 272
Nahualate River, 71
Nahuatl, Aztec language, 251, 257
Naj Tunich, 73
Navarrete, Carlos, 87, 89, 98
Nebaj, Guatemala, 71, 76, 80
Negro ("Black") River, 65, 251, 254; Middle, 69–72; Upper, 67–69. *See also* Chixoy River
Nine Places, 256, 257, 261
Nonoalco, 259
northern highlands: ceramics, 107, 110–118, *112*; exotic feathers, 165–166; ties to Salinas de los Nueve Cerros, 84, 108, 111–114, 167. *See also* Cancuen/Transversal breakaway network
Northern Transversal Strip: associations with Pacific Coast, 47, 258–259, 261, 271–275; associations with Underworld, 25, 251; economics, 1, 5–6, 11, 12–13, 15, 17–18, 21, 24, 27–30, 36, 37, 41, 105–119, 152–166, *153*, *160*, 167–168, 178; history, 2, 3, 6, 15–16, 37, 67, 120, 187–188, 209–212; location, 2, 206, 207–208, 249, *250*; paleoecology, 2, 206, 207–208, 213; ritual pilgrimage and cave use, 5, 6–7, 18, 90, 121
Nueve Cerros Ridge (Nine Hills or Bolonppeluitz), 84, 192, *192*, 197, 199–200, 206, 211

Obando Acuña, Luis, 111
obsidian, 21, 144, 150–151, 168; El Chayal source, 18, 21, 97, 144–145, 150–151, 168; exchange, 4, 12, 17; Ixtepeque source, 22, 144–145, 168; Mexican sources, 97, 146–147, *148*, 168; northern Verapaces and El Quiche source, 22; Pachuca obsidian source, 168; San Martin Jilotepeque (SMJ) source, 18, 21, 97, 144–145, 149, 150, 168; from Zaragoza, Puebla, 27, 168
ocarinas, 82
Olmec, 85; were-jaguar clefts, 199
Olmeca-Xicalanca, 259
Orion, 252–253, 264
oxbow lakes, 214, 225
Oxib'chipek, Guatemala, 114, 116

Pachuca, Mexico, obsidian source, 97, 146–147, *148*, 168
Pacot, Sacapulas, 70
Paddler Gods, 130–134, *131*
Palenque, Chiapas, 12, 258; association with Copan, 142; K'inich Ahkal Mo' Naab III, 271; Pakal sarcophagus, 158, 191; potential trade routes, 98
Pan Amaq' Ik'i (Place of the Peoples of the Darkness), 267
Papasca, Sacapulas Valley, 70
Paris Codex, 253, 265
Pasión River: and Altar de Sacrificios, 85; and Cancuen sacred urban landscape, 82, 106, 178, 179, 181, 184; and Candelaria Caves, 178; and Chixoy River Basin, 178; Middle Pasión projects, *20*, 24–25; and Salinas River, 65; "superhighway" of western lowlands, 63; trade route, 16, 25; Tres Islas shrine, 5, 18
pataxte, 154
patronyms, 249
Paynes Creek, Belize, 160, *160*, 167
Peten Itza, Lake, 222–223, 248
Peten Sedimentary Basin, geography as outcome of tectonic displacements, 207–208

Petexbatun Region, 12, 17, 24, 178–179
Piedras Negras, 85
pih (sack), 172
pilgrimage, 6, 42, 62, 118, 170, 190
pilgrims, 50, 181
Pinelo, Antonio de León de, 258
Pismachi, early K'iche' capital, 68
plumbate pottery: Tohil, 77, 267; at Yalambojoch, 97
Poaceae plants, and fire regimes, 242
Popol Vuh, 68, 69, 203, 249, 250–253, 264–265, 268, 270, 275
Poqomchi' language, 271
Poqomchi' Maya: Kaweq surnames, 270; and K'iche' Federation, 79; toponym Beleju' or Nine Peaks, 256
Poqom language, 270
Poqom Maya: capital Nim Poqom, 274; founding of Kaminaljuyu, 256; and K'iche' Federation, 79, 169; part of Chama population, 270; in San Cristóbal Verapaz, 270; *Título del Barrio de Santa Ana*, 270
Proskouriakoff, Tatiana, 71, 142
Pueblo Viejo Chixoy, 72, 77, 79
Puerto Arturo, Lake, 222
Puleston Axe, 195
Purula Valley, 80
Putun Maya, 257, 259–261
pyrite, 17, 97

Q'anjob'alan language, 101
Qawa Tzuul-Taq'aa, association with God L, 252
Q'eqchi': cities, 81; food preparation, 238; historical transmission of knowledge of household gardens, 237, 238; language, 200, 251–252, 270–271; mythology of, 268–270; people, 163, 164, 169, 171, 173–175, 203, 238, 245, 262; toponym, 251; trade connections with other Maya groups, 237; villages, 218, 237
Quen Santo: ceramics, 96–97; history, 6, 89–90; mirror backs, 6; obsidian, 97; ritual and pilgrimage, 6–7, 90, *99*; settlement patterns, 93, *94*, 95, 99–100; stone sculptures, 98
Quetzalcoatl, cult of (Feathered Serpent), 259. See also k'uk'umatz
quetzals, 4, 8, 80, 84, 105; harvesting, 165, 166; location, 165, 166; trade and tribute, 166, 170–171
Quixal Hydroelectric Dam, 67, 72, 79
Q'umarkaj, 67–69, *68*, 70, 72, 77

Rabinal Valley, 253, 274
Rancho Viejo, 100
Rands, Robert, 142
Rapa Nui, 223
Raxruha Viejo: ceramics, 50, 51–52, 105, 110, 115–116; history, 10, 46–48, 50, 51–53, 107; material culture, 50, 118; settlement patterns, 48–49, *49*
Recinos, Adrian, 264
reeds, 181–182, 195
reflector (mirror) backs, 97
refugia, 209
Reilly, F. Kent III, 62
Relación de las Cosas de Yucatán (Landa, Bishop Diego de), 261–263, 275
Relación Geográfica de Ek' Balam, 265, 268
Ribas, Fray Diego de, 164
Rice, Prudence M., 150
Río Laguna Biosphere Reserve, 222
rock art, 99

Sacapulas, 65, 69–72; control, 70; part of K'iche' empire, 71; pre- and post-conquest sites, 69–70; referred to as Tuja or Tujal, 69; saltworks, 69, 71, 85, 159, *160*, 168
Sacchaná, inscribed stelae, 98
Sacpuy, central Peten, 248
Sahagún, Bernardino: *citlaltlachtli* (Stellar Ballcourt), 252; merchants who sold false cacao, 172
Sajkabaja, El Quiche, Guatemala, 271
Sak Witz, White Mountain, 46, *47*, 60

Salama Valley, 16
Salazar, Fray Gabriel, 173, 258
Salinas de los Nueve Cerros: ceramics, 7–8, 108–109, *109*, 111–114, 115–116, *117*, 118, 143, 160, *161*, 167, 171; connections, 84, 108, 111–114, 167, 261, 266, 274, 275; environmental history, 207, 211, 222, 223, 225–229, *230*, 242, 245; figurines, 8; firewood, 212, 244; history, 4, 6, 83, 163, 242, 245, 256, 257, 265, 271; land management, 8, 194, 195, 211–212, 218, 229–239, 240, 242, 244; obsidian, 50, 145–146, 147, *148*, 149; pollen, 232–234; ritual pilgrimage and cave ceremonies, 6–7; sacred urban landscape, 177, 192, *192*, 193, *193*, 194, 197, 199–204, *202*, 205; salt brine stream, 204; salt dome, 83, 84, 106, 159, 192, 193, 197, 199–204, 205, 211, 213, 245, 254; salted fish, 82, 152; salt production and exchange, 6, 9, 17, 18, 65, 106, 109, 159–164, *161*, 168, 175, 198, 200, *203*, 205, 254, 256; settlement patterns, 65, 84–85, 106, 108, 111–114, 147, 149, 150, 159, 167, 190–192, *192*, 193–198, 200, *201*, *202*, 204, 254; toponym, 256. *See also* Nueve Cerros Ridge (Nine Hills or Bolonppeluitz)
Salinas de Magdalena, 72
Salinas River, 83
Salsipuedes River, 246
salt production and exchange, 4, 8, 12; Colonial period, 163–165; markets, 167–168; methods, 159–163; Sacapulas, 69, 71, 159, 160; Salinas de los Nueve Cerros, 105, 159–163, 175–176; San Mateo Ixtatan, 159, *160*, 168; symbolism, 197–198; Yucatan, 159, 164, *266*, 274–275
San Cristóbal Verapaz, 65, 270
San Francisco Hills, 178
San Juan Acala, Coban, 258
San Lorenzo Lake, 91

San Marcos, Coban, 163, 258
San Martin Jilotepeque (SMJ) obsidian source, 18, 21, 97, 144–145, 149
San Mateo Ixtatan salt source, 159, *160*, 168
San Pedro Carcha, 250
San Simón complex, Raxruha Viejo ceramics, 110
Santa Amelia River, 179
Santa Cruz Quiche, 67
Santa Cruz Ridge, 107
Santa Isabel River Valley, 107
Santa Lucia Lachua, 147, 218
Santa Lucía Vieja, 84–85
Santa Marta Salinas, 216, 226–227, *227*
Santo Tomás Nim Xol, *barrio* of Coban, 250
Sapotaceae, 231, 235
Saqb'im, 274
scarlet macaw feathers, 165
Schele, Linda, 191
Schortman, Edward, 23
sculpture, 7, 87, 98, *99*, 142; associated with caves, 6–7, 115; Cancuen, 48, 53, 179; Chacula Region, 6, 99; Chinkultic, Chiapas, Mexico, 98, 100; Chuitinamit, 70; Los Cerritos-Chijoj, 77; Quen Santo, 93, 98; Raxruha Viejo, 118; Yukatek influence, 246–247
Sebol, 64; ceramics, 105, 110; location, 107, 117, 118; ritual use of multiple caves, 107
Sebol River, 53, 63, 107
Seler, Eduard, 2, 3, 83, 87, 89, 96, 97, 98, 101
Selva Lacandona, 98, 102
Semetabaj, Guatemala, 21, 150
Sepur formation, 208
serpent, 134, 156, 256, 264, 273
Serpent Maw at Ek' Balam, 268
Serpent Star, 264
Sesakkar, 54–56, 64, 107; ceramics, 55, 105; location, 107, 117, 118; settlement patterns, *54*, 54–55
Sharer, Robert J., 16
Sierra de los Cuchumatanes, 87, 98, 102, 117, 206, 207, 208

Sierra Lacandon, 206
Sierra Madre mountains, 156
Skyband Bench, Copan, 125, *126*, 129, 139, 141
Sky Turtle, 252
Smith, A. Ledyard, 1, 69, 70
Smith, Robert E., 80
snake, 264, 273, *273*. *See also* Fire Snakes
"social jade," 97
Soconusco: cacao production, 156, 158, 172–173, 175; obsidian importation, 150
Solanaceae plants, in household gardens, 231, 234, 235
Sonsonate, cacao production, 172, 175
southern depocenter (Chapayal Basin), 207–208
southern lowlands: ceramic, 3–4, 111, *112*, 113; collapse of, 83; corbeled vault, 92; import of El Chayal obsidian and highland jade, 17–18, 21; import of salt from Salinas de los Nueve Cerros, 5; likely route between the Chixoy River headwaters and the southern lowlands, 66; major consumer of cacao from highlands, 156; population estimates, 21; principal consumers of highland goods during the later Preclassic and the Classic periods, 12–13, 21, 41, 82, 84, 106; salt sources in and around, *160*; schematic of partnership forms in the development of networks, 34
Spanish colonialism: cacao's use as a "coin of the realm" taken up by colonial Spanish authorities, 172; Chixoy-Salinas River as important trade route, 258; decline of regional trade in salt, achiote, feathers, and cacao, 171, 175–176; illicit trade among Maya and Spaniards of European-produced items for Indigenous commodities, 172–175; Spanish practice of *reducción*, 250; Transversal provision for general needs of consumption of the lowland population in Colonial records, 37, 64, 71, 155, 169–170

speleothems, 99
Spondias, 231, *233*, 235, 242
star, 98, 264, 273
Stone, Andrea, 135, 137–138
Stuart, David, 132
Sukitan (Chocola) on Middle Nahuala River, 272
sun, 125, 130, 155, 179, 182, 204, 253, 262–263, 268, 270
Sun gods: Old Sun God, 125; Sun God/Lunar Maize God, 125, *127*; Sun Hero, 262, 263; Sun of the Day, 268 (*See also* Jun Ajpuuh, Sun of the Day); Sun of the Night, 268, 270

Tabasco, 14; and Acallan, 257; Cancuen ceramics from, 27, 56–57; exchange of metal tools for tribute goods in Transversal, 169–170; Peten connection to, 98; in Peten Sedimentary Basin, 207
Tajal Chan Ahk, Cancuen ruler: associations, 46, *47*, 60, 178, 251–253, *252*, 263, 264, 268; ballcourt of, 184
Tayasal, 248
Tenochtitlan: *chinampa* (floating garden) system, 195; double water temples, 186; plazas of, ideological power, 204. *See also* Aztec Empire
Teotihuacan, 26, 204, 253, 256; toponym Chiconauhtlan, Nine Place, 256–257
Theobroma cacao. *See* cacao
Thompson, J. Eric S., 257, 259–260, 263
Tikal: archaeological study of, 12; architectural groups, 191; quetzal skeletons, 166; relationship with Teotihuacan, 26; trade routes, 5, 25, 247; workshops, 5, 17–18, 97
Título del Barrio de Santa Ana, 270
Título de Totonicapán, 169
Tohil Plumbate pottery, 77, 267
Tojolabales, cultural and linguistic group, 101
Tollan, "The Place of Reeds," 26, 195
Toniná, 98, 100–102, 142

tools: flake tools, 146; igneous groundstone, 4; metal, in exchange for tribute products, 169–170; salt-refining, 115, 162–163
toponyms, 249, 250–251, 256, 266
Toribio, Friar Romo González, 274
Tovilla, Martín Alfonso, 164, 171
traders, 50, 261
"Transversal" ceramic tradition, 80
Tres Islas, 5, 18, 45; ceramics, 114, 116
Tres Lagunas, 93, 94
Triada del chocolate (achiote, cacao, and vanilla), cultural transmission of to Q'eqchi' Maya, 238
tribute economy, *154*, 168–169; "fairs," 170; metal tools, 169–170; "paradigmatic five" elite tributes, 168–169, *169*; for perishable goods, 168–171; quetzal feathers collected, *154*, 168–169, *169*, 170–171; tribute bearers and tributes in painted scenes and murals, 168–169, *169*; tributes received by K'iche' Federation, 169, 171
Trilete spores, 240, 243
Trinitario cacao, 239
Tucuru, Verapaz, 165
Tula, 26, 195
turtle, 192, 194, 195, 253, 264. *See also* Sky Turtle; Turtle Star
Turtle Star, 264
Tzeltal language, 100–101
Tz'utujil lineage, 264, 274
tzuul (mountain), 251–252. See also *witz*

Uaxac Canal, 90, 93, 97, 101
Uaxactun, 12
Underworld, 199; associated with water, 25, 194, 196, 251; ballcourts as figurative entrance to, 183–184, 203, 251; cacao association with, 154, *154*, 158; Cerro Tortugas salt dome as gateway to, 199, 200, 204, 205; denizens of on Hun Nal Ye stone coffer, *131*, 131–132; entrance to Xibalba, 63, 251, *268*, 270; Fireplace, 263; God L as God of, 134–135, 249, 252–253; Northern Transversal Strip as entrance to or realm of, 25, 251. *See also* Xibalba
Unin Witz: material culture, 97; settlement patterns, 88, 90, *90*
Upper Pasión, 12, 17, 19, 25, 26, 64, 114, 246; network, 17, 26, 31, 36
Uspantan, Chamac, 271
Usumacinta: figurine style, 127; region, 91, 94, 98
Usumacinta River, 7, 65, *66*, 94, 159, 168, 178, 246, 256, 275; River Basin, 89, 91–92, 101–102; sites on, 67, 85, 91, 92, 126, 264; trade, 258–259; transport, 249, 258
Uxpanapa Arc, Veracruz-Oaxaca, Mexico, 209, 220

vanilla, 105, 158, 174; and *Triada del chocolate*, 158, 238
Vázquez, Friar Francisco, *Crónica de la Provincia del Santísimo Nombre de Jesús de Guatemala*, 274
Velasco, Capitan Juan de Santiago, 164
Veracruz, 26–27, 47, 56–58, 60, 209, 222
Verapaz: as Acallan, 257, 258, 259; achiote exportation, 159; Cahabon, 165; cloud forests as source of quetzal feathers, 165, 166, 171; conversion to Christianity, 163; Poqom, 270; pyrite from "biotopo del quetzal" area, 17; Tucuru, 165; Verapaz-style ceramics and figurines, 36, 67, 74; wealth of *alcaldes mayores* from trading Spanish goods for cacao and achiote, 174
Vico, Fray Domingo de, 164
Villagutierre Soto-Mayor, Juan de, *History of the Conquest of the Province of the Itza*, 174
Virú Valley, Peru, 191
Vista Hermosa, Guatemala, 216, 226–227, *227*

war, 32, 35; at Cancuen, 46, *47*, 48, 60;

Chontalpa and Itza, 156; warfare, 6, 17, 25, 170, 259. *See also* Guatemalan Civil War
Wari Camp, Belize, 186
warrior: Acallan (warrior) at Chichen Itza, *260*; Coyote lineage, 274; dedicated architecture for, 204; Fox lineage, 271; kings, 100; lineages, 271–272, 274; with merchants, as protection, 256; of the sun, 268; Weasel lineage, 272, 274
water, sacred to Maya and Mesoamerica, 194–196. *See also* Cancuen, sacred urban landscape; Maya sacred worldview; Salinas de los Nueve Cerros, sacred urban landscape
wattle and daub walls, 92
Watul, Lord, 263
Wauchope, Robert, 67
Weasel lineage, 271, 272, 274
were-jaguar, 199
Willey, Gordon, 190–191
witz (mountain), 48, *49*. See also *tzuul* (mountain)
women, 128, 158, 187
workshop(s): empty, perhaps for feather working, 171; figurine, 82; imitation ceramic-ware production, 118; industrial, 204; jade at Cancuen, 30, 31, 52–53, 57, 61, 114, 190; obsidian and jade at Tikal, 17; salt-working, 163
"world system" approach, 23

Xacbal River, *211*, 217, 225
Xajil (coyote warriors), 274
Xbalanque. *See* Balam Q'e
Xecaltoj, Sacapulas Valley, 70
Xibalba: association with ballgame, 262, 263; association with color black, 251, 266; association with Salinas de los Nueve Cerros, 266; black road the Hero Twins selected as path into Xibalba, 251; and divine hearth, 253, *254*, 263; entrance to geographical Underworld, 63, 251; Hero Twins' death and rebirth as sun and moon, 253, 263, 268; historical geographical region, 249–254; Jun Ajpuuh, 263, 268; in Landa's *Relación de las Cosas de Yucatan*, 261–263, 275; origins of both Kanek' and Kaweq lineages in historical Xibalba, 264, 275. *See also* Underworld
Xicalanco: connection with Chixoy River, 258–259; historic trading area and port, 257; peoples from, 261
Xiuhcoatl, four Fire Snakes, 253, *255*
xiuhmolpilli, stick bundles depicted in *Codex Borbonicus*, 172, 253, *254*, 263
Xiuhteuctli, 253, *255*
Xmukane, 249, 252–253, 264–265, 270, 275
xochitl (birth of the sun Mexican glyph), 263
Xokmo' Maya, 173, 175, 237
Xolchun, Sacapulas, 69, 70
Xolcoxoy, Sacapulas, 69
Xolpacol, Sacapulas, 70
Xoltinamit, Sacapulas, 70
Xpiyakok, *Popol Vuh*, 252–253, 264, 265
X-ray fluorescence (XRF), 96–97, 146–147, 148
Xultun, 188

yajaw (subordinate noble), 46. See also *ajaw*; *kaloomte* (high king); *k'uhul ajaw* (holy lord)
Yalambojoch, Chacula Region, 88; ballcourts, 92; ceramics, 96, 97, 98; obsidian, 97
Yal Tzimin, Chacula Region, 96
Yaxchilan, 85
Yaxha, central Peten, 248
yearbearer system, 261, 271
Yib'anh Kolan Xak, Chacula Region, 88, 92, 96
Yich'aak K'ak, ruler of Calakmul, *169*
Yolnhajab', Lake, 92, 96
Yucatan Peninsula, 258, 275–276; cacao growth in, 156; relations with Transversal and Salinas del los Nueve Cerros, 261,

264, 271, 274, 275–276; saltworks, 159, 164, *266*, 274–275; Yukatek migration along the Mopan River tributaries, 246–249, *248*. See also Kanek' lineage
Yukatek language/speakers, 164, 173, 248, 251, 253, 257, 264, 271, 276
Yuxquen, Chacula Region, 96

Zacualpa, Middle Chixoy, 76
Zaculeu, Middle Chixoy, 76
Zaragoza, Puebla, 27, 57, 60, 168
Zender, Marc, 135, 137–138
Zorita, Alonso de, 155
Zygnemataceae algal zygospores, 215, 222–223, 239